Everyday Encounters

FROM THE WADSWORTH SERIES IN COMMUNICATION STUDIES

EVERYDAY ENCOUNTERS

An Introduction to Interpersonal Communication

JULIA T. WOOD

The University of North Carolina, Chapel Hill

Wadsworth Publishing Company

I(T)P™ **An International Thomson Publishing Company**

Belmont • Albany • Bonn • Boston • Cincinnati • Detroit • London
Madrid • Melbourne • Mexico City • New York • Paris
San Francisco • Singapore • Tokyo • Toronto • Washington

Communication Studies Editor: Todd R. Armstrong
Editorial Assistants: Laura A. Murray and
Michael Gillespie
Project Development Editor: Lewis DeSimone
Production Editor: Vicki Friedberg
Text and Cover Designer: Carolyn Deacy
Print Buyer: Barbara Britton
Permissions Editor: Robert M. Kauser

Copy Editor: Melissa Andrews
Page Makeup: Rosa+Wesley Design Associates
Photo Researcher: Stephen Forsling
Illustrator: Precision Graphics
Cover Illustration: © Nancy Doniger
Compositor and Color Separation: York Graphic Services
Printer: Von Hoffman Press, Inc.

COPYRIGHT © 1996 by Wadsworth Publishing Company
A Division of International Thomson Publishing Inc.
I(T)P The ITP logo is a trademark under license.

Printed in the United States of America
  2 3 4 5 6 7 8 9 10–00 99 98 97

For more information, contact Wadsworth Publishing Company.

Wadsworth Publishing Company
10 Davis Drive
Belmont, California 94002, USA

International Thomson Publishing Europe
Berkshire House 168-173
High Holborn
London, WC1V 7AA, England

Thomas Nelson Australia
102 Dodds Street
South Melbourne 3205
Victoria, Australia

Nelson Canada
1120 Birchmount Road
Scarborough, Ontario
Canada M1K 5G4

International Thomson Editores
Campos Eliseos 385, Piso 7
Col. Polanco
11560 México D.F. México

International Thomson Publishing GmbH
Königswinterer Strasse 418
53227 Bonn, Germany

International Thomson Publishing Asia
221 Henderson Road
#05-10 Henderson Building
Singapore 0315

International Thomson Publishing Japan
Hirakawacho Kyowa Building, 3F
2-2-1 Hirakawacho
Chiyoda-ku, Tokyo 102, Japan

All rights reserved. No part of this work covered by the copyright hereon may be reproduced or used in any form or by any means—graphic, electronic, or mechanical, including photocopying, recording, taping, or information storage and retrieval systems—without the written permission of the publisher.

Library of Congress Cataloging-in-Publication Data

Wood, Julia T.
    Everyday encounters : an introduction to interpersonal
  communication / Julia T. Wood.
        p.   cm.
    Includes bibliographical references and index.
    ISBN 0-534-26106-X
    1. Interpersonal communication. 2. Interpersonal relations.
  I. Title.
  BF637.C45W656   1995
  153.6–dc20
                                95-7555

For Michelle

*Who teaches me to appreciate the adventure and
magic in everyday life.*

*Humankind has not woven the web of life. We are but
one thread within it. Whatever we do to the web, we
do to ourselves.* CHIEF SEATTLE

STWK 1110

STWK

Brief Contents

stock info

Contents

Part One

THE FABRIC OF INTERPERSONAL COMMUNICATION

6 / *Mindful Listening 147*

Part Two

WEAVING COMMUNICATION INTO RELATIONSHIPS

8 / *Managing Conflict in Relationships 207*

Preface

Everyday Encounters offers a distinct alternative to existing textbooks for the introductory course in interpersonal communication. It is unique in its emphasis on theories, research, and skills that are anchored in the field of communication and in its attention to significant trends in social life in the 1990s.

Focus on Communication Research and Theory

In the 1970s, when interpersonal communication was a very young intellectual area, research was limited. Because theoretical and research foundations for courses were not abundant, the content of most texts and courses either extended general principles of communication to interpersonal contexts or relied primarily on research in fields other than communication.

Although interpersonal communication continues to draw from other disciplines, by now it is a substantive field in its own right, complete with a base of knowledge, theories, and research anchored in communication. The maturation of interpersonal communication as an intellectual area is evident in the substantial original research published in academic journals, as well as in the steady stream of scholarly books. It is clear that interpersonal communication is no longer a derivative field.

Textbooks for introductory communication courses no longer need to rely primarily on research and theories developed by scholars outside of the communication field. *Everyday Encounters* reflects a strong focus on research in the communication discipline. For example, my discussions of personal relationships highlight Leslie Baxter's extensive research on relational dialectics. I also weave into all chapters emergent knowledge of gender differences in communication. These and other topics in current communication inquiry are integrated into this book. As a result, students who read it will gain an appreciation of the scope and depth of scholarship in the field of communication.

Attention to Significant Social Trends

Social diversity is not merely a timely trend, a new buzz word, or a matter of "political correctness." Instead, social diversity is a basic fact of life in the United States, a country (like many others) enriched by a cornucopia of people, heritages, customs, and ways of interacting. *Everyday Encounters* reflects and addresses social diversity by weaving it into the basic fabric of interpersonal communication.

Infusing diversity into communication requires more than tacking paragraphs on gender or race onto conventional approaches to topics. In writing this book, I have woven awareness of race, class, gender, age, and sexuality into discussions of communication theory and skills. For example, in exploring self-concept, I give detailed attention to race, gender, and sexual orientation as core facets of identity that shape how individuals communicate and interpret the communication of others. In examining patterns of interaction in families, I include research on families that are not white and middle class. Chapter 10 on romantic relationships includes parallel attention to heterosexual and gay and lesbian relationships. Rather than highlighting the attention to diversity with diversity boxes or separate features, I have blended diverse social groups, customs, and lifestyles into the book as a whole.

Social diversity is not the only significant social trend that affects and is affected by interpersonal communication. *Everyday Encounters* addresses communication challenges, confusions, and issues that are part of personal and social life in the 1990s. There is a full chapter on friendships, which have assumed enlarged importance in the face of marriages that often break down and families that are usually geographically dispersed. The chapter on romantic relationships addresses abuse and violence between intimates, and it discusses using communication to negotiate safer sex in an era shadowed by HIV and AIDS. I also include a discussion of communication in long-distance relationships, which are part of many of our lives.

Special Features of Everyday Encounters

I've already mentioned two distinctive features of this book: emphasis on communication research and theories and attention to social diversity as integral to interpersonal communication. In addition to those features, there are other facets of the book that are designed to make it engaging and useful to students.

First, I adopt a conversational tone so that students realize there is a real person behind the words they're reading and studying. I share with students some of the communication challenges and encounters that surface in my life. The conversational writing style is also intended to invite students to interact with ideas on a personal level.

My voice is not the only one that students will encounter in this book. Every chapter is enhanced by commentaries written by students in my classes. The experiences, insights, and concerns expressed by these students broaden the conversation to include a large range of perspectives.

Everyday Encounters also includes two pedagogical features that promote development of interpersonal communication skills. Each chapter includes several "Put It in Practice" exercises, which encourage students to apply concepts and principles discussed in the text to their own lives. Each chapter also includes a number of "Check It Out" features, which highlight interesting research and examples of interpersonal communication in everyday life.

Additional Resources for Instructors

Accompanying *Everyday Encounters* are four instructional resources. An extensive *Instructor's Resource Manual* supplements the textbook. The manual discusses philosophical and pragmatic considerations involved in teaching the introductory course in interpersonal communication. It also includes suggestions for course emphases, sample syllabi, exercises and films appropriate for each chapter, masters for overheads of diagrams in the textbook, and a bank of test items. Full-color transparency acetates of figures, diagrams, and charts are available upon adoption, as is a videotape that demonstrates everyday applications of principles and skills covered in this book. Computerized testing is also available.

Acknowledgments

Although only my name appears as the author of this book, many people have contributed to it. I am especially indebted to Todd Armstrong, my editor at Wadsworth. From start to finish, he has been a guiding spirit for this book. As an editor, he gave direction to the overall project, made insightful suggestions for refining early drafts, and inspired selection of the textile art that graces the pages of this book. As a friend, he provided personal support, enthusiasm, and encouragement.

Also essential to the birth of this book were the professionals at Wadsworth who transformed an unembroidered manuscript into a finely crafted book. Specifically, I thank Vicki Friedberg, Melissa Andrews, Bob Kauser, Stephen Forsling, Carolyn Deacy, Emma Nash, Gladys Rosa-Mendoza, and the invincible Laura Murray, who made sure nothing fell through the cracks.

In addition to the editorial team at Wadsworth, I am grateful to the many students and teachers who reviewed versions of the manuscript and whose comments and suggestions improved the final content of the book. I thank Patricia Amason, University of Arkansas; Lucinda Bauer,

University of North Carolina at Chapel Hill; Betsy W. Bach, University of Montana; Cherie L. Bayer, Indiana University; Kathryn Carter, University of Nebraska, Lincoln; Joseph S. Coppolino, Nassau Community College; Laverne Curtis-Wilcox, Cuyahoga Community College; Michelle Miller, University of Memphis; John Olson, Everett Community College; William Foster Owen, California State University, Sacramento; Nan Peck, Northern Virginia Community College, Annandale Campus; Mary Jo Popovici, Monroe Community College; Sharon A. Ratliffe, Golden West College; Susan Richardson, Prince George's Community College; Cathey S. Ross, University of North Carolina, Greensboro; Kristi A. Schaller, Georgia State University; Michael Wallace, Indiana University/Purdue University at Indianapolis; and the students at North Virginia Community College, Annandale Campus, and University of Arkansas who class tested the book.

Writing this book was not only a professional activity, it was also a personal engagement that benefited from the generous support of individuals who make up my family of choice. At the top of that list is Robbie Cox, my partner in love, life, and adventure for over twenty years. He cheered me on when writing was going well and bolstered my confidence when it was not. He provided a critical ear when I wanted a sounding board and privacy when I was immersed in writing. Along with Robbie, I am fortunate to have the support of my sister Carolyn and my friends Nancy and Sue. And, of course, I must acknowledge my feline alter ego, Scrambles, who is the only member of my family who keeps me company when I am writing at 2 or 3 in the morning.

Guide to Learning

Before you begin using *Everyday Encounters* in your communication course, I'd like to give you a short tour of the text and its special features. *Everyday Encounters* incorporates an impressive amount of current communication theory and research. Throughout the text I've blended this vital conceptual material with skill-building discussions to give you a deeper understanding of how the dynamics of interpersonal communication affect your daily life.

I also address the opportunities and challenges of living in today's multicultural world by incorporating social diversity into the basic discussions of interpersonal communication. In *Everyday Encounters* you'll find the subjects of race, class, gender, age, and sexuality woven into the core material. You'll also find comments from a broad range of students whose voices personalize and bring into focus many interpersonal communication issues discussed in the text.

I hope you'll take a few minutes to peruse the next five pages for a quick overview of the unique features and character of *Everyday Encounters*. My goal in writing this book is to provide you with an accessible introduction to the theory, research, and skills that are vital to effective interpersonal communication in everyday life. Enjoy the dialogue!

Communication Theory and Research Highlighted

I've integrated into the text a wealth of current data related specifically to the field of communication that supports and explains the skills you're encouraged to develop. You'll find that your expanded knowledge of communication will help you in all manner of interpersonal encounters.

are differences in your social, cultural, and physiological resources for perceiving. Remembering that perceptions are subjective curbs the tendency to think our perceptions are the only valid ones.

Avoid Mindreading

Because perception is subjective, people differ in what they notice and in what it means to them. One of the most common problems in interpersonal communication is **mindreading**, which is assuming we understand what another person thinks or perceives. When we mindread, we don't check with another person to see what he or she is thinking. Instead, we act as if we know what's on another's mind, and this can get us into considerable trouble. Gottman and his colleagues identify mindreading as one of the behaviors that contributes to interpersonal tension (Gottman, 1993; Gottman, Notarius, Gonso, & Markman, 1976). The danger of mindreading is that we may misinterpret others and have no way of checking on the accuracy of our perceptions. Sometimes we do understand one another but sometimes we don't.

Consequently, for the most part mindreading is more likely to harm than help interpersonal communication. Consider a few examples. One person might say to her partner, "I know you didn't plan anything for our anniversary because it doesn't matter to you." Whether or not the partner made plans, it's impossible to guess motives or to know why the partner forgot if indeed she or he did. One friend might say to another, "You were late coming over because you're still mad about what happened yesterday." The speaker is guessing reasons for the friend's tardiness and could well be wrong. Mindreading also occurs when we say things such as "I know why you're upset" (Has the person said she or he is upset?) or "You don't care about me anymore" (maybe the other person is too preoccupied or worried to be as attentive as usual). We also mindread when we tell ourselves we know how somebody else will feel or react, or what he or she will do. The truth is we don't really know—we're only guessing. When we mindread, we impose our perspectives on others instead of allowing them to say what they think. This can cause misunderstandings as well as resentment, since most of us prefer to speak for ourselves.

© 1995 M. C. Escher/Cordon Art—Baarn, Holland. All rights reserved.

The social world that we share with others is a world we have imagined together and agreed to believe in.
ELIZABETH JANEWAY

Chapter 3
Perception and
Communication
87

A Documented Examination of Mindreading

This excerpt on mindreading from *Chapter 3: Perception and Communication*, supported by research references, offers you guidelines for improving perception and communication.

© 1995 M. C. Escher/Cordon Art—Baarn, Holland. All rights reserved.

Check It Out

THE WHORF-SAPIR VIEW OF LANGUAGE

Studies by anthropologists reveal that our perceptions are guided by language. The language of the Hopi Indians makes no distinction between stationary objects and moving processes, whereas English uses nouns and verbs respectively. The English word *snow* is the only word we have to define frozen, white precipitation that falls in the winter. In Arctic cultures where snow is a major aspect of life, there are many words to define snow that is powdery, icy, dry, wet, and so forth. The distinctions are important to designate which snows allow safe travel.

Source: Whorf, B. (1956). *Language, thought, and reality.* New York: MIT Press/John Wiley.

---

ine a person as an ..., a gourmet cook, or ...rects our attention ...rson. We might talk ...about wilderness leg...ments with the ... the chef, and ex... en with the father. ... Asian American or a ... we notice about the ...many other aspects ...perceive and interact ... ow we define them. ... n we respond to a ...y represents who he ...mbol to define some...many other aspects of ...dividuals totalize gay ...tional preference is ... a person. Interest...erosexuals on the ...alizing also occurs ... saying "He's a ... She's preppy," or "He's just a jock." Totalizing is ...g. When we stereotype someone, we define ...racteristics of a group. When we totalize others, ...y are by spotlighting a single aspect of their

JAMAL

I know all about totalizing. A lot of people relate to me as black, like that's all I am. Sometimes in classes, teachers ask me to explain the "African American perspective" on something, but they don't ask me to explain my perspective as a premed major or a working student. I am an African American, but that's not all I am.

The symbols we use to define experiences in our relationships affect how we think and feel. In a recent study, my colleagues and I asked romantic couples how they defined differences between them (Wood, Dendy, Dordek, Germany, & Varallo, 1994). We found that some individuals define differences as positive forces that energize a relationship and keep it interesting. Others define differences as problems or barriers to closeness. There was a direct connection between how partners defined differences and how they acted. Partners who viewed differences as constructive approached disagreements with curiosity, interest, and a hope for growth through discussion. On the other hand, partners who labeled differences as problems tended to deny differences and to avoid talking about them.

Chapter 4
The World of Words
103

The Role of Symbols

In this excerpt from *Chapter 4: The World of Words*, research conducted by a group of communication scholars sheds light on how the symbols we use in thinking about our relationships influence how we perceive and feel about those relationships.

Social Diversity Woven into the Fabric of the Text

Every chapter and virtually every topic present race-ethnicity, class, and gender as key elements of identity affecting interpersonal communication.

A Societal Look at Gender

This discussion of gender from *Chapter 2: Communication and the Creation of Self* gives you an enlightening view of the topic from a societal perspective.

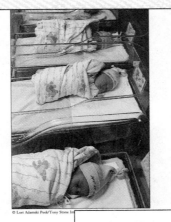

education, and businesses are dominated by Caucasian men, while people of color and women continue to fight overt and covert discrimination in admission, hiring, and advancement. The color of one's skin makes a difference in how society treats us, our material lives, and who we are told we are.

DERRICK

If my mama told me once, she told me a million times: "You got to work twice as hard to get half as far because you're black." I knew that my skin was a strike against me in this society since I can remember knowing anything. When I asked why blacks had to work harder, Mama said, "Because that's just how it is." I guess she was telling me that's how this society looks on African Americans.

Gender is another important category in Western culture. Historically, men have been more valued and considered more rational, competent, and entitled to privilege than women. In the 1800s, women were not allowed to own property, gain professional training, or vote. It was considered appropriate for a husband to beat his wife; the phrase "rule of thumb" comes from the law that stated a man could beat his wife as long as he used a stick no larger than the size of his thumb. Even on the verge of the twenty-first century, women and men are not considered equal in many societies. Some scholars argue that gender is the most important aspect of personal identity in Western culture (Fox-Genovese, 1991). From pink and blue blankets hospitals wrap around newborns to differential salaries earned by women and men, gender is a major facet of identity. Given the importance our society places on gender, it is no wonder that one of the first ways children learn to identify themselves is by their sex (Wood, 1996). When I asked my four-year-old niece Michelle who she was, her immediate response was "I'm a girl." Only after naming her sex did she describe her family, her likes and dislikes, and other parts of herself.

Western cultures have strong gender prescriptions. Girls and women are expected to be caring, deferential, and cooperative, while boys and men are supposed to be independent, assertive, and competitive (Wood, 1994d). Consequently, women who assert themselves or compete are likely to receive social disapproval, be called "bitches," and otherwise reprimanded for violating gender prescriptions. Men who refuse to conform to social views of masculinity and who are gentle and caring risk being labeled wimps. Our gender, then, makes a great deal of difference in how others view us and how we come to see ourselves.

© Lori Adamski Peek/Tony Stone Im...

---

hierarchy of the firm, the higher up your office was—literally. I mean, the president and vice presidents—six of them—had the whole top floor, while there were forty or more interns crowded onto my floor.*

As Jerry's observations indicate, space also expresses power relations. Individuals who have power usually command more space than individuals with lesser power. The connection between power and space is evident in the fact that most bosses have large, spacious offices while their secretaries have smaller offices or workstations, even though they have to manage far more material than bosses. Homes also reflect power differences among family members. Adults usually have more space than children, and men more often than women have their own rooms and sit at heads of tables.

Power may also be exerted through silence, a powerful form of nonverbal communication. By not responding, men sometimes discourage others from speaking and clear the way to talk about their own preferred topics (DeFrancisco, 1991). In extreme form, power is nonverbally enacted through violence and abuse, activities that men are more likely to commit than women (Wood, 1994d).

Responsiveness, liking, and power are dimensions of relational-level meanings that are communicated primarily through nonverbal behaviors.

© Anne Dowie

In a full heart there is room for everything, and in an empty heart there is room for nothing.
ANTONIO PORCHIA

Nonverbal Communication Reflects Cultural Values

Like verbal communication, nonverbal patterns reflect communication rules of specific cultures. This implies that the majority of nonverbal actions are not instinctive, but are learned as we are socialized in particular cultures. We've already noted a number of differences between nonverbal behaviors encouraged in feminine and masculine communication cultures. In addition to diversity among cultures within our country, nonverbal behaviors vary from one country to another. As you might expect, dissimilarities reflect distinct cultural values.

Have you ever seen the bumper sticker that says "If you can read this, you're too close"? That slogan proclaims North Americans' fierce territoriality. We prize private space, and we resent, and sometimes fight, anyone who trespasses on what we consider our turf. In cultures where individuality is a less pronounced value, people are less territorial. For instance, Brazilians stand close in shops, buses, and elevators and when they bump into each other they don't apologize or draw back (Wiemann & Harrison, 1983).

Cultural Traits and Nonverbal Communication

This excerpt from *Chapter 5: The World Beyond Words* examines the effect of culture on nonverbal communication.

Student Commentaries

Interspersed throughout the body of the text are commentaries collected from a broad spectrum of students. I've included them to personalize theories and practices that are covered in the text.

Yih-Tang Lin's commentary in the Introduction is a vivid example of how easily miscommunication occurs, especially on a multicultural level.

sexual standard the culture represents as natural. However, heterosexuals often do not understand their sexual orientation in relation to homosexuality. Similarly, African Americans, Asians, and other people of color realize how they differ from European Americans more than European Americans perceive how they differ from people of color. We can also see our competitive attitude toward athletics in a new light by learning about the Japanese preference for ties in sports events so that neither side loses face. It is difficult to be aware of whiteness, heterosexuality, middle-class status, or competitive perspectives on sports because cultural practices make those appear natural and right in our lives. Thus, learning about people in other cultures and people who are outside of what the culture defines as mainstream inevitably teaches us about the mainstream as well.

The diversity of our society offers both opportunities and challenges. Differences in gender, race, class, cultural heritage, sexual preference, age, physical abilities, and spiritual beliefs present us with a rich array of perspectives on identity and interaction. Exploring variations among us enhances our appreciation of the range of human behavior and the options open to us in our own lives. At the same time, diversity can complicate interaction, because people may communicate in dissimilar ways and misunderstand one another as Yih-Tang Lin notes in her commentary.

YIH-TANG LIN

When I first came here to school I was amazed at how big the rooms in dormitories are, so I remarked on this. All of the Americans had a laugh at that and thought I was joking. In my country, individuals have very little space, and houses are tight together. The first time an American disagreed with me I felt angry that he would make me lose face. We don't ever contradict another person directly. I have had many miscommunications in this country.

The process of socialization teaches each of us how to communicate and interpret what others say and do. This means that communication goals and styles vary according to the values and norms of particular social groups. Latinas and Eastern Europeans may have learned different ways of disclosing personal information, just as women and men may have been socialized into different styles of friendship. For this reason, we cannot simply tack discussions of diversity onto existing understandings of interaction.

© John Coletti/Stock, Boston

© Betty Press/Woodfin Camp & Associates, Inc.

© Craig Aurness/Woodfin Camp & Associates, Inc.

We are all different facets of the same reality, different parts of the one whole, just as the numerous waves rising and falling in the ocean are interrelated transformations of the one ocean.
THICH THIEN-AN

others can provide models. If you know someone you think is particularly skillful in supporting others, observe her or him carefully to identify particular communication skills. You may not want to imitate this person exactly, but observing will make you more aware of concrete skills involved in supporting others. You may choose to tailor some of the skills others display to suit your personal style.

Set Realistic Goals

Although it is true that willpower can do marvelous things, it does have limits. We need to recognize that trying to change how we see ourselves works only when our goals are realistic. If you are shy and want to be more extroverted, it is reasonable to try to speak up more and socialize more often. On the other hand, it may not be reasonable to set the goal of being the life of the party.

Realistic goals require realistic standards. Often dissatisfaction with ourselves stems from unrealistic expectations. In a culture that emphasizes perfectionism, it's easy to be trapped into expecting more than is humanly possible. If you define a goal of being a totally perfect communicator in all situations, you are setting yourself up for failure. It's more reasonable and more constructive to establish a series of realistic small goals that can be met. You might focus on improving one of the skills of communication competence we discussed in Chapter 1. When you are satisfied with your ability at that skill, you can move on to a second one.

Remembering our discussion of social comparison, it's also important to select reasonable measuring sticks for ourselves. It isn't realistic to compare your academic work to that of a certified genius. It is reasonable to measure your academic performance against others who have intellectual abilities similar to your own. Setting realistic goals and selecting appropriate standards of comparison are important to bring about change in yourself.

KENDRICK

I really got bummed out my freshman year. I had been the star on my high school basketball team, so I came to college expecting to be a star here too. The first day of practice, I saw a lot of guys who were better than I was. They were incredible. I felt like nothing. When I got back to my room, I called my mom and told her I was no good at basketball here. She told me I couldn't expect to compete with guys who had been on the team for a while and who had gotten coaching. She asked how I stacked up against just the other first-year players, and I said pretty good. She told me they were the ones to compare myself to.

Kendrick's commentary from *Chapter 2: Communication and the Creation of Self* shows how interpersonal communication issues surface in your everyday life.

Hands-On Help

You'll find the two learning tools displayed below placed liberally throughout *Everyday Encounters*. In fact, both aids appear in each chapter. I hope you'll take advantage of the useful information and practice they offer because they can help you raise your communication consciousness and expand your interpersonal skills.

Check It Out

A KALEIDOSCOPIC CULTURE

The city of Atlanta, Georgia, which didn't even have a pizza parlor until 1959, by 1990 had a Korean Chamber of Commerce, a Hmong church, Hispanic yellow pages, Baptist churches for Romanians and Haitians, and a Chinese community center (p. 11).

Atlanta is home to 4,000 Vietnamese, 10,000 Indians, 25,000 Koreans, 30,000 Chinese, and 100,000 Hispanics (p. 11). Currently, white citizens are in the minority in Atlanta and many major cities in the United States. Between 1980 and 1990, the Hispanic population in the United States grew by over 50%, while the Asian or Pacific Islander population grew by over 100% in the same decade.

Source: Bates, E. (1994, fall). Beyond black and white. *Southern Exposure*, pp. 11–15.

© David Young-Wolff/PhotoEdit

class, gender, spirituality, and sexual orientation shape your communication. My race provides me with greater understanding of Caucasian values and perspectives than of those held by women and men of color. However, being of one race doesn't mean that I, or you, can't develop understanding of and respect for the experiences of people of other races.

Because I am middle class, I have been fortunate not to suffer economic deprivation (except when I was a poor graduate student!). Yet I interact with many working-class people, and I've gained some insight into the views, values, concerns, and pleasures that make up the fabric of their lives. Although my heterosexuality implies that I don't have personal experience in gay and lesbian relationships, I have learned a good deal about them from gay and lesbian friends of mine. All of us are limited by our own identities and the experiences and understandings they have given us. Yet, this doesn't mean we have to be ignorant of all those who are different from us. In fa[...] a range of people, th[...] important similarities [...] differences.

Diversity in Interpersona[...]

In introducing mysel[...] context of a highly di[...] diversity is one of the [...] of our era. Making u[...] ple of many races, et[...] socioeconomic classes, genders, ages, spiritual i[...] orientations.

The social diversity of modern life fosters t[...] more obvious one is increased understanding of [...] tives and behaviors that differ from our own. L[...] portant is the insight into ourselves that comes [...] who differ from us in certain ways. For instance[...] "normal" as being European American, heterose[...] young. Gay and lesbian orientations are often se[...] culturally created norm of heterosexuality. This [...] individuals understand their sexual orientations [...]

Part I
The Fabric of Interpersonal
Communication

6

"Check It Out" Boxes

This "Check It Out" box from the Introduction documents the growing cultural diversity of Atlanta, Georgia.

There are two differences between I-language and you-language. First, I-statements own responsibility, whereas you-statements project it onto another person. Second, I-statements offer considerably more description than you-statements. You-statements tend to be accusations that are very abstract. This is one of the reasons they're ineffective in promoting change. I-statements, on the other hand, provide concrete descriptions of behaviors that we dislike without directly blaming the other person for how we feel.

Some people feel awkward when they first start using I-language. This is natural, since most of us have learned to rely on you-language. With commitment and practice, however, you can learn to communicate with I-language. Once you feel comfortable using it, you will find that I-language has many advantages. It is less likely than you-language to make others defensive, so I-language opens the doors for dialogue. I-language is also more honest. We deceive ourselves when we say "You made me feel . . ." since others don't control how we feel. Finally, I-language is more empowering than you-language. When we say you did this or you made me feel that, we give control of our emotions to others. This reduces our personal power and, by extension, our motivation to change what is happening. Using I-language allows you to own your own feelings while also explaining to others how you interpret their behaviors.

TABLE 4.2 I- and You-Language	
You-Language	**I-Language**
You hurt me.	I feel hurt when you ignore what I say.
You make me feel small.	I feel small when you tell me that I'm selfish.
You're really domineering.	When you shout, I feel dominated.
You humiliated me.	I felt humiliated when you mentioned my problems in front of our friends.

Put It in Practice

USING I-LANGUAGE

For the next three days, whenever you use you-language, try to rephrase what you said or thought in I-language. How does this change how you think and feel about what's happening? How does using I-language affect interaction with others? Are others less defensive when you own your feelings and describe, but don't evaluate, their behaviors? Does I-language facilitate working out constructive changes?

Now that you're tuned into I- and you-language, monitor how you feel when others use you-language about you. When a friend or romantic partner says "You make me feel . . . ," do you feel defensive or guilty? Try teaching others to use I-language so that your relationships can be more honest and open.

Chapter 4
The World of Words

115

"Put It in Practice" Activities

This sample "Put It in Practice" activity from *Chapter 4: The World of Words* raises your awareness of the subtleties of language and how they can affect your relationships.

Additional Study Aids

I've included the following learning aids in each chapter to further enhance your study of interpersonal communication.

Who are you? Throughout our lives we ponder this question. We answer it one way at one time, then change our answer as we ourselves change. At the age of five, perhaps you defined yourself as your parents' daughter or son. That view of yourself implicitly recognized sex, race, and social class as parts of your identity. In high school, you may have described yourself in terms of academic strengths ("I'm good at math and science"), athletic endeavors ("I'm a forward on the team"), leadership positions ("I'm president of the La Rosa Club"), friends and romantic partners ("I'm going steady with Cam"), or future plans ("I'm starting college next year"; "I'm going to be an attorney"). Now that you're in college, it's likely you see yourself in terms of a major, a career path, and perhaps a relationship you hope will span the years ahead. You've probably also made some decisions about your sexual orientation, spiritual commitments, and political beliefs.

As you think about the different ways you've defined yourself over the years, you'll realize that the self is not a constant entity that is fixed early and then remains stable. Instead, the self is a process that evolves and changes continuously. Like the New Leaf on the previous page, the self emerges and is reborn throughout our lives. Among the influences that form and re-form ourselves are interactions with others and our reflections on them. In this chapter, we will explore how the self is formed and changed in the process of communicating with

© Anne Dowie

What Is the Self?

The **self** arises in communication and is a multi involves importing and acting from social persp complicated definition, as we will see it directs portant propositions about what, in fact, *is* very

The Self Arises in Communication

Communication is essential to developing a self clear understandings of who they are and what develop selves in the process of communicating who we are. Just as countries sometimes import countries, individuals import ideas about themse culture around them. As we import others' pers we come to share their perceptions of the world

From the moment we enter the world, we do, we learn how they see us, and we take their selves. Once we have internalized the views of generalized other, we engage in internal dialog ourselves of social perspectives. Through the p

Part I
The Fabric of Interpersonal
Communication

42

Chapter Introductions

I often open chapters with questions about your life or scenarios familiar to you as a way to introduce the chapter and preview its content. This introduction from *Chapter 2: Communication and the Creation of Self* is bound to get you thinking about the chapter's main issue: your self.

---

own feelings and thoughts by using I-language. Third, we should respect others as the experts on what they feel and think and not presume we know what they mean or share their experiences. The fourth principle is to strive for clarity by choosing appropriate degrees of abstraction, qualifying generalizations, and indexing evaluations, particularly ones applied to people.

SUMMARY

In this chapter, we discussed the world of words and meaning—the uniquely human universe that we inhabit because we are symbol users. Because symbols are arbitrary, ambiguous, and abstract, they have no inherent meanings. Instead, we actively construct meaning by interpreting symbols based on perspectives gleaned through interaction with others and our personal experiences. We also punctuate to create meaning in communication.

Instead of existing only in the physical world of the here and now, we use symbols to define, evaluate, and classify ourselves, others, and our experiences in the world. In addition, we use symbols to think hypothetically, so we can consider alternatives and simultaneously inhabit all three dimensions of time. Finally, symbols allow us to self-reflect so that we can monitor our own behaviors.

Although members of a society share a common language, we don't all use it the same way. Communication cultures, which exist both within and between countries, teach us rules for talking and interpreting others. Because communication rules vary among cultures based on gender, race, and class, we can't assume others use words just as we do.

The final section of this chapter discussed principles for improving effectiveness in verbal communication. Because words can mean different things to various people and because different communication cultures instill distinct rules for interacting, misunderstandings are always possible. To minimize them, we should engage in dual perspective, own our thoughts and feelings, respect what others say about how they think and feel, and monitor abstractness, generalizations, and static evaluations.

In the next chapter, we continue our discussion of the world of human communication by exploring the fascinating realm of nonverbal behavior.

KEY TERMS

Arbitrary
Ambiguous
Abstract
Communication rules
Regulative rules

Constitutive rules
Punctuation
Totalizing
Loaded language
Static evaluation

120

Chapter Summaries

Chapter summaries reiterate and condense the main issues of each chapter in a few paragraphs. This summary is from *Chapter 4: The World of Words.*

End-of-Chapter Key Terms

After each chapter summary is a list of key terms found in that chapter. These are also repeated in a complete glossary at the end of the text. Review these terms on your own to gauge your understanding of the chapter content.

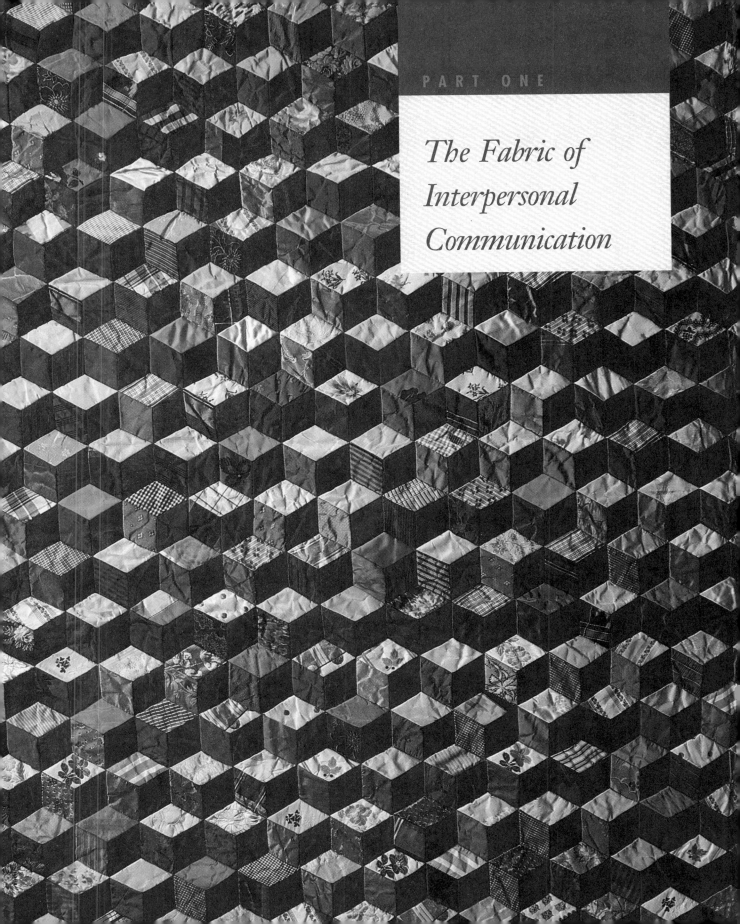

The Fabric of Interpersonal Communication

Starting the Conversation

$\mathcal{W}$hen I was twenty years old, something happened that profoundly changed the rest of my life: I took an introductory course in interpersonal communication. A new world of meaning opened up for me as I learned about the power of communication to enhance or harm relationships. The more courses I took, the more fascinated I became, so I decided to make a career of studying and teaching interpersonal communication. I wrote *Everyday Encounters* because I wanted to awaken you to the wonder of interpersonal communication as my first course awakened me.

In these opening pages, I'll introduce you to the field of interpersonal communication, to myself, and to the special context of our everyday encounters in this era.

The Field of Communication

The field of communication has a long and distinguished intellectual history. It dates back to ancient Greece where great philosophers such as Aristotle and Plato taught rhetoric, or public speaking, as a skill for participating in civic life. In the 2,000 years since the field was founded, it has expanded to encompass many kinds of interaction including small-group discussion, family communication, oral traditions, and interpersonal communication.

In recent years, interest in interpersonal communication has mushroomed, making it one of the largest and most vibrant areas in the entire discipline. Student demand for courses in interpersonal communication is rising. Scholars have responded by conducting more and more research and offering a greater number of classes that help students learn to interact effectively in everyday encounters.

The impressive theory and research generated by scholars of communication over the past two thousand years are the fabric from which I wove this book. Reflecting the intellectual maturity of the field, communication theory and research offer rich insight into the importance of interpersonal communication to individual identity and personal relationships. In the chapters that follow, we'll learn what scholars have discovered about how communication affects our self-concepts and our relationships with others. We'll also discover how different kinds of communication create defensive or supportive climates and how they promote constructive or unproductive ways of managing conflict.

© Tom Levy/Photo 20-20

We are more alike, my friends, than we are unalike.
MAYA ANGELOU

© Billy Barnes

Because communication in its many forms is central to personal and social life, the concerns of the communication field intersect with those of other disciplines interested in human behavior. Thus, research in communication contributes to and draws from work in fields such as psychology, sociology, anthropology, and counseling. The interdisciplinary mingling of ideas enriches the overall perspective on human interaction that you will find in *Everyday Encounters*.

A Personal Introduction

When I was an undergraduate, most of the books I read seemed distant and impersonal. I never had the feeling a real human being had written them, and authors never introduced themselves except by stating their titles. Certainly that's no way to begin a book about interpersonal communication! Instead, I'd rather create a more personal basis for interaction between you and me.

So that you may know something about the person who has written your book, let me introduce myself. I'm in my early forties, and I'm more excited now about life and its possibilities than ever before. Particularly, teaching and talking with students enrich my life and fuel my energies. My students are never-failing sources of insight and vision. Because my students teach me so much, I've included many of their reflections in this book. You'll encounter these in the chapters that follow. It's likely that you'll agree with some of my students' comments, disagree with others, and want to think further about still others. However you respond to their ideas, I suspect that you, like I, will find them interesting, insightful, and often challenging.

Now, some twenty-three years since I took my first course in interpersonal communication, I am more fascinated by and committed to this field than ever. I love teaching principles and skills that enhance students' effectiveness in everyday encounters. I also find that what I teach enriches my own life by allowing me to be more effective in my interactions with others. In addition, I enjoy conducting research to learn more about communication. A number of my studies are reflected in this book.

Although teaching, research, and writing occupy a great deal of my time, I have other interests as well. I cherish close relationships and spend much time with friends and my partner, Robbie Cox. (My cat, Scrambles, and I are also devoted to each other!) The relationships in my life continuously enlarge my understandings of human nature and the vital role of interpersonal communication in our lives.

I am European American, southern, middle class, heterosexual, and deeply committed to spiritual practice. Each facet of my identity shapes how I communicate and how I think about interaction, just as your race,

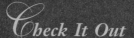
A KALEIDOSCOPIC CULTURE

The city of Atlanta, Georgia, which didn't even have a pizza parlor until 1959, by 1990 had a Korean Chamber of Commerce, a Hmong church, Hispanic yellow pages, Baptist churches for Romanians and Haitians, and a Chinese community center (p. 11).

Atlanta is home to 4,000 Vietnamese, 10,000 Indians, 25,000 Koreans, 30,000 Chinese, and 100,000 Hispanics (p. 11). Currently, white citizens are in the minority in Atlanta and many major cities in the United States. Between 1980 and 1990, the Hispanic population in the United States grew by over 50%, while the Asian or Pacific Islander population grew by over 100% in the same decade.

Source: Bates, E. (1994, fall). Beyond black and white. *Southern Exposure*, pp. 11–15.

© David Young-Wolff/PhotoEdit

class, gender, spirituality, and sexual orientation shape your communication. My race provides me with greater understanding of Caucasian values and perspectives than of those held by women and men of color. However, being of one race doesn't mean that I, or you, can't develop understanding of and respect for the experiences of people of other races.

Because I am middle class, I have been fortunate not to suffer economic deprivation (except when I was a poor graduate student!). Yet I interact with many working-class people, and I've gained some insight into the views, values, concerns, and pleasures that make up the fabric of their lives. Although my heterosexuality implies that I don't have personal experience in gay and lesbian relationships, I have learned a good deal about them from gay and lesbian friends of mine. All of us are limited by our own identities and the experiences and understandings they have given us. Yet, this doesn't mean we have to be ignorant of all those who are different from us. In fact, the more I interact with a range of people, the more I discover we have important similarities as well as interesting differences.

Diversity in Interpersonal Life

In introducing myself, I've placed myself in the context of a highly diverse society. This social diversity is one of the distinguishing features of our era. Making up Western society are people of many races, ethnicities, physical abilities, socioeconomic classes, genders, ages, spiritual inclinations, and sexual orientations.

The social diversity of modern life fosters two types of insight. The more obvious one is increased understanding of and respect for perspectives and behaviors that differ from our own. Less obvious but equally important is the insight into ourselves that comes from learning about those who differ from us in certain ways. For instance, Western cultures define "normal" as being European American, heterosexual, middle class, and young. Gay and lesbian orientations are often seen as deviations from the culturally created norm of heterosexuality. This means that gay and lesbian individuals understand their sexual orientations in relation to the heterosexual standard the culture represents as natural. However, heterosexuals often do not understand their sexual orientation in relation to homosexuality. Similarly, African Americans, Asians, and other people of color realize how they differ from European Americans more than European Americans perceive how they differ from people of color. We can also see our competitive attitude toward athletics in a new light by learning about the Japanese preference for ties in sports events so that neither side loses face. It is difficult to be aware of whiteness, heterosexuality, middle-class status, or competitive perspectives on sports because cultural practices make those appear natural and right in our lives. Thus, learning about people in other cultures and people who are outside of what the culture defines as mainstream inevitably teaches us about the mainstream as well.

The diversity of our society offers both opportunities and challenges. Differences in gender, race, class, cultural heritage, sexual preference, age, physical abilities, and spiritual beliefs present us with a rich array of perspectives on identity and interaction. Exploring variations among us enhances our appreciation of the range of human behavior and the options open to us in our own lives. At the same time, diversity can complicate interaction, because people may communicate in dissimilar ways and misunderstand one another as Yih-Tang Lin notes in her commentary.

© John Coletti/Stock, Boston

© Betty Press/Woodfin Camp & Associates, Inc.

YIH-TANG LIN

When I first came here to school I was amazed at how big the rooms in dormitories are, so I remarked on this. All of the Americans had a laugh at that and thought I was joking. In my country, individuals have very little space, and houses are tight together. The first time an American disagreed with me I felt angry that he would make me lose face. We don't ever contradict another person directly. I have had many miscommunications in this country.

© Craig Aurness/Woodfin Camp & Associates, Inc.

We are all different facets of the same reality, different parts of the one whole, just as the numerous waves rising and falling in the ocean are interrelated transformations of the one ocean.

THICH THIEN-AN

The process of socialization teaches each of us how to communicate and interpret what others say and do. This means that communication goals and styles vary according to the values and norms of particular social groups. Latinas and Eastern Europeans may have learned different ways of disclosing personal information, just as women and men may have been socialized into different styles of friendship. For this reason, we cannot simply tack discussions of diversity onto existing understandings of interaction.

Instead, we must weave awareness of diversity into the basic fabric of interpersonal communication. Each identity and communication style contributes to the overall fabric of interpersonal communication in our everyday lives.

In this book, we will consider many ways in which diversity intersects with communication. We'll discover, for instance, that women and men, in general, listen differently and rely on distinct types of communication to create closeness. We'll also learn that race and ethnicity influence personal styles of communication. To appreciate diversity in interpersonal communication, we will consider differences among people as natural and important dimensions of our everyday encounters.

Diversity is not something we add to communication, but is a basic part of what communication means and how we engage in it. Rather than adding understandings of diversity onto conventional views of communication, we will weave differences among us into discussions of how we communicate and how we interpret others' communication. This means, for example, we can't discuss principles of listening and conflict and then tack on a few words about ethnicity or gender. Instead, we want to consider how gender integrally affects the way we listen and how ethnic identity influences orientations to conflict. Because many Eastern cultures view conflict as disruptive and offensive, some Asian Americans may be reluctant to be as assertive as many Westerners. It's important for us to understand that Westerners' assertiveness and Easterners' more yielding styles of communicating reflect the values and norms of different cultures. This highlights the fact that effective communication isn't the same everywhere. Instead, what is effective depends on cultural values and standards. Weaving diversity into how we think about interpersonal communication enlarges understandings of both communication and the range of people and perspectives it involves. Cherrie, a student in one of my courses, makes this point effectively in her commentary.

C H E R R I E

I am Hispanic, and I am tired of classes and books that ignore my people. Last year I took a course in family life, and all we talked about was Western middle-class families. Their ways are not my ways. A course on family should be about many kinds of families. I took a course in great literature, and there was only one author who was not Western and only three who were women. It's not true that only white men write great literature.

Weaving the Book

I've written this book in a conversational tone, because I hope you and I will interact personally about ideas in the pages that follow. Another reason I chose to use a personal tone is that I want you to understand there is a real person behind the words you read. Like you, I am interested in interpersonal communication, and I am continuously trying to figure out how to be more effective in my everyday encounters with others. In this book, I share some of the ideas and skills that enhance my interactions, and I hope you will find them valuable in your life.

In addition to my voice, you'll encounter the voices of students like Cherrie and Yih-Tang Lin in this book. Woven throughout the pages that follow are reflections from my students' communication journals. In reading their commentaries, you'll discover that some of them are much like you and others are quite different. I believe we can learn from both those who are similar to us and those who differ from us. Regardless of whether you agree with the commentaries written by my students, they provide a rich source of ideas and learning. I think you will find, as I do, that it is enlarging to encounter a range of perspectives and issues relevant to interpersonal interaction.

Learning about interpersonal communication involves encounters with others, ourselves, and the world of ideas. I've woven these three kinds of encounters into the text as student commentaries and features that are titled "Put It in Practice" and "Check It Out." The commentaries invite you to encounter others and their perspectives. "Put It in Practice" features invite you to apply material discussed in the text to your own life. Finally, the "Check It Out" boxes spotlight interesting research and news items about interpersonal communication. Each of these features is woven into the text, just as encounters with ourselves, others, and ideas are woven into the fabric of our everyday lives.

The metaphor of weaving is also reflected in the artwork that opens each chapter. The weavings and other fabric art in this book reflect the experiences, values, and talents of people in many different cultures—from Japan to the United States, from the United Kingdom to India. You'll also notice the art reflects diverse artistic traditions—from folk crafts, as in the alphabet quilt that introduces Chapter 4, to elaborate textile art, as in the Furisode kimono shown at the beginning of Chapter 5. In selecting these images, I hope to emphasize the rich diversity of our world and the different ways in which distinct kinds of art express ideas, feelings, and human life. If you wish to know more about the art, page 314 provides credits and information on each chapter-opening image.

Everyday Encounters is my way of giving back to all of the students who have taught me so much. It's also a way to contribute to the field that continues to enrich my life and to make teaching communication a continuous joy for me. I hope this book will enhance your appreciation of the power of interpersonal communication in our relationships. I also hope it will motivate you to apply the principles and skills presented here in your everyday life.

Julia T. Wood

Julia T. Wood
Nelson Hairston Distinguished Professor
The University of North Carolina at Chapel Hill

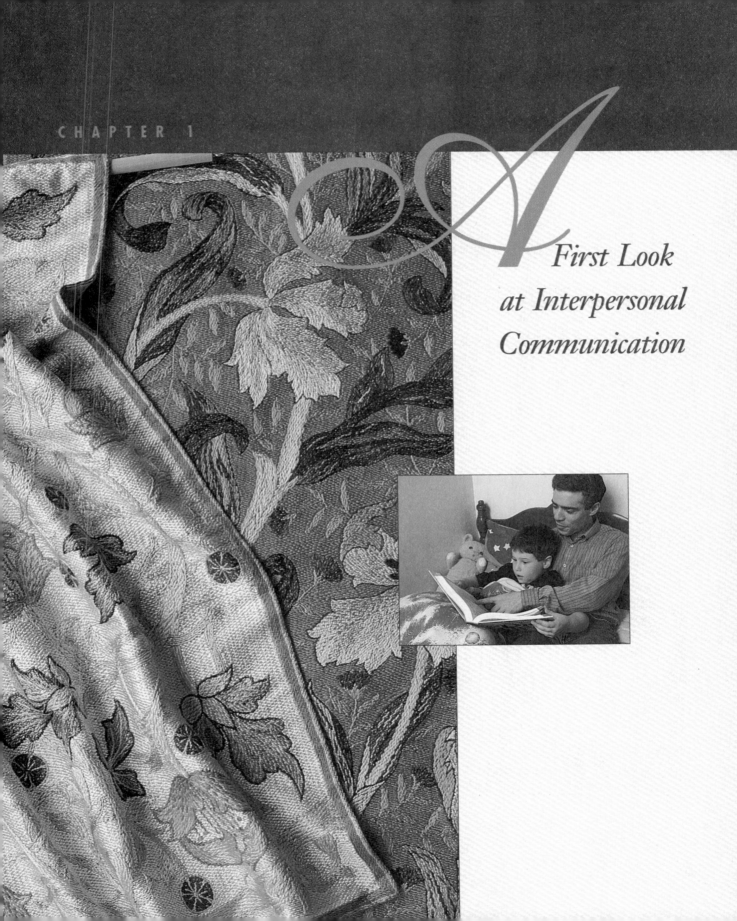

CHAPTER 1

A First Look at Interpersonal Communication

*Y*ou've been interviewing for two months, and so far, you haven't gotten a single job offer. After another interview that didn't go well, you run into a close friend who asks what's wrong. Instead of just offering quick sympathy, your friend suggests the two of you go to lunch and talk. Over sandwiches, you disclose that you're starting to worry you won't find a job and you wonder what's wrong with you. Your friend listens closely and lets you know she cares about your concerns. Then she tells you about other people she knows who also haven't gotten job offers. All of a sudden you don't feel so alone. She reminds you how worried you felt last term when you were struggling with that physics course and then you made a B on the final. Listening to her, your sagging confidence begins to recover. Before leaving, she helps you come up with new strategies for interviewing. You feel whole and hopeful again by the time you leave.

This scenario reveals the importance of interpersonal communication in our everyday lives. We count on others who are special to us to care about what is happening in our lives and to help us sort through problems and concerns. We want them to share our worries, as well as our joys. In addition, we need others to encourage our growth. Friends and romantic partners who believe in us often enable us to overcome self-defeating patterns and to become more the selves we want to be. And sometimes we just want to hang out with people we like and trust. Interpersonal communication is common to the many ways close relationships contribute to our lives.

Interpersonal communication is the foundation of personal identity and growth, and it is a primary basis of building connections with others. Effective communication enlarges us as individuals and enhances the quality of relationships, whereas ineffective communication diminishes us personally and can poison, or even destroy, our relationships. We engage in communication to develop identities, establish connections, deepen ties over time, and work out problems and possibilities. In short, interpersonal communication is central to our everyday lives and our happiness. It is the lifeblood of meaningful relationships.

Reprinted by permission of Tribune Media Services.

In this chapter, we take a first look at interpersonal communication. We'll start by considering how communication meets important human needs. We will then distinguish interpersonal communication from communication in general. Next we will identify principles and skills of effective interpersonal communication. After reading this chapter, you should understand what interpersonal communication is (and is not), why it matters in our lives, and the skills and principles of competent interpersonal communication.

The Interpersonal Imperative

Have you ever thought about why we communicate with others? There are many reasons we seek interaction and many human needs it meets. Abraham Maslow (1968), a psychologist, described human needs as arranged in a hierarchy in which more basic needs must be satisfied before we can focus on ones that are more abstract (Figure 1.1). As we will see, communication is a primary means to meeting each level of human need.

Physical Needs

At the most basic level, humans need to survive, and communication helps us meet this need. To survive, babies must alert others when they are hungry or in pain. And others must respond to these needs or babies will die. As we grow older, we still communicate to meet survival needs. We discuss medical problems with doctors in order to stay well, and effectiveness in communicating affects what jobs we get and how much income we earn to pay for basic needs such as medical care, food, and water.

At times we all rely on others. We might need assistance to understand difficult material in courses, fix a short in our stereo, learn a new computer program, or develop effective interviewing strategies. In each case, we communicate to gain assistance. Through communication we meet basic needs whether those are gaining food and water or engaging in sex, which Maslow considered a basic human need. Sometimes we also have to persuade

© A. Sieveking/Petit/Photo Researchers, Inc.

We start out in our lives as little children, full of light and the clearest vision.

BRENDA UELAND

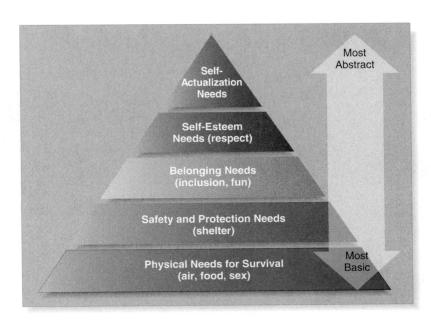

FIGURE 1.1 *Maslow's Hierarchy of Needs*

Doonesbury © 1994 G. B. Trudeau. Reprinted with permission of Universal Press Syndicate. All rights reserved.

others to comply with our requests by explaining why they should or how helping us will help them. This too requires communication skill.

Safety Needs

We also meet safety needs through communication. If your roof is leaking or termites have invaded your apartment, you must talk with the rental agent to have the problem solved so that you have safe shelter. In an era under the shadow of AIDS, couples have to talk with each other about safer sex. Being able to discuss private and difficult issues surrounding sex is essential to our safety.

NAVITA

It's funny, but it's harder to talk about sex than to have it. I'm having to learn how to bring up the topic of safety and how to be assertive about protection. I used not to do that because it's embarrassing, but I'd rather be embarrassed than dead.

Communication skills also allow us to protect ourselves from damaging, or even deadly, environmental toxins. Residents in communities with toxic waste dumps have to communicate with officials and media to correct environmental toxins that endanger their physical survival and safety.

Belonging Needs

The third level in Maslow's hierarchy is belonging, or social, needs. All humans seek others to be happy, to enjoy life, and to enrich experiences. We want others' company, acceptance, and affirmation, and we want to give acceptance and affirmation to others. The alternative is loneliness, which can be very painful. Interaction with others provides us with a sense of social fit ("I'm one of the group"), structures time ("It's fun to shoot hoops with Pat"), and introduces us to perspectives that broaden our own views ("I never saw it that way").

CHAD

I never had a label for it before, but a lot of my communication is for belonging needs. When I feel down or bored, I find one of my friends and we hang out. It doesn't matter what we do, or whether we do anything really. Sometimes it's just important to have somebody to hang with.

The connection between good relationships and well-being is demonstrated by a great deal of research. For instance, one study found that people who lack strong social ties are 200 to 300% more likely to die prematurely (Narem, 1980). Another report concluded that heart disease is far more prevalent in people who do not have strong interpersonal relationships than in ones who do (Ruberman, 1992). Researchers have also found a strong link between having few friends and problems such as depression, anxiety, and fatigue (Hojat, 1982; Jones & Moore, 1989). A particularly dramatic finding is that people who are deprived of interaction often hallucinate, lose physiological coordination, and become depressed and disoriented (Wilson, Robick, & Michael, 1974). This research confirms that isolation is one of the cruelest forms of punishment.

Self-Esteem Needs

Moving up the hierarchy, we find self-esteem needs, which are concerned with being valued. We want others to respect us, and we want to

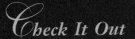

GHADYA KA BACHA

In 1954, a young, naked boy who was starving found his way to the hospital at Balrampur, India. He showed no ability to interact with people and had heavy calluses as if he moved on all fours. In addition, there were scars on the boy's neck as if he had been dragged by animals. The boy, named Ramu by the hospital staff, spent most of his time playing with a stuffed animal as a wild animal might in its lair. He showed no interest in communicating; indeed, he seemed to feel no connection with other people. Only twice did Ramu seem excited. Once was when he was taken to see wolves at a zoo, and the other time was when he saw a dog.

Ramu would howl when he smelled raw meat in the hospital kitchen over 100 yards from his room—far too great a distance for the human sense of smell to detect a scent. Ramu also didn't eat like a human: He tore meat apart and lapped milk from a container. Most of the doctors and scientists who examined Ramu concluded he was a wolf boy who had grown up in the wild and been socialized by wolves. He had no concept of himself as a person. Instead, he saw himself as a wolf and was more interested in interacting with animals than humans, who were not "his kind." Thus, doctors referred to Ramu as Ghadya Ka Bacha, the Indian term for wolf boy.

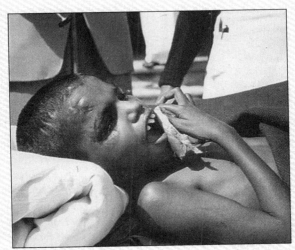

Archive Photos/APA

© 1982. *The Far Side* cartoon by Gary Larson is reprinted by permission of Chronicle Features, San Francisco, CA. All rights reserved.

respect ourselves. As we will see in Chapter 2, communication is the primary way we figure out who we are and who we can be. We gain our first sense of self from others who communicate how they see us. Parents tell children they are pretty or plain, smart or slow, good or bad, difficult or helpful. As parents communicate their perceptions, children begin to form images of themselves. This process continues throughout life as we see ourselves reflected in others' eyes. We learn who we are by how others see us, communicate with us, and respond to us. The story of *Ghadya Ka Bacha*, the "wolf boy," demonstrates that communicating with others is essential to self-concept—and even to human identity (Shattuck, 1980).

Self-Actualization Needs

According to Maslow, the most abstract human needs are for self-actualization. By this he meant that each of us wants to grow throughout life and to realize our unique potential. As humans, we seek more than survival, safety, belonging, and esteem. We also thrive on growth. Each of us wants to cultivate new dimensions in our lives, enlarge our perspectives, engage in challenging and different experiences, and learn new skills. We want to become our fullest selves by realizing our unique potential.

Communication fosters our growth as individuals. It is often in interaction with others that we first recognize possibilities for who we can be—ones that hadn't occurred to us. Others also introduce us to new experiences and ways of thinking, and we are enlarged by these. In addition, we use communication to experiment with new versions of ourselves. Sometimes we talk with others about goals and challenges we are embracing. At other times we try out new styles of identity without calling explicit attention to what we're doing. We see how others respond and decide whether we like the effects of the new identity or whether we need to go back to the drafting board.

LASHELLE

A person who changed my life was Mrs. Dickenson, my high school history teacher. She thought I was really smart, and she helped me see myself that way. I'd never considered myself all that intelligent, and I sure hadn't thought I would go to college, but Mrs. Dickenson helped me to see a whole new image of who I could be. She stayed after school a lot of days to talk to me about my future and to help me get ready for the SAT. If it weren't for her, I wouldn't be in college now.

© Nita Winter

We must recognize the whole gamut of human potentialities, and so weave a less arbitrary social fabric, one in which each diverse human gift will find a fitting place.

MARGARET MEAD

Others also help us self-actualize through inspiration and teaching. Gandhi, for instance, was a model of strength that didn't depend on aggression. Seeing him embody passive resistance with grace and impact inspired thousands of Indians to define themselves as passive resisters. Years later in the United States, the Reverend Martin Luther King, Jr., followed Gandhi's example with his nonviolent resistance of racism. Religious leaders such as Lao-tzu, Confucius, Jesus, Mohammad, and Buddha are also models who inspire people to grow personally. As we interact with teachers and leaders who inspire us, we may come to understand their visions of the world and of themselves and may weave those into our own self-concepts.

Living in a Diverse Society

To the needs Maslow identified, I would add a sixth one. In the 1990s, we need to know how to live effectively in a richly diverse society. Our world includes people of different ethnicities, genders, social classes, sexual preferences, ages, and abilities. To function effectively in a world

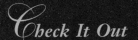
Check It Out

RELIGIONS AROUND THE WORLD

Although Christianity dominates in Western societies, around the world a number of religions are vital and growing.

Buddhism, founded by Siddhartha Gautama in southern Nepal in the sixth and fifth centuries B.C., has over 307 million followers. The Buddhist religion emphasizes the interdependence of all living beings and seeks to reduce suffering in the world.

Confucianism has nearly 6 million followers today. Founded by Confucius, a Chinese philosopher, in the sixth and fifth centuries B.C., this religion stresses the relationships among individuals, families, and society based on *li*, or proper behavior, and *jen*, or sympathetic attitudes.

Hinduism dates back to 1500 B.C. when indigenous religions of India combined with Aryan religions. Hindus believe in a strict caste system, which ranks people into different classes that one progresses through in a series of incarnations. Today there are over 6 million Hindus.

Judaism is traced back to Abraham, Isaac, and Jacob, who were the decendants of Judah, in the year 2000 B.C. Jews believe that the human condition can be bettered by following the teachings of the Jewish Bible, which is the Old Testament. The *Torah* is an especially revered portion of the Jewish Bible. Today there are approximately 18 million followers of Judaism.

Taoism was founded in China by Lao-tzu, who is said to have been born in 604 B.C. Taoism encourages living simply, spontaneously, and in harmony with nature. Because Taoism has been actively diminished since the Communist revolution, it is difficult to know how many followers there are.

Shinto is an ancient indigenous religion of Japan that existed prior to the fifth century B.C. Shintos, who number approximately three and a half million today, believe in multiple spiritual beings and deities, called *kami*, and they give loyalty to societies believed to be favored by the *kami*.

Source: *New York Public Library Desk Reference*. (1989). New York: Simon & Schuster and Songstone Press, pp. 189–191.

UPI/Bettmann

Justice cannot be for one side alone, but must be for both.
ELEANOR ROOSEVELT

marked by diversity, we rely on communication. Through interaction with others, we learn about experiences and lifestyles that differ from our own. In addition, we share our experiences and values with people who seem unlike us in certain ways. Through interaction, diverse individuals come to understand their differences and to recognize them as opportunities for growth.

Like the other needs in Maslow's hierarchy, living in a diverse world becomes salient to us when we meet more basic needs. As long as we need food, shelter, and a sense of belonging, engaging diversity may not be salient to us. When more basic needs are met, however, we recognize the importance of appreciating diversity. It's also the case that learning to engage diversity may help us meet some of our more basic needs. For example, our safety may depend on communicating with someone from a different culture, and we may meet belonging needs by joining groups with people who represent a range of ethnicities, religions, sexual orientations, and so forth. As we stand on the brink of the twenty-first century, one of the most vital functions of communication is helping us understand and participate in a diverse world.

Put It in Practice

COMMUNICATION AND YOUR NEEDS

How do the needs we've discussed show up in your life? To find out, try this:

First, keep a diary of your communication for the next three days. Note the people you talk to, what is said, and how you feel about each interaction.

After you've completed a three-day diary, go back through and classify each interaction according to one of the six needs we discussed. How much of your communication focuses on each need?

Physical survival	Self-esteem
Safety	Self-actualization
Belonging	Living in a diverse society

Defining Interpersonal Communication

So far we've seen that communication is a primary way to meet a range of human needs. There are many kinds of communication, however, and not all are interpersonal. We now want to clarify what interpersonal communication is.

When asked to distinguish interpersonal communication from communication in general, many people say that interpersonal communication involves fewer people, often just two. Although much interpersonal communication involves only two or three individuals, this isn't a precise way to define interpersonal communication. If it were, then an exchange between a shopper and a salesclerk would be interpersonal, but a family conversation wouldn't be.

Some people suggest that intimate contexts define interpersonal communication. Using this standard, we would say that a couple on a first date in a romantic restaurant engages in more interpersonal communication than an established couple in a shopping mall. Clearly, context doesn't tell us what is distinct about interpersonal communication.

What distinguishes interpersonal communication is a special quality of interaction. This emphasizes what happens between people, not where they are or how many are present. For starters, then, we can say interpersonal communication is a special type of interaction. This is best understood by thinking about a communication continuum.

© Serge Attal/Sygma

FIGURE 1.2 *The Communication Continuum*

A Communication Continuum

We can begin to understand the special character of interpersonal communication by tracing the meaning of the word *interpersonal*. It is derived from the prefix *inter* meaning "between" and the word *person*, so interpersonal communication literally occurs between persons. In one sense, all communication happens between persons, yet actually many interactions don't involve us personally. Communication exists on a continuum from impersonal to interpersonal (Figure 1.2).

A lot of our communication doesn't require that we or others interact personally. Sometimes we don't acknowledge others as persons at all, but treat them as objects. In other instances, we interact with others in stereotypical or role-bound ways, but don't deal with them as distinct persons. And with a select few we communicate in deeply personal ways. These distinctions were captured in poetic terms by the philosopher Martin Buber (1970) who distinguished among three levels of communication: I–It, I–You, and I–Thou.

I–It Communication   In an I–It relationship, we treat others very impersonally, almost as objects. In **I–It communication*** we do not acknowledge the humanity of other persons; we may not even affirm their existence. Salespeople, servers in restaurants, and clerical staff are often treated

---

*Boldface terms are defined in the glossary at the end of the book.

not as people, but as instruments to take orders and produce what we want. We also tend not to have personal conversations with phone solicitors. In the extreme form of I–It relationships, others are not even acknowledged. When a homeless person asks for money for food, some people do not even respond, but look through and beyond the person as if she or he isn't there. In dysfunctional families, parents may ignore children, thereby treating the children as its, not as unique individuals. Students on large campuses may also feel they are treated as its, not as persons. Jason, a sophomore in one of my classes, makes this point.

JASON

One thing that really bothers me about this school is that I get treated like a number a lot of the time. When I go to see my adviser, he asks what my social security number is—not what my name is. Most of my professors don't even know my name. We all knew each other in high school, and all the teachers called on us by name. It felt more human there. Sometimes I feel like an it on this campus.

I–You Communication The second level that Buber identified is **I–You communication**, which accounts for the majority of our interactions. I–You communication is midway between impersonal and interpersonal communication. People acknowledge one another as more than objects, but they don't fully engage each other as unique individuals. For example, suppose you go shopping and a salesclerk asks, "May I help you?" Chances are you won't have a deep conversation with the clerk, but you might treat him or her as more than an it. Perhaps you say, "I'm just browsing today. You know how it is at the end of the month—no money." The clerk might laugh and commiserate about how money gets tight by the end of each month. In this interaction, you and the clerk treat each other as more than its: The clerk doesn't treat you as a faceless shopper, and you don't treat the clerk as just an agent of the store.

I–You relationships may also be more personal than interactions with salesclerks. For instance, we talk with others in our classes and on our sports teams in ways that are somewhat personal. Interaction is still guided by our roles as peers, members of a class or team, and students. Yet we do affirm their existence and recognize them as individuals within those roles. Teachers and students often talk personally, yet stay within their social roles and don't reveal their private selves. We communicate in less depth with most people in our social circles than with those we love most. Casual friends, work associates, and distant family members typically engage in I–You communication.

I–Thou Communication The most rare kind of relationship involves **I–Thou communication**. Buber regarded this as the highest form of human dialogue because each person affirms the other as cherished and unique. When we interact on an I–Thou level, we meet others in their wholeness and individuality. Instead of dealing with them as occupants of social roles, we see them as unique human beings whom we know and accept in their totality. Also, in I–Thou communication we don't mask ourselves; instead, we open ourselves fully, trusting others to accept us as we are with virtues and vices, hopes and fears, strengths and weaknesses.

Buber believed that only in I–Thou relationships do we become fully human, which for him meant we discard the guises we use most of the time and allow ourselves to be completely genuine in interaction (Stewart, 1986). Much of our communication involves what Buber calls "seeming," in which we're preoccupied with our image and careful to manage how we present ourselves. In I–Thou relationships, however, we engage in "being," in which we reveal who we really are and how we really feel. For Buber, only I–Thou communication is fully interpersonal for only in I–Thou encounters do we meet each other as whole, existential persons.

I–Thou relationships are not commonplace, because we can't afford to reveal ourselves totally to everyone all of the time. We also don't want to be completely open or to form deeply personal ties with everyone. Thus, I–Thou relationships and the communication in them are rare and special. They represent fully interpersonal relationships.

© Mugshots/Gabe Palmer/The Stock Market

In love there are two things—bodies and words.
JOYCE CAROL OATES

Put It in Practice

COMMUNICATION IN YOUR RELATIONSHIPS

Consider how Buber's theory of communication applies to your life. Identify someone with whom you have each kind of communication: I–It, I–You, I–Thou. Describe what needs and values each relationship satisfies.

How does communication differ among the relationships? What don't you say in I–It and I–You relationships that you do say in I–Thou relationships? How do different levels of communication affect the closeness you feel with others?

Definition

Now that we realize there are degrees of interpersonalness, let's develop a specific definition. **Interpersonal communication** *is a selective, systemic, unique, and ongoing process of interaction between individuals who reflect and build personal knowledge of one another as they create meanings.* We'll discuss key terms in this definition so that we share understanding of interpersonal communication.

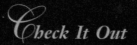

ANTI-NOISE

It's estimated that more than 9 million workers are exposed to dangerous levels of noise that have effects ranging from increased fatigue to loss of hearing. Until recently companies recognized only the most excessive forms of noise. However, there are serious dangers from low-frequency noises such as rumblings from motors, engines and fans. Low-frequency noise pollution affects not only office workers, but others. For example, groundskeepers are bombarded by 85+ decibels from lawn mowers and other machines.

Awareness of the dangers of noise has spawned a new line of work: noise consulting. Noise consultants help employers identify hazardous noise levels and recommend ways to reduce dangers. The newest remedy is a noise cancellation device that produces *anti-noise*, which is equal but opposite sound waves to block noise. Early tests indicate anti-noise is more effective than earplugs.

Source: Labor letter. (1994, July 16). *Wall Street Journal*, p. A1.

Selective   First, as we noted above, fully interpersonal communication is not something we engage in or desire with everyone. Instead, we invest the effort and take the risks of being genuinely open with only a few people. As Buber realized, the majority of our communication is relatively superficial and occurs on I–It or I–You levels. This is fine, since I–Thou relationships require more time, energy, and courage than we want to offer to everyone.

Systemic   Interpersonal communication is also **systemic**, which means it takes place within various systems. All communication occurs in contexts that influence what happens and the meanings we assign to communication. The communication between you and me right now is embedded in multiple systems including the interpersonal communication course, academic institutions, and U.S. society. Each of these systems influences what we expect of each other, what I write, and how you interpret what you read. The ways people communicate also vary across cultures. Whereas North Americans tend to communicate assertively and look at one another, in many Asian societies assertion and eye contact are considered rude. Native Americans are traditionally less verbal than Americans of European heritage.

Consider an example of the systemic character of communication. Suppose Ian gives Cheryl a solid gold pendant and says, "I wanted to show how much I care about you." What do his words mean? That depends in large part on the systems in which he and Cheryl interact. If Ian and Cheryl just started dating, an extravagant gift means something different than if they've been married for twenty years. On the other hand, if they don't have an established relationship and Cheryl is engaged to Manuel, Ian's gift may mean something else. What if Ian beat Cheryl the day before? Perhaps then the gift is to apologize, not to show love. If Ian is rich, a solid gold pendant may be less awesome than if he is short on cash. Systems that affect what this communication means include Cheryl and Ian's relationship, their socioeconomic classes, cultural norms for gift-giving, and Cheryl's and Ian's personal histories. All of these contexts affect their interaction and what it means.

Because interpersonal communication is systemic, situation, time, people, culture, personal histories, and so forth interact to affect meanings. We can't just add up the various parts of a system to understand their impact on communication. Instead, we have to recognize that all parts of a system interact, so that each part affects all others. In other words, elements of communication systems are interdependent; each is tied to all of the others.

We should also realize that all systems include **noise**, which is anything that distorts communication or interferes with individuals' understandings of one another. Noise in communication systems, just like other kinds of noise, complicates understanding. Also, like other kinds of noise, noise in communication systems is both inevitable and unavoidable. We should simply be aware that it exists and try to compensate for the difficulties it causes.

© David M. Grossman/Photo Researchers, Inc.

There are three kinds of noise. Physical noise includes extreme temperatures, hunger that keeps us from concentrating, fatigue, or crowded conditions. Psychological noises occur in us and affect how we communicate and how we interpret others. For instance, if you are preoccupied with a problem, you may be inattentive. Likewise, prejudice, cultural differences, and defensive feelings can interfere with communication. Our needs may also affect how we interpret others. For example, if we really need affirmation or love, we may be predisposed to perceive others as communicating more commitment than they really do. Finally, semantic noise exists when words themselves are not mutually understood. Authors sometimes create semantic noise by using jargon or unnecessarily technical language. For instance, to discuss noise I could write that communication can be egregiously obstructed by phenomena extrinsic to an exchange that actuate misrepresentations and symbolic incongruities. Although that sentence may be accurate, it's not clear because it's filled with semantic noise.

CARMELLA

I wish professors would learn about semantic noise. I really try to pay attention in class and to learn, but the way some faculty talk makes it impossible to understand what they mean, especially if English is a second language. I wish they would remember that we're not specialists like they are, so we don't know all the technical words.

When we say that communication is systemic, then, we mean three things. First, all communication occurs within multiple systems that affect meanings. Second, all parts and all systems of communication are interdependent, so they affect one another. Finally, all communication systems have noise that may be physical, psychological, or semantic.

Unique Interpersonal communication is also unique. In relationships that go beyond social roles, every person is unique and, therefore, irreplaceable. We can substitute people in I–It and even I–You relationships (one clerk can ring up purchases as well as another; we can get another racquetball buddy), but we can't replace intimates. When we lose intimates, we find new friends and romantic partners, but they aren't interchangeable with the ones we lost.

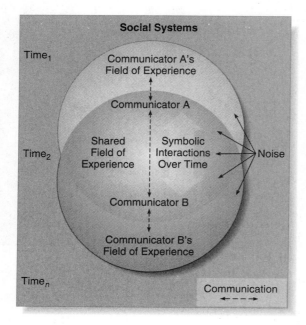

Social Systems

Time₁ — Communicator A's Field of Experience

Communicator A

Shared Field of Experience | Symbolic Interactions Over Time → Noise

Time₂

Communicator B

Communicator B's Field of Experience

Timeₙ

Communication

FIGURE 1.3
Model of Communication
(Adapted from Wood, 1992)

Just as every person is unique, so is each friendship and romantic relationship. Each develops its own distinctive patterns and rhythms and even special vocabulary that are not part of other interpersonal relationships. In the process of becoming close, people work out personal roles and rules for interaction, and these may deviate from general social rules and roles. With one friend you might go roller blading and get together for athletic events and insult each other in jest. With a different, equally close friend you might talk openly about feelings. My sister Carolyn and I constantly play jokes on each other and engage in verbal duels in which we try to one-up each other. With my other sister these forms of communication create problems (as I discovered!). My communication with each sister reflects not only who we are as unique persons, but also our particular relationships. In other words, interpersonal communication involves persons in relation to each other.

Ongoing Process   Interpersonal communication is an ongoing, continuous **process**. This means, first, that interpersonal communication evolves over time, becoming more interpersonal as individuals interact. Friendships and romantic relationships gain depth and significance over the course of time, and they may also decline in quality over time. Because relationships are dynamic, they don't stay the same, but continuously change just as we do.

An ongoing process also has no discrete beginnings and endings. Figure 1.3 highlights the processual character of interpersonal communication by including time as a dynamic feature that changes. Suppose a friend stops by and confides in you about a troubling personal problem. When did that communication begin? Although it may seem to have started when the friend came by, earlier interactions may have led the friend to feel it was safe to talk to you and that you would care about the problem. We can't be sure when this communication began. Similarly, we don't know where it will end. Perhaps it ends when the friend leaves, but perhaps it doesn't. Maybe your response to the problem helps your friend see new options. Maybe what you learn changes how you feel toward your friend. Because communication is ongoing, we can never be sure when it begins and ends, as Kate illustrates.

KATE

It's really true about not knowing where communication stops. I'm a resident adviser for my dorm, and last year a freshman came in to talk. I started to ask her to come back later, because I was trying to finish a paper, but she looked so upset that I put it aside. She asked me what I planned to do when I got out of college and if things ever got so rough I just wanted to call it quits. I couldn't figure out what was bothering her, but I felt like I needed to keep talking. I told her about a counselor on campus who helped me through a bad time. After an hour or so, she thanked me for my time and left. A few months later, her best friend told me that she'd been considering killing herself and talking with me was what stopped her.

Because interpersonal interaction is a process, what happens between people is linked to both past and future. In our earlier example, the meaning of Ian's gift reflects prior interactions between him and Cheryl, and their interaction about the gift will affect future interactions. All of our communication occurs in three temporal dimensions—past, which affects what happens now; present; and future, which is molded by what occurs in this moment (Dixson & Duck, 1993). How couples handle early arguments affects how they deal with later ones; what happened in a relationship last week shapes interaction today. Past, present, and future are always interwoven in communication.

The ongoing quality of interpersonal communication also suggests that we can't stop the process, nor can we edit or unsay what has been said. In this sense, communication is irreversible—we can't take it back. Interpersonal communication is always evolving, changing, moving ever onward.

Interaction   Interpersonal communication is a process of interaction between people. Unlike electronic communication in which one person sends a message and another receives it, in interpersonal communication each person both sends and receives communication. As you speak to a friend, your friend smiles; while a teacher explains an idea, you nod to show you understand; as your parent scolds you, you wrinkle your brow resentfully. In interpersonal encounters, all parties communicate continuously and simultaneously.

The interactive nature of interpersonal communication implies that responsibility for effectiveness is shared among communicators. We often say, "You didn't express yourself clearly" or "You misunderstood me," as if understanding rests with a single person. In reality, responsibility for good communication is shared. Effectiveness requires people who are speaking to use language carefully and be sensitive to others' responses both during and after they speak. At the same time, someone who is listening has a responsibility to try to understand and to give feedback to the other person. Alone, neither person can make interaction successful. Because interpersonal communication is an ongoing, interactive process, all participants share responsibility for its effectiveness.

Individuals   From Buber we learned that fully interpersonal communication involves engaging others as individuals unlike any other persons. Interpersonal communication involves more than speaking from social roles (teacher–student; boss–employee; customer–salesclerk). Instead, to engage in interpersonal communication, we must treat others and be treated by them as individuals. This is possible only if we learn who they are and they come to understand us as distinct individuals, unlike anyone else. We can't automatically communicate with others as full, unique individuals because

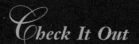

PILLOW TALK

Counselors have discovered what couples have long known—that private codes of communication are part and parcel of intimacy. Recent studies indicate that most intimate partners develop private vocabularies to express themselves to each other in unique ways. Couples report having private nicknames for one another ("the redhead," "noodle brain"), special codes for indicating they want to make love ("want to read in bed tonight?"), and teasing routines and mock insults used to show affection.

What researchers also discovered is that closeness between partners seems linked to how extensive a private language they have developed. Thus, it may be that communication is not only the messenger of loving feelings, but also the creator.

Source: Public pillow talk. (1987, October). *Psychology Today*, p. 18.

we don't know them personally when we first meet. Instead, we come to understand the unique fears and hopes, problems and joys, needs and abilities of persons as we interact with them meaningfully over a period of time. As trust builds, people disclose personal information that allows insight into their unique selves.

Personal Knowledge   Interpersonal communication both reflects and creates personal knowledge. To connect as unique individuals, we have to get to know others personally. You can't interact with someone as a full person until you know something about that person. Over time, as we move toward more fully interpersonal relationships, our communication is based increasingly on personal knowledge. My sisters feel differently about exchanging verbal insults and tricks because of experiences in their lives. As each of them revealed her history and feelings, I adapted my communication to reflect my personal knowledge of each of them.

Interpersonal communication also creates personal knowledge. As our relationships with others deepen, we build trust and learn how to communicate in ways that make each other feel comfortable and safe. In turn, the personal knowledge that allows us to do this encourages us to self-disclose further: We share secrets, fears, and experiences that we don't tell to just anyone. This is part of what Buber meant by "being" with others. Personal knowledge is a process—one that grows and builds on itself over time as people communicate interpersonally.

LIZELLE

What I like best about long-term relationships is all the layers that develop. I know the friends I've had since high school in so many ways. I know what they did and felt and dreamed in high school, and I know them as they are now. They have the same kind of in-depth knowledge of me. We tell each other everything, so it sometimes seems that my deepest friends know me better than I know myself.

Meanings   The heart of interpersonal communication is shared meanings between people (Duck, 1994a, 1994b). We don't just exchange words when we communicate. Instead, we create meanings as we figure out what each other's words and behaviors stand for, represent, or imply. Meanings grow out of histories of interaction between unique persons. For example, my partner, Robbie, and I are both continuously overcommitted, and we worry about the pace of each other's life. Often one of us says to the other "bistari, bistari." That phrase means nothing to you unless you know Nepalese and can translate it as meaning "slow down, go gradually." When one of us says "bistari," we not only suggest slowing down, but also remind ourselves of our special time living and trekking in Nepal. Most close friends and romantic partners develop vocabularies that have meaning only to them.

You might have noticed that I refer to meaning*s*, not just one meaning. This is because all interpersonal communication has two levels of meaning (Watzlawick, Beavin, & Jackson, 1967). The first level, called the **content meaning**, deals with literal or denotative meaning. Content meanings concern information. If a parent says to a five-year-old child, "Clean your room now," the content meaning is that the room is to be cleaned.

The second level of meaning is the **relational level of meaning**. This refers to what communication expresses about relationships between communicators. The relational meaning of "Clean your room now" is that the parent has the right to order the child—they have an unequal power relationship. If the parent had said, "Would you mind cleaning your room?" the relational meaning would have suggested a more equal relationship. Assume a friend says, "You're the only person I can talk to about this," and then discloses something that is worrying him. The content level includes the actual issue itself and the information that you're the only one with whom he will discuss this issue. But what has he told you on the relationship level? He has communicated that he trusts you, he considers you special, and he perhaps expects you to care about his troubles.

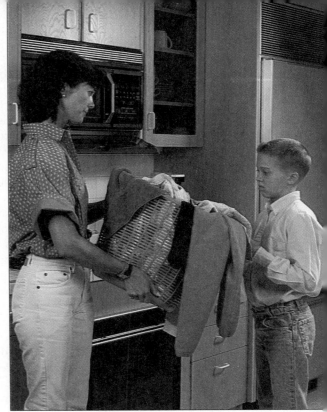

© Jeffry W. Myers/Stock, Boston

ANI

My father needs to learn about relational meanings. Whenever I call home, he asks me if anything's wrong. Then he asks what the news is. If I don't have news to report, he can't understand why I'm calling. Then Mom gets on the phone, and we talk for a while about stuff—nothing important, just stuff. I don't call to tell them big news. I just want to touch base and feel connected.

Scholars have identified three general dimensions of relational-level meanings (Wood, 1994d). The first dimension is responsiveness, and it refers to how aware of others and involved with them we are. Perhaps you have talked to people who shuffled papers and glanced at a clock. If so, you probably felt they weren't interested in you or the conversation. Low responsiveness is communicated on the relational level of meaning when people don't look at us or when they are preoccupied with something other than talking with us. Higher responsiveness is communicated by eye contact, head nods, and feedback that indicates involvement.

A second dimension of relational meaning is liking, or affection. This concerns the degree of positive or negative feeling that is communicated. Although liking may seem synonymous with responsiveness, the two are actually distinct. We may be responsive to people we don't like but have to pay attention to, and we are sometimes preoccupied and unresponsive to people we care about. We communicate that we like or dislike others by what we actually say as well as by tone of voice, facial expressions, how close we sit to them, and so forth.

Power or control is the third dimension of relational meaning. This refers to the power balance between communicators. A parent may say to a five-year-old, "Clean your room because I say so, that's why." This communicates that the parent has greater power than the child—the power to tell the child what to do. Friends and romantic partners sometimes engage in covert power struggles on the relational level. One person suggests going to movie X and then to dinner at the pizza parlor. The other responds by saying she doesn't want to see that movie and isn't in the mood for pizza. They could be arguing on the content level about their different preferences for the evening. If arguments over what to do are recurrent and heated, however, chances are the couple is negotiating power. In interpersonal relationships, the relational level of meaning is often the most important, for it sets the tone for interaction and how people feel about each other.

Put It in Practice

LEVELS OF MEANING

For the next forty-eight hours, focus on relational meanings in your communication. Record examples of the following:

1. Communicating responsiveness
2. Communicating lack of responsiveness
3. Expressing liking
4. Expressing dislike
5. Announcing superiority
6. Showing subordination
7. Expressing equality

What does this tell you about the relational issues being negotiated and expressed in your relationships?

In sum, we have seen that communication exists on a continuum, ranging from impersonal to interpersonal. We have also defined interpersonal communication as a selective, systemic, unique, and ongoing process of interaction between individuals who reflect and build personal knowledge of one another as they create meanings. Meanings, we have seen, reflect histories of interaction and involve both content and relational levels. Building on this definition, we're now ready to identify basic principles of interpersonal communication.

Principles of Interpersonal Communication

The definition of interpersonal communication and our discussion of reasons we communicate suggest six basic principles. Understanding these will help you communicate more effectively in a variety of contexts.

We Cannot Not Communicate

Whenever people are together, they communicate. We cannot avoid communicating when we are with others, because they interpret what we do and say as well as what we don't do and don't say. Even if we choose to be silent, we're communicating. What we mean by silence and how others interpret it will depend on cultural backgrounds. Because Westerners are more verbal than most cultural groups, they are likely to regard silence as a signal of uneasiness, anger, or disinterest. Native Americans and members of many Eastern societies might interpret silence as a sign of thought or respect. Either way, silence communicates.

Although others sometimes misunderstand what we mean, they still respond to our presence and what we do and don't say and do. Even when we don't intend to communicate, we do so. We may be unaware of a grimace that gives away our disapproval or an eye roll that shows we dislike someone, but we are communicating nonetheless. Unconscious communication particularly occurs on the relational level of meaning as we express feelings about others through subtle, often nonverbal communication. Regardless of whether we aim to communicate and whether others understand our intentions, we continuously, unavoidably communicate.

Communication Is Irreversible

Perhaps you have been in heated arguments in which you lost your temper and said something you later regretted. It could be that you hurt someone or revealed something about yourself you meant to keep private. Later you might have tried to repair the damage by apologizing, explaining what you said, or denying what you revealed. But you couldn't erase your communication; you couldn't unsay what you said.

© Phyllis Picardi/Stock, Boston

The fact that communication is irreversible means that what we say and do matters. It has impact. The irreversibility of interpersonal communication underlines our earlier discussion of communication as an ongoing process that reflects what has gone before and shapes what will follow. Once we say something to another person, that becomes part of the relationship. Remembering this principle keeps us aware of the importance of choosing when to speak and what to say—or not say!

Meanings Are Constructed in Interpersonal Communication

Human beings construct the meanings of their communication. The significance of communication doesn't lie in words and nonverbal behaviors. Instead, meaning arises out of how we interpret one another. This calls our attention to the fact that humans are symbol-users, which sets us apart from other creatures (Mead, 1934; Wood, 1992).

As we will see in Chapter 4, **symbols** such as words have no inherent or true meanings. Instead, we have to interpret symbols. What does it mean if someone says, "You're crazy"? To interpret the comment, you have to consider the context (a counseling session, a party, after a daredevil stunt), who said it (a friend, a psychiatrist, an enemy), and the words themselves, which may mean various things (a compliment on your zaniness, disapproval, a medical diagnosis).

In interpersonal communication, people continuously interpret each other. Although typically we're not aware that we assign meanings, inevitably we do so. Someone you have been dating suggests you need some space from each other; a friend starts turning down invitations to get together; someone you barely know asks you to dinner. The meanings of such communications are neither self-evident nor inherent in the words. Instead, we construct their significance. In close relationships, partners gradually coordinate meanings so that they have shared understandings of issues and feelings important to their connection. When a relationship begins, one person may regard confrontation as healthy and the other may avoid arguments. Over time, partners come to share meanings for conflict—what it is, how to handle it, and whether it threatens the relationship or is a path to growth. The meaning of conflict, as well as other aspects of communication, is shaped by cultural backgrounds. Americans, for example, value confrontation more than many Asians do, so conflict means different things to each group.

BYRON

Sometimes my buddies and I will call each other "boy" or even "black boy," and we know we're just kidding around. But if a white calls me "boy," I get real mad. It doesn't mean the same thing when they call us "boy" that it does when we call ourselves "boy."

Even one person's meanings vary over time and in response to experiences and moods. If you're in a good mood, a playful jibe might strike you as funny or as an invitation to banter, but the same remark might hurt or anger you if you're feeling down. The meaning of the jibe, like all communication, is not preset or absolute. Meanings are created by people as they communicate in specific contexts.

Interpersonal Communication Develops and Sustains Relationships

Interpersonal communication is the primary way we build, refine, and transform relationships. Communication is not merely a mechanism we use to convey preexisting meanings. Instead, it is a creative process of generating meanings. Partners talk to work out expectations, understandings of how to act with one another, which topics and styles of communicating are appropriate and which are off limits, and what the relationship itself is. Is it a friendship or a romantic relationship? How much and in what ways can we count on each other? How do we handle disagreements—confront them, ignore them, or use indirect strategies to restore harmony? What are the bottom lines—the "shalt not" rules for what counts as unforgivable betrayal? What counts as caring—words, deeds, both? What do certain responses, words, and strategies mean? Because communication has no intrinsic meanings, we must generate our own in the course of interaction. Steve Duck (1994a, 1994b), a relationship scholar, maintains that communication is relationships—that interaction is the crux of what a relationship is and what partners mean to each other.

Communication also allows us to construct, or reconstruct, individual and joint histories. For instance, when people fall in love, they often redefine former loves as "mere infatuations" or "puppy love," but definitely not the real thing. In the United States, marriage may be defined as a joining of two individuals. In many societies, however, marriage is regarded as a union of two families or communities. In some societies, marriage is not an individual choice, but a relationship arranged by parents. When something goes wrong in a relationship, partners may work together to define what happened in a way that allows them to continue. Marriage counselors report that couples routinely work out face-saving explanations for affairs so that they can stay together in the aftermath of infidelity (Scarf, 1987). As partners communicate thoughts and feelings, they generate shared meanings for themselves, their interaction, and their relationship.

Communication is also the primary means by which intimates construct a future for themselves, and a vision of shared future is one of the most powerful ties that link people (Dixson & Duck, 1993). Romantic couples often dream together by talking about the family they plan and how they'll be in twenty years. Likewise, friends discuss plans for the future and promise reunions if they must move apart. Communication allows us to express and share dreams, imaginings, and memories and to make all of these part of the joint world of relational partners. In her interpersonal communication journal, Karen, one of my students, explained how communication made the future of her relationship seem more real.

KAREN

I love talking about the future with my fiancé. Sometimes we talk for hours about the kind of house we'll have and what our children will be like and how we'll juggle two careers and a family. I know everything won't work out exactly like we think now, but talking about it makes me feel so close to Dave and like our future is real.

Interpersonal Communication Is Not a Panacea

As we have seen, we communicate to satisfy many of our needs and to create relationships with others. Yet it would be a mistake to think communication is a cure-all. Often it can help us work out problems and disagreements, but it isn't a panacea for everything that ails us and our relationships. Many problems can't be solved by talk alone. Communication by itself won't end hunger, abuses of human rights around the globe, racism, or physical diseases. Neither can words alone bridge irreconcilable differences between people or erase the hurt of betrayals. Although good communication may increase understanding and help us find solutions to problems, it is not a cure-all. We should also realize that the idea of "talking things through" is distinctly Western. Not all societies think it's wise or useful to communicate about relationships or to talk extensively about feelings. Just as interpersonal communication has many strengths and values, it also has limits, and its effectiveness is shaped by cultural contexts.

Interpersonal Communication Effectiveness Can Be Learned

One of the most important principles of interpersonal communication is that we can become more effective if we invest personal effort to learn and practice good communication skills. It is erroneous to believe that effective communicators are born, that some people just have a natural talent and others don't. Although some people have extraordinary talent in athletics or music, all of us can become competent athletes and respectable musicians. Likewise, some people may seem naturally gifted at communicating, but all of us can become competent communicators. This book and the course that you are taking should sharpen your understandings of how interpersonal communication works and should help you learn skills that will enhance your personal effectiveness in relating to others.

The six principles we have identified clarify what interpersonal communication is and is not and suggest ways to become more skillful in our own communicative endeavors. Building on all we have covered, we turn now to guidelines for becoming competent in interpersonal communication.

Guidelines for Interpersonal Communication Competence

Sometimes we handle interactions well, while in other cases we are ineffective. What are the differences between effective and ineffective communication? Scholars define **interpersonal communication competence** as the ability to communicate in ways that are interpersonally effective and appropriate. Effectiveness involves achieving the goals we have for specific interactions. In different situations, your goals might be to explain an idea, comfort a friend, stand up for your position, negotiate a raise, or persuade someone to change behaviors. The more effectively you communicate, the more likely you'll be competent in achieving your goals.

Competence also emphasizes appropriateness. This means that competent communication is adapted to particular situations and individuals. Language that is appropriate at a party with friends may not be appropriate in a job interview. Somewhat reserved communication is appropriate with people with whom we have I–You relationships, whereas more open communication is appropriate in I–Thou relationships. Appropriateness also involves contexts. It may be appropriate to kiss an intimate in a private setting, but not in a classroom. Similarly, many people choose not to argue in front of others, but prefer to engage in conflict when they are alone. Five skills are closely tied to competence in interpersonal communication: developing a range of communication skills, adapting communication appropriately, engaging in dual perspective, monitoring communication, and committing to interpersonal communication.

Ability to Use a Range of Behaviors

No one style of communication is best in all circumstances, with all people, or for dealing with all issues. Because what is effective varies, we need to have a broad repertoire of communication behaviors. Consider the different skills required for interpersonal communication competence in several situations: To comfort someone, we need to be soothing and compassionate. To negotiate a good deal on a car, we need to be assertive and firm. To engage constructively in conflict, we need to listen and defuse defensive climates. To support a friend who is depressed, we need to affirm that individual, demonstrate we care, and encourage the friend to talk about his or her problems. To grow closer to others, we need to know how and when to disclose personal information and how to express our caring

© Robert Brenner/PhotoEdit

in ways others appreciate. Sometimes it's effective to accommodate another person, yet in other cases we need to compromise or work out mutual solutions. Because no single set of skills composes interpersonal communication competence, we need to learn a range of communicative abilities.

Ability to Adapt Communication Appropriately

Being able to communicate in a range of ways doesn't make us competent unless we also know which kinds of communication are suitable in specific moments. For instance, knowing how to be both assertive and deferential isn't useful unless we can figure out when each style of communication is appropriate. Although there isn't a neat formula for adapting communication appropriately, it's generally important to consider personal goals, context, and the individuals with whom we communicate.

Your goals for communication are a primary guideline for selecting appropriate behaviors. If your purpose in a conversation is to give emotional support to someone, then it isn't effective to talk at length about your own experiences. On the other hand, if you are trying to let someone understand you better, talking in depth about your life is effective. If your goal is to win an argument and get your way, it may be competent to assert your point of view, point out flaws in your partner's ideas, and refuse to compromise. If you want to work through conflict in a way that doesn't harm a relationship, however, other communication choices might be more constructive.

M A R Y   M A R G A R E T

I think I need to work on figuring out when to be assertive and when not to be. For most of my life I wasn't at all assertive, even when I should have been. Last spring, though, I was so tired of having people walk all over me that I signed up for a workshop on assertiveness training. I learned how to assert myself, and I was really proud of how much more I would stand up for myself. The problem was that I did it all the time, regardless of whether something really mattered enough to be assertive. Just like I was always passive before, now I'm always assertive. I need to figure out a better way to balance my behaviors.

Context is another influence on decisions of when, how, and about what to communicate. It is appropriate to ask your doctor about symptoms during an office exam, but it isn't appropriate to do so when you see the doctor in a social situation. Timing is an important aspect of context, since there are often better and worse times to bring up various topics. When a friend is feeling low, that's not a good time to criticize, although at another time criticism might be constructive. Children are geniuses at timing, knowing to wait until parents are in a good mood to ask for favors or new toys.

Remembering Buber's discussion of the I–Thou relationship, we know it is important to adapt what we say and how we say it to particular individuals. As we have seen, interpersonal communication increases our knowledge of others. Thus, the more interpersonal a relationship is, the more we can adapt our communication to unique partners. Abstract communicative goals such as supporting others call for quite distinct behaviors in regard to specific individuals. What feels supportive to one friend may not to another. One of my closest friends withdraws if I challenge her ideas, yet another of my friends relishes challenges and the discussions they prompt. What is effective in talking with them varies. We have to learn what our intimates need, what upsets and pleases them, and how they interpret various kinds of communication. Scholars refer to the ability to adapt messages effectively to particular individuals as **person-centered** communication (Bernstein, 1974; Burleson, 1987; Zorn, 1995). Appropriately adapted communication, then, is sensitive to goals, contexts, and others.

Ability to Engage in Dual Perspective

One of the most important aspects of competent interpersonal communication is the ability to engage in **dual perspective**, which is understanding another person's perspective, beliefs, thoughts, and/or feelings (Phillips & Wood, 1983; Wood, 1992). When we adopt dual perspective, we understand how someone else thinks and feels about issues. To meet another person in genuine dialogue, we must be able to realize how that person views himself or herself, the situation, and his or her thoughts and feelings. We may personally see things much differently, and we may want to express our perceptions. Yet we also need to understand and respect the other person's perspective.

People who cannot take the perspectives of others are egocentric. They impose their perceptions on others and interpret others' experiences through their own eyes. Consider an example. Roberto complains that he is having trouble writing a paper for his communication class. His friend Raymond responds, "All you have to do is outline the theory and then apply it. That's a snap." "But," says Roberto, "I've always had trouble writing. I just block when I sit down to write." Raymond says, "That's silly. Anyone can do this. It just took me an hour or so." Raymond has failed to understand how Roberto sees writing. If you have trouble writing, then composing a paper isn't a snap, but Raymond can't get beyond his own comfort with writing to understand Roberto's different perspective.

ASHA

Sometimes it's very difficult for me to understand my daughter. She likes music that sounds terrible to me, and I don't like the way she dresses sometimes. For a long time I judged her by my own values about music and dress, but that really pushed us apart. She kept saying, "I'm not you. Why can't you look at it from my point of view?" Finally, I heard her, and now we both try to understand each other's point of view. It isn't always easy, but you can't have a relationship on just one person's terms.

As Asha says, engaging in dual perspective isn't necessarily easy, since all of us naturally see things from our own point of view and in terms of our own experiences. Yet, like other communication skills, we can learn how to do it. Three guidelines can help you increase your ability to take the perspective of others. First, be aware of the tendency to see things from your own perspective, and resist that inclination. Second, listen closely to how others express their thoughts and feelings so that you gain clues of what things mean to them and how they feel. Third, ask others to explain how they feel, what something means to them, or how they view a situation. Asking questions and probing for details communicates on the relational level that you are interested and that you want to understand. Making a commitment to engage in dual perspective and practicing the three guidelines just discussed will enhance your ability to recognize and respond to others' perspectives.

Put It in Practice

DEVELOPING DUAL PERSPECTIVE

Practice the guidelines for improving dual perspective. During the next two days, do the following in conversations.

1. Identify your own perspective on issues that others talk about. What do you think about the issues?

2. Try not to impose your thoughts and feelings. Suspend them long enough to hear the other person.

3. Pay close attention to what the other person says. How does she or he describe feelings, thoughts, and views? Listen carefully to the other person without translating his or her communication into your own language.

4. Ask questions. Ask the other person "What do you mean?" "How does that feel to you?" "How do you see the issue?" "What do you think about the situation?"

5. Notice what you learn by suspending your own perspective and working to understand the other person.

Ability to Monitor

The fourth ability that affects interpersonal communication competence is **monitoring**, which is the capacity to observe and regulate your own communication (Wood, 1992, 1995c). Most of us do this much of the time. Before bringing up a touchy topic, you remind yourself not to get defensive and not to get pulled into counterproductive arguing. During the discussion, your partner says something that upsets you. You think of a really good zinger, but stop yourself from saying it because you don't want to hurt the other person. Later, you're feeling defensive, so you prompt yourself to stay open. In each instance, you monitored your communication.

Monitoring occurs both before and during interaction. Often before conversations we indicate to ourselves how we feel and what we do and don't want to say. During communication we stay alert and edit our thoughts before expressing them. Our ability to monitor allows us to adapt communication in advance and gauge our effectiveness as we interact.

Of course, we don't monitor all of the time. When we are with people who understand us or when we are talking about unimportant topics, we don't necessarily need to monitor communication with great care. Sometimes, however, not monitoring can result in communication that hurts others or that leads us not to think well of ourselves. In some cases, failure to monitor results from getting caught up in the dynamics of interaction. We simply forget to keep a watchful eye on ourselves, and so we say things we shouldn't. In addition, some people have poorly developed monitoring skills. They have limited awareness of how they come across to others. Communication competence involves learning to attend to feedback from others and to monitor the impact of our communication as we interact with others.

Commitment to Interpersonal Communication

The final requirement for interpersonal competence is commitment to communication. Without a firm decision to try to meet another in honest, genuine dialogue, all of the other skills are insufficient. To commit to interpersonal communication means four things. First, it means you care about a relationship and are willing to invest energy in communicating with your partner. Second, you must commit to the other as a unique and valuable individual. This implies you can't dismiss the other's feelings as wrong, inappropriate, or silly. Instead, you must honor the person and the feelings he or she expresses, even if you feel differently. Third, commitment involves caring about yourself and your ideas and feelings. Just as you must honor those of others, so too must you respect yourself and your own perspective. Finally, competent communicators are committed to the communication process itself. They realize that it is interactive and always evolving, and they are willing to deal with that complexity. In addition, they are sensitive to multiple levels of meaning and to the irreversibility of communication. Commitment, then, is vital to relationships, others, ourselves, and communication.

In sum, interpersonal communication competence is the ability to communicate in ways that are interpersonally effective and appropriate. Five requirements for competence are developing a range of communication skills, adapting them appropriately to goals, others, and situations, engaging in dual perspective, monitoring communication and its impact, and committing to interpersonal communication.

Put It in Practice

IMPROVING COMMUNICATION COMPETENCE

Are you satisfied with your proficiency at each skill?

1. How competent are you in various communication skills?
2. Describe communication situations in which you don't feel you are as competent as you'd like to be.
3. How well do you adapt your communication to different goals, situations, and people?
4. How consistently and effectively do you engage in dual perspective when interacting with others? How can you tell when you really understand another's point of view?
5. How well do you monitor your communication so that you gauge how you come across to others?
6. Describe your commitments to others, relationships, yourself, and the interpersonal communication process.

Consider which aspects of communication competence you would most like to improve, and make a contract with yourself to work on those during this course.

SUMMARY

In this chapter, we launched our study of interpersonal communication. We began by noting that communication is essential to our survival and happiness. Communicating with others allows us to meet basic needs for survival and safety, as well as more abstract human needs for inclusion, esteem, self-actualization, and participation in a socially diverse world.

We learned that not all communication is interpersonal and that communication exists on a continuum that ranges from impersonal (I–It) to interpersonal (I–Thou). Fully interpersonal communication occurs when individuals engage each other as full, unique human beings who create meanings on both content and relational levels.

We discussed six principles of interpersonal communication. First, it is impossible not to communicate. Whether or not we intend to send certain messages and whether or not others understand our meanings, communication always occurs when people are together. Second, communication is irreversible because we cannot unsay and undo what passes between us and others. The third principle maintains that meanings don't reside in words, but rather in how we interpret them. Fourth, we use communication to develop and sustain relationships. In fact, it's fair to say communication is essential to relationships, since it is in the process of interacting with others that we develop expectations, understandings, and rules to guide relationships. Fifth, although communication is powerful and important, it is not a cure-all. Like all phenomena, it has limits. The final principle is that effectiveness in interpersonal communication can be learned through committed study and practice of principles and skills.

Competent interpersonal communicators interact in ways that are effective and appropriate. This means that we should adapt our ways of communicating to specific goals, situations, and others. Effectiveness and appropriateness require us to recognize and respect differences that reflect personal and cultural backgrounds. Guidelines for doing this include developing a range of communication skills, adapting communication sensitively, engaging in dual perspective, monitoring our own communication, and acting out of a deep commitment to interpersonal communication and its impor-

tance in building and sustaining relationships. In later chapters of this book, we will focus on developing the skills that enhance interpersonal communication competence.

KEY TERMS

I–It communication
I–You communication
I–Thou communication
Interpersonal
   communication
Systemic
Noise
Process
Content meaning

Relational level of meaning
Symbols
Interpersonal
   communication
   competence
Person-centered
   communication
Dual perspective
Monitoring

CHAPTER 2

Communication and the Creation of Self

© Anne Dowie

ho are you? Throughout our lives we ponder this question. We answer it one way at one time, then change our answer as we ourselves change. At the age of five, perhaps you defined yourself as your parents' daughter or son. That view of yourself implicitly recognized sex, race, and social class as parts of your identity. In high school, you may have described yourself in terms of academic strengths ("I'm good at math and science"), athletic endeavors ("I'm a forward on the team"), leadership positions ("I'm president of the La Rosa Club"), friends and romantic partners ("I'm going steady with Cam"), or future plans ("I'm starting college next year"; "I'm going to be an attorney"). Now that you're in college, it's likely you see yourself in terms of a major, a career path, and perhaps a relationship you hope will span the years ahead. You've probably also made some decisions about your sexual orientation, spiritual commitments, and political beliefs.

As you think about the different ways you've defined yourself over the years, you'll realize that the self is not a constant entity that is fixed early and then remains stable. Instead, the self is a process that evolves and changes continuously. Like the New Leaf on the previous page, the self emerges and is reborn throughout our lives. Among the influences that form and re-form ourselves are interactions with others and our reflections on them. In this chapter, we will explore how the self is formed and changed in the process of communicating with others.

What Is the Self?

The **self** arises in communication and is a multidimensional process that involves importing and acting from social perspectives. Although this is a complicated definition, as we will see it directs our attention to some important propositions about what, in fact, *is* very complicated—the self.

The Self Arises in Communication with Others

Communication is essential to developing a self. Infants aren't born with clear understandings of who they are and what their value is. Instead, we develop selves in the process of communicating with others who tell us who we are. Just as countries sometimes import materials from other countries, individuals import ideas about themselves from the people and culture around them. As we import others' perspectives inside ourselves, we come to share their perceptions of the world and ourselves.

From the moment we enter the world, we interact with others. As we do, we learn how they see us, and we take their perspectives inside ourselves. Once we have internalized the views of particular others and the generalized other, we engage in internal dialogues in which we remind ourselves of social perspectives. Through the process of internal dialogues, or conversations with ourselves, we enforce the social values we have learned and the views of us that others communicate. How we perceive ourselves reflects the image of us that is reflected in others' eyes.

Self-Fulfilling Prophecy   One particularly powerful way in which communication shapes the self is **self-fulfilling prophecy,** which is acting in ways that bring about our expectations or judgments of ourselves. If you have done poorly in classes where teachers didn't seem to respect you, and done well with teachers who thought you were smart, then you know what self-fulfilling prophecy is. The prophecies that we act to fulfill are usually first communicated by others. However, because we import others' perspectives into ourselves, we may label ourselves as they do and then act to fulfill our own labels. We may try to live up or down to the ways others define us and the ways we define ourselves. A friend of mine constantly remarks that he is unattractive. As a child he was overweight, and his family constantly called him "fatty" and "tubby." Later he had to wear braces and endure the nickname "silvermouth." Now my friend is slender and has a great smile, but he can't see that. He still sees himself in terms of outdated labels. As a result, he avoids smiling and doesn't buy nice clothes, saying "What's the point?" He accepted others' judgments that he was unattractive and continues to fulfill the prophecy by seeing himself as less attractive than he is now.

Like my friend, many of us believe things about ourselves that are inaccurate. Sometimes labels that were once true aren't any longer, but we continue to believe them. In other cases the labels were never valid, but we are trapped by them anyway. Unfortunately, children are often called slow or stupid when the real problem is that they have physiological difficulties such as impaired vision or hearing or they are from other cultures and struggling with a second language. Even when the true source of difficulty is discovered, it may be too late if the children have already adopted a destructive self-fulfilling prophecy. If we accept others' judgments, we may fulfill their prophecies.

Communication with three kinds of others is especially influential in shaping self concept.

Check It Out

A POSITIVE PROPHECY

For years, Georgia Tech ran a Challenge program, which was a bridge course designed to help disadvantaged students succeed academically. Yet when administrators reviewed the records, they found that students enrolled in Challenge did no better than disadvantaged students who didn't attend.

Norman Johnson, a special assistant to the president of Tech, explained the reason for the dismal results of Challenge. He said, "We were starting off with the idea the kids were dumb. We didn't say that, of course, but the program was set up on a deficit model." Then Johnson suggested a new strategy: "Suppose we started with the idea that these youngsters were unusually bright, that we had very high expectations of them."

Challenge teachers were then trained to expect success from their students and to communicate their expectations through how they treated students. The results were impressive: In 1992, 10% of the first-year Challenge students had perfect 4.0 averages for the academic year. That 10% was more than all of the minority students who had achieved 4.0 averages in the entire 1980–1990 decade. By comparison, only 5% of the students who didn't participate in Challenge had perfect averages. When teachers expected Challenge students to do well and communicated those expectations, the students in fact did do well—a case of a positive self-fulfilling prophecy.

Source: Raspberry, W. (1994, July 5). Major gains in minorities' grades at Tech. *Raleigh News and Observer,* p. 9A.

EMOTIONAL ABUSE

© David Young-Wolff/PhotoEdit

Andrew Vachss is an attorney and author who has devoted his life to helping children who have been abused. He has worked with children who have been sexually assaulted, physically maimed, abandoned, starved, and otherwise tortured. Yet, Vachss regards emotional abuse as the worst harm of all. He says,

Of all the many forms of child abuse, emotional abuse may be the cruelest and longest-lasting of all. Emotional abuse is the systematic diminishment of another. It may be intentional or subconscious (or both), but it is always . . . designed to reduce a child's self-concept to the point where the victim considers himself unworthy—unworthy of respect, unworthy of friendship, unworthy of the natural birthright of all children: love and protection. . . . [T]here is no real difference between physical, sexual, and emotional abuse. All that distinguishes one from the other is the abuser's choice of weapons. (p. 4)

Source: Vachss, A. (1994, August 28). You carry the cure in your own heart. *Parade*, pp. 4–6.

Communication with Family Members   For most of us, family members are the first and most important influence on how we see ourselves. Because family interaction dominates our early years, it usually sculpts the foundations of our self-concepts. Parents and other family members communicate who we are and what we are worth through direct definitions, scripts, and attachment styles.

Direct definition, as the name implies, is communication that explicitly tells us who we are by labeling us and our behaviors. Parents and other family members define us by how they describe us. For instance, parents might say "You're my little girl" or "You're a big boy," and thus communicate to the child what sex it is. Having been labeled boy or girl, the child then pays attention to other communication about boys and girls to figure out what it means to be a certain sex. Family members guide our understandings of gender by instructing us in what boys and girls do and don't do. Parents' own gender stereotypes are typically communicated to children, so daughters may be told "Good girls don't play rough," "Be nice to your friends," and "Don't mess up your clothes." Sons, on the other hand, are more likely to be told "Go out and get 'em," "Stick up for yourself," and "Don't cry." As we hear these messages, we pick up our parents' and society's gender expectations.

Family members provide direct communication about many aspects of who we are through statements they make. Positive labels enhance our self-esteem: "You're so smart," "You're sweet," "You're great at soccer." Negative labels can damage children's self-esteem: "You're a trouble maker," "You're stupid," and "You're impossible" are messages that demolish a child's sense of self-worth.

Direct definition also takes place as family members respond to children's behaviors. If a child clowns around and parents respond by saying "What a cut-up; you really are funny," the child learns to see herself or himself as funny. If a child dusts furniture and receives praise ("You're great to help me clean the house"), being helpful to others is reinforced as part of the child's self-concept. From direct definition, children learn what parents value, and this shapes what they come to value. For instance, in my family, intelligence was a primary value:

To be smart was good, and to be less than smart was unacceptable. I was great at outdoor activities such as building tree houses and leading "jungle expeditions" through the woods behind our home. Yet my parents were indifferent to my aptitudes for adventures and physical activity. What they stressed was learning and reading. I still have vivid memories of being shamed for a B in reading on my first-grade report card. Just as intensely I recall the excessive praise heaped on me when I won a reading contest in fourth grade. By then I had learned what I had to be to get approval from my family. Through explicit labels and responses to our behaviors, family members provide direct definitions of who we are and—just as important—who we are supposed to be.

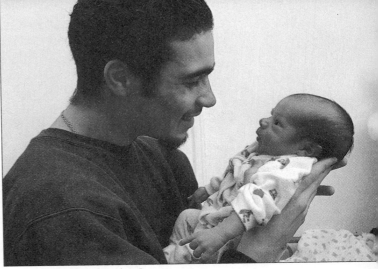
© Margaret Miller/Photo Researchers, Inc.

Your children are not your children. They are the sons and daughters of Life's longing for itself.

KAHLIL GIBRAN

Identity scripts are another way family members communicate who we are. Psychologists define identity scripts as rules for living and identity (Berne, 1964; Harris, 1969). Like the scripts for plays, identity scripts define our roles, how we are to play them, and basic elements in the plot of our lives. Think back to your childhood to identify some of the principal scripts that operated in your family. Did you learn "We are responsible people," "Save your money for a rainy day," "Always help others," "Look out for yourself," or "Live by God's word"? These are examples of identity scripts people learn in families.

Most psychologists believe that the basic identity scripts for our lives are formed very early, probably by age five. This means that fundamental understandings of who we are and how we are supposed to live are forged when we have virtually no control. We aren't allowed to co-author or even edit our initial identity scripts, because adults have power and children aren't conscious of learning scripts. It is largely an unconscious process by which we internalize scripts that others write, and we absorb them with little, if any, awareness. As adults, however, we are no longer passive tablets on which others can write out who we are. We have the capacity to review the identity scripts that were given to us and to challenge and change those that do not fit the selves we now choose to be.

Put It in Practice

REFLECTING ON YOUR IDENTITY SCRIPTS

To take control of our own lives, we must first understand influences that shape it currently. Identify identity scripts your parents taught you.

1. First, recall explicit messages your parents gave you about "who we are" and "who you are." Can you hear their voices telling you codes you were expected to follow?

2. Next, write down the scripts. Try to capture the language your parents used in teaching the scripts.

3. Now review each script. Which ones make sense to you today? Are you still following any that are irrelevant to your present life? Do you disagree with any of them?

4. Finally, commit to changing scripts that aren't productive for you or that conflict with values you hold.

We *can* rewrite scripts once we are adults. To do so, we must become aware of what our families taught us and take responsibility for scripting our own lives.

Finally, parents communicate who we are through their **attachment styles,** which are patterns of parenting that teach us who we and others are and how to approach relationships. From extensive studies of interaction between parents and children, John Bowlby (1973, 1988) developed a theory that we learn attachment styles in our earliest relationships. In these formative relationships, others communicate how they see us, others, and relationships.

Most children form their first human bond with a parent, usually the mother, since women do more of the caregiving in our society (Wood, 1994e). Clinicians who have studied attachment styles believe that the first bond is especially important because it forms expectations for later relationships (Ainsworth, Blehar, Waters, & Wall, 1978; Bartholomew & Horowitz, 1991; Miller, 1993). Four distinct attachment styles have been identified. A **secure attachment style** is the most positive. This style develops when the caregiver responds in a consistently attentive and loving way to a child. In response, the child develops a positive sense of self-worth ("I am lovable") and a positive view of others ("People are loving and can be trusted"). People with a secure attachment style tend to be outgoing, affectionate, and able to handle the challenges and disappointments of close relationships without losing self-esteem.

A **fearful attachment style** is cultivated when the caregiver in the first bond communicates in negative, rejecting, or even abusive ways to a child. Children who are treated this way often infer that they are unworthy of love and that others are not loving. Thus, they learn to see themselves as unlovable and others as rejecting. Not surprisingly, people with a fearful attachment style are apprehensive about relationships. Although they often want close bonds with others, they fear others will not love them and that they are not lovable. Thus, as adults they may avoid others or feel insecure in relationships.

ZONDI

In South Africa where I was born, I learned that I was not important. Most daughters learn this. My name is Zondomini, which means between happiness and sadness. The happiness is because a child was born. The sadness is because I am a girl, not a boy. I am struggling now to see myself as worthy.

A **dismissive attachment style** is also promoted by caregivers who are disinterested, rejecting, or abusive toward children. Yet, people who develop this style do not accept the caregiver's view of them as unlovable. Instead, they dismiss others as unworthy. Consequently, children develop a positive view of themselves and a low regard for others and relationships. This leads them to a defensive view of relationships as unnecessary and undesirable.

A final pattern is the **anxious/resistant attachment style,** which is the most complex of the four. Each of the other three styles results from some consistent pattern of treatment by a caregiver. The anxious/resistant style, however, is fostered by *inconsistent* treatment from the caregiver. Sometimes the adult is loving and attentive, yet at other times she or he is indifferent or rejecting. The caregiver's communication is not only inconsistent, but also unpredictable. He or she may respond positively to something a child does on Monday and react negatively to the same behavior on Tuesday. An accident that results in severe punishment one day may be greeted with indulgent laughter on another day. Naturally, this unpredictability creates great anxiety in a child who depends on the caregiver (Miller, 1993). Because children tend to assume others are right and they are wrong, they believe they are the source of any problem—they are unlovable or deserve others' abuse. In her commentary, Noreen explains how inconsistent behaviors from her father confused and harmed her as a child.

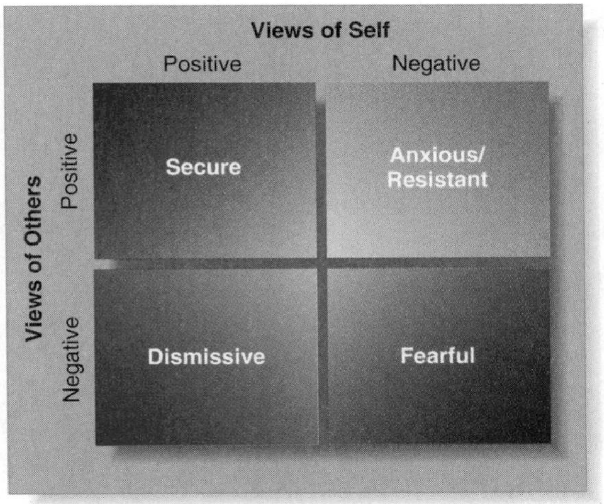

FIGURE 2.1 *Styles of Attachment*

N O R E E N

When I was little, my father was an alcoholic, but I didn't know that then. All I knew was that sometimes he loved me and played with me and sometimes he would shout at me for nothing. Once he told me I was his sunshine, but later that same night he told me he wished I'd never been born. Even though now I understand the alcohol made him act that way, it's still hard to feel I'm okay.

In adult life, individuals who have an anxious/resistant attachment style tend to be preoccupied with relationships. On one hand, they know others can be loving and affirming. On the other hand, they realize that others can hurt them and be unloving. Reflecting the pattern displayed by the caregiver, people with an anxious/resistant attachment style are often inconsistent themselves. One day they invite affection; the next day they rebuff it and deny needing closeness. Figure 2.1 shows the four attachment styles.

The attachment styles we learned in our first close relationship tend to persist (Bartholomew & Horowitz, 1991; Belsky & Pensky, 1988; Bowlby, 1988). However, this is not inevitable. We can modify our attachment

Leigh M. Wilco

Living in process is being open to insight and encounter.
SUSAN SMITH

styles by challenging unconstructive views of us communicated in our early years and by forming relationships that foster secure connections today.

Communication with Peers   A second major influence on our self-concepts is communication with peers. From childhood playmates to work associates, friends, and romantic partners, we interact with peers throughout our lives. As we do, we gain information about how others see us, and this affects how we see ourselves. The term **reflected appraisal** refers to the idea that we reflect the appraisals that others make of us. If others communicate that they think we are smart, we are likely to reflect that appraisal in how we act and think about ourselves. If others communicate that they see us as dumb or unlikable, we may reflect their appraisals by thinking of ourselves in those ways. Reflected appraisals of peers join with those of family members and shape the images we have of ourselves.

A second way in which communication with peers affects self-concept is through **social comparison,** which involves comparing ourselves with others to form judgments of our own talents, abilities, qualities, and so forth. Whereas reflected appraisals are based on how others view us, social comparisons are our own use of others as measuring sticks for ourselves. We gauge ourselves in relation to others in two ways. First, we compare ourselves to others to decide whether we are like them or different from them. Are we the same age, color, religion? Do we hang out with the same people? Do we have similar backgrounds, political beliefs, and social commitments? Assessing similarity and difference allows us to decide with whom we fit. Research has shown that people generally are most comfortable with others who are like them, so we tend to gravitate toward those we regard as similar (Pettigrew, 1967; Whitbeck & Hoyt, 1994). This can, however, deprive us of diverse perspectives of people whose experiences and beliefs differ from our own. When we limit ourselves only to people like us, we impoverish the social perspectives that form our own understandings of the world.

We also use social comparison to gauge ourselves in relation to others. Because there are no absolute standards of beauty, intelligence, musical talent, athletic ability, and so forth, we measure ourselves in relation to others. Am I as good a batter as Hendrick? Do I play the guitar as well as Sam? Am I as smart as Serena? Am I as attractive as Jana? Through comparing ourselves to others, we crystallize a self-image based on how we measure up on various criteria. This is normal and necessary if we are to develop realistic self-concepts. However, we should be wary of using inappropriate standards of comparison. It isn't realistic to judge our attractiveness in relation to stars and models or our athletic ability in relation to professional players.

Put It in Practice

REVIEWING YOUR SOCIAL COMPARISONS

Find out if your social comparisons are realistic. First, write "I am" six times. Complete the first three sentences with words that reflect positive views of yourself. Complete the fourth through sixth sentences with words that express negative views of yourself. For example, you might write, "I am kind," "I am smart," "I am responsible," "I am clumsy," "I am selfish," and "I am impatient."

Next, beside each sentence write the names of two people you use to judge yourself on each quality. For "I am kind," you would list people you use to measure kindness. List your social comparisons for all self descriptions.

Now, review the names and qualities. Are any of the people unrealistic comparison points for you? If so, whom might you select to make more realistic social comparisons?

© Zimbel/Monkmeyer

Communication with Society   The third influence on our self-concepts is interaction with society in general. As members of a shared social community, we are influenced by its values, judgments, and perspectives. The perspectives of society (generalized other) are revealed to us in two ways. First, they surface in interactions with others who have internalized cultural values and pass them onto us. In the course of conversation we learn how society regards our sex, race, and class, and what society values in personal identity. As we interact with others, we encounter not just their particular perspectives, but also the perspective of the generalized other as they reflect it.

Broadly shared social perspectives are also communicated to us through media and institutions that reflect cultural values. For example, when we read popular magazines and go to movies, we are inundated with messages about how women and men are supposed to look and act. The desirable women are invariably thin, beautiful, and deferential, while attractive men are strong, in charge, and successful (Faludi, 1991). Mediated communication infuses our lives, telling us over and over again how we are supposed to be and providing us with a basis for assessing ourselves.

The institutions that organize our society further convey social perspectives by the values they uphold. For example, our judicial system reminds us that as a society we value laws and punish those who break them. The institution of Western marriage communicates society's view that when people marry they become a single unit, which is why joint

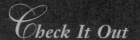

FEMININITY—MUSLIM STYLE

© Christina Dameyer/Photo 20-20

The standards of feminine beauty aren't the same worldwide, so we shouldn't judge the appearance of women in one culture by the standards of femininity in another culture. United States citizens are quick to criticize Muslim women as oppressed because they prefer the *hijab* that covers them. However, Muslims may see their modest form of dressing as less oppressive than American women's quest for beauty. In a 1984 issue of *Mahjubah: The Magazine for Moslem Women*, this observation appeared:

> *If women living in western societies took an honest look at themselves, such a question [why Muslim women cover themselves] would not arise. They are the slaves of appearance and the puppets of a male chauvinistic society. Every magazine and news medium tells them how they should look and behave. They should wear glamorous clothes and make themselves beautiful for strange men to gaze and gloat over them. So the question is not why Muslim women wear* hijab, *but why the women in the West, who think they are so liberated, do not wear* hijab.

Source: Cited in Ferrante, J. (1992). *Sociology: A global perspective*. Belmont, CA: Wadsworth.

ownership of property is assumed for married couples. In other societies, marriages are arranged by parents, and newlyweds become part of the husband's family. The number of schools and the levels of education inform us that as a society we value learning. At the same time, institutional processes reflect prevailing social prejudices. For instance, we may be a lawful society, but wealthy defendants can often buy better "justice" than poor ones. Similarly, although we claim to offer equal educational opportunities to all, students whose families have money and influence can often get into better schools than students whose families are without such resources. These and other values are woven into the fabric of our culture, and we learn them with little effort or awareness. Reflecting carefully on social values allows us to make conscious choices about which ones we will accept for ourselves.

Put It in Practice

IDENTIFYING SOCIAL VALUES IN MEDIA

Select four popular magazines. Record the focus of articles and advertisements in the magazines. What do the articles and ads convey about what is valued in the United States? What themes and types of people are emphasized?

If you have a magazine aimed primarily at one sex, consider what cultural values it communicates about gender. What do articles in it convey about how women or men are regarded and what they are expected to be and do? Ask the same questions about advertisements. How many ads aimed at women focus on being beautiful, looking young, losing weight, taking care of others, and attracting men? How many ads aimed at men emphasize strength, virility, success, and independence?

To extend this exercise, scrutinize the cultural values that are conveyed by television, films, billboards, and news stories. Pay attention to who is highlighted and how different genders, races, and professions are represented.

We have seen that the self arises in communication. From interaction with family members, peers, and society as a whole, we are taught the prevailing values of our culture and of particular others who are significant in our lives. These perspectives become part of who we are. We'll now discuss more briefly other premises about the self.

The Self Is Multidimensional

There are many dimensions, or aspects, of the human self. You have an image of your physical self—how large, attractive, and athletic you are. In addition, you have perceptions of your cognitive self including your intelligence and aptitudes. You also have an emotional self-concept. Are you sensitive or not? Are you easily hurt? Are you generally upbeat or cynical? Then there is your social self, which involves how you are with others. Some of us are extroverted and joke around a lot or dominate interactions, while others prefer to be less prominent. Our social selves also include our social roles—daughter or son, student, worker, parent, or partner in a committed relationship. Finally, each of us has a moral

© Spencer Grant/Stock, Boston

self consisting of our ethical and spiritual beliefs, the principles we believe in, and our overall sense of morality. Although we use the word *self* as if it referred to a single entity, in reality the self is made up of many dimensions.

The Self Is a Process

Virtually all researchers and clinicians who have studied human identity conclude that we are not born with selves, but instead we acquire them. George Herbert Mead, a distinguished social psychologist, was among the first to argue that humans do not come into the world with a sense of themselves. Babies literally have no **ego boundaries,** which define where an individual stops and the rest of the world begins (Chodorow, 1989). To an infant, being held by a father is a single sensation in which it and the father are blurred. A baby perceives no boundaries between its mouth and a nipple or its foot and the tickle by a mother. As infants have a range of experiences and as others respond to them, they gradually begin to see themselves as distinct from the external environment. This is the beginning of a self-concept—the realization that one is a separate entity.

Within the first year or two of life, as infants start to differentiate themselves from the rest of the world, the self begins to develop. Babies, then toddlers, then children devote enormous energy to understanding

© Esbin-Anderson/The Image Works

To forget one's ancestors is to be a brook without a source, a tree without a root.

CHINESE PROVERB

who they are. They actively seek to define themselves and to become competent in the identities they claim (Kohlberg, 1958; Piaget, 1932/1965). For instance, little girls and boys start working early on being competent females and males, respectively. They scan the environment, find models of females and males, and imitate and refine their performances of gender. In like manner, children figure out what it takes to be smart, strong, attractive, and responsible, and they work to become competent in each. Throughout our lives, we continue the process of defining and presenting our identities. The ways we define ourselves vary as we mature. Struggling to be a swimmer at age four gives way to being popular in high school and being a successful professional and partner in adult life.

Some people feel uneasy with the idea that the self is a process, not a constant entity. We want to believe there is some stable, enduring core that is our essence—our true, unchanging identity. Of course, we all enter the world with certain biological abilities and limits, which constrain the possibilities of who we can be. Someone without the genes to be tall and coordinated, for instance, is probably not going to be a basketball superstar, and a person who is tone deaf is unlikely to perform in Carnegie Hall. Beyond genetic and biological limits, however, we have considerable freedom in sculpting who we will be. The fact that we change again and again during our lives is evidence of our capacity to be self-renewing and ever-growing beings.

The Self Imports and Acts from Social Perspectives

In studying how infants acquire selves, Mead realized that we import social perspectives to form views of ourselves. He used the word *import* to indicate that we take into ourselves views that originally come from others. We rely on two kinds of social perspectives to define ourselves and to guide how we think, act, and feel.

Particular Others The first perspectives that affect us are those of **particular others.** As the term implies, these are specific individuals who are significant to us. Mothers, fathers, siblings, and often day-care providers are particular others who are significant to most infants. In addition, some families, particularly those of people of color, include aunts, uncles, grandparents, and others who live together. Hispanic and African American families, in general, have more extended families than do most European

Part I
The Fabric of Interpersonal Communication

52

Americans, so children in these families often have a greater number of particular others who affect how they come to see themselves (Gaines, 1995).

CLARK

My brother Alan was really significant in my life. He was four years older than I, and I thought he was perfect. I wanted to be just like him, and I remember imitating what he did and how he talked so that I could be manly. When he said I did something well, I was so proud, and when Alan made fun of me I worked harder to get it right. I think I still see myself through his eyes a lot.

As babies interact with particular others in their world, they learn how others see them. This is the beginning of a self-concept. Notice that the self starts from outside—from others' views of who we are. Recognizing this, Mead said that we must first get outside ourselves to get into ourselves. By this he meant that the only way we can see ourselves is from the perspectives of others. We first see ourselves in terms of how particular others see us. If parents communicate to a child that she or he is special and cherished, the child will come to see herself or himself as worthy of love. On the other hand, children whose parents communicate that they are not wanted or loved may come to think of themselves as unlovable. Earlier in this chapter, we discussed this process as reflected appraisal. It has also been called the "looking glass self," since others are mirrors who reflect who we are (Cooley, 1912). Reflected appraisals are not confined to childhood, but continue throughout our lives. Sometimes a teacher first sees potential that students have not recognized in themselves. When the teacher communicates that a student is talented in a particular area, the student may come to see himself or herself that way. Later, as you enter professional life, you will encounter coworkers and bosses who reflect their appraisals of you—you're on the fast track, average, or not suited to your position. The appraisals of us that others communicate shape our sense of who we are.

Put It in Practice

REFLECTING ON REFLECTED APPRAISALS

To understand how reflected appraisals have influenced your self-concept, try this exercise.

1. First, list five words that describe ways you see yourself. Examples are *responsible, ambitious, unattractive, clumsy, funny, intelligent, shy,* and *athletic.*
2. Next, identify the particular individuals who have been and are especially significant in your life. Try to list at least five individuals who have or do matter to you.

THE CONSTRUCTION OF RACE IN AMERICA

The term *white* wasn't used to describe race or identity until Europeans colonized the United States. They invented the label white as a way to increase solidarity among European settlers who actually had diverse ethnic backgrounds. By calling themselves "white," these diverse groups could gloss over differences among them and use their common skin hue to distinguish themselves from people of color. *White*, in other words, is a term that was created to legitimize slavery.

During the time when slavery was an institution in the United States southern plantation owners invented a system of racial classification known as "the one drop rule." According to this system, a person with as little as one drop of African blood was classified as black. Thus, racial divisions were established, though arbitrarily.

Source: Bates, E. (1994, fall). Beyond black and white. *Southern Exposure*, pp. 11–15.

Reprinted by permission of Steve Kelley, *The San Diego Union-Tribune.*

3. Now, think about how these special people communicated to you about the traits you listed in step 1. How did they express their appraisals of what you defined as important parts of yourself?

Can you trace how you see yourself to the appraisals reflected by particular others in your life?

Generalized Other   The second social perspective that influences how we see ourselves is called the **perspective of the generalized other.** The generalized other is the collection of rules, roles, and attitudes endorsed by the whole social community in which we live (Mead, 1934). In other words, the generalized other represents the views of society. The process of socialization is one in which individuals internalize the perspective of the generalized other and thus come to share that perspective. In U.S. culture, the perspective of the generalized other views murder, rape, robbery, and embezzlement as wrong, and each of us learns that as we participate in the society. In addition, we learn which aspects of identity society considers important, how society views various social groups, and by extension, how it views us as members of specific groups. Modern Western culture emphasizes gender, race, affectional preference, and socioeconomic class as central to personal identity (Andersen & Collins, 1992; Wood, 1995b, 1996).

In Western society, race is considered a primary aspect of personal identity. The race that has been historically favored and privileged in the United States is Caucasian. In the early years of this country's life, it was considered normal and right for white men to own black women, men, and children and to require them to work for no wages and in poor conditions. Later, it was considered "natural" that white men could vote but black men could not. White men had rights to education, professional jobs, ownership of property, and other basic freedoms that were denied blacks. Even today, Caucasian privilege continues: White children often have access to better schools with more resources than do people of color. The upper levels of government, education, and businesses are dominated by Caucasian men, while people of color and women continue to fight overt and covert discrimination in admission, hiring, and advancement. The color of one's skin makes a difference in how society treats us, our material lives, and who we are told we are.

DERRICK

If my mama told me once, she told me a million times: "You got to work twice as hard to get half as far because you're black." I knew that my skin was a strike against me in this society since I can remember knowing anything. When I asked why blacks had to work harder, Mama said, "Because that's just how it is." I guess she was telling me that's how this society looks on African Americans.

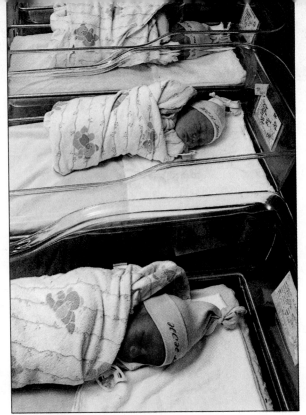

© Lori Adamski Peek/Tony Stone Images, Inc.

Gender is another important category in Western culture. Historically, men have been more valued and considered more rational, competent, and entitled to privilege than women. In the 1800s, women were not allowed to own property, gain professional training, or vote. It was considered appropriate for a husband to beat his wife; the phrase "rule of thumb" comes from the law that stated a man could beat his wife as long as he used a stick no larger than the size of his thumb. Even on the verge of the twenty-first century, women and men are not considered equal in many societies. Some scholars argue that gender is the most important aspect of personal identity in Western culture (Fox-Genovese, 1991). From pink and blue blankets hospitals wrap around newborns to differential salaries earned by women and men, gender is a major facet of identity. Given the importance our society places on gender, it is no wonder that one of the first ways children learn to identify themselves is by their sex (Wood, 1996). When I asked my four-year-old niece Michelle who she was, her immediate response was "I'm a girl." Only after naming her sex did she describe her family, her likes and dislikes, and other parts of herself.

Western cultures have strong gender prescriptions. Girls and women are expected to be caring, deferential, and cooperative, while boys and men are supposed to be independent, assertive, and competitive (Wood, 1994d). Consequently, women who assert themselves or compete are likely to receive social disapproval, be called "bitches," and otherwise reprimanded for violating gender prescriptions. Men who refuse to conform to social views of masculinity and who are gentle and caring risk being labeled wimps. Our gender, then, makes a great deal of difference in how others view us and how we come to see ourselves.

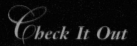

CREATING CLASS

Around the world, societies create systems of classifying people. Relatively open systems, such as the United States' view of classes, allow interaction among different classes and assume individuals can move from one class to another. In contrast, caste classifications are closed systems that assume individuals are locked into the social status ascribed to them at birth and that strongly discourage interaction among members of different castes.

Apartheid, an Afrikaans word that means apartness, has prevailed in South Africa for hundreds of years and was made the official policy of the country in 1948. Once the Nationalists, a conservative white political party, seized power, they legislated hundreds of laws to enforce rigid racial separation in virtually every area of life and to support domination of the country by the white minority.

In 1990, South Africa abolished the Separate Amenities Act, which had mandated separate and unequal cemeteries, parks, trains, hotels, hospitals, and so forth for whites and blacks. Other discriminatory practices and laws are gradually being dismantled in South Africa.

Sources: Ferrante, J. (1992). *Sociology: A global perspective.* Belmont, CA: Wadsworth. Wren, C. S. (1990, October 16). A South Africa color bar falls quietly. *New York Times,* pp. Y1, Y10.

ALLISON

When I was real young, I was outside playing in a little swimming pool one day. It was hot and my brothers had their shirts off, so I took mine off too. When my mother looked up and saw me, she went berserk. She told me to get my shirt back on and act like a lady. That's when I knew that girls have to hide and protect their bodies, but boys don't.

A third aspect of identity that is salient in our culture's eyes is sexual orientation. Historically and today, heterosexuality is viewed as the normal sexual orientation, and lesbians, bisexuals, and gays are regarded as abnormal. Society communicates this viewpoint not only directly, but also through privileges given to heterosexuals but denied to gays, lesbians, and bisexuals. For example, a woman and man who love each other can be married and have their commitment recognized religiously and legally. Two men or two women who love each other and want to be life partners are denied social and legal recognition (Wood, 1995c). Heterosexuals can cover partners on insurance policies and inherit from them without paying taxes, but people with other sexual preferences cannot. To be homosexual or bisexual in modern Western culture is to be socially devalued. However, many gays and lesbians reject and resist negative social views of their identity, and they form communities that support positive self-images.

A fourth peg of identity in our society is socioeconomic class. Because the United States is a class-conscious society, the class we belong to affects everything from how much money we make, to the kinds of schools, jobs, and lifestyle choices we see as possibilities for ourselves. Class is difficult to point to because, unlike sex and race, it is not visible. Class isn't just the amount of money a person has. It's a basic part of how we understand the world and how we think, feel, and act. Class affects which stores, restaurants, and schools are part of our life. It influences who our friends are, where we live and work, and even what kind of car we drive (Langston, 1992).

GENEVA

I may be in a first-class university, but I don't fit with most of the folks here. That hits me in the face every day. I walk across campus and see girls wearing shoes that cost more than all four pairs I own. I hear students talking about restaurants and trips that I can't afford. Last week I heard a guy complaining about being too broke to get a CD player for his car. I don't own a car. I don't know how to relate to these people who have so much money. I do know they see the world differently than I do.

Class influences which needs we focus on in Maslow's hierarchy. For example, people with economic security have the resources and leisure time to contemplate higher level needs such as self-actualization. They can afford therapy, yoga, spiritual development, and elite spas to condition their bodies. These are not feasible for people who are a step away from

© Ann McQueen/The Picture Cube

poverty. Members of the middle and upper classes assume they will attend college and enter good professions, yet these are often not realistic options for working-class people (Langston, 1992). Guidance counselors may encourage academically gifted working-class students to go to work or pursue vocational education after high school, while middle-class students of average ability are routinely steered toward good colleges and status careers. In patterns such as this, we see how the perspective of the generalized other shapes our identities and our concrete lives.

Race, gender, sexual preference, and class are primary in our society's views of individuals and their worth. In thinking about these four social constructions of identity, it's important to realize they intersect with one another. Race interacts with gender, so that women of color experience double oppression and devaluation in our culture (Higginbotham, 1992; Lorde, 1992). Class and sexual preference also interact: Homophobia, or fear of homosexuals, is particularly pronounced in the working class, so a lesbian or gay person in a poor community may be socially ostracized (Langston, 1992). Class and gender are also interlinked, with women being far more likely to live at the poverty level than men (Stone, 1992). Gender and race intersect, so that black men have burdens and barriers not faced by white men (Gibbs, 1992). All facets of our identity interact.

Although race, gender, sexual preference, and socioeconomic class are especially salient in social views of identity and worth, there are many other views of the general society that we learn and often internalize. For instance, Western societies clearly value intelligence, ambition, rugged individualism, and competitiveness. People who do not conform to these social values receive less respect than those who do. Another value our society endorses is slimness, particularly in Caucasian women. Being slim (and beautiful) is considered very important, and those who don't measure up are often shunned and regarded as less worthy than those who do. Because society places such emphasis on slenderness in women, eating disorders are epidemic, and as many as 80 out of 100 fourth-grade girls diet—and most of them are well within normal weight limits (Wolf, 1991). Because preoccupation with self is a luxury of class, the quest for thinness is more pronounced among Caucasian women than women of color and in middle and upper classes more than working classes (Wood, 1994d). Society imposes physical requirements on men as well. Strength and sexual prowess are two expectations of "real men," which may explain why increasing numbers of men are having pectoral implants and penis enlargement surgery. People not born with bodies society favors may feel compelled to construct them!

Put It in Practice

INTERNALIZING THE GENERALIZED OTHER

Which views of the generalized other have you internalized?

1. How do you evaluate women? How important is physical appearance to your judgments?

2. How do you evaluate men? To what extent do strength and ambitiousness affect your judgments?

3. What were you taught about African Americans, Hispanics, and members of Asian cultures? Which of the views you were taught have you imported into yourself?

4. How do you see heterosexuals, bisexuals, gays, and lesbians? How did you develop these views?

Are there social perspectives and attitudes that you hold but don't really respect or like? If so, consider challenging them and re-forming those parts of yourself.

As we interact with particular others and participate in general social life (the generalized other), we learn what and whom our society values. Social perspectives, however, do not remain outside of us. In most cases, we import them into ourselves, and we thus come to share the views and values generally endorsed in our society. In many ways this is useful, even essential, for collective life. If we all made up our own rules about when to stop and go at traffic intersections, car accidents would skyrocket. If each of us operated by our own code for lawful conduct, there would be no shared standards regarding rape, murder, robbery, and so forth. Life would be chaotic.

Yet not all social views are as constructive as traffic rules and criminal law. The generalized other's unequal valuing of different races, genders, and sexual preferences fosters discrimination against whole groups of people whose only fault is not being what society defines as normal or good. Each of us has a responsibility to exercise critical judgment about which social views we personally accept and use as guides for our own behaviors, attitudes, and values. This leads to a third proposition about the self.

Social Perspectives on the Self Are Constructed and Variable

We have seen that we gain a sense of personal identity and an understanding of social life by encountering and internalizing social perspectives of particular others and the generalized other. This could lead you to think that our self-concepts are determined by fixed social values. As we will see, however, this isn't the case. Social views are constructed and variable, so they can be changed.

Constructed Social Views   Social perspectives are constructed in particular cultures at specific times. What a society values does not reflect divine law, absolute truth, or the natural order of things. The values that are endorsed in any society are arbitrary and designed to support dominant ideologies, or the beliefs of those in power. For example, it was to white plantation owners' advantage to define Africans as slaves and as inferior human beings. Doing so supported the privileges that white landowners enjoyed. Similarly, it was to men's advantage to deny women the right to vote, since doing so preserved men's power to control the laws of the land. By approving of heterosexuality and not homosexuality, the culture supports a particular, arbitrary family ideal. When we reflect on widely endorsed social values, we realize that they tend to serve the interests of those who are privileged by the status quo.

Variable Social Views   The constructed and arbitrary nature of social values becomes especially obvious when we consider how widely values differ among cultures. For example, in Sweden, Denmark, and Norway, marriages between members of the same sex are allowed and are given full legal recognition. Prescriptions for femininity and masculinity also vary substantially across cultures. In some places, men are emotional and dependent, and women are assertive and emotionally controlled. In many countries south of the United States, race is less prominent than in North America, and mixed-race marriages are common and accepted.

Check It Out

A CROSS-CULTURAL LOOK AT SEXUAL IDENTITY

The Navajo and Mohave Indian tribes gave special respect to *nadles*, who were considered neither male nor female, but a combination of the two sexes. The identity of nadle was sometimes conferred at birth on babies born with ambiguous genitals. Nadle was also an identity that individuals could choose later in life. When working on weaving or other tasks assigned to women, nadles dressed and acted as women. When engaged in male activities, nadles dressed and acted as males. Nadles could marry either women or men. Within their tribes, nadles were regarded as very wise and were given special privileges and deference.

Source: Olien, M. (1978). *The human myth*. New York: Harper & Row.

The Bettmann Archive

The individualistic ethic so prominent in the United States is not valued or considered normal in many other countries, particularly Asian and African ones (Gaines, 1995). There are also countries in which heterosexuality is not the only sexual preference regarded as normal. Some cultures even recognize more than two genders!

Social meanings also vary across time within single cultures. For example, in the 1700s and 1800s, women in the United States were defined as too delicate to engage in hard labor. During the World Wars, however, women were expected to do "men's work" while men were at war. When men returned home, society once again decreed that women were too weak to perform in the labor market, and they were reassigned to home and hearth. The frail, pale appearance considered feminine in the 1800s gave way to robust, fleshy ideals in the 1940s as embodied by Marilyn Monroe. Today a more athletic body is one of the ideals prescribed for women.

Social prescriptions for men have also varied. The rugged he-man who was the ideal in the 1800s disposed of unsavory rustlers and relied on his physical strength to farm wild lands. After the Industrial Revolution, physical strength and bravado gave way to business acumen, and money replaced muscle as a sign of manliness. Today, as our society struggles with changes in women, men, and families, the ideals of manhood are being revised yet again. Increasingly, men are expected to be involved in caring for children and to be sensitive as well as independent and strong.

The meaning of homosexuality has also been revised over time in Western culture. Until fairly recently, our society strongly disapproved of gays, lesbians, and bisexuals, so most nonheterosexuals did not publicly acknowledge their affectional preference. Although much prejudice still exists, it is gradually diminishing. As we noted earlier, homosexual marriages are recognized in some places around the world. Laws protecting lesbians and gays against housing and job discrimination are also being enacted. As social views of homosexuality change, more and more gays and lesbians are openly acknowledging their sexuality.

The meaning our society assigns to different races has also varied markedly over our history as a nation. African Americans who once had no basic rights now have the same legal rights as Caucasians. Hispanics, Latinas and Latinos, Asians, and other peoples of color are increasingly recognized and valued in the United States. Although racial ignorance and its product, bigotry, still haunt our nation's life, they are lessening. Today many teachers recognize the strengths of students of various races. As the generalized other's perspective on diverse ethnicities enlarges, people of color gain more positive reflected appraisals of their identity than was the case years ago.

Other socially constructed views are also variable. In the 1950s and 1960s, people with disabilities were often kept in their homes or put in institutions. Today, many schools endorse mainstreaming, which places students who have physical or mental handicaps in classrooms in regular schools. Sensitivity to people who have special problems grows as nonhandicapped students learn to see and be around people with disabilities.

The Bettmann Archive

The meaning of age has also varied during different epochs in U.S. history. In the 1800s, the average life span was less than sixty years, and it was not uncommon for people to die in their forties or fifties. Then fifty was considered old, but today fifty is not regarded as so old. The average life span today is nearly seventy, making fifty seem considerably less old. In the 1800s, people typically married in their teens, and they often had five or more children before reaching thirty. Today many people wait until their thirties to begin having children, and parents in their forties aren't considered "too old."

Changeable Social Views   Our discussion suggests that social perspectives are changeable. As we have seen, they have, in fact, changed significantly over time. Social perspectives are fluid and respond to individual and collective efforts to weave new meanings into the fabric of social life. From 1848 until 1920, many women fought to change social views of women, and they succeeded in gaining rights for women to vote, attend universities, and so forth. In the 1960s, civil rights activism launched nationwide rethinking of actions and attitudes toward nonwhites. The battle to recognize and value gays and lesbians is more recent, yet already it has altered social perspectives. Each of us has the responsibility to speak out against social perspectives that we perceive as wrong or harmful. By doing so we participate in the ongoing process of refining who we are as a society.

JENNIFER

My parents are pretty straight-laced and conservative. They brought me up to think homosexuals are sinners and whites are better than any other race. But I don't think like that now, and I've been speaking my mind when I'm home to visit my folks. At first they got angry and said they didn't send me to college to get a bunch of crazy liberal ideas, but gradually they are coming around a little. I think I am changing how they think by voicing my views.

In sum, meanings for facets of identity are socially created. Because they are arbitrary constructions, they vary over time and across cultures. This highlights the power of individuals and groups to shape social understandings that make up the generalized other. Just as our culture shapes who we are, so too do we shape it. In the final section of this chapter, we consider guidelines for improving our self-concepts.

Guidelines for Improving Self-Concept

So far we have explored how we form our self-concepts through interaction with others and participation in society. Although this information helps us understand how we developed our current views of ourselves, it doesn't tell us a great deal about how we might transform aspects of our self-concepts that are unconstructive and hold us back. As we will see, there are ways to strengthen our identities.

Make a Firm Commitment to Change

The first principle for changing self-concept is the most difficult and most important. You must make a firm commitment to cultivating personal growth. This isn't as easy as it might sound. A firm commitment involves more than saying "I want to be better" or "I want to like myself more." Saying these sentences is simple. What is more difficult is actually investing energy and effort to bring change about. A firm commitment requires that we keep trying. From the start, you need to realize that changing how you think of yourself is a major project.

It is difficult to change self-concept for two reasons. First, doing so requires continuous effort. Because the self is a process, it is not formed in one fell swoop, and it cannot be changed in a moment of decision. We have to be willing to invest effort in an ongoing way. In addition, we must realize at the outset that there will be setbacks, and we can't let them derail our resolution to change. Last year a student said she wanted to be more assertive, so she began speaking up more often in class. When a professor criticized one of her contributions, her resolution folded. Changing how we see ourselves is a long-term process.

A second reason it is difficult to change our self-concepts is that the self resists change. Morris Rosenberg (1979), a psychologist who has studied self-concept extensively, says that most humans tend to resist change and that we also seek esteem or a positive view of ourselves. The good news is that we want esteem or a positive self-image; the bad news is that we find it difficult to change, even in positive directions. Interestingly, Rosenberg and others have found that we are as likely to hold onto negative self-images as we are positive ones. Apparently, consistency itself is comforting. If you realize in advance that you may struggle against change, you'll be prepared for the tension that accompanies personal growth. Because change is a process and the self resists change, a firm commitment to improving your self-concept is essential.

Gain Knowledge as a Basis for Personal Change

Commitment alone is insufficient to bring about constructive changes in who you are. In addition, you need knowledge of several types. First, you need to understand how your self-concept was formed. In this chapter, we've seen that much of how we see ourselves results from socially constructed values. Based on what you've learned, you can exercise critical judgment about which social perspectives to accept and which to resist. For instance, you may not wish to go along with our society's evaluations of race, gender, sexual preference, and class.

TINA

One social value I do not accept is that it's good to be as thin as a rail if you're female. A lot of my girlfriends are always dieting. Even when they get weak from not eating enough, they won't eat because they'll gain weight. I know several girls who are bulimic, which is really dangerous, but they are more scared of gaining a pound than of dying. I just flat refuse to buy into this social value. I'm not fat, but I'm not skinny either. I'm not as thin as models, and I'm not aiming to be. It's just stupid to go around hungry all the time because society has sick views of beauty for women.

Second, you need to know what changes are desirable and how to bring them about. Often our ideas about changing ourselves are too vague and abstract to be useful. For instance, "I want to be more skillful at intimate communication" or "I want to be a better friend" are very abstract objectives. You can't move toward such fuzzy goals until you know something about the talk that enhances and impedes intimacy and what people value in friends. Books such as this one will help you pinpoint concrete skills that facilitate your own goals for personal change. Someone who wants to be a better friend might focus on developing empathic listening skills and creating supportive communication climates. The goal of being adept at intimate communication requires learning how to self-disclose appropriately, manage conflict constructively, and engage in dual perspective. In later chapters, we will discuss these and other specific skills that advance interpersonal communication competence in particular relationships and settings.

In addition to reading this book and learning from your class, there are other ways to gain knowledge to help you set and achieve goals of personal improvement. One very important source of knowledge is other people. Talking with others is a way to learn about relationships and what people want in them. Others can also provide useful feedback on your interpersonal skills and your progress in the process of change. Finally, others can provide models. If you know someone you think is particularly skillful in supporting others, observe her or him carefully to identify particular communication skills. You may not want to imitate this person exactly, but observing will make you more aware of concrete skills involved in supporting others. You may choose to tailor some of the skills others display to suit your personal style.

Set Realistic Goals

Although it is true that willpower can do marvelous things, it does have limits. We need to recognize that trying to change how we see ourselves works only when our goals are realistic. If you are shy and want to be more extroverted, it is reasonable to try to speak up more and socialize more often. On the other hand, it may not be reasonable to set the goal of being the life of the party.

Realistic goals require realistic standards. Often dissatisfaction with ourselves stems from unrealistic expectations. In a culture that emphasizes perfectionism, it's easy to be trapped into expecting more than is humanly possible. If you define a goal of being a totally perfect communicator in all situations, you are setting yourself up for failure. It's more reasonable and more constructive to establish a series of realistic small goals that can be met. You might focus on improving one of the skills of communication competence we discussed in Chapter 1. When you are satisfied with your ability at that skill, you can move on to a second one.

Remembering our discussion of social comparison, it's also important to select reasonable measuring sticks for ourselves. It isn't realistic to compare your academic work to that of a certified genius. It is reasonable to measure your academic performance against others who have intellectual abilities similar to your own. Setting realistic goals and selecting appropriate standards of comparison are important to bring about change in yourself.

KENDRICK

I really got bummed out my freshman year. I had been the star on my high school basketball team, so I came to college expecting to be a star here too. The first day of practice, I saw a lot of guys who were better than I was. They were incredible. I felt like nothing. When I got back to my room, I called my mom and told her I was no good at basketball here. She told me I couldn't expect to compete with guys who had been on the team for a while and who had gotten coaching. She asked how I stacked up against just the other first-year players, and I said pretty good. She told me they were the ones to compare myself to.

Assess Yourself Fairly

Being realistic also involves making fair assessments of ourselves. This requires us to place judgments in context and to see ourselves as in process. To assess ourselves effectively, we need to understand not just our discrete qualities and abilities, but also how all of the parts of us fit together to form the whole self. One of the ways we treat ourselves unfairly is to judge particular abilities out of context. For example, my friend Meg is a very accomplished writer, but she faults herself constantly for not spending as much time as her neighbor in volunteer activities. Meg's neighbor doesn't work outside of the home, so she has more time to volunteer for social causes. The lesson here is that we have to appreciate our particular skills and weaknesses in the overall context of who we are. It might be reasonable for my friend to acknowledge she doesn't volunteer a great deal of time if she also recognizes her impressive achievements in writing. However, when judging her writing she compares herself to Marilyn French, Pat Conroy, Marge Piercy, and other writers of national stature. Meg's self-assessment is unrealistic because she compares herself to people who are extremely successful in particular spheres of life, yet she doesn't notice that her models are not especially impressive in other areas. As a result, she mistakenly feels she is inadequate in most ways. In our efforts to improve self-concept, then, we should acknowledge our strengths and virtues as well as parts of ourselves we wish to change.

A key foundation for improving self-concept is accepting yourself as in process. Earlier in this chapter, we saw that one characteristic of the human self is that it is continuously in process, always becoming. This implies several things. First, it means you need to accept who you are now as a starting point. You don't have to like or admire everything about yourself, but it is important to accept who you are today as a basis for going forward (Wood, 1992). The self that you are results from all of the interactions, reflected appraisals, and social comparisons you have made during your life. You cannot change your past, but neither do you have to be bound by it forever. Only by realizing and accepting who you are now can you move ahead.

Accepting yourself as in process also implies that you realize you can change. Who you are is not who you will be in five or ten years. Because you are in process, you are always changing and growing. Don't let yourself be hindered by defeating self-fulfilling prophecies or the mindtrap that you cannot change (Rusk & Rusk, 1988). You can change if you set realistic goals, make a genuine commitment, and then work for the changes you want. Remember that you are not fixed as you are; you are always in the process of becoming.

Create a Supportive Context for Change

Just as it is easier to swim with the tide than against it, it is easier to change our views of ourselves when we have some support for our efforts. You can do a lot to create an environment that supports your growth by choosing contexts and people who help you realize your goals.

First think about settings. If you want to improve your physical condition, it makes more sense to go to intramural courts than to hang out in bars. If you want to lose weight, it's better to go to restaurants that serve healthy foods and offer light choices than to go to cholesterol castles. If you want to become more extroverted, you need to put yourself in social situations, rather than in libraries. But libraries are a better context than parties if your goal is to improve academic performance.

B O B

I never drank much until I got into this one group at school. All of them drank all the time. It was easy to join them. In fact, it was pretty hard not to drink and still be one of the guys. This year I decided I was drinking too much, and I wanted to stop. It was hard enough not to keep drinking, since the guys were always doing it, but what really made it hard was the ways the guys got on me for abstaining. They let me know I was being uncool and made me feel like a jerk. Finally, to stop drinking, I had to get a different apartment.

Who we are with has a great deal to do with how we see ourselves and how worthy we feel we are. This means we can create a supportive context by consciously choosing to be around people who believe in us and encourage our personal growth. It's equally important to steer clear of people who pull us down or say we can't change. In other words, people who reflect positive appraisals of us enhance our ability to improve who we are.

One way to think about how others' communication affects how we feel about ourselves is to realize that others can be uppers, downers, and vultures. **Uppers** are people who communicate positively about us and who reflect positive appraisals of our self-worth. They notice our strengths, see our progress, and accept our weaknesses and problems without discounting us. When we're around uppers, we feel more upbeat and positive about ourselves. Uppers aren't necessarily unconditionally positive in their communication. A true friend can be an upper by recognizing our weaknesses and helping us work on them. Instead of putting us down, an upper believes in us and helps us believe in ourselves and our capacity to change. Identify two uppers in your life.

Downers are people who communicate negatively about us and our self-worth. They call attention to our flaws, emphasize our problems, and put down our dreams and goals. When we're around downers, we tend to feel down about ourselves. Reflecting their perspectives, we're more aware of our weaknesses and less confident of what we can accomplish when we're around downers. Identify two downers in your life.

Calvin & Hobbes © 1995 Watterson. Dist. by Universal Press Syndicate. Reprinted with permission. All rights reserved.

Vultures are an extreme form of downers. They not only communicate negative images of us, but actually attack our self-concepts just as actual vultures prey on their victims (Simon, 1977). Sometimes vultures initiate harsh criticism of us. They say, "That outfit looks dreadful on you" or "You really blew that one." In other cases, vultures pick up on our own self-doubts and magnify them. They find our weak spots and exploit them; they pick us apart by focusing on sensitive areas in our self-concept. For example, a friend of mine is inefficient in managing his time and is very sensitive about this. I once observed a coworker pick him apart just as a vulture picks apart its prey. The coworker said, "I can't believe this is all you've done. You're the most unproductive person I've ever known. What a waste! Your output doesn't justify your salary." That harangue typifies the attack on self-worth that vultures enjoy. By telling us we are inadequate, vultures demolish our self-esteem. Can you identify vultures in your life?

Reflect on how you feel about yourself when you're with uppers, downers, and vultures. Can you see how powerfully others' communication affects your self-concept? You might also think about the people for whom you are an upper, downer, or vulture.

Others aren't the only ones whose communication affects our self-concepts. We also communicate with ourselves, and our own messages influence our esteem. One of the most crippling kinds of self-talk we can engage in is **self-sabotage.** This involves telling ourselves we are no good, we can't do something, there's no point in trying to change, and so forth. We may be repeating judgments others made of us, or may be inventing negative self-fulfilling prophecies ourselves. Either way, self-sabotage defeats us because it undermines belief in ourselves. Self-sabotage is poisonous; it destroys our motivation to change and grow. We can be downers or even vultures, just as others can be. In fact, we can probably do more damage to our self-concepts than others can because we are most aware of our vulnerabilities and fears. This may explain why vultures were originally described as people who put themselves down.

We can also be uppers for ourselves. We can affirm our worth, encourage our growth, and fortify our sense of self-worth. Positive self-talk builds motivation and belief in yourself. It is also a useful strategy to interrupt and challenge negative messages from yourself and others. The next time you hear yourself saying "I can't do . . . " or someone else says "You'll never change," challenge the self-defeating message with self-talk. Say out loud to yourself, "I can do it. I will change." Use positive self-talk to resist counterproductive communication about yourself.

Before leaving this discussion, we should make it clear that improving your self-concept is not facilitated by uncritical positive communication. None of us grows and improves when we listen only to praise, particularly if it is less than honest. The true uppers in our lives offer constructive criticism as a way to encourage us to reach for better versions of ourselves. In sum, improving your self-concept requires being in contexts that support growth and change. Seek out experiences and settings that foster belief in yourself and the changes you desire. Also, recognize uppers, downers, and vultures in yourself and others, and learn which people and which kinds of communication assist you in achieving your own goals for self-improvement.

SUMMARY

In this chapter, we explored the self as a process that evolves over the course of our lives. We saw that the self is not present at birth, but develops as we interact with others. Through communication we learn and import social perspectives, both those of particular others and those of the generalized other, or society as a whole. Reflected appraisals, direct definitions, and social comparisons are communication processes that shape how we see ourselves and how we change over time. The perspective of the generalized other includes social views of aspects of identity, including race, gender, sexual preference, and class. These, however, are arbitrary social constructions that we may challenge once we are adults. When we resist counterproductive social views, we promote change in society.

The final section of the chapter focused on ways to improve self-concept. Guidelines for doing this are to make a firm commitment to personal growth, acquire knowledge about desired changes and concrete skills, set realistic goals, assess yourself fairly, and create contexts that support the changes you seek. Transforming how we see ourselves is not easy, but it is possible. We can make amazing changes in who we are and how we feel about ourselves when we embrace our human capacity to make choices.

KEY TERMS

Self
Self-fulfilling prophecy
Direct definition
Identity scripts
Attachment styles
Secure attachment style
Fearful attachment style
Dismissive attachment style
Anxious/resistant attachment style

Reflected appraisal
Social comparison
Ego boundaries
Particular others
Perspective of the generalized other
Uppers
Downers
Vultures
Self-sabotage

CHAPTER 3

Perception and Communication

his chapter focuses on meaning, which is the heart of communication. To understand how humans create meanings for themselves and their activities, we need to explore relationships between perception and communication. As we will see, these two processes interact so that each affects the other in an ongoing cycle of influence. Like the quilt on the previous page, perception is a complex blend of many elements. In other words, perception shapes how we understand others' communication and how we ourselves communicate. At the same time, communication influences our perceptions of people and situations. The two processes are intricately intertwined in the overall quilt of perception. Before reading further, try to connect the nine dots at left. You may use no more than four lines, the lines must be straight, and the lines must be connected to one another.

To understand how perception and communication interact, we will first discuss the three-part process of perception. Next, we'll consider factors that affect our perceptions. Finally, we will explore ways to improve our abilities to perceive and communicate effectively.

Before we get into those topics, let's return to the nine dots problem. Could you solve it? Most people who have trouble solving the problem are stymied because they label the nine dots a square, and they try to connect the dots staying within the boundaries of a square. However, it's impossible to connect the dots with four straight lines if you define them as a closed square. One solution appears at the end of the chapter, on page 92.

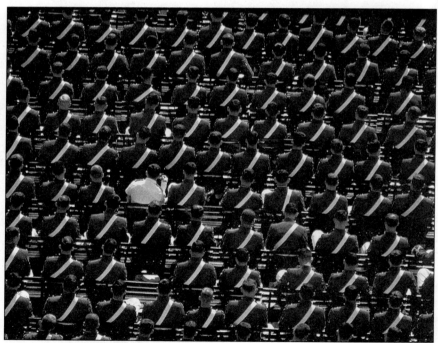

© James Holland/Stock, Boston

This exercise makes an important point about the topics we'll consider in this chapter. The label "square" affects how you perceive the nine dots. In the same fashion, our words affect how we perceive others, situations, and ourselves. At the same time, our perceptions, which are always incomplete and subjective, shape what things mean to us and the labels we use to describe them. As long as we perceive the nine dots as a square, we won't be able to solve the problem. Similarly, we communicate with others according to how we perceive and define them, and we may miss opportunities when our labels limit what we perceive. In the pages that follow, we want to unravel the complex relationships between perception and communication.

"May I suggest that in today's group-therapy session we all work on our contact with reality."
Reprinted courtesy *Omni* Magazine © 1979.

Human Perception

When we talk about perception, we're concerned with how we make sense of the world and what happens in it. **Perception** is an active process of selecting, organizing, and interpreting people, objects, events, situations, and activities. The first thing to notice about this definition is that perception is an active process. We are not passive receivers of what is "out there" in the external world. Instead, we actively work to make sense of ourselves, others, and our interactions. To do so, we select only certain things to notice, and then we organize and interpret what we have selectively noticed. What anything means to us depends on which aspects of it we attend to and how we organize and interpret what we notice. Thus, perception is not a simple matter of recording external reality. Instead, we actively interact with the world to construct what it means to us.

Perception consists of three processes—selecting, organizing, and interpreting. These processes are continuous, so they blend into one another. They are also interactive, so each of them affects the other two.

Selection

Stop for a moment and notice what is going on around you right now. Is there music in the background or perhaps several different kinds of music from different places? Is the room warm or cold, messy or clean, large or small, light or dark? Is there laundry in the corner waiting to be washed? Can you smell anything—food being cooked, the stale odor of cigarette smoke, traces of cologne? Who else is in the room and nearby? Do you hear other conversations? Is the window open? Can you hear muted sounds of activities outside? Now think about what's happening inside you:

FIGURE 3.1 *Perception*

Are you alert or sleepy, hungry, comfortable? Do you have a headache or an itch anywhere? On what kind of paper is your book printed? Is the type large, small, easy to read? How do you like the size of the book, the colors used, the design for inserts in the text?

Chances are that you weren't conscious of most of these phenomena when you began reading the chapter. Instead, you focused on reading and understanding the material in the book. You narrowed your attention to what you defined as important in this moment, and you were unaware of many other things going on around you. This is typical of how we live our lives. We can't attend to everything in our environment, because there is simply far too much there, and most of it isn't relevant to us at a particular time.

We select stimuli to attend to based on a number of factors. First, some qualities of external phenomena draw attention. For instance, we notice things that **STAND OUT** because they are larger, more intense, or more unusual than other phenomena. So we're more likely to hear a loud voice than a soft one and to notice someone in a bright shirt than someone in a drab one. Change also compels attention, which is why we may take for granted all of the pleasant interactions with a friend and notice only the tense moments.

Sometimes we deliberately influence what we notice by indicating things to ourselves (Mead, 1934). In fact, in many ways education is a process of learning to indicate to ourselves things we hadn't seen. Right now you're learning to be more conscious of the selectiveness of your perceptions, so in the future you will notice this more on your own. In English courses, you learn to notice how authors craft characters and use words to create images. Women's Studies classes heighten awareness of the consistent absence of women in conventional accounts of history. In every case, we learn to perceive things we previously didn't recognize. Take a look at Figure 3.1. What do you see?

Suzanne illustrates how we can use selective perception to our advantage.

SUZANNE

I decided to use the information about selective attention to stop smoking. Usually when I smoked, I noticed how relaxing it was to puff a cigarette and how much I liked the flavor. But this week when I lighted up, I would focus on the burning smell of the match. Then I would notice how the smoke hurt my eyes when it rose from a cigarette. I also noticed how nasty ashtrays look with butts in them and how bad a room smells when I've been smoking in it. Once I really paid attention to everything I disliked about cigarettes, I was able to stop. I haven't had one in six days!

What we select to notice is also influenced by who we are and what is going on in us. Our motives and needs affect what we see and don't see. If you've just broken up with a partner, you're more likely to notice attractive people at a party than if you are in an established relationship. Motives also explain the oasis phenomenon in which thirsty people stranded in a desert see an oasis although none really exists. Our expectations further affect what we notice. We are more likely to perceive what we expect to perceive and what others have led us to anticipate. This explains the self-fulfilling prophecy that we discussed in Chapter 2. A child who is told she is unlovable may perceive herself that way and may notice rejecting but not affirming communication from others. We selectively tune in to only some stimuli, so that we simplify the complexities of the total reality in which we live.

Check It Out

EXPECTATIONS AND PERCEPTION

In a class experiment, racially prejudiced and unprejudiced Caucasians were asked to describe African Americans pictured in photographs. The prejudiced viewers "saw" stereotypical racial characteristics such as broadness of noses and fullness of lips, even when those features were not objectively present. The unprejudiced viewers did not notice stereotypical racial qualities. This study demonstrates how powerfully our expectations can mold what we see.

Source: Secord, P. F., Bevan, W., & Katz, B. (1956). The Negro stereotype and perceptual accentuation. *Journal of Abnormal and Social Psychology, 54,* 78–83.

Organization

Once we have selected what to notice, we must make sense of it. We don't simply collect perceptions and string them together randomly; instead, we organize them in meaningful ways. The most developed and useful theory for explaining how we organize experience is **constructivism,** which states that we organize and interpret experience by applying cognitive structures called schemata. Originally developed by Kelly in 1955, constructivism has been elaborated by scholars in communication and psychology. We rely on four schemata to make sense of interpersonal phenomena: prototypes, personal constructs, stereotypes, and scripts.

Prototypes   **Prototypes** are knowledge structures that define the most clear or representative examples of some category (Fehr, 1993, p. 89). For example, you probably have a prototype of great teachers, boring teachers, true friends, and perfect romantic partners. Each of these categories is exemplified by a person who is the ideal case—that's the prototype. We use prototypes to place others in categories—Jane is a confidante, Burt is someone to hang out with, Corina is a romantic interest, Elvira is an enemy. Each category of people is exemplified by one person who best represents the whole group.

DAMION

The person who is my ideal of a friend is my buddy Jackson. He stood by me when I got into a lot of trouble a couple of years ago. I got mixed up with some guys who used drugs, and I started using them too. Pretty soon the coach figured out what was going on, and he suspended me from the team.

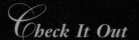

THE CULTURAL PROTOTYPE OF LOVE

Beverly Fehr and her colleagues report that the North American prototype of love centers on five qualities: trust, caring, honesty, friendship, and respect. Passionate feelings and qualities, although often desired and appreciated, are not central to the cultural prototype of love. Instead, companionship, caring, and consideration exemplify cultural views of love.

Sources: Fehr, B. (1993). How do I love thee: Let me consult my prototype. In S. W. Duck (Ed.), *Understanding relationship processes, 1: Individuals in relationships* (pp. 87–122). Newbury Park, CA: Sage. Fehr, B., & Russell, J. A. (1991). Concept of love viewed from a prototype perspective. *Journal of Personality and Social Psychology, 60,* 425–438.

I felt like I was finished when he did that, and then I really got into drugs. But Jackson wouldn't give up on me, and he wouldn't let me give up either. He took me to a drug center and went there with me every day for three weeks. He never turned away when I was sick or even when I cried most of one night when I was getting off the drugs. He just stood by me. Once I was straight, Jackson went with me to see the coach about getting back on the team.

Prototypes define categories by identifying ideal cases. We classify people by asking which of our prototypes they most closely resemble. Prototypes organize our perceptions by allowing us to place people and other phenomena in broad categories. We then consider how close they are to the prototype, or exemplar, of that category.

Personal Constructs   Personal constructs are "mental yardsticks" that allow us to measure people and situations along bipolar dimensions of judgment (Kelly, 1955). Examples of personal constructs are intelligent–unintelligent, kind–unkind, interesting–boring, arrogant–modest, assertive–passive, and attractive–unattractive. To size up an individual, we measure her or him by personal constructs that we use to distinguish among people. How intelligent, kind, or attractive is this person? Whereas prototypes help decide into which broad category a person or event fits, personal constructs let us make more detailed assessments of particular qualities of phenomena we perceive. The personal constructs we rely on fundamentally shape our perceptions, because we define something only in terms of how it measures up on the constructs we use. Thus, we may not notice qualities of people that aren't covered by the constructs we apply.

NAI LEE

One of the ways I look at people is by whether they are independent or related to others. That is one of the first judgments I make of others. In Korea we are not so individualistic or independent as people in the United States. We think of ourselves more as members of families and communities than as individuals. The emphasis on independent identity was the first thing I noticed when I came to this country, and it is still an important way I look at people.

Stereotypes   Stereotypes are predictive generalizations about people and situations. Based on the category in which we place someone or something and how it measures up against personal constructs we apply, we predict what it will do. For instance, if you define someone as a liberal, you might stereotype her or him as likely to vote Democratic, support social legislation, be pro-environment, and so forth. You may have stereotypes of fraternity and sorority members, athletes, and people from other cultures. The stereotypes you have don't necessarily reflect actual similarities among people. Instead, stereotypes are based on our perceptions of similarities among people. We may perceive similarities that others don't, and we may fail to perceive commonalities that are obvious to others.

WINOWA

People have a stereotype of Native Americans. People who are not Native Americans think we are all alike—how we look, how we act, what we believe, what our traditions are. But that isn't true. The Crow and Apache are as different as people from Kenya and New York. Some tribes have a history of aggression and violence; others have traditions of peace and harmony. We worship different spirits and have different tribal rituals and customs. All of these differences are lost when people stereotype us all into one group.

© Kim Newton/Woodfin Camp and Associates, Inc.

Stereotypes may be accurate or inaccurate. In some cases we have incorrect understandings of a group, and in other cases individual members of a group don't conform to the behaviors typical of a group as a whole. Although we need stereotypes in order to predict what will happen around us, they can be harmful if we forget that they are based on our perceptions, not objective reality.

PHYLLIS

I'll tell you what stereotype really gets to me: the older student. I'm thirty-eight and working on my degree, and everyone at this college treats me like a housewife who's dabbling in courses. The students treat me like their mother, not a peer. And the faculty are even worse sometimes. I've had several professors who don't take my questions or my work seriously. One even said to me that I shouldn't worry about grades, since I didn't have to plan a career like the younger students. Well, I am planning a career, I am a student, and I am serious about my work.

Scripts The final cognitive schemata we use to organize perceptions is **scripts,** which are guides to action based on our experiences and observations of interaction. Scripts consist of a sequence of activities that define what we and others are expected to do in specific situations. Many of our daily activities are governed by scripts, although we're often unaware of them. You have a script for greeting casual acquaintances as you walk around campus ("Hey, how ya doing?" "Fine—can't complain," "See ya"). You also have scripts for dating, managing conflict, talking with professors, dealing with clerks, and hanging out with friends. Scripts organize perceptions into lines of action.

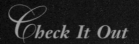

THE CENSUS BUREAU'S DILEMMA

Systems of organizing or classifying are arbitrary constructions invented by humans. Yet we sometimes act as if the ways we have classified things are intrinsically right. Consider the dilemma of the Census Bureau, which finds that its method of classifying races no longer works.

The mushrooming diversity of our country has created problems for the Census Bureau and other demographic trackers. The racial categories currently used were created in 1978, and they are no longer adequate to classify people with diverse languages, cultures, and ethnic heritages. It is inappropriate to lump diverse groups into single categories such as Asian (Japanese, Chinese, Taiwanese, Nepalese, and so on) or Native American (Crow, Apache, Lumbee, and so on). The prevailing classifications also count Middle Easterners as white and Alaskans as Alaskan natives, rather than American natives. Another deficiency of existing categories is their inability to acknowledge people who have multiracial identities—and this may be the majority of us.

Social critic Eric Bates (1994, p. 15) asks, "Counting and grouping people by racial categories helps us fight discrimination—but does it also perpetuate racism by institutionalizing false racial distinctions? Can we preserve 'race' as a useful statistical device and yet find ways to acknowledge that such measurements can never truly reflect our rich diversity as a people?"

Prototypes, personal constructs, stereotypes, and scripts are cognitive schemata that organize our thinking about people and situations. We use them to make sense of what we notice and to figure out how we and others will act in particular situations. All four cognitive schemata reflect the perspectives of particular others and the generalized other. As we interact with people, we internalize our culture's ways of classifying, measuring, and predicting phenomena and its norms for acting in various situations.

Social perspectives are not always accurate or constructive, so we shouldn't accept them unreflectively. For instance, if your parents engaged in bitter, destructive quarreling, you may have learned a script for conflict that will undermine your relationships. Similarly, cultural views of nonmainstream groups are often negative and inaccurate, so we should assess them critically before using them to organize our own perceptions and direct our own activities.

Put It in Practice

SIZING UP OTHERS

Pay attention to the cognitive schemata you use the next time you meet a new person. First notice how you classify the person. Do you categorize her or him as a potential friend, date, bureaucrat, neighbor? Next, identify the constructs you use to assess the person. Do you focus on physical characteristics (attractive–unattractive), mental qualities (intelligent–unintelligent), psychological features (secure–insecure), and/or interpersonal qualities (eligible–committed)? Would different constructs be prominent if you used a different prototype to classify the person? Now, note how you stereotype the person. What do you expect him or her to do based on the prototype and constructs you've applied? Finally, identify your script—how you expect interaction to unfold between you.

Interpretation

People, interactions, and situations have no intrinsic meaning. Instead, we assign meaning by interpreting what we have noticed and organized. **Interpretation** is the subjective process of explaining perceptions in ways that let us make sense of them. To interpret the meaning of another's actions, we construct explanations for what she or he does.

Attributions   **Attributions** are explanations of why things happen and why people act as they do (Heider, 1958; Kelley, 1967). Attributions have four dimensions. The first is internal/external locus, which attributes what a person does to either internal factors (he's angry) or external factors (the traffic jam frustrated him). The second dimension is stable/unstable, which explains actions as the result of stable factors that won't change (she's a Type A person) or temporary occurrences (she acted that way because she just had a fight with the boss). Global/specific is the third dimension, and it defines behavior as the result of a general pattern (he's an angry person) or a specific instance (he gets angry about sloppy work). Finally, there is the dimension of responsibility, which attributes behaviors to either factors people can control (she doesn't try to overcome her depression) or ones they cannot (she is depressed because of a chemical imbalance). In judging whether others can control their actions, we decide whether to hold them responsible for what they do.

Self-Serving Bias   Research indicates that we tend to construct attributions that serve our personal interests (Hamachek, 1992; Sypher, 1984). Thus, we are inclined to make internal, stable, and global attributions for our positive actions and our successes. We're also likely to claim good results come about because of personal control we exerted. For example, you might say that you did well on a test because you are a smart (internal and stable) person who is always responsible (global) and studies hard (personal control). On the other hand, we tend to avoid taking responsibility for negative actions and failures by attributing them to external, unstable, and specific factors that are beyond personal control. To explain a failing grade on a test, you

---

Check It Out

ATTRIBUTIONAL PATTERNS AND RELATIONSHIP SATISFACTION

Investigations have shown that happy and unhappy couples have distinct attributional styles. Happy couples make relationship-enhancing attributions. Individuals attribute nice things a partner does to internal, stable, and global reasons. "She got the film for us because she is a good person who always does sweet things for us." Unpleasant things a partner does are attributed to external, unstable, and specific factors. "He yelled at me because all of the stress of the past few days made him not himself."

Unhappy couples employ reverse attributional patterns. They explain nice actions as results of external, unstable, and specific factors. "She got the tape because she had some extra time this particular day." Negative actions are seen as stemming from internal, stable, and global factors. "He yelled at me because he is a nasty person who never shows any consideration to anybody else."

Negative attributions fix pessimistic views and undermine motivation to improve a relationship. Whether positive or negative, attributions may be self-fulfilling prophecies.

Sources: Bradbury, T. N., & Fincham, F. D. (1990). Attributions in marriage: Review and critique. *Psychological Bulletin, 107,* 3–33. Fletcher, G. J., & Fincham, F. D. (1991). Attribution in close relationships. In G. J. Fletcher & F. D. Fincham (Eds.), *Cognition in close relationships* (pp. 7–35). Hillsdale, NJ: Lawrence Erlbaum.

© 1994 Cathy Guisewite. Reprinted by permission of Universal Press Syndicate. All rights reserved.

might say that you did poorly because the professor (external) put a lot of tricky questions on that test (unstable, specific factor) so that all of your studying didn't help (outside of personal control). In other words, our misconduct results from outside forces that we can't help, but all the good we do reflects our personal qualities and efforts. This **self-serving bias** can distort our perceptions, leading us to take excessive personal credit for what we do well and to abdicate responsibility for what we do poorly. When we make faulty attributions for our behaviors, we form an unrealistic image of ourselves and our abilities.

CHICO

When I do badly on a test or paper, I usually say either the professor was unfair or I had too much to do that week and couldn't study like I wanted to. But when my friends do badly on a test, I tend to think they're not good in that subject or they aren't disciplined or whatever.

We've seen that perception involves three interrelated processes. The first of these, selection, involves noticing certain things and ignoring others out of the total complexity of what is going on. The second process is organization where we use prototypes, personal constructs, stereotypes, and scripts to order what we have selectively perceived. Finally, we engage in interpretation to make sense of the perceptions we have gathered and organized. Attributions are a primary way we explain what we and others do. Although we discussed each of these processes separately, in reality they may occur in different orders and they interact continuously. Thus, our interpretations shape the knowledge schemata we use to organize experiences, and the ways we organize perceptions affect what we notice and interpret. For instance, in her commentary earlier in this chapter, Nai Lee's interpretations of Westerners' individualism were shaped by the schemata she learned in her Korean homeland. Also, reliance on the construct of individualistic–communal shaped what she noticed about Americans. Now that we understand the complex processes involved in perception, we're ready to consider a range of factors that influence what and how we perceive.

Influences on Perception

Recently I attended the first meeting of a student–faculty group that wanted to start a new leadership development program on campus. At the end of the session, the facilitator said, "This has been a great first meeting. Participation was so high!" Beside me, a young African American woman grumbled, "Yeah—white participation." I then noticed there were only three African American students, one Asian American student, and no faculty of color. Thinking back, I realized none of the minority students had spoken during the meeting. As a member of the majority group, I hadn't realized how few people of color were in the room, and I hadn't noticed that none of them spoke. The African American student beside me had perceived the meeting differently than I initially did, because her ethnicity and personal experiences on a campus dominated by whites made her attentive to racial dynamics I didn't notice.

As this example illustrates, everyone doesn't perceive situations and people in the same way. In this section, we consider some of the influences on our perceptions.

Physiology

The most obvious reason perceptions vary among people is that we differ in our sensory abilities and physiologies. The five senses are not the same for all of us. Music that one person finds deafening is barely audible to another. Salsa that is painfully hot to one diner may seem mild to someone else. On a given day on my campus, students wear everything from shorts

© LeDuc/Monkmeyer

*Deafness has left me acutely
aware of both the duplicity that
language is capable of and the
many expressions the body
cannot hide.*

TERRY GALLOWAY

and sandals to jackets, indicating they have different sensitivities to cold. Some people have better vision than others, and some are color-blind. These differences in sensory abilities affect our perceptions.

Our physiological states also influence perception. If you are tired, stressed, or sick, you're likely to perceive things more negatively than you normally would. For instance, a playful insult from a friend might anger you if you're feeling down, but wouldn't bother you if you felt good. Also, you might attribute a sick friend's behaviors to unstable and specific causes rather than to enduring personality. Each of us has our own biorhythm, which influences the times of day when we tend to be alert and fuzzy. I'm a morning person, so that's when I prefer to teach classes and write. I am less alert and creative late in the day. Thus, I perceive things in the morning that I simply don't notice when my energy level declines.

Age is another factor that influences our perceptions. The older we get, the more rich a perspective we have for perceiving life and people. Thus, compared to a person of twenty, someone who is sixty has a more complex fund of experiences to draw on in perceiving. You probably think nothing of paying seventy-five cents for a can of soda, but I recall buying it for a quarter when I was younger. To me, the current prices seem high because I have a comparison point that you don't. The extent of discrimination still experienced by women and minorities understandably discourages many college students. I am more hopeful than some of them because I have seen many changes in my lifetime. When I attended college, women were not admitted on an equal basis with men and almost all students of color attended minority colleges. When I entered the job market, few laws protected women and minorities against discrimination in hiring, pay, and advancement. The substantial progress made during my life leads me to perceive current inequities as changeable.

Culture

A **culture** consists of beliefs, values, understandings, practices, and ways of interpreting experience that are shared by a number of people. It is a set of taken-for-granted assumptions that form the pattern of our lives and that guide how we think, feel, and act. The influence of culture is so pervasive that it's hard to realize how powerfully it shapes our perceptions. Perhaps the best way to recognize the assumptions of our own culture is to travel to other places where values, understandings, and codes of behavior are different.

Consider a few aspects of modern Western culture that influence our perceptions. One characteristic of our culture is the emphasis on technology and its offspring, speed. We expect things to happen fast—almost instantly. Whether it's instant photos, five-minute copying, or one-hour martinizing, we live at an accelerated pace (Wood, 1995c). We send letters by express mail, jet across the country, and microwave meals. Social commentators suggest that the cultural emphasis on speed may diminish patience and thus our willingness to invest in long-term projects, such as relationships (Toffler, 1970, 1980). In countries such as Nepal and Mexico, life proceeds at a more leisurely pace, and people spend more time talking, relaxing, and engaging in low-key activity.

North America is also a fiercely individualistic culture in which personal initiative is expected and rewarded. Other cultures, particularly many Asian ones, are more communal, and identity is defined in terms of one's family, rather than as an individual quality. Because families are more valued in communal cultures, elders are given greater respect and care than they often receive in the United States. The difference between communal and individualistic cultures is also evident in child-care policies. More communal countries have policies that reflect the value they place on families. In every developed country except the United States, new parents, including adoptive parents, are given at least six weeks of paid parental leave, and some countries provide nearly a year's paid leave (Wood, 1994d).

© Keren Su/Stock, Boston

Patterns of the past echo in the present and resound through the future.
DHYAN YWAHOO

Put It in Practice

CULTURAL VALUES

How do values in Western culture affect your everyday perceptions and activities? See if you can trace concrete implications of these cultural values:

Example: Competition. This value is evident in concrete practices such as competitive sports, grading policies, and attempts to get the last word in casual conversations.

1. Productivity
2. Individualism
3. Speed
4. Youth
5. Wealth

With others in your class discuss the impact of cultural values on your day-to-day perceptions and activities.

Standpoint In recent years, scholars have realized that we are affected not only by the culture as a whole, but by our particular location within the culture (Haraway, 1988; Harding, 1991). *Standpoint* refers to your point of view as it is influenced by your social circumstances. **Standpoint theory**

© B. Daemmrich/The Image Works

claims that a culture includes a number of social groups that distinctively shape perceptions, identities, and opportunities of members. As we saw in Chapter 2, race, gender, class, and sexual preference are primary ways that Western culture groups people. Although we may all realize that our society attaches differential value to different social groups, each of us is only one race, class, and sex. The way we perceive the world and ourselves is shaped by our experiences as members of the particular groups to which we belong. This is why the African American woman at the student–faculty meeting noticed the absence of participation by people of color and I didn't.

In an early discussion of standpoint, the philosopher Georg Hegel (1807) pointed out that standpoints reflect power positions in social hierarchies. To illustrate, he noted that the institution of slavery is perceived very differently by masters and slaves. Extending Hegel's point, we can see that those in positions of power have a vested interest in preserving the system that gives them privileges. Thus, they are unlikely to perceive its flaws and inequities. On the other hand, those who are disempowered by a system are able to see inequities and discrimination (Harding, 1991).

Women and men, as social groups, have different standpoints. For instance, the caregiving we generally associate with women is not due to maternal instinct, but rather to the social role of mother, which teaches women to care for others, notice who needs what, and defer their own needs (Ruddick, 1989). Other researchers have discovered that men who are in caregiving roles become nurturing, accommodative, and sensitive to others' needs as a consequence of being in the social role of caregiver (Kaye & Applegate, 1990).

JANICE

I'll vouch for the idea of standpoint affecting how we communicate. I was always a pretty independent person. Some people even thought I was kind of selfish, because I really would prioritize myself. Then I had my first baby, and I stayed home with him for a year. I really changed—and I mean in basic ways. I believed that my most important job was to be there for Timmy, and so my whole day focused on him. He was the person I thought about first, not myself. I learned to hear the slightest difference in his cries, so I could tell when he was hungry or needed his diapers changed or wanted company. When I went back to work after a year, a lot of my former colleagues said I was different—much more attentive and sensitive to what they said and more generous with my time than I had been. I guess I developed new patterns of communication as a result of mothering.

Gendered standpoints are also evident in marital conflict. Researchers have found that conflict lessens wives' love for husbands more than it lessens husbands' love for wives (Huston, McHale, & Crouter, 1985; Kelly, Huston, & Cate, 1985). This makes sense when we realize that husbands generally exercise more power over decision making, so they usually prevail in conflict. Naturally, the winners of conflicts are more satisfied with relationships than losers are!

Gendered standpoints are also obvious in the effort that women and men in general invest in maintaining relationships. Socialized into the role of "relationship expert," women are expected by others and themselves to take care of relationships (Tavris, 1992; Wood, 1993, 1994d). They are supposed to know when something is wrong and to resolve the tension. This may explain why women tend to be more aware than men of problems in relationships (Brehm, 1992).

Put It in Practice

EXPLORING STANDPOINTS

To become more aware of diverse perspectives on social life, talk with someone whose standpoint differs from your own. Discuss how you and the other person think about families, careers, and attending college. Explore how the individual perceives college life and activities on campus. How do these perceptions differ from your own? Does interaction with this person give you new perspectives on familiar things in your life?

Both our membership in an overall culture and our standpoint as members of particular social groups shape how we perceive people, situations, events, and ourselves.

Social Roles

Our perceptions are also shaped by our social roles. Both the training that we receive to fulfill a role and the actual demands of the role affect what we notice and how we interpret and evaluate it. My perceptions of my classes focus on how interested students seem, whether they appear to have read material, and whether what they're learning is useful in their lives. Students have told me that they think about classes in terms of number and difficulty of tests, whether papers are required, and whether the professor is interesting. We have different perspectives on what classes are. In working on this book, I've focused on ideas, whereas Todd, my editor, thinks about layout, design features, and marketing issues that don't occur to me.

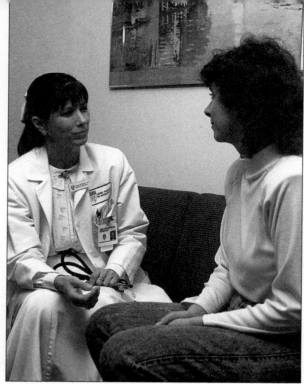

© Frank Siteman/The Picture Cube

The professions people enter influence what they notice and how they think and act. Prior to her professional training, my sister Carolyn did not seem to have highly developed analytic thinking skills. However, after law school she was extremely analytic, and her conversational style shifted to be more argumentative, logical, and probing. Physicians are trained to be highly observant of physical symptoms, and they may detect a physical problem before the person who has it. Once at a social gathering, a friend of mine who is a physician asked me how long I had had a herniated disk. Shocked, I told him I didn't have one. "You do," he insisted, and, sure enough, a few weeks later a disk ruptured. His medical training enabled him to perceive subtle changes in my posture and walk that I hadn't noticed.

Cognitive Abilities

In addition to physiological, cultural, and social influences, perception is also shaped by our cognitive abilities. How elaborately we think about situations and people and the extent of personal knowledge of others we have affect how we select, organize, and interpret experiences.

Cognitive Complexity   People differ in the number and type of knowledge schemata they use to organize and interpret people and situations. **Cognitive complexity** refers to the number of constructs (remember, these are bipolar dimensions of judgment) used, how abstract they are, and how elaborately they interact to shape perceptions. Most children have fairly simple cognitive systems. They rely on few schemata; focus more on concrete categories than abstract, psychological ones; and often are not aware of relationships among different perceptions. For instance, toddlers often call any and every adult male "daddy," because they haven't learned more complex ways to distinguish among men.

Adults also differ in cognitive complexity, and this affects the accuracy of our perceptions. If you can think of people only as nice or mean, you have a limited range for perceiving the motives of others. Similarly, people who focus on concrete data tend to have less sophisticated understandings than people who also perceive psychological data. For example, you might notice that a person is attractive, tells jokes, and talks to others easily. These are concrete perceptions. At a more abstract, psychological level, you might reason that the concrete behaviors you observe reflect a secure, self-confident personality. This is a sophisticated explanation because it provides a rich perception of why the individual acts as she or he does.

What if you later find out that the person is very quiet in classes? Someone with low cognitive complexity would have difficulty integrating the new information into prior observations. Either the new information would be dismissed because it doesn't fit or the most recent data would replace the former perception and the person would be redefined as shy. A more cognitively complex person would integrate all of the information into a coherent account. Perhaps a cognitively complex individual would conclude that the person is very confident in social situations, but less secure in academic ones.

Research has shown that cognitively complex individuals are flexible in interpreting complicated phenomena and are able to integrate new information into how they think about people and situations. Individuals who are less cognitively complex are likely to ignore discrepant information that doesn't fit with their impressions or to throw out old ideas and replace them with new impressions (Crockett, 1965; Delia, Clark, & Switzer, 1974). Either way they fail to recognize some of the nuances and inconsistencies that are part of human nature. The complexity of our cognitive systems affects how intricately we perceive people and interpersonal situations.

© Craig Aurness/West Light

Person-Perception   **Person-perception** is related to cognitive complexity, since it requires abstract thinking and a breadth of schemata. Person-perception refers to the ability to perceive another as a unique and distinct individual apart from social roles and generalizations. Our ability to perceive others as unique depends both on general ability to make cognitive distinctions and on how well we know particular others. Recalling the discussion of I–Thou relationships in Chapter 1, you may remember that these are relationships in which people know and value each other as unique individuals. To do so, we must learn about another, and this requires considerable time and interaction. As we get to know another better, we gain insight into how she or he differs from others in a group ("Rob's not like other political activists," "Ellen's more interested in people than most Computer Science majors"). The more we interact with another and the greater variety of experiences we have together, the more insight we gain into her or his motives, feelings, and behaviors. As we come to understand others as individuals, we fine-tune our perceptions of them. Consequently, we're less likely to rely on stereotypes to perceive them. This is why we often communicate more effectively with people we know well than with strangers or casual acquaintances.

STEVE

You really have to know somebody on an individual basis to know what she or he likes and wants. When I first started dating Sherry, I sent her red roses to let her know I thought she was special. That's the "lovers' flower," right? It turns out that was the only flower her father liked, and they had a million red roses at his funeral. Now they make Sherry sad because they remind her he's dead. I also took her chocolates once, then later found out she's allergic to chocolate. By now I know what flowers and things she likes, but my experience shows that the general rules don't always apply to individuals.

Person-perception is not the same as empathy. **Empathy** is the ability to feel with another person—to feel what she or he feels in a situation. Feeling with another is an emotional response that some scholars believe is not really possible. Our feelings tend to be guided by our own emotional tendencies and experiences, so it may be impossible to feel what another person feels. What we can do is realize that another is feeling something and connect as well as we can based on our own, different experiences. A more realistic goal is to learn to adopt dual perspective so that we adapt our communication to other people's frames of reference (Phillips & Wood, 1983; Wood, 1982, 1995a, 1995c). With commitment and effort, we can learn a lot about how others see the world, even if that differs from how we see it.

When we take the perspective of others, we try to grasp what something means to them and how they perceive things. This requires suspending judgment at least temporarily. We can't appreciate someone else's perspective when we're imposing our evaluations of whether it is right or wrong, sensible or crazy. Instead, we have to let go of our own perspective and perceptions long enough to enter the world of another person. Doing this allows us to understand issues from the individual's point of view, so that we can communicate more effectively with her or him. At a later point in interaction we may choose to express our own perspective or to disagree with another's views. This is appropriate and important in honest communication, but voicing our own views is not a substitute for the equally important skill of recognizing another's perspective.

In sum, we've seen that many factors influence perception and account for differences among people in perceptions. Differences based on physiology, culture and standpoint, social roles, and cognitive abilities affect what we perceive and how we interpret others and experiences. In the final section of the chapter, we consider ways to improve the accuracy of our perceptions.

Guidelines for Improving Perception and Communication

Perception is a foundation of interpersonal communication. Yet, as we have seen, many factors influence how accurately we perceive others and situations. To be a competent communicator, it's important to form perceptions carefully and check their accuracy. We'll discuss six guidelines for improving the accuracy of perceptions and, ultimately, the quality of interpersonal communication.

Recognize That All Perceptions Are Subjective

What you've read so far makes it clear that our perceptions are inevitably subjective. Each of us perceives from a particular perspective that is shaped by our physiology, culture, standpoint, social roles, and cognitive abilities. This means that what we perceive is always partial and subjective. It is partial because we cannot perceive everything, but instead select only certain aspects of phenomena to notice. We then organize and interpret those selected stimuli in personal ways that are necessarily incomplete. Perception is also subjective, since it is influenced by individual background and physiology and our personal modes of interpretation.

Objective features of reality have no meaning until we notice, interpret, and evaluate them. It is our perceptions that construct meanings for the people and experiences in our lives. An outfit perceived as elegant by one person may appear cheap to another. A teacher one student regards as fascinating may put someone else to sleep. A weekend camping trip may be a joy to an outdoors person and an ordeal to an individual not accustomed to roughing it. There is no truth or falsity to perceptions—they represent only what things mean to individuals. Thus, when you and another person disagree about something, neither of you is wrong or crazy. It's more likely that you have attended to different things and that there are differences in your social, cultural, and physiological resources for perceiving. Remembering that perceptions are subjective curbs the tendency to think our perceptions are the only valid ones.

Avoid Mindreading

Because perception is subjective, people differ in what they notice and in what it means to them. One of the most common problems in interpersonal communication is **mindreading,** which is assuming we understand what another person thinks or perceives. When we mindread, we don't check with another person to see what he or she is thinking. Instead, we act as if we know what's on another's mind, and this can get us into considerable trouble. Gottman and his colleagues identify mindreading as one of the

© 1995 M. C. Escher/Cordon Art—Baarn, Holland. All rights reserved.

The social world that we share with others is a world we have imagined together and agreed to believe in.

ELIZABETH JANEWAY

behaviors that contributes to interpersonal tension (Gottman, 1993; Gottman, Notarius, Gonso, & Markman, 1976). The danger of mindreading is that we may misinterpret others and have no way of checking on the accuracy of our perceptions. Sometimes we do understand one another but sometimes we don't.

Consequently, for the most part mindreading is more likely to harm than help interpersonal communication. Consider a few examples. One person might say to her partner, "I know you didn't plan anything for our anniversary because it doesn't matter to you." Whether or not the partner made plans, it's impossible to guess motives or to know why the partner forgot if indeed she or he did. One friend might say to another, "You were late coming over because you're still mad about what happened yesterday." The speaker is guessing reasons for the friend's tardiness and could well be wrong. Mindreading also occurs when we say things such as "I know why you're upset" (Has the person said she or he is upset?) or "You don't care about me anymore" (maybe the other person is too preoccupied or worried to be as attentive as usual). We also mindread when we tell ourselves we know how somebody else will feel or react, or what he or she will do. The truth is we don't really know—we're only guessing. When we mindread, we impose our perspectives on others instead of allowing them to say what they think. This can cause misunderstandings as well as resentment, since most of us prefer to speak for ourselves.

CONSUELA

Mindreading drives me crazy. My boyfriend does it all the time, and he's wrong as often as he's right. Last week he got tickets to a concert because he "knew" I'd want to go. Maybe I would have if I hadn't already planned a trip that weekend, but he never checked on my schedule. A lot of times when we're talking, he'll say something, then before I can answer he says, "I know what you're thinking." Then he proceeds to run through his ideas about what I'm thinking. Usually he's off base, and then we get into a sideline argument about why he keeps assuming what I think instead of asking me. I really wish he would ask me what I think.

Check Perceptions with Others

The third guideline follows directly from the first two. Because perceptions are subjective and mindreading is an ineffective way to figure out what others think, we need to check our perceptions with others. In the first example above, it would be wise to ask, "Did you forget our anniversary?" If the partner did forget, then the speaker might ask, "Why do you think you forgot?" The partner may not know why or the reasons may not be satisfactory, but asking is a better way to open a productive dialogue than accusing a partner of bad motives.

Perception checking is an important communication skill because it helps people arrive at mutual understandings of each other and their relationships. To check perceptions, you should first state what it is that you have noticed. For example, a person might say, "Lately you've seemed less attentive to me." Then the person should check to see whether the other perceives the same thing: "Do you feel you've been less attentive?" Finally, it's appropriate to ask the other person to explain her or his behavior. In the example, the person might ask, "Why do you think you're less attentive?" (If the partner doesn't perceive that she or he is less attentive, the question would be "Why have you wanted to be together less often and seemed distracted when we talk?") When checking perceptions, it's important to use a tentative tone, rather than a dogmatic or accusatory one. This minimizes defensiveness and encourages good discussion. Just let the other person know you've noticed something and would like him or her to clarify his or her perceptions of what is happening and what it means.

Put It in Practice

PERCEPTION CHECKING

To gain skill in perception checking (and all communication behaviors), you need to practice. Try this:

1. Monitor your tendencies to mindread, especially in established relationships in which you feel you know your partners well.

2. The next time you catch yourself mindreading, stop. Instead, tell the other person what you are noticing and invite her or him to explain how she or he perceives what's happening. First, find out whether your partner agrees with you about what you noticed. Second, if you agree, then find out how your partner interprets and evaluates the issue.

3. Engage in perception checking for two or three days so that you have lots of chances to see what happens. When you've done that, reflect on the number of times your mindreading was inaccurate.

4. How did perception checking affect interaction with your friends and romantic partners? Did you find out things you wouldn't have known if you'd engaged in mindreading?

Distinguish Between Facts and Inferences

Competent interpersonal communication also depends on distinguishing facts from inferences. A fact is an objective statement based on observation. An inference involves an interpretation that goes beyond the facts.

THE TRUTH, THE WHOLE TRUTH, AND NOTHING BUT THE TRUTH

Research indicates that eyewitness testimony may not be as accurate as we often assume. Studies show that witnesses' perceptions are shaped by the language attorneys use.

In one experiment, viewers were shown a film of a traffic accident and then were asked, "How fast were the cars going when they *smashed* into each other?" Other viewers were asked how fast the cars were going when they *bumped* or *collided*. Viewers testified to significantly different speeds depending on which word was used in the question.

In a separate experiment, viewers were shown a film of a traffic accident and then filled out a questionnaire that included questions about things that had not actually been on the film. Viewers who were asked, "Did you see *the* broken headlight?" more frequently testified they saw it than did viewers who were asked, "Did you see *a* broken headlight?"

The accidents that viewers "saw" were shaped by the words used to describe them.

Source: Trotter, R. J. (1975, October 25). "The truth, the whole truth, and nothing but . . . " *Science News, 108,* 269.

For example, a student consistently comes to class late and sits at the back of the room, sometimes dozing off during discussions. The teacher might think, "That student is rude and unmotivated." The facts are that the student comes late, sits toward the rear of the classroom, and sometimes falls asleep. Defining the student as "rude and unmotivated" is an inference that goes beyond the facts. The fact might be that the student is tired because he or she has a job that ends right before the class.

It's easy to confuse facts and inferences because we sometimes treat the latter as the former. When we say, "The student is rude," we've made a statement that sounds factual, and we may then regard it that way ourselves. To avoid this tendency, substitute more tentative words for *is*. For instance, "The student seems rude" or "This student may be being rude" are more tentative statements that keep the speaker from treating an inference as a fact.

Put It in Practice

USING TENTATIVE LANGUAGE

To become more sensitive to our tendencies to confuse facts and inferences, pay attention to the language you use for the next twenty-four hours when you describe people and interactions. Listen for words like *is* and *are* that imply factual information. Do you find there are instances in which more tentative language would be more accurate?

Now extend your observations to other people and the language they use. When you hear others say, "she is," "they are," or "he is," are they really making factual statements or are they making inferences?

Monitor the Self-Serving Bias

Earlier in this chapter, we discussed the self-serving bias, which involves attributing our successes and nice behaviors to internal and stable qualities in us that we control and attributing our failures and bad behaviors to external, unstable factors beyond our control. Because this bias can distort perceptions, we need to monitor it carefully. Try to catch yourself in the act of explaining away your failures or adverse behaviors as not your fault and taking personal credit for accomplishments that were helped along by luck or situational factors.

Monitoring the self-serving bias also has implications for how we perceive others. Just as we tend to judge ourselves generously, we may also be inclined to judge others too harshly. Monitor your perceptions to see whether you attribute others' successes and admirable actions to external factors beyond their control, and their shortcomings and blunders to internal factors they can (should) control. If you do this, substitute more generous explanations for others' behaviors and notice how that affects your perceptions of them.

Monitor Labels

Words crystallize perceptions. Until we label an experience, it remains nebulous and less than fully formed in our thinking. Only when we name our feelings and thoughts do we have a clear way to describe and think about them. But just as words crystallize experiences, they can also freeze thought. Once we label our perceptions, we may respond to our own labels rather than actual phenomena.

Consider this situation. Suppose you get together with five others in a study group, and a student named Andrea monopolizes the whole meeting with her questions and concerns. Leaving the meeting, one person says, "Gee, Andrea is so selfish and immature! I'll never work with her again." Another person responds, "She's not really selfish. She's just insecure about her grades in this course, so she was hyper in the meeting." Chances are these two people will perceive and treat Andrea differently depending on whether they label her selfish or insecure. The point is that the two people don't respond to Andrea herself, but to the words they use to label their perceptions of her.

Effective communicators realize that the words they use influence their perceptions. In Chapter 4, we consider in depth how language affects perception. For now, remember that when we engage in interpersonal communication, we abstract only certain aspects of the total reality around us. Our perceptions are one step away from reality, since they are always partial and subjective. We move a second step from reality when we label a perception. We move even further from the actual reality when we respond not to behaviors or our perceptions of them, but instead to the label we impose. This process can be illustrated as a ladder of abstraction (Figure 3.2), a concept emphasized by one of the first scholars of interpersonal communication (Hayakawa, 1962, 1964).

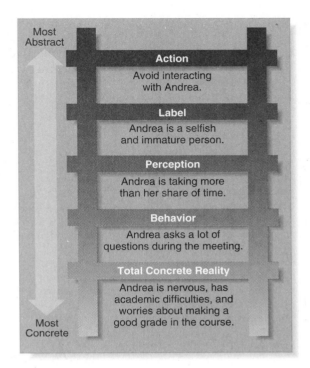

FIGURE 3.2
Perception, Communication, and Abstraction

Perceiving accurately is neither magic nor an ability that some people just naturally have. Instead, it is a communication skill that can be developed. Following the five guidelines we have discussed will allow you to make more careful and accurate perceptions in interpersonal communication situations.

SUMMARY

In this chapter, we've explored human perception, a process that involves selecting, organizing, and interpreting experiences. These three processes are not separate in practice; instead, they interact so that each one affects the others. What we selectively notice affects what it is that we interpret and evaluate. At the same time, our interpretations become a lens that influences what we notice in the world around us. Selection, interpretation, and evaluation interact continuously in the process of perception.

We have seen that perception is influenced by many factors. Our sensory capacities and our physiological condition affect what we notice and how astutely we recognize stimuli around us. In addition, our cultural backgrounds and standpoints in society shape how we see and interact with the world. Social roles are another influence on perception. Thus, our professional training and our roles in families affect what we notice and how we organize and interpret it. Finally, perception is influenced by cognitive abilities including cognitive complexity, person-perception, and perspective taking.

Understanding how perception works provides a foundation for improving our perceptual capacities. We discussed six guidelines for improving the accuracy of perceptions. First, realize that all perceptions are subjective, so there is no absolutely correct or best understanding of a situation or a person. Second, because people perceive differently, we should avoid mindreading or assuming we know what others are perceiving. Third, it's a good idea to check perceptions, which involves stating how you perceive something and asking how another person does. Avoiding the self-serving bias is also important, since it can lead us to perceive ourselves too charitably and to perceive others too harshly. A fifth guideline is to distinguish facts from inferences.

Perception is a process of abstracting in which we move further and further away from the concrete reality as we select, organize, interpret, evaluate, and label phenomena. We need to know when we are making factual descriptions and when we are making inferences that require checking. The final guideline is to monitor how language shapes perceptions. The labels we use, which are abstractions from what actually exists, affect how we perceive people and situations. Just as we can't see how to solve the nine dots problem if we label the dots a square, so we cannot see aspects of ourselves and others when our labels limit our perceptions. Realizing this encourages us to be more sensitive to the power of language and to make more considered word choices.

What we have covered in this chapter allows us to understand how we perceive others and situations and how we might improve our perceptual skills. In the next chapter, we explore the power of language in greater depth, and we will see how what we say affects our interpersonal relationships.

KEY TERMS

Perception	Self-serving bias
Constructivism	Culture
Prototypes	Standpoint theory
Personal constructs	Cognitive complexity
Stereotypes	Person-perception
Scripts	Empathy
Interpretation	Mindreading
Attributions	

Solution to the problem on p. 70:

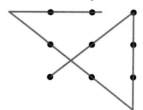

CHAPTER 4

The World of Words

*M*any children in the United States have heard the nursery rhyme "Sticks and stones can break my bones, but words can never hurt me." By now, most of us have figured out that isn't true. Words can hurt us, sometimes very deeply. Words can also enchant, comfort, teach, amuse, and inspire us. We use language to plan, dream, remember, evaluate, and reflect on ourselves and the world around us. Words, in short, are powerful aspects of everyday life.

The human world is a world of words and meanings. Just as the alphabet quilt shown on the preceding page weaves images together to create meaning, so do we weave words together to create meaning in our lives. We use words to express ourselves and to give meaning to our lives and activities. In this chapter, we take a close look at the verbal dimension of communication and how it affects personal identity and interpersonal interaction. We begin by defining symbols and symbolic abilities. Next we explore different communication cultures to appreciate how various social groups communicate. We close the chapter by discussing guidelines for effective verbal communication.

Symbols and Meaning

As we discovered in our discussion of perception, we do not deal with raw reality most of the time. Instead, we abstract only certain parts of reality to notice and label. After we label experiences, we respond to our labels, not to the experiences themselves. This means that our perceptions and experiences are filtered through symbols. To appreciate the importance of symbols in our lives, we'll discuss what they are and how they affect us personally and interpersonally.

The Nature of Symbols

Symbols are arbitrary, ambiguous, abstract representations of other phenomena. For instance, your name is a symbol that represents you. House is a symbol that stands for a particular kind of building. Love is a symbol that represents intense feelings. All language and much nonverbal behavior is symbolic, but not all symbols are language. Art, music, and objects also are symbols that stand for feelings, thoughts, and experiences.

Symbols Are Arbitrary   Symbols are **arbitrary,** which means they are not intrinsically connected to what they represent. For instance, the word *Julia* has no necessary or natural connection to me. All of our symbols are arbitrary because we could easily use other symbols as long as we all agreed on their meanings. Certain words seem right because as a society we agree to use them in particular ways, but they have no natural correspondence with their referents. Further, meanings change over time.

© John Grimes

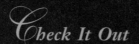
HOW WORDS HURT US

To realize how powerfully words can affect us, consider how you feel about the following words:

Drunk	Alcoholic	Problem drinker	Person with a disease
Nigger	Negro	Black	African American
Kike	Hebrew	Jew	Jewish person
Queer	Fag	Homosexual	Gay/lesbian
Chick	Bimbo	Girl	Woman
God squader	Jesus freak	Bible belter	Christian

In the 1950s, *gay* meant lighthearted and merry; today it is generally understood to refer to homosexuals. The majority of publishers and dictionaries no longer allow male-generic language, which uses male terms (*chairman, postman, mankind*) to represent both women and men. Our language also changes as we invent new words. African Americans began using *disrespect* as a verb to describe behaviors that demean someone. By now, the term *disrespect* has entered the general language.

Symbols Are Ambiguous   Symbols are also **ambiguous,** which means their meanings aren't clear-cut or fixed. There are variations in what words mean. A *good friend* means someone to hang out with to one person and someone to confide in to another. The term *nice clothes* means different things to people in the working class and people who are very affluent. Christmas, Hanukkah, and Thanksgiving carry distinct connotations for people who have families and those who don't. *Affirmative action* has different meanings for people who have experienced discrimination and ones who have not. Although the words are the same, what they mean varies as a result of individuals' unique experiences.

Although words don't mean exactly the same thing to everyone, within a culture many symbols have an agreed-on range of meanings (Mead, 1934). In learning language, we learn not only words but the meanings and values of our society. Thus, all of us know that dogs are four-footed creatures, but each of us also has personal meanings based on dogs we have known and our experiences with them.

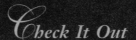

OUR MULTICULTURAL LANGUAGE

Although the term *multicultural* has only recently come into popular usage, our society and our language have always been multicultural. See if you recognize the cultural origins of the following everyday words.

1. brocade	6. silk
2. chocolate	7. skunk
3. cotton	8. gingham
4. klutz	9. noodle
5. khaki	10. zombie

Answers: 1. Spanish; 2. Nahuatl (Native American); 3. Arabic; 4. Yiddish; 5. Hindi; 6. Greek; 7. Algonquian (Native American); 8. Malay; 9. German; 10. Congo.

Source: Carnes, J. (1994, spring). An uncommon language. *Teaching Tolerance*, 56–63.

The ambiguity of symbols explains why misunderstandings so often arise in interpersonal communication. We tend to assume that words mean the same thing to others as they do to us. Recently, a friend of mine told her three-year-old daughter she needed to be more responsible about putting away her toys. Later we discovered the little girl had tucked all of her stuffed animals into beds around the house. That's what being more responsible meant to her.

RON

A while ago I told my girlfriend I needed more independence. She got all upset because she thought I didn't love her anymore and was pulling away. All I meant was that I need some time with the guys and some for just myself. She said that the last time a guy said he wanted more independence, she found out he was dating others.

Ambiguity frequently surfaces in friendships and romantic relationships. Martina tells her boyfriend that he's not being attentive, meaning that she wants him to listen more closely to what she says. However, he infers she wants him to call more often and open doors for her. The word *love* means different things to people brought up in abusive and nonabusive families. Similarly, spouses often have different meanings for "doing their share" of home chores. To most women, it means doing half of the work, but to men it tends to mean doing more than their fathers, which is still less than their wives do (Hochschild with Manchung, 1989).

According to a relationship counselor, a common problem between intimates is language that creates ambiguity (Beck, 1988). A wife asks her husband to be more loving, but she and he have different understandings of what being more loving means. Suggesting that a friend should be more sensitive doesn't provide a very clear idea of what you want. To minimize the problems of ambiguity, it's important to be as clear as possible when communicating. Thus, it's more effective to say "I would like for you to look at me and give feedback when I'm talking" than to say "I wish you'd be more attentive."

Put It in Practice

COMMUNICATING CLEARLY

To express yourself clearly, it's important that you learn to translate ambiguous words into concrete language. Practice translating with the statements below.

Example: Ambiguous language: You are rude.
Clear language: I don't like it when you interrupt me.

Ambiguous Language

You're conceited.

I want more freedom.

Let's have a low-key evening.

We need to be closer.

Julia T. Wood

Symbols Are Abstract   Finally, symbols are **abstract,** which means they are not concrete or tangible. They stand for ideas, people, events, objects, feelings, and so forth, but they are not the things they represent. In Chapter 3, we discussed the process of abstraction whereby we move further and further away from concrete reality. The symbols we use vary in abstractness. *Scrambles* is the name of the particular cat who lounges on the back of my chair while I'm writing. *Cat* is a more abstract label for her. *Animal* is even more abstract.

As our symbols become increasingly abstract, the potential for confusion mushrooms. One of the ways this happens is overgeneralization. Couple counselor Aaron Beck (1988) reports that overly general language distorts how partners think about a relationship. They may make broad, negative statements such as "You never go along with my preferences" or "You always interrupt me." In most cases, such statements are overgeneralizations that are not entirely accurate. Yet by symbolizing experience this way, partners frame how they think about it. Researchers have shown that we are more likely to recall behaviors that are consistent with how we've labeled people than ones that are inconsistent (Fincham & Bradbury, 1987). When we say a friend is always insensitive, we'll probably remember all of the occasions in which she or he was insensitive, and we'll overlook times when she or he was sensitive.

Bobby Patton and Kurt Ritter (1976), two communication scholars, suggest that misunderstandings can be minimized by using specific language. It's clearer to say "I wish you wouldn't interrupt when I'm talking" than "Don't be so dominating."

Principles of Verbal Communication

Now that we understand symbols are arbitrary, ambiguous, and abstract representations of other phenomena, we can consider three principles of verbal communication.

Interpretation Creates Meaning Because symbols are abstract, ambiguous, and arbitrary, their meanings are never self-evident or absolute. Instead, we have to think about symbols to figure out what they mean. We construct meanings in the process of interacting with others and through dialogues we carry on in our own heads (Duck, 1994a, 1994b; Shotter, 1993). The process of constructing meaning is itself symbolic, since we rely on words to think about what things mean.

Interpretation is an active, creative process we use to make sense of words. If we say "dinner" to a dog, the dog will respond in a predictable manner because *dinner* has a fixed, exact meaning to the dog. To us, however, the word *dinner* may mean many things—time for family talk, a romantic experience, a struggle to stick to a diet, or tension from strained relations among people present at the meal. For humans, words are ambiguous and layered with multiple meanings. Although we're usually not conscious of the effort we invest to interpret words, we continuously engage in the process of constructing meanings.

When somebody says "Blow off," you have to think about the comment and the person who made it to decide whether it's an insult, a friendly needling, or a colloquial way to say you are out of line. What the words mean also depends on the self-esteem and previous experiences of the individual who is told to blow off. Individuals who are secure and have high self-esteem are not as likely to be hurt as individuals who have less self-confidence. Relational-level meanings rely especially on understandings of the person speaking and the context of communication. Because symbols require interpretation, communication is an ongoing process of creating meanings.

D O N I K A

It took me a long time to understand certain words in my fiancé's family. When I first met them, I heard them talk about the wife's career, but I knew she did not work. In the family, they say her career is keeping track of all the children. They also talked about the husband's hobby of being broke. I thought this meant he spent a lot of money on collecting stamps or something, but what they mean is he likes to give to causes and this takes much money. It took several visits for me to understand the family vocabulary.

Communication Is Rule-Guided Verbal communication is patterned by unspoken but broadly understood rules (Argyle & Henderson, 1985; Schiminoff, 1980). **Communication rules** are shared understandings of what communication means and what behaviors are appropriate in various situations. For example, we understand that people take turns speaking and that we should speak softly in libraries. In the course of interacting with our families and others, we unconsciously absorb rules that guide how we communicate and how we interpret others' communication. According to Miller (1993), children begin to understand and follow communication rules by the time they are one to two years old.

© Paul Mozell/Stock, Boston

There are two kinds of rules that govern communication (Cronen, Pearce, & Snavely, 1979; Pearce, Cronen, & Conklin, 1979). **Regulative rules** regulate interaction by specifying when, how, where, and with whom to talk about certain things. For instance, Westerners know not to interrupt when someone else is speaking, but in more informal settings, interruptions may be appropriate. In other cultures, there are strong rules against interrupting in any contexts. Some families have a rule that people cannot argue at the dinner table. Families also teach us rules about how to communicate in conflict situations (Honeycutt, Woods, & Fontenot, 1993; Jones & Gallois, 1989; Yerby, Buerkel-Rothfuss, & Bochner, 1990). Regulative rules also define when, where, and with whom it's appropriate to show affection and disclose private information. Regulative rules vary across cultures so that what is considered appropriate in one society may be regarded as impolite or offensive elsewhere.

YUMIKO

I try to teach my children to follow the customs of my native Japan, but they are learning to be American. I scold my daughter, who is seven this year, for talking loudly and speaking when she has not been addressed, but she tells me all the other kids talk loudly and talk when they wish to talk. I tell her it is not polite to look directly at others, but she says everyone looks at others here. She communicates as an American, not a Japanese.

Constitutive rules define what communication means by specifying how certain communicative acts are to be counted. We learn what signifies respect (paying attention), affection (kisses, hugs), and rudeness (interrupting). We also learn what communication is expected if we want to be perceived as a good friend (showing support, being loyal), a responsible employee (meeting deadlines, developing strong reports), and a desirable romantic partner (showing respect and trust, being faithful, sharing confidences). We learn constitutive and regulative rules from both particular others and the generalized other. Like regulative rules, constitutive ones are shaped by cultures. Boasting outrageously about personal abilities is considered egotistical and offensive by most Caucasians. Among African Americans, however, this form of communication, often called "woofing," is viewed as a way of showing verbal wit.

© Bob Daemmrich/Stock, Boston

Put It in Practice

COMMUNICATION RULES

Think about the regulative and constitutive rules you follow in your communication. For each item below identify two rules you learned.

Regulative Rules

List rules that regulate how you:

1. Talk with elders
2. Interact at dinner time
3. Have first exchanges in the morning
4. Greet casual friends on campus
5. Talk with professors

Constitutive Rules

How do you communicate to show:

1. Respect
2. Love
3. Disrespect
4. Support

   After you've identified your rules, talk with others in your class about the rules they follow. Are there commonalities among your rules that reflect broad cultural norms? What explains differences in individuals' rules?

Everyday interaction is guided by rules that tell us when to speak, what to say, and how to interpret others' communication. Our social interactions, which involve I–It and I–You relationships, tend to adhere to rules that are widely shared in our society. Interaction between intimates also follows rules, but these may not be broadly shared by members of the culture. Intimate partners negotiate private rules to guide how they communicate and what certain things mean (Wood, 1982, 1995c). Couples craft personal rules for whether and how to argue, express love, make decisions, and spend time together (Beck, 1988; Fitzpatrick, 1988).

It's important to understand that we don't have to be aware of communication rules in order to follow them. For the most part, we're really not conscious of the rules that guide how, when, where, and with whom we communicate about various things. We may not realize we have rules until one is broken and we become aware that we had an expectation. A study by DeFrancisco (1991) revealed that between spouses there was a clear pattern in which husbands interrupted wives and were unresponsive to topics wives initiated. The couples were unaware of the rules, but their communication nonetheless sustained the pattern. Becoming aware of communication rules empowers you to change ones that don't promote good interaction, as Emily's commentary illustrates.

EMILY

My boyfriend and I had this really frustrating pattern about planning what to do. He'd say, "What do you want to do this weekend?" And I'd say, "I don't know. What do you want to do?" Then he'd suggest two or three things and ask me which of them sounded good. I would say they were all fine with me, even if they weren't. And this would keep on forever. Both of us had a rule not to impose on the other, and it kept us from stating our preferences, so we just went in circles about any decision. Well, two weekends ago, I talked to him about rules, and he agreed we had one that was frustrating. So we invented a new rule that says each of us has to state what we want to do, but the other has to say if that is not okay. It's a lot less frustrating to figure out what we want to do since we agreed on this rule.

FIGURE 4.1 *The Demand–Withdraw Pattern*

Punctuation Affects Meaning   We punctuate communication to interpret meaning. We're not talking about the kind of punctuation you study in grammar classes, although punctuation of communication is also a way of marking a flow of activity into meaningful units. In writing we use commas, periods, and semicolons to define where ideas stop and start and where pauses are needed. Similarly, in interpersonal communication, **punctuation** defines beginnings and endings of interaction episodes (Watzlawick et al., 1967).

To decide what communication means, we must establish its boundaries. Usually this involves deciding who started the interaction. When we don't agree on punctuation, problems may arise. If you've ever heard children arguing about who started a fight, you understand the importance of punctuation. A common instance of conflicting punctuation is the demand–withdraw pattern (Bergner & Bergner, 1990; Christensen & Heavey, 1990; James, 1989). In this pattern, one person tries to create closeness with personal talk, and the other strives to maintain autonomy by avoiding intimate discussion (Figure 4.1). The more the first person pushes for personal talk ("Tell me what's going on in your life," "Let's talk about our future") the further the second withdraws ("There's nothing to tell," "I don't want to talk about the future," silence). Each partner punctuates interaction as starting with the other's behavior. Thus, the demander thinks "I pursue because you withdraw" and the withdrawer thinks "I withdraw because you pursue."

There is no absolutely correct punctuation, since it depends on subjective perceptions. When partners don't agree on punctuation, they don't share meanings for what is happening between them. To break out of unconstructive cycles, such as demand–withdraw, partners need, first, to realize they may punctuate differently and, second, to discuss how each of them experiences the pattern. This reminds us of a guideline discussed in Chapter 2: Perspective-taking is essential to effective communication.

Put It in Practice

PUNCTUATING INTERACTION

The next time you and another person get in an unproductive cycle, stop and discuss how each of you punctuates interaction.

1. What do you define as the start of interaction?
2. What does the other person define as the beginning?
3. What happens when you learn about each other's punctuation? How does this affect understanding between you?

The meaning of verbal communication arises out of personal interpretations, communication rules, and punctuation. These three principles highlight the creativity involved in constructing meaning. We're now ready to probe how verbal communication affects us and our relationships.

Symbolic Abilities

The ability to use symbols allows humans to live in a world of ideas and meanings. Instead of just reacting to our concrete environments, we think about them and sometimes transform them. Philosophers of language have identified five ways symbolic capacities affect our lives (Cassirer, 1944; Langer, 1953, 1979). As we discuss each, we'll consider how to realize the constructive power of symbols and minimize the problems they can prompt.

Symbols Define

The most basic symbolic ability is definition. We use symbols to define experiences, people, relationships, feelings, and thoughts. As we saw in Chapter 3, the definitions we impose shape what things mean to us. When we label someone, we focus attention on particular aspects of that person and her or his activities, and we necessarily obscure other aspects of who she or he is. We might define a person as an environmentalist, a teacher, a gourmet cook, or a father. Each definition directs our attention to certain aspects of the person. We might talk with the environmentalist about wilderness legislation, discuss class assignments with the teacher, swap recipes with the chef, and exchange stories about children with the father. If we define someone as an Asian American or a Latina, then that may be all we notice about the person, although there are many other aspects of her or him. We tend to perceive and interact with people according to how we define them.

Totalizing occurs when we respond to a person as if one label totally represents who he or she is. We fix on one symbol to define someone and fail to recognize many other aspects of who he or she is. Some individuals totalize gay men and lesbians as if affectional preference is the only important facet of a person. Interestingly, we don't totalize heterosexuals on the basis of their sexuality. Totalizing also occurs when we dismiss people by saying "He's a Republican," "She's old," "She's preppy," or "He's just a jock." Totalizing is not the same as stereotyping. When we stereotype someone, we define him or her in terms of characteristics of a group. When we totalize others, we negate most of who they are by spotlighting a single aspect of their identity.

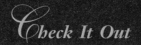

THE WHORF-SAPIR VIEW OF LANGUAGE

Studies by anthropologists reveal that our perceptions are guided by language. The language of the Hopi Indians makes no distinction between stationary objects and moving processes, whereas English uses nouns and verbs respectively. The English word *snow* is the only word we have to define frozen, white precipitation that falls in the winter. In Arctic cultures where snow is a major aspect of life, there are many words to define snow that is powdery, icy, dry, wet, and so forth. The distinctions are important to designate which snows allow safe travel.

Source: Whorf, B. (1956). *Language, thought, and reality.* New York: MIT Press/John Wiley.

JAMAL

I know all about totalizing. A lot of people relate to me as black, like that's all I am. Sometimes in classes, teachers ask me to explain the "African American perspective" on something, but they don't ask me to explain my perspective as a premed major or a working student. I am an African American, but that's not all I am.

The symbols we use to define experiences in our relationships affect how we think and feel. In a recent study, my colleagues and I asked romantic couples how they defined differences between them (Wood, Dendy, Dordek, Germany, & Varallo, 1994). We found that some individuals define differences as positive forces that energize a relationship and keep it interesting. Others define differences as problems or barriers to closeness. There was a direct connection between how partners defined differences and how they acted. Partners who viewed differences as constructive approached disagreements with curiosity, interest, and a hope for growth through discussion. On the other hand, partners who labeled differences as problems tended to deny differences and to avoid talking about them.

NONDISCRIMINATION IN HOUSING

Whoops! Real estate ads may lead to lawsuits if they contain language that offends certain groups. "Great view" excludes persons with visual impairments; "walking distance to shops" offends people in wheelchairs; "master bedroom" suggests sexism; "family room" discriminates against child-free couples and singles; and "newlyweds" excludes gay and lesbian couples who cannot be legally wed.

In 1994, Pennsylvania's Association of Realtors, Newspaper Association, and Human Relations Commission issued a list of about seventy-five unacceptable words and phrases for real estate ads. Among the forbidden terms:

bachelor pad	couples	mature
children	traditional	senior citizens
private	newlyweds	exclusive

© Donna Binder/Impact Visuals

A number of communication scholars have shown that the language we use to think about relationships affects what happens in them (Duck, 1985, 1994a, 1994b; Honeycutt, 1993; Spencer, 1994). People who consistently use negative labels to describe their relationships heighten awareness of what they don't like and diminish perceptions of what they do like (Cloven & Roloff, 1991). It's also been shown that partners who focus on good facets of their relationships are more conscious of virtues in partners and relationships and less bothered by imperfections (Bradbury & Fincham, 1990; Fletcher & Fincham, 1991).

These studies show us that our definitions of relationships can create self-fulfilling prophecies. Because verbal language is ambiguous, arbitrary, and abstract, there are multiple ways we can define any experience. Once we select a label, we tend to see the experience in line with our label. This suggests we should reconsider definitions that undermine healthy self-concepts and interpersonal relationships.

Symbols Evaluate

Symbols are not neutral, but laden with values. This is an intrinsic quality of symbols. In fact, it's impossible to find words that are completely neutral or objective. We describe people we like with language that accents their good qualities and downplays their flaws. Just the reverse is true of our descriptions for people we don't like. Restaurants use positive words to heighten the attractiveness of menu entrees. A dish described as tender London Broil gently sautéed in natural juices and topped with succulent mushrooms sounds more appetizing than one described as dead cow carcass cooked in blood and topped with fungus grown in compost and manure.

Of course, there are degrees of evaluation in language. We might describe people who speak their minds as assertive, outspoken, courageous, or authoritarian. Each word has a distinct connotation. In recent years, we have become more sensitive to how symbols can hurt people. Most individuals with disabilities prefer not to be called disabled, since that totalizes them in terms of a disability. The term *African American* emphasizes cultural heritage, whereas *black* focuses on skin color.

Designations for homosexuals are currently in transition. The term *homosexual* has negative connotations and even more so do words like *fairy* and *faggot*. Some gays and lesbians use the term *sexual orientation* to suggest they didn't choose their sexuality. Others use the term *sexual preference* to indicate their sexuality is a matter of choice, not genetics. Still others speak of *affectional preference* to signal that their commitment concerns the entire realm of affection, not just sexual activity.

Loaded language is words that strongly slant perceptions and, thus, meanings. For example, radio personality Rush Limbaugh refers to feminists as Feminazis, which inaccurately implies feminists are also Nazis. Loaded language also encourages negative views of older citizens. Terms such as *geezer* and *old fogies* incline us to regard older people with contempt or pity. Alternatives such as *senior citizen* and *mature person* reflect more respectful attitudes.

Check It Out

REAPPROPRIATING LANGUAGE

An interesting communicative phenomenon is the reappropriation of language. This happens when a group reclaims terms others use to degrade it and treats those terms as positive self-descriptions. Reappropriation intends to take the sting out of a term that others use pejoratively.

Some feminists and women musicians have reappropriated the term *girl* to define themselves and to resist the general connotations of childishness.

Some gays have reappropriated the term *queer* and are using it as a positive statement about their identity.

The writer Reynolds Price developed cancer of the spine that left him paraplegic. He scoffs at terms such as *differently abled* and *physically challenged* and refers to himself as a cripple and others as "temporarily able-bodied."

MAYNARD

I'm as sensitive as the next guy, but I just can't keep up with what language offends what people anymore. When I was younger, "Negro" was an accepted term, then it was black, and now it's African American. Sometimes I forget and say "black" or even "Negro," and I get accused of being racist. It used to be polite to call females girls, but now that offends a lot of the women I work with. Just this year I heard that we aren't supposed to say "blind" or "disabled" anymore; we're supposed to say "visually impaired" and "differently abled." I just can't keep up.

Probably many of us have sympathy with Maynard, who was fifty-four years old when he took a course with me. It is hard to keep up with changes in language, and it's inevitable that we will occasionally offend someone unintentionally. Nonetheless, we should try to learn what terms hurt or insult others and avoid using those. It's also advisable for us to tell others when they've referred to us with a term that we dislike. As long as we speak assertively but not confrontationally, it's likely that others will respect our ideas.

Symbols Organize Perceptions

We use symbols to organize our perceptions. As we saw in Chapter 3, we rely on cognitive schemata to classify and evaluate experiences. How we organize experiences affects what they mean to us. For example, your prototype of a good friend affects how you judge particular friends.

When we place someone in the category of friend, the category influences how we interpret the friend and his or her communication. An insult is likely to be viewed as teasing if made by a friend, but a call to battle if made by an enemy. The words don't change, but their meaning varies depending on how we organize them.

The organizational quality of symbols also allows us to think about abstract concepts, such as justice, integrity, and good family life. We use broad concepts to transcend specific, concrete activities and to enter the world of conceptual thought and ideals. Because we think abstractly, we don't have to consider every specific object and experience individually. Instead, we can think in general terms.

Our capacity to abstract can also distort thinking. A primary way this occurs is stereotyping, which is thinking in broad generalizations about a whole class of people or experiences. Examples of stereotypes are "sorority women are preppy," "teachers are smart," "jocks are dumb," "feminists hate men," "religious people are good," and "conflict is bad." Notice that stereotypes can be positive or negative generalizations.

Common to all stereotypes is classifying an experience or person into a category based on general knowledge of that category. When we use stereotypical terms such as *African Americans, lesbians, white males,* and *working class,* we may see only what members of each group have in common and not perceive differences among individuals. What's lost is the uniqueness of the individual person. Clearly, we have to generalize. We simply cannot think about each and every thing in our lives as a specific instance. However, stereotypes can blind us to important differences among phenomena we lump together. Thus, it's important to reflect on stereotypes and to stay alert to differences among things we place in any category.

"Well, then, if 'commandments' seems too harsh to me, and 'guidelines' seems too wishy-washy to you, how about 'The 10 Policy Statements'?"

Reprinted from *The Chronicle of Higher Education.*
By permission of Mischa Richter and Harald Bakken.

Symbols Allow Hypothetical Thought

Where do you hope to be five years from now? What is your fondest childhood memory? To answer these questions, you must think hypothetically, which means to think about experiences and ideas that are not part of your concrete, present situation. Because we can think hypothetically, we can plan, dream, remember, set goals, consider alternative courses of action, and imagine possibilities.

Hypothetical thought is possible because we use symbols. When we symbolize, we name ideas so that we can hold them in our minds and reflect on them. We can contemplate things that currently have no real existence, and we can remember ourselves in the past and project ourselves into the future. Our ability to live simultaneously in all three dimensions of time explains why we can set goals and work toward them even though there is nothing tangible about them in the moment (Dixson & Duck, 1993). For example, you've invested many hours studying and writing papers because you have the idea of yourself as someone with a college degree. The degree is not real now, nor is the self that you will become once you have the degree. Yet the idea is sufficiently real to motivate you to work hard for many years.

Julia T. Wood

Close relationships rely on ideas of history and future. One of the strongest glues for intimacy is a history of shared experiences (Bellah, Madsen, Sullivan, Swindler, & Tipton, 1985; Wood, 1995c). Just knowing that they have weathered rough times in the past helps partners get through trials in the present. Belief in a future also sustains intimacy. We interact differently with people we don't expect to see again than with ones who are continuing parts of our lives. Talking about the future also knits intimates together because it makes real the idea that more lies ahead (Acitelli, 1993; Duck, 1990).

*Love just doesn't sit there,
like a stone, it has to be made,
like bread; re-made all the time,
made new.*
URSULA K. LE GUIN

Thinking hypothetically helps us improve who we are. In Chapter 2, we noted that one guideline for improving self-concept is accepting yourself as in process. This requires you to remember how you were at an earlier time, to appreciate progress you've made, and to keep an ideal image of how you want to be in the future to fuel continued motivation for improving yourself.

DUK-KYONG

Sometimes I get very discouraged that I do not yet know English perfectly and that there is much I still do not understand about customs in this country. It helps me to remember that when I came here two years ago I did not speak English at all, and I knew nothing about how people act here. Seeing how much progress I have made helps me not to be discouraged with what I do not know yet.

Symbols Allow Self-Reflection

Just as we use symbols to reflect on what goes on outside of us, we also use them to reflect on ourselves. Humans don't simply exist and act. Instead, we think about our existence and reflect on our actions. Mead (1934) considered self-reflection to be the basis for human selfhood. He believed that our capacity to look at ourselves and our activities was responsible for civilized society.

According to Mead, there are two aspects to the self. First, there is the I, which is the spontaneous, creative self. The I acts impulsively in response to inner needs and desires, regardless of social norms. The ME is the socially conscious part of the self that monitors and moderates the I's impulses. The ME reflects on the I from the social perspectives of others. The I is impervious to social conventions and expectations, but the ME is keenly aware of them. In an argument, your I may want to hurl a biting insult at someone you don't like, but your ME censors that impulse and reminds you that it's impolite to put others down.

Mead regarded the ME as the reflective part of the self. The ME reflects on the I, so we simultaneously author our lives as the I acts and reflect on them as the ME analyzes the I's actions. This means we can think about who we want to be and set goals for becoming the self we desire. We can feel shame, pride, and regret for our actions—emotions that are possible because we self-reflect. We can control what we do in the present by casting ourselves forward in time to consider how we might later feel about our actions.

Self-reflection also empowers us to monitor ourselves, a skill we discussed in Chapter 1. When we monitor ourselves we (the ME) notice and evaluate our (the I's) actions and may modify them based on our judgments (Phillips & Wood, 1983; Wood, 1992). For instance, during a discussion with a friend you might say to yourself, "Gee, I've been talking nonstop about me and my worries and I haven't even asked how she's doing." Based on your monitoring, you might inquire about your friend's life. When interacting with people from different cultures, we monitor by reminding ourselves they may not operate by the same values and communication rules that we do. Self-reflection allows us to monitor our communication and adjust it to be effective.

Put It in Practice

I—ME DIALOGUES

To see how the I and the ME work together, monitor your internal dialogues. These are conversations in your head as you consider different things you might say and do.

Monitor your I—ME dialogues as you talk with a professor, a close friend, and a romantic partner. What creative ideas and desires does your I initiate? What social controls does your ME impose? What urges and whims occur to your I? What social norms does your ME remind you of?

How do the I and the ME work together? Does one sometimes muffle the other? What would be lost if your I became silent? What would be missing if your ME disappeared?

Self-reflection also allows us to manage our image, or the identity we present to others. Because we reflect on ourselves from social perspectives, we are able to consider how we appear in others' eyes. When talking with

Julia T. Wood

teachers, you may consciously present yourself as respectful, attentive, and studious. When interacting with parents, you may repress some of the language and topics that surface in discussions with your friends. When communicating with someone you'd like to date, you may choose to be more attentive and social than you are in other circumstances. Continuously, we adjust how we present ourselves so that we sculpt our image to fit particular situations and people.

MYRELLA

I have a really bad temper that can get me into serious trouble if I'm not careful. Sometimes I feel like telling someone off or exploding or whatever, but I stop myself by thinking about how bad I'll look if I do it. I remind myself that others might see me as hysterical or crazy or something, and that helps me to check my temper.

Summing up, we use symbols to define, classify, and evaluate experiences; to think hypothetically; and to self-reflect. Each of these abilities helps us create meaning in our personal and interpersonal lives.

Communication Cultures

Although all humans use symbols, we don't all use them in the same way. As we have seen, symbols are social conventions whose meanings we learn in the process of interacting with others. For this reason, people from different cultures use communication in different ways and attach different meanings to particular communicative acts.

A communication culture exists when people share norms about how to use talk and what purposes it serves (Labov, 1972). Members of communication cultures share perspectives on communication that outsiders do not have, which is why cross-cultural communication is sometimes difficult.

Communication cultures are not defined by countries or geographical locations, but by shared understandings of how to communicate. Among the communication cultures that coexist in Western society are Native Americans, gay men, women and men, and people with disabilities. Each of these co-cultures has its own distinct understandings of communication. For example, in general, African Americans engage in more dramatic and elaborate verbal play than European Americans. Signifying, playing the dozens, and woofing, or braggadocio, are positive verbal activities in African American culture, yet the Caucasian mainstream doesn't recognize, much less appreciate, these forms of communication.

TABLE 4.1 Rules of Gender Communication Cultures

Feminine Communication Rules	Masculine Communication Rules
1. Include others. Use talk to show interest in others, and respond to their needs.	1. Assert yourself. Use talk to establish your identity, expertise, knowledge, and so on.
2. Use talk cooperatively. Communication is a joint activity, so people have to work together. It's important to invite others into conversation, wait your turn to speak, and respond to what others say.	2. Use talk competitively. Communication is an arena for proving yourself. Use talk to gain and hold attention, to wrest the talk stage from others; interrupt and reroute topics to keep you and your ideas spotlighted.
3. Use talk expressively. Talk should deal with feelings, personal ideas, and problems and should build relationships with others.	3. Use talk instrumentally. Talk should accomplish something such as solving a problem, giving advice, or taking a stand on issues.

Gender Communication Cultures

Of the many communication cultures that exist, gender has received particularly intense study. Because we know more about it than other communication cultures, we'll explore gender as an example of communication culture. Researchers have investigated both how women and men are socialized into separate communication cultures and how their communication differs in practice. One of the earliest studies showed that children's games are a primary agent of gender socialization (Maltz & Borker, 1982). Typically, children's play is sex-segregated, and there are notable differences between the games the sexes tend to play.

Games girls favor, such as house and school, involve few players; require talk to negotiate how to play, since there aren't clear-cut guidelines; and depend on cooperation and sensitivity between players. Baseball, soccer, and war, which are typical boys' games, require more players and have clear goals and rules, so less talk is needed to play. Most boys' games are highly competitive both between teams and for individual status within teams. Interaction in games teaches boys and girls distinct understandings of why, when, and how to use talk. Table 4.1 summarizes rules of feminine and masculine communication cultures.

Research on adult women's and men's communication reveals that the rules taught through child play remain with us. For instance, women's talk is generally more expressive and focused on feelings and personal issues, whereas men's talk tends to be more instrumental and competitive (Aries, 1987; Beck, 1988; Coates & Cameron, 1989; Johnson, 1989; Treichler & Kramarae, 1993; Wood, 1994c, 1994d). Another general difference between the sexes is the basis of relationships. For men, activities tend to be the primary foundation of close friendships and romantic relationships (Swain, 1989; Wood & Inman, 1993). Thus, men typically cement friendships through doing things together and for one another. For women, communication is the primary foundation of relationships. Talk is not only a means to instrumental ends, but also an end in itself. For many women, communicating is the essence of building and sustaining closeness (Aries, 1987; Becker, 1987; Riessman, 1990).

Given the differences between how women and men, in general, use communication, it's hardly surprising that the sexes often misunderstand one another. One clash between gender communication cultures occurs when women and men discuss problems. Typically, if a woman tells a man about something that is troubling her, his response is to offer advice or a solution (Tannen, 1990; Wood, 1994d, 1996). His view of communication as instrumental leads him to show support by doing something. Because feminine cultures see communication as a way to build connections with others, however, women often want empathy and discussion of feelings before advice is useful. Thus, women sometimes feel men's responses to their concerns are uncaring and insensitive. On the other hand, men may feel frustrated when women offer empathy and support instead of advice for solving problems. In general, men are also less comfortable making personal disclosures, which women regard as an important way to enhance closeness (Aries, 1987; Wood & Inman, 1993).

© Snitzer/Stock, Boston

Words form the thread on which we string our experiences.
ALDOUS HUXLEY

Another conundrum in interaction between men and women concerns different styles of listening. Socialized to be responsive and expressive, women tend to make listening noises such as "um hm," "yeah," and "I know what you mean" when others are talking (Tannen, 1990; Wood, 1996). This is how they show they are attentive and interested. Masculine culture, however, doesn't emphasize using communication responsively, so men tend to make fewer listening noises when another is talking. Thus, women sometimes feel men aren't listening to them because men don't symbolize their attention in the ways women have learned and expect.

Perhaps the most common complication in gender communication occurs when a woman says "Let's talk about us." To men this often means trouble, because they interpret the request as implying there is a problem in a relationship. For women, however, this is not the only—or even the main—reason to talk about a relationship. Feminine communication cultures regard talking as the primary way to create relationships and build closeness (Riessman, 1990). In general, women regard talking about a relationship as a way to celebrate and increase intimacy. Socialized to use communication instrumentally, however, men tend to think talking about a relationship is useful only if there is some problem to be resolved (Acitelli, 1988, 1993). For men, the preferred mode of enhancing closeness is to do things together. Suzie's commentary illustrates this gender difference.

SUZIE

Gender cultures explain a big fight my boyfriend and I had. We've been dating for three years, and we're pretty serious, so I wanted our anniversary to be really special. I suggested going out for a romantic dinner where we could talk about the relationship. Andy said that sounded dull, and he wanted to go to a concert where there would be zillions of people. At the time, I thought that meant he didn't care about us like I do, but maybe he feels close when we do things together instead of when we just are together.

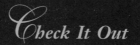

BLACK TALK

Geneva Smitherman is a linguist who studies distinctive features of African American oral traditions. In her 1994 book, *Black Talk: Words and Phrases from the Hood to the Amen Corner,* Smitherman documents the richness and uniqueness of African American language. The following is a sampling from *Black Talk:*

Chill: Relax.

Sweet: Outstanding.

All that: Excellent, great, all that something seems to be. Example: That woman is bad. She is definitely all that.

Amen corner: Place in black churches where traditionally elders, especially women, sit.

Drop a dime: Tell on someone who is doing something wrong or illegal; reporting the person.

Git ovah: Refers to making it over to a spiritually good life after struggling to overcome sin.

Jump salty: Become angry.

Mojo: Originally, mojo was a magical charm. In modern usage it refers to [a] source of personal magic that an individual may draw upon to put others under a spell.

Scared of you: A compliment that acknowledges another person's achievements. Example: I'm scared of you now that you've been promoted.

That how you living? This is a criticism that asks why someone is acting a particular way.

Source: Smitherman, G. (1994). *Black talk: Words and phrases from the hood to the amen corner.* Boston: Houghton Mifflin.

Other Communication Cultures

Gender, of course, is not the only communication culture, and communication between men and women is not the only kind of interaction that may be plagued by cross-cultural misunderstandings. Research indicates that communication patterns vary among social classes. For example, working-class people tend to use shorter, simpler sentences, less elaborate explanations, and more conventional grammar than members of the middle class (Bernstein, 1973).

Communication cultures are also shaped by race and ethnicity so that different groups engage in distinct communication patterns. A recent report on African American speech indicates that it is typically more assertive than that of European Americans (Ribeau, Baldwin, & Hecht, 1994). What African Americans consider authentic, powerful exchanges may be perceived as antagonistic by individuals from different communication cultures. The rappin' and stylin' of African Americans is not practiced (or understood) by most European Americans. Another feature of African American speech is extensive verbal play in which members play the dozens (a game of exchanging insults), speak indirectly, and use highly dramatic language. These forms of verbal play are thought to be valves for aggression and creativity that oppressed groups cannot safely express explicitly (Garner, 1994). As a group, African Americans are more oriented toward collective interests such as family or race than are European Americans, who tend to be more individualistic (Gaines, 1995). As a rule, African Americans also communicate more interactively than European Americans (Weber, 1994). This explains why African Americans call out responses such as "Tell it," "All right," and "Keep talking," during speeches, church sermons, and classes. What Caucasians regard as interruptions of a speaker, many African Americans perceive as positive participation in communication.

APPRECIATING COMMUNICATION CULTURES

Were you socialized into a gender culture? Are the gender communication rules we've discussed evident in how you communicate and interpret others? What about your ethnic and racial culture? Identify rules you learned for being polite, showing interest, and indicating disapproval.

After thinking about your own communication cultures, talk with people from different communication cultures. Identify differences in the rules you follow for public and private interaction. Do you recognize communication rules that explain differences between how you and others talk?

© Goldberg/Monkmeyer

Although people may use the same language, they don't all use it in the same way. Within our country, different communication cultures teach distinct rules about how, when, why, and with whom to talk. Recognizing and respecting different communication cultures increases our ability to participate competently in a diverse culture.

Language is a living thing.
We can feel it changing.
GILBERT HIGHET

Guidelines for Improving Verbal Communication

We've explored what symbols are and how they may be used differently in distinct communication cultures. Building on these understandings, we can now consider guidelines for improving effectiveness in verbal communication.

Engage in Dual Perspective

The single most important guideline for effective verbal communication is to engage in dual perspective. This involves recognizing another person's perspective and taking that into account as you communicate. Effective interpersonal communication is not a solo performance, but a relationship between people. Awareness of others and their viewpoints should be reflected in how we speak. For instance, it's advisable to refrain from using

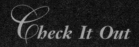

MISSING THE BOAT

Communication scholar Wen Shu Lee (1994) reports that one of the greatest barriers to cross-cultural communication is idioms. Although people from other cultures learn formal English, they often aren't taught slang and jargon. Examples of idioms that confuse nonnative speakers are *kick the bucket, hang a right, flip the bird, miss the boat*, and *get up to speed.*

Source: Lee, W. S. (1994). On not missing the boat: A processual method for intercultural understanding of idioms and lifeworld. *Journal of Applied Communication Research, 22,* 141–161.

a lot of idioms when talking with someone for whom English is a second language. Similarly, instead of giving advice when a woman tells him about a problem, a man who uses dual perspective might realize empathy and supportive listening are likely to be more appreciated. The point is that competent communicators acknowledge and respect the perspectives of those with whom they interact.

We don't need to abandon our own perspectives to accommodate those of others. In fact, it would be as unconstructive to stifle your own views as to ignore those of others. Dual perspective, as the term implies, consists of two perspectives. It requires understanding both our own and another's point of view and giving voice to each when we communicate. Most of us can accept and grow from differences, but we seldom feel affirmed if we are unheard or disregarded. Understanding and heeding others' viewpoints in how you communicate paves the way for affirming relationships.

Own Your Own Feelings and Thoughts

We often use verbal language in ways that obscure our responsibility for how we feel and what we think. For instance, people say "You made me mad" or "You hurt me" as if what they feel is caused by someone else. On a more subtle level, we sometimes blame others for our responses to what they say. "You're so demanding" really means that you feel put upon by what someone else wants or expects. The sense of feeling pressured by another's expectations is in you, not the other person. Even though others' behaviors can influence us, they can't really determine how we feel.

Our feelings and thoughts result from how we interpret others' communication. Although how we interpret what others say may lead us to feel certain ways, others do not directly cause our responses. In certain contexts, such as abusive relationships, others may powerfully shape how we think and feel. Yet even in these extreme situations, we need to remember that we, not others, are responsible for our feelings. Telling others they make you feel some way is likely to arouse defensiveness, which doesn't facilitate healthy interpersonal relationships.

Effective communicators take responsibility for themselves by using language that owns their thoughts and feelings. They claim their feelings and do not blame others for what happens in themselves. To take responsibility for your own feelings, rely on I-language, rather than you-language. Table 4.2 gives examples of the difference.

There are two differences between I-language and you-language. First, I-statements own responsibility, whereas you-statements project it onto another person. Second, I-statements offer considerably more description than you-statements. You-statements tend to be accusations that are very abstract. This is one of the reasons they're ineffective in promoting change. I-statements, on the other hand, provide concrete descriptions of behaviors that we dislike without directly blaming the other person for how we feel.

Some people feel awkward when they first start using I-language. This is natural, since most of us have learned to rely on you-language. With commitment and practice, however, you can learn to communicate with I-language. Once you feel comfortable using it, you will find that I-language has many advantages. It is less likely than you-language to make others defensive, so I-language opens the doors for dialogue. I-language is also more honest. We deceive ourselves when we say "You made me feel . . ." since others don't control how we feel. Finally, I-language is more empowering than you-language. When we say you did this or you made me feel that, we give control of our emotions to others. This reduces our personal power and, by extension, our motivation to change what is happening. Using I-language allows you to own your own feelings while also explaining to others how you interpret their behaviors.

TABLE 4.2 I- and You-Language	
You-Language	**I-Language**
You hurt me.	I feel hurt when you ignore what I say.
You make me feel small.	I feel small when you tell me that I'm selfish.
You're really domineering.	When you shout, I feel dominated.
You humiliated me.	I felt humiliated when you mentioned my problems in front of our friends.

Put It in Practice

USING I-LANGUAGE

For the next three days, whenever you use you–language, try to rephrase what you said or thought in I–language. How does this change how you think and feel about what's happening? How does using I–language affect interaction with others? Are others less defensive when you own your feelings and describe, but don't evaluate, their behaviors? Does I–language facilitate working out constructive changes?

Now that you're tuned into I- and you–language, monitor how you feel when others use you–language about you. When a friend or romantic partner says "You make me feel . . . ," do you feel defensive or guilty? Try teaching others to use I–language so that your relationships can be more honest and open.

© Alan Carey/The Image Works

Every word we speak causes a reaction in people around us.
THICH THIEN-AN

Respect What Others Say About Their Feelings and Ideas

Has anyone ever said to you, "You shouldn't feel that way"? If so, you know how infuriating it can be to be told that your feelings aren't valid, appropriate, or acceptable. It's equally destructive to be told our thoughts are wrong. When someone says, "How can you think something so stupid?" we feel disconfirmed. Effective communicators don't disparage what others say about what they feel and think. Even if you don't feel or think the same way, you can still respect another person as the expert on her or his own perspective.

One of the most disconfirming forms of communication is speaking for others when they are able to speak for themselves. Recently, I had a conversation with a couple at a party in which one person spoke for another. The man in the couple said, "She's having trouble balancing career and family," "She's really proud of sticking with her exercise program," and "She's worried about how to take care of her parents now that their health is declining." His wife, who was with us, wasn't allowed to say where she had trouble, felt pride, or experienced worry. His automatic tendency to answer questions I addressed to her left her voiceless. The same pattern occurs when parents speak for children by responding to questions the children could answer. Generally, it's arrogant and disempowering to speak for others.

Just as we should not speak for others, we also should not assume we understand how they feel or think. As we have seen, our distinct experiences and ways of interpreting life make each of us unique. We seldom, if ever, completely grasp what another person feels or thinks. Although it is supportive to engage in dual perspective, it isn't supportive to presume we fully grasp what's happening in someone else, especially when he or she differs from us in important ways.

It's particularly important not to assume we understand people from other cultures, including ones within our society. Recently, an Asian woman in one of my classes commented on discrimination she faces, and a Caucasian man in the class said, "I know what you mean. Prejudice really hurts." Although he meant to be supportive, his response angered the woman, who retorted, "You have no idea how I feel, and you have no right to act like you do until you've been female and nonwhite." When we claim to share what we haven't experienced, we take away from others' lives and identities.

Respecting what others say about what they feel and think is a cornerstone of effective interpersonal communication. We also grow when we open ourselves to perspectives, feelings, and thoughts that differ from our own. If you don't understand what others say, ask them to elaborate. This shows you are interested and respect their expertise or experience. Inviting others to clarify, extend, or explain their communication enlarges understanding between people.

Strive for Accuracy and Clarity

Because symbols are arbitrary, abstract, and ambiguous, the potential for misunderstanding always exists. In addition, individual and cultural differences foster varying interpretations of words. Although we can't completely eliminate misunderstandings, we can minimize them.

Being Aware of Levels of Abstraction

Misunderstanding is less likely when we are conscious of levels of abstraction. Much confusion results from language that is excessively abstract. For instance, assume a professor says, "Your papers should demonstrate a sophisticated conceptual grasp of material and its pragmatic implications." Would you know how to write a paper to satisfy the professor? Probably not, because the language is very abstract and unclear. Here's a more concrete description: "Your papers should include definitions of the concepts and specific examples that show how they apply in real life." With this more concrete statement, you would have a clear idea of what the professor expected.

Abstract language is not always inadvisable. As we have seen, abstract language allows us to generalize, which is necessary and useful. The goal is to use a level of abstraction that suits particular communication objectives and situations. Abstract words are appropriate when speakers and listeners have similar concrete knowledge about what is being discussed. For example, a couple that has been dating might talk about "lighthearted comedies" and "heavy movies" as shorthand ways to refer to two film genres. Because they have seen many movies together, they have shared referents for the abstract terms *lighthearted* and *heavy*, so confusion is unlikely. Similarly, long-term friends can say "Let's just hang out" and understand the activities implied by the abstract term *hang out*.

Check It Out

RESPECTING OTHERS' EXPERIENCES

Marsha Houston, an accomplished communication scholar, explains how claiming understanding can diminish a person. She writes that white women should never tell African American women that they understand black women's experiences. Here's Houston's explanation:

> I have heard this sentence completed in numerous, sometimes bizarre, ways, from "because sexism is just as bad as racism," to "because I watch the 'Cosby Show,'" to "because I'm also a member of a minority group. I'm Jewish . . . Italian . . . overweight." . . .
> Similar experiences should not be confused with the same experience; my experience of prejudice is erased when you identify it as "the same" as yours (p. 138).

Source: Houston, M. (1994). When black women talk with white women: Why dialogues are difficult. In A. González, M. Houston, & V. Chen (Eds.), *Our Voices: Essays in culture, ethnicity, and communication* (pp. 133–139). Los Angeles: Roxbury.

More concrete language is useful when communicators don't have shared experiences and interpretations. For example, early in a friendship the suggestion to "hang out" would be more effective if it included specifics: "Let's hang out today—maybe watch the game and go out for pizza." In a new dating relationship, it would be clearer to say, "Let's get a lighthearted movie like *Sister Act*. I don't want anything heavy like *The Piano* or *Schindler's List*." Providing examples of general terms clarifies meanings.

Abstract language is particularly likely to lead to misunderstandings when people talk about changes they want in one another. Concrete language and specific examples help individuals have similar understandings of which behaviors are unwelcome and which ones are wanted. For example, "I want you to be more helpful around the house" does not explain what would count as being more helpful. Is it vacuuming and doing laundry? Shopping for groceries? Fixing half of the meals? It isn't clear what the speaker wants unless more concrete descriptions are supplied. Likewise, "I want to be closer" could mean the speaker wants to spend more time together, talk about the relationship, do things together, have a more adventurous sex life, or any number of other things. Vague abstractions promote misunderstanding if individuals don't share concrete referents.

Qualifying Language   Another strategy for increasing the clarity of communication is to qualify language. Two types of language require qualification. First, we should qualify generalizations so that we don't mislead ourselves or others into mistaking a general statement for an absolute one. "Politicians are crooked" is a false statement because it overgeneralizes. A more accurate statement would be "A number of politicians have been shown to be dishonest." Qualifying reminds us of limitations on what we say.

Put It in Practice

QUALIFYING LANGUAGE

Study the qualified and unqualified statements below.

Unqualified	Qualified
Foreign cars are better than American ones.	Hondas and Mazdas generally require less maintenance than Fords and Chevys.
Science courses are harder than humanities courses.	Most students find Chemistry tougher than Music.
Television is violent.	Many commercial programs include a lot of violence.

Practice your skill in qualifying language by providing appropriate restrictions for the overgeneralizations below.

Unqualified

Teaching assistants aren't as good as professors.

Affirmative action gives jobs to unqualified people.

Men are more competitive than women.

Textbooks are boring.

We should also qualify language when describing and evaluating people. The term **static evaluation** refers to assessments that suggest something is unchanging or static. These are particularly troublesome when applied to people. Ann is selfish. Don is irresponsible. Bob is generous. Vy is dependent. Whenever we use the word *is*, we suggest something is inherent and fixed. In reality, we aren't static, but continuously changing. A person who is selfish at one time may not be at another. An individual who is irresponsible on one occasion may be responsible in other situations. Indexing is a technique developed by early communication scholars to remind us that our evaluations apply only to specific times and circumstances (Korzybski, 1958). To index, we would say Ann$_{June 6, 1997}$ acted selfishly, Don$_{on the task committee}$ was irresponsible, Bob$_{in college}$ was generous, and Vy$_{in her relationships with men in high school}$ was dependent. See how indexing ties description to a specific time and circumstance? Mental indexing reminds us that we and others are able to change in remarkable ways.

KEN

Parents are the worst for static evaluations. When I first got my license seven years ago, I had a fender bender and then got a speeding ticket. Since then I've had a perfect record, but you'd never know it from what they say. Dad's always calling me "hot rodder," and Mom goes through this safety spiel every time I get ready to drive somewhere. You'd think I was the same now as when I was sixteen.

Effective interpersonal communication is accurate and clear. We've considered four principles for improving the effectiveness of verbal communication. Engaging in dual perspective is the first principle and a foundation for all others. A second guideline is to take responsibility for our own feelings and thoughts by using I-language. Third, we should respect others as the experts on what they feel and think and not presume we know what they mean or share their experiences. The fourth principle is to strive for clarity by choosing appropriate degrees of abstraction, qualifying generalizations, and indexing evaluations, particularly ones applied to people.

SUMMARY

In this chapter, we discussed the world of words and meaning—the uniquely human universe that we inhabit because we are symbol users. Because symbols are arbitrary, ambiguous, and abstract, they have no inherent meanings. Instead, we actively construct meaning by interpreting symbols based on perspectives gleaned through interaction with others and our personal experiences. We also punctuate to create meaning in communication.

Instead of existing only in the physical world of the here and now, we use symbols to define, evaluate, and classify ourselves, others, and our experiences in the world. In addition, we use symbols to think hypothetically, so we can consider alternatives and simultaneously inhabit all three dimensions of time. Finally, symbols allow us to self-reflect so that we can monitor our own behaviors.

Although members of a society share a common language, we don't all use it the same way. Communication cultures, which exist both within and between countries, teach us rules for talking and interpreting others. Because communication rules vary among cultures based on gender, race, and class, we can't assume others use words just as we do.

The final section of this chapter discussed principles for improving effectiveness in verbal communication. Because words can mean different things to various people and because different communication cultures instill distinct rules for interacting, misunderstandings are always possible. To minimize them, we should engage in dual perspective, own our thoughts and feelings, respect what others say about how they think and feel, and monitor abstractness, generalizations, and static evaluations.

In the next chapter, we continue our discussion of the world of human communication by exploring the fascinating realm of nonverbal behavior.

KEY TERMS

Arbitrary	Constitutive rules
Ambiguous	Punctuation
Abstract	Totalizing
Communication rules	Loaded language
Regulative rules	Static evaluation

CHAPTER 5

The World Beyond Words

*P*at sprawled in the chair, legs spread wide apart. Pat pulled a slice of pizza from the box and took a large bite, using a hand to wipe away cheese and grease. After swallowing the pizza, Pat chugged a Budweiser and belched loudly.

Robin sat with crossed legs at the table, relishing the pizza on the plate. After nibbling the first slice, Robin used a napkin to dab at traces of cheese and grease, then sipped a beer, suppressing the burp it prompted.

What do you know about Robin and Pat other than that they like pizza and beer? Even though nothing in the descriptions identified gender, you probably guessed that Pat was male and Robin was female. Your inferences about sex were based on nonverbal behaviors. Pat was sprawled with legs open, while Robin sat with legs crossed. Pat ate pizza from a box, chugged beer, and belched, whereas Robin ate from a plate, sipped beer, and suppressed a burp. Our culture accepts it when males, but not females, belch, sit with legs spread apart, and chug beer.

If we saw a woman guzzling beer, wiping her face with her hand, sitting with legs widely spread, and belching, we'd regard her as distinctly unfeminine. Gender is not simply a matter of physiology, but is something we perform day in and day out in our lives. Recognizing this, West and Zimmerman (1987) note that we behave in ways that announce we are feminine or masculine. We also use nonverbal behaviors to express race, class, and sexuality as facets of identity. The Furisode kimono shown at the opening of this chapter includes nonverbal indicators that the courtier is a member of the upper class (the fine horse he rides, the richly worked robes with satin stitching). Clothes, possessions, and other nonverbal symbols communicate a great deal about who we are.

The world beyond words is an important dimension of interpersonal communication. The nonverbal system accounts for 65 to 93% of the total meaning of communication (Birdwhistell, 1970; Mehrabian, 1981). This suggests that nonverbal behaviors often have more impact than verbal ones on how we communicate and perceive others' communication.

In this chapter, we explore the fascinating world beyond words that is so much a part of interpersonal life. To launch our exploration, we will examine principles of nonverbal communication. Next, we'll discuss types of nonverbal behavior. Guidelines for improving effectiveness in nonverbal communication complete the chapter.

© Anne Dowie

Principles of Nonverbal Communication

Nonverbal communication is all aspects of communication other than words themselves. It is more than gestures and body language. In addition, nonverbal communication includes *how* we utter words (inflection, volume), features of environments that affect meaning (temperature, lighting), and objects that affect personal images and interaction patterns (dress, jewelry, furniture). Like verbal communication, nonverbal behavior is ambiguous, abstract, and arbitrary. Thus, we can't be sure what a smile or gesture means, and we can't guarantee that others understand the meanings we intend to express with our actions.

Also like verbal communication, our nonverbal behavior and our interpretations of others' nonverbal behavior are governed by rules of particular cultures. For this reason, our actions tend to reflect and reproduce understandings and values of the particular cultures to which we belong. For instance, dress considered appropriate for women varies across cultures, with miniskirts accepted in the United States and veils required in other societies. Eye contact also varies among cultures so that what is polite gazing in one context may be intrusive and rude in another. Four principles of nonverbal communication provide insight into how it affects meaning in interpersonal interaction.

Nonverbal Behaviors Can Supplement or Replace Verbal Communication

Communication researchers have identified five ways in which nonverbal behaviors interact with verbal communication (Malandro & Barker, 1983). First, nonverbal behaviors may repeat verbal messages. For example, you might say "yes" while nodding your head. Second, nonverbal behaviors may highlight verbal communication. For instance, you can emphasize particular words by speaking more loudly, and you can indicate you mean something sarcastically by tone of voice. Third, we use nonverbal behavior to complement

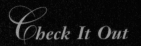
Check It Out

THE CASE OF CLEVER HANS

In the 1900s, Herr von Osten trained his horse Hans to count by tapping his front hoof. Hans learned quickly and was soon able to multiply, add, divide, subtract, and perform complex mathematical calculations. He could even count the number of people in a room or the number of people wearing eyeglasses. Herr von Osten took Hans on a promotional tour. At shows he would ask Hans to add 5 and 8, divide 100 by 10, and do other computations. In every case, Hans performed flawlessly, leading others to call him "Clever Hans." Because some doubters thought Clever Hans's feats involved deceit, proof of his mathematical abilities was demanded.

The first test involved computing numbers that were stated on stage by people other than von Osten. Using his hoof, Hans pounded out the correct answers. However, he didn't fare so well on the second test in which one person whispered a number into Hans's left ear and a different person whispered a number into his right ear. Hans was told to add the two numbers and pound out the sum, an answer not known by anyone present. Hans couldn't solve the problem. On further investigation, it was deduced that Hans could solve problems only if someone he could see knew the answer. When Hans was given numbers and asked to compute them, viewers leaned forward and tensed their bodies as Hans began tapping his hoof. When Hans tapped the correct number, onlookers relaxed their body postures and nodded their heads, which Hans took as a signal to stop tapping.

Hans was clever, not because he could calculate but because he could read nonverbal communication of people.

Source: Sebeok, T. A., & Rosenthal, R. (Eds.). (1981). *The Clever Hans phenomenon: Communication with horses, whales, apes and people.* New York: New York Academy of Sciences.

or add to words. When you see a friend, you might say "I'm glad to see you" and underline the verbal message with a warm embrace. Fourth, nonverbal behaviors may contradict verbal messages, as when someone says "Nothing's wrong" in a frosty, hostile tone of voice. Finally, we sometimes substitute nonverbal behaviors for verbal ones. For instance, you might roll your eyes to indicate you disapprove of something. In all of these ways, nonverbal behaviors augment or replace verbal communication.

Nonverbal Behaviors Can Regulate Interaction

In conversations, we generally know when someone else is through speaking and it is our turn to talk. We also sense when a professor welcomes discussion from students and when the professor is in a lecture mode. We can even perceive when a professor or friend expects or wants us specifically to enter conversation. Seldom do explicit, verbal cues tell us when to speak and keep silent. When talking, friends typically don't say "Your turn to talk" or hold up signs saying "I am through now." Instead, turn-taking in conversation is regulated nonverbally (Malandro & Barker, 1983). We signal we don't want to be interrupted by averting our eyes or by maintaining a speaking volume and rate that thwart interruption. When we're through talking, we look back to others to signal "Okay, now somebody else can speak." We invite specific individuals to speak by looking directly at them, often after asking a question.

Although we aren't usually aware of nonverbal actions that regulate interaction, we rely on them to know when to speak and when to remain silent. Without conscious realization, we signal others they should enter a conversation or wait until we're through speaking. We send and respond to subtle nonverbal cues whenever we communicate with others.

Nonverbal Behaviors Often Establish Relational-Level Meanings

You'll recall that in Chapter 1, we discussed two levels of meaning that are always present in communication. To review, the content level of meaning concerns actual information or literal meaning. The relational level of meaning defines individuals' identities and relationships between people. More than verbal language, nonverbal communication conveys relational-level meanings (Keeley & Hart, 1994). In fact, communication scholars refer to nonverbal communication as the "relationship language" and note that it, more than verbal messages, expresses the overall feeling of relationships (Burgoon, Buller, Hale, & deTurck, 1984; Sallinen-Kuparinen, 1992). There are three dimensions of relationship-level meanings that are conveyed primarily through nonverbal communication (Mehrabian, 1981). As we will see, how we express and interpret each of these dimensions varies among different communication cultures.

Responsiveness   One facet of relational-level meaning is responsiveness. Through eye contact, facial expressions, and body posture, we indicate our interest in others' communication. Westerners signal interest by holding eye contact and assuming an attentive posture. To express lack of interest or boredom, we decrease visual contact and adopt a passive body position. Also, synchronicity, or harmony, between people's postures and facial expressions reflects how comfortable they are with each other (Berg, 1987; Capella, 1991). We're more likely to feel that others are involved with us if they look at us, nod, and lean forward than if they gaze around the room, look bored, and fiddle with papers as we speak (Miller & Parks, 1982).

© Bob Daemmrich/Stock, Boston

ALLAN

The most useful professional development seminar I've ever had was on listening. Our instructor showed us how to sit and look at people to show we were interested. We learned that most men don't show their interest with head nods and eye contact. That explained to me why some of the women I supervise complained that I never seemed interested when they came to talk to me. It wasn't that I wasn't interested. I just didn't show it with my nonverbal behavior.

Different communication cultures teach members distinct rules for showing responsiveness. Because feminine culture emphasizes building relationships by expressing interest in others, women generally display greater emotional responsiveness than men (Montgomery, 1988; Ueland, 1992). In addition to communicating their own feelings nonverbally, women are generally more skilled than men in interpreting others' emotions (Hall, 1978; Noller, 1986). African Americans also tend to be more skilled than Caucasians in reading emotions, which suggests decoding is a survival strategy for those who have historically had subordinate standpoints (women and minorities). Prisoners, another subordinate group, also show strong decoding capacity (Wood, 1994e). The well-being and sometimes physical safety of those with low power depend on being able to decipher the feelings and intentions of those with more power.

Liking   A second dimension of relational meaning is liking. Nonverbal behaviors are keen indicators of how positively or negatively we feel toward others. Smiles and friendly touching tend to indicate positive feelings, while frowns and belligerent postures express antagonism (Keeley & Hart, 1994). In addition to these general rules shared in Western society,

EXASPERATED?
TRY TO THINK OF YOUR MATE AS A CROSS-CULTURAL EXPERIENCE!

I AM **NOT** TRYING TO BE ALOOF—I'M A GODDAMNED CAT, OKAY?!

© Jennifer Berman. Used by permission.

more specific rules are instilled by particular communication cultures. Masculine cultures emphasize emotional control and independence, so men are less likely than women to use nonverbal behavior that reveals how they feel. Reflecting the values of feminine culture, women, in general, sit closer to others and engage in greater eye contact than men (Montgomery, 1988; Reis, Senchak, & Solomon, 1985). They are also more openly expressive of their inner feelings, since that is encouraged in feminine communication cultures. Women are also more likely than men to initiate hand-holding and touch others to show affection. Liking is also communicated between marriage partners. Happy couples sit closer together and engage in more eye contact than unhappy couples (Miller & Parks, 1982; Noller, 1986).

CARLA

I swear, it's so hard to figure out what guys think of you. When you're around a guy, he's like Mr. Stone Face, so he doesn't give away anything about how he feels. I can't tell by how he acts if a guy likes me or is interested. My girlfriends say the same thing—guys are just inscrutable. Girls aren't like that at all. If we like someone, we smile and let him or her know instead of acting distant and aloof.

Power The third aspect of relational-level meanings is power. We rely greatly on nonverbal behaviors to assert dominance and to negotiate for status and influence (Henley, 1977). Given what we have learned about gender communication cultures, it is not surprising that men typically exceed women in efforts to exert control. Men assume greater amounts of space and use greater volume and more forceful gestures to assert their ideas (Hall, 1987; Major, Schmidlin, & Williams, 1990). Men are also more likely than women to use gestures and touch to symbolize control (Henley, 1977; Leathers, 1986). The prerogative to touch another reflects power, so individuals with power touch those with lesser power. For instance, bosses touch secretaries far more often than secretaries touch bosses (Spain, 1992).

JERRY

Last summer I had an internship with a big accounting firm in Washington, and space really told the story on status. Interns like me worked in two large rooms on the first floor with partitions to separate our desks. New employees worked on the second floor in little cubicles. The higher up you were in the hierarchy of the firm, the higher up your office was—literally. I mean, the president and vice presidents—six of them—had the whole top floor, while there were forty or more interns crowded onto my floor.

© Anne Dowie

As Jerry's observations indicate, space also expresses power relations. Individuals who have power usually command more space than individuals with lesser power. The connection between power and space is evident in the fact that most bosses have large, spacious offices while their secretaries have smaller offices or workstations, even though they have to manage far more material than bosses. Homes also reflect power differences among family members. Adults usually have more space than children, and men more often than women have their own rooms and sit at heads of tables.

Power may also be exerted through silence, a powerful form of nonverbal communication. By not responding, men sometimes discourage others from speaking and clear the way to talk about their own preferred topics (DeFrancisco, 1991). In extreme form, power is nonverbally enacted through violence and abuse, activities that men are more likely to commit than women (Wood, 1994d).

Responsiveness, liking, and power are dimensions of relational-level meanings that are communicated primarily through nonverbal behaviors.

In a full heart there is room for everything, and in an empty heart there is room for nothing.
ANTONIO PORCHIA

Nonverbal Communication Reflects Cultural Values

Like verbal communication, nonverbal patterns reflect communication rules of specific cultures. This implies that the majority of nonverbal actions are not instinctive, but are learned as we are socialized in particular cultures. We've already noted a number of differences between nonverbal behaviors encouraged in feminine and masculine communication cultures. In addition to diversity among cultures within our country, nonverbal behaviors vary from one country to another. As you might expect, dissimilarities reflect distinct cultural values.

Have you ever seen the bumper sticker that says "If you can read this, you're too close"? That slogan proclaims North Americans' fierce territoriality. We prize private space, and we resent, and sometimes fight, anyone who trespasses on what we consider our turf. In cultures where individuality is a less pronounced value, people are less territorial. For instance, Brazilians stand close in shops, buses, and elevators and when they bump into each other they don't apologize or draw back (Wiemann & Harrison, 1983).

THE SPORTS CULTURE AND DEVALUING OF WOMEN

Is disregard for women actually encouraged in sports? Mariah Nelson, author of *The Stronger Women Get, the More Men Love Football*, suggests that the sports culture trains men to derogate women. Consider:

Girls and women who want to play sports with boys are ridiculed, sexually harassed, and excluded.

College stars and professional athletes learn to expect pretty women to "escort" them. A good-looking date is an important nonverbal indicator of status.

Locker room talk centers on discussions of women's bodies and graphic descriptions of sexual conquests.

Studies of locker room talk found that men spoke of women as objects and tried to outdo one another in telling about their sexual performances.

Athletes who talk about serious relationships with women or speak respectfully of women are often ridiculed by their teammates for becoming "too female."

One coach at a major college once remarked after his team lost a game, "I'm going to go home and beat my wife."

Source: Nelson, M. B. (1994, June 23). Violence from the locker room. *Raleigh News and Observer*, p. 13A.

SANDY

I was so uncomfortable when I traveled to Mexico last year. People just crammed into buses even when all the seats were taken. They pushed up together and pressed against each other. I felt they were really being rude, and I was uptight about having people on top of me like that. I guess it was a cultural difference like we learned, but it sure made me uneasy at the time. I never knew how territorial I was until I felt my space was being invaded.

Norms for touching also reflect cultural values. In one study, Americans, who are relatively reserved, were observed engaging in an average of only two touches an hour. The emotionally restrained British averaged zero touches per hour. Parisians, long known for their emotional expressiveness, touched 110 times per hour. Puerto Ricans touched most, averaging 180 touches an hour (Knapp, 1972).

Patterns of eye contact also reflect cultural values. In North America, frankness and assertion are valued, so meeting another's eyes is considered appropriate and a demonstration of personal honesty. Yet in many Asian and northern European countries, direct eye contact is considered abrasive and disrespectful (Hall, 1968). In Brazil, eye contact is often so intense that people from the United States consider it rude. Imagine the confusion this causes in intercultural business negotiations.

Four principles provide a foundation for understanding nonverbal communication. First, nonverbal behavior can supplement or replace verbal communication. Second, nonverbal behaviors can regulate interaction. Third, nonverbal behavior is more powerful than verbal behavior in expressing relational-level meanings. Finally, nonverbal communication reflects cultural values and, thus, is learned rather than instinctive. We're now ready to explore types of nonverbal behavior that make up this intricate communication system.

Types of Nonverbal Behaviors

Because so much of our interaction is nonverbal, this system includes many types of communication. In this section, we will consider nine forms of nonverbal behavior, noticing how we use each to establish relationships and to express personal identity and cultural values.

Face and Body Motion

Kinesics is a technical term that refers to body position and body motions, including those of the face. Clearly, we signal a great deal about how we see ourselves by how we hold our bodies. Someone who stands erectly and walks confidently announces self-assurance, whereas someone who slouches and shuffles may seem to be saying "I'm not very sure of myself." We also communicate moods with body posture and motion. For example, someone who walks quickly with a resolute facial expression appears more determined than someone who saunters along with an unfocused gaze. We sit more rigidly when we are nervous or angry and adopt a relaxed posture when we feel at ease.

Body postures may signal whether we are open to interaction. Someone who sits with arms crossed and looks downward seems to say, "Don't bother me." That's also a nonverbal strategy students sometimes use to dissuade teachers from calling on them in classes. To invite interaction, Westerners look at others and smile, signaling that conversation is welcome. Yet in many Asian societies, direct eye contact and smiling at nonintimates might be considered disrespectful. We also use gestures to signal what we think of others. We use a hand gesture to indicate okay and a different gesture to communicate contempt.

Our faces are intricate communication messengers. The face alone is capable of over 1,000 distinct expressions that result from variations in tilt of the head and movements of the eyebrows, eyes, and mouth (Eckman, Friesen, & Ellsworth, 1971). Our eyes can shoot daggers of anger, issue challenges, or radiate feelings of love. With our faces we can indicate disapproval (scowls), doubt (raised eyebrows), admiration (warm eye gazes), and resistance (stares). The face is particularly powerful in conveying responsiveness and liking (Keeley & Hart, 1994; Patterson, 1992).

One of the most important interpersonal aspects of kinesics concerns how we position ourselves relative to others and what our positions say about our feelings toward them. Couples communicate dissatisfaction by increaing distance and by decreasing smiles and eye gazes (Miller & Parks, 1982). We also use nonverbal behaviors, such as smiles, close seating, and warm gazes, to signal we like others and are happy with them (Walker & Trimboli, 1989).

Check It Out

HOW TO DISCOURAGE ASSAULT

Many criminals are highly skilled at interpreting nonverbal behavior. Their success in getting away with crimes depends on their ability to read others. Convicted thieves report that they don't pick victims randomly, but instead carefully select whom to rob. They look for people whose walks signal unsureness and whose posture and face suggest passivity. Some people announce they're good targets, declared one career thief. The best way to avoid being picked as a victim is to walk confidently, hold your head upright, and meet others' eyes without staring. Above all, never appear unsure or lost—particularly if you are!

© Anne Dowie   © Anne Dowie

The eyes have one language everywhere.
GEORGE HERBERT

Put It in Practice

COMMUNICATING CLOSENESS

To become more aware of subtle nonverbal behaviors that reflect intimacy, try this. Watch a television show and keep a careful record of characters' kinesic communication.

1. How close do characters who are intimate stand or sit to one another? How close do characters who are antagonistic stand or sit? What is the distance between characters who are just meeting or who have casual relationships?

2. Watch patterns of eye contact between characters who are intimates, enemies, and casual acquaintances. How often do they look at each other? How long is eye gaze maintained in each type of relationship?

3. Notice facial expressions for characters who do and don't like each other. How often do they smile or stare?

As a class, discuss what your observations reveal about kinesic communication and relational-level meanings.

For good reason, poets call the eyes "the mirrors of the soul." Our eyes communicate some of the most important and complex messages about how we feel about others. If you watch infants, you'll notice that they focus on others' eyes. Babies become terrified if they can't see their mothers' eyes, but they aren't bothered when other parts of their mothers' faces are hidden (Spitz, 1965). Even as adults, we tend to look at eyes to judge emotions, honesty, interest, and self-confidence.

Touch

Touch is the first of our five senses to develop (Leathers, 1976), and many communication scholars believe touching and being touched are essential to a healthy life. Research on dysfunctional families reveals that mothers touch babies less often and less affectionately than mothers in healthy families. In disturbed families, mothers tend to push children away, nonverbally signaling rejection (Birdwhistell, 1970). In contrast, babies who are held closely and tenderly tend to develop into self-confident adults who have secure attachment styles (Main, 1981).

Touching also communicates power and status. People with high status touch others and invade others' spaces more than people with less status (Henley, 1977). Cultural views of women as more touchable than men are reflected in gendered patterns of contact. Parents touch sons less often and more roughly than they touch daughters (Condry, Condry, & Pogatshnik, 1983). These patterns early in life teach the sexes different rules for using touch and interpreting touches from others. As adults, women tend to engage in touch to show liking and intimacy (Montgomery, 1988), while men rely on it to assert power and control (Henley, 1977; Leathers, 1986). For example, women frequently hug others and touch the hands and arms of friends during conversation. Men are more likely than women to use touch aggressively to exert power over others or to repel physical aggression by others. Feminine training to be nice to others and preserve relationships explains why women may be reluctant to object to touching, even if it is unwanted. These gendered patterns contribute to sexual harassment where women are often the targets of unwelcome touch (LePoire, Burgoon, & Parrott, 1992), as Claire's commentary illustrates.

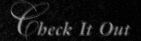
Check It Out

FREEDOM OF (NONVERBAL) SPEECH

Nonverbal communication has been costly for some sports stars. When German midfielder Stefan Effenberg made an obscene gesture to fans during a World Cup match in the summer of 1994, his coach promptly kicked him off the squad.

The season before, Miami Dolphins linebacker Bryan Cox flipped an obscene gesture in Buffalo. The NFL slapped him with a $10,000 fine that was later reduced to $3,000.

Private companies such as athletic teams can make their own rules. However, in the United States, nonverbal behavior is protected by freedom of speech laws. Thus, Louis Sirkin, a First Amendment attorney, successfully defended a motorist who insulted a traffic officer with an obscene hand gesture.

Source: Be civil. (1994, July 5). *Wall Street Journal*, p. A1.

CLAIRE

There's a guy where I work who really bothers me. He doesn't really cross a clear line, but it seems like he's always brushing against me. Like when he comes to my desk, he leans over just enough that his chest presses against me. Sometimes he touches my arm or hand when he's showing me a paper, and the other day he stood behind me to show me how to run a new spreadsheet program. He had both arms around me when it would have been easier to work the mouse if he'd sat on the side. I've never said anything because I don't want to hurt his feelings or seem hysterical or something, but it really bothers me.

Check It Out

HELP WITH EATING DISORDERS

Preoccupation with weight can rob you of vitality and, in extreme form, endanger your life. If you are obsessed with weight or have an eating disorder, help is available either from the health center on your campus or from national organizations such as these:

American Anorexia Bulimia Association
418 E. 76th Street
New York, NY 10021

Center for the Study of Anorexia and Bulimia
1 West 91st Street
New York, NY 10024

National Anorexic Aid Society
1925 East Dublin-Granville Road
Columbus, OH 43229

Physical Appearance

Western culture places an extremely high value on physical appearance. For this reason, most of us notice how others look, and we form initial evaluations based on their appearance, over which they have limited control. We first notice obvious physical qualities such as sex and race. After interpreting these, we then form judgments of how attractive others are and make inferences about their personalities. In one study, researchers found that people associate plump, rounded bodies with laziness and weakness. Thin, angular physiques were thought to reflect youthful, hard-driven, nervous, stubborn personalities, and athletic body types were seen as indicating strong, adventurous, self-reliant personalities (Wells & Siegel, 1961).

Cultures stipulate ideals for physical form. Currently in the West, the cultural ideals emphasize thinness and softness in women and muscularity and height in men (Wolf, 1991). Further, many women feel greater pressure to meet the cultural ideal, since they are judged more in terms of attractiveness, while men are judged on the basis of accomplishments (Spitzack, 1990, 1993). This general cultural standard is qualified by ethnic identity. In traditional African societies, full-figured bodies are perceived as symbolizing health, prosperity, and wealth, which are all desirable (Villarosa, 1994). African Americans who embrace this value accept or prefer women who weigh more than the current ideal for Caucasians (Root, 1990; Thomas, 1989).

ANDREA

Nearly all of the girls I know have eating problems. Some constantly diet, and a lot of others binge and purge. We're all afraid to gain any weight— afraid that guys won't want to date us if we weigh even a little extra. Usually I stick to dieting, but if I eat too much I do throw it up. I hate that, but it's better than being fat.

Class membership further modifies ethnic values concerning weight. In 1994, *Essence* magazine reported that African American women who were either affluent or poor were likely to have strong black identities that allowed them to resist Caucasian preoccupations with thinness. On the other hand, middle-class African American women who are upwardly mobile are more inclined to deemphasize their ethnic identities to get ahead, and they are more susceptible to obsessions with weight and eating disorders (Villarosa, 1994).

Artifacts

Artifacts are personal objects we use to announce our identities and personalize our environments. We craft our image by how we dress and what objects, if any, we carry and use. Nurses and physicians wear white and frequently drape stethoscopes around their necks; professors travel with briefcases, while students more often tote backpacks. White-collar professionals tend to wear tailored outfits and dress shoes, whereas blue-collar workers more often dress in jeans or uniforms and boots. The military requires uniforms that define individuals in terms of the group. In addition, stripes and medals signify rank and accomplishments.

© Don Smetzer/Tony Stone Images, Inc.

We also use artifacts to define our territories. To claim our spaces, we fill them with objects that matter to us and that reflect our experiences and values. Lovers of art adorn their homes with paintings and sculptures that announce their interests and personalize their private space. Religious families often express their commitments by displaying pictures of holy scenes and the Bible, the Koran, or another sacred text. We exhibit artifacts that symbolize important relationships and experiences in our lives. For example, many people have pictures of family members in their offices and homes. On my writing desk, I have a photograph of my sister Carolyn; an item that belonged to my father; the first card my partner, Robbie, ever gave me; and a jar of rocks from a beach where I retreat whenever possible. These artifacts personalize my desk and remind me of people and experiences I cherish.

JENETTA

Whenever I move, the first thing I have to do is get out the quilt that my grandmother made. Even if it is summer and I won't use the quilt, I have to unpack it first and put it out where I can see it. She brought me up, and seeing that quilt is my way of keeping her in my life.

In her book *Composing a Life*, Mary Catherine Bateson (1990) comments that we turn houses into homes by filling them with what matters to us. We make impersonal spaces familiar and comfortable by imprinting them with our artifacts. We use mugs given to us by special people, nurture plants to enliven indoor spaces, surround ourselves with books and magazines that announce our interests, and sprinkle our world with objects that reflect what we care about.

Artifacts communicate important relational meanings. We use them to announce our identities and to express how we perceive and feel about others. Although clothing has been more unisex in recent years, once you venture beyond the campus context, gendered styles are evident. To declare gender, we dress to meet cultural expectations of men and women.

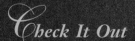
HOW COLORS AFFECT MOOD

How much is mood influenced by color? Research reports these relations between colors and moods (Wexner, 1954):

Red	Exciting, stimulating
Blue	Secure, comfortable, soothing
Orange	Distressed, upset, disturbed
Brown	Dejected, unhappy, melancholy
Green	Calm, serene, peaceful
Black	Powerful, strong, defiant
Yellow	Cheerful, joyful, jovial
Purple	Dignified, stately

© Richard Hutchings/PhotoEdit

Thus, women sometimes wear makeup, dresses that may have lace or other softening touches, skirts, high-heel shoes, jewelry, and hose, all of which conform to the cultural ideal of women as decorative objects. Typically, men wear less, if any, jewelry, and their clothes and shoes are functional. Flat shoes allow a person to walk comfortably or run if necessary; high heels don't. Men's clothing is looser and less binding, and it includes pockets for wallets, change, keys, and so forth. In contrast, women's clothing tends to be more tailored and often doesn't include pockets, making a purse necessary.

We also use artifacts to establish racial identity. In recent years, marketers have offered more ethnic clothing and jewelry, so people of color can more easily acquire artifacts that express their distinctive cultural heritages. In addition, African Americans often dress more stylishly and dramatically than Caucasians and may even engage in "stylin'," which is dressing to appear as if you are well off, especially if you aren't (Ribeau et al., 1994). Stan explained to Caucasians in my class what stylin' means within the African American culture. I asked him to write out his explanation so that I could include it here.

STAN

We have to do stylin' if we want any respect in this society. It's not like we're putting on airs or trying to be something we're not. What it is is a way to challenge stereotypes about our race. Whites think blacks are lazy, ugly, and uncultivated, and they've tried to make us see ourselves that way too. But we defy their stereotypes when we dress fine. We say to ourselves and to whites that we look good. That's why brothers and sisters do stylin'.

Others also use artifacts to communicate how they see us. Many hospitals still swaddle newborns in blue and pink blankets to designate sex. Even though many parents today try to be nonsexist, many still send gender messages through the toys they give children. In general, parents, and especially fathers, give sons toys that encourage rough play (trains) and competitiveness (baseball gloves, toy weapons), whereas they give daughters toys that cultivate nurturing (dolls) and attention to appearance (makeup kits, frilly clothes) (Caldera, Huston, &

O'Brien, 1989; Lytton & Romney, 1991; Pomerleau, Bolduc, Malcuit, & Cossette, 1990). Gifts are conventional ways to say "you matter to me." Some objects are invested with cultural meanings as well: Engagement rings and wedding bands signify commitment. We also symbolize that we're connected to others by wearing their clothes, as when women wear male partners' shirts or partners exchange sweatshirts.

Put It in Practice

ARTIFACTUAL GENDER MESSAGES

What kinds of toys did your parents give you? Did they ever discourage you from playing with particular kinds of toys? Did you ask for toys that aren't ones society prescribes for your gender—boys asking for dolls, girls for train sets? Did your parents let you have the toys?

Now think about the clothing your parents gave you. If you're a woman, did your parents expect you to wear frilly dresses and stay clean? If you're a man, did your parents give you clothes meant for rough play and getting dirty?

SPEED EATING

To make a profit, restaurants have to get people in and out as quickly as possible. Studies indicate that one way to do this is the strategic use of music (Bozzi, 1986).

Researchers played music in a cafeteria and observed patrons over sixteen days. On the first day, the researchers played fast instrumental music with 122 beats per minute. The next day, slow instrumentals with fifty-six beats a minute were played. On the third day, there was no music. The researchers repeated the sequence for sixteen days while they observed.

When no music was played, people ate the slowest, averaging 3.23 bites per minute. When slow music accompanied dining, customers ate somewhat more quickly—3.83 bites per minute. When fast music was played, diners sped up their eating to 4.4 bites per minute. When questioned, diners said they hadn't noticed any differences in background music. Even though they weren't conscious of environmental factors, they responded to them by how they behaved.

Environmental Factors

Environmental factors are another nonverbal influence on interpersonal interaction. Environmental factors are elements of settings that affect how we feel and act. For instance, we respond to architecture, colors, room design, temperature, sounds, smells, and lighting. Rooms with comfortable chairs invite relaxation, whereas rooms with stiff chairs prompt formality. Dimly lit rooms can enhance romantic feelings, although dark rooms can be depressing. We feel solemn in churches and synagogues with their somber colors and sacred symbols such as crosses and menorahs.

We tend to feel more lethargic on sultry summer days and more alert on crisp fall ones. Delicious smells can make us feel hungry, even if we weren't previously interested in food. Our bodies synchronize themselves to patterns of light, so that we feel more alert during daylight than during the evening. In settings where people work during the night, extra lighting and even artificial skylights are used to simulate daylight so that workers stay alert.

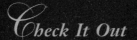

ROOM ENOUGH TO GROW . . . AND GROW

Americans' love of space and lots of it is obvious in changing housing patterns. Consider this: Lori and Ron Simek spent over $650,000 to build a four-bedroom, six-bathroom, 5,700-square-foot "cabin" near Yellowstone Park. They will be the only occupants.

In 1994, nearly half of the homes constructed in the United States exceeded 3,000 square feet and were lived in by couples who had no children at home. This reflects a dramatic change in the housing patterns in the United States. Since 1969, the average size of a new single-family home has jumped by 33%—from 1,400 square feet to 2,100 square feet. During this time period, the size of the average U.S. family has decreased by the same 33%—from 3.6 people in 1969 to 2.7 people in 1994.

Source: Templin, N. (1994, October 17). Wanted: Six bedrooms, seven baths for empty nesters. *Wall Street Journal*, pp. B1, B7.

"*Sorry, Ridgely, but this area is my personal space.*"

© 1994 by Sidney Harris. *The Wall Street Journal*.

Think about restaurants in which you've eaten. The environment of most fast-food restaurants encourages customers to eat quickly and move on, whereas more expensive restaurants are set up to promote longer stays and spending extra money on wines and desserts. For the same reason, fast-food restaurants are brightly lit and have fast music, if any. Finer restaurants tend to have dim lighting and soft, slow music, which encourages diners to linger.

Proxemics and Personal Space

Proxemics refers to space and how we use it (Hall, 1968). Every culture has norms for using space and for how close people should be to one another. In the United States, we interact with social acquaintances from a distance of 4 to 12 feet, but are comfortable with 18 inches or less between us and close friends and romantic partners (Hall, 1966). When we are angry with someone, we tend to move away from her or him and to resent it if she or he approaches us.

Space also announces status, with greater space being assumed by those with higher status (Henley, 1977). Substantial research shows that women and minorities generally have less space than Caucasian men in our society (Spain, 1992). The prerogative to invade someone else's personal space is also linked to power, with those having greater power also being most likely to trespass into others' territory (Henley, 1977). Responses to invasions of space also reflect power, with men likely to respond aggressively when their space is invaded (Fisher & Byrne, 1975). This reflects gendered socialization, which encourages women to defer and accommodate and men to vie for status.

How people arrange space reflects how close they are and whether they want interaction. Couples who are very interdependent tend to have greater amounts of common space and less individual space in their homes than do couples who are more independent (Fitzpatrick, 1988; Fitzpatrick & Best, 1979; Werner, Altman,

& Oxley, 1985; Werner & Haggard, 1985). Similarly, families that value interaction arrange furniture to invite conversation and eye contact. Less interactive families arrange furniture to discourage conversation. Chairs may be far apart and may face televisions instead of each other (Burgoon, Buller, & Woodhall, 1989; Keeley & Hart, 1994). People also invite or discourage interaction by how they arrange office spaces. Some of your professors may have desks that face the door and a chair beside the desk for open communication with students; other professors may have desks turned away from the door and may position chairs across from their desks to preserve status and distance.

Put It in Practice

WHAT DOES YOUR SPACE SAY?

Survey your room or apartment. Is furniture arranged to promote or discourage interaction? How much space is common, and how much is reserved for individuals? Is space divided evenly among you and your roommate(s), or do some people have more space than others?

Now think about your home. How is the space arranged there? Is there a living room or family room? If so, is furniture set up to invite interaction? Is there a lot, a little, or a moderate amount of common space?

How do spatial arrangements in your home and your room or apartment regulate interaction and reflect the styles and status of people who live there?

Check It Out

ENVIRONMENTAL RACISM

The term *environmental racism* arose to describe a pattern whereby toxic waste dumps and hazardous plants are disproportionately located in low-income neighborhoods and communities of color. Whether this is deliberately planned or not, many industries expose our most vulnerable communities to pollutants and carcinogens that seldom affect middle- and upper-class neighborhoods. The pattern is very clear: The space of minorities and poor people can be invaded and contaminated, but the territory of more affluent citizens cannot be.

Source: Robert Cox, President of the National Sierra Club, 1994–1996, personal communication.

© Jon Riley/Tony Stone Images, Inc.

Television has proved that people will look at anything, rather than at each other.

ANN LANDERS

Chronemics

Chronemics refers to how we perceive and use time to define identities and interaction. Nonverbal scholar Nancy Henley (1977) reports that we use time to negotiate and convey status. She has identified a cultural rule that stipulates important people with high status can keep others waiting. Conversely, people with low status are expected to be punctual in Western society. It is standard practice to have to wait, sometimes a good while,

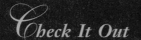
CULTURAL VIEWS OF TIME

North Americans and Germans differ in the time they invest in work. The typical job in Germany requires thirty-seven hours a week, and a minimum of five weeks' paid leave annually is guaranteed by law. Stores close on weekends and four of five week nights so that workers can have leisure time. In the United States, jobs typically require forty-four to eighty hours a week, and many workers can't take more than a week's leave at a time. Further, many North Americans take second jobs even when their first jobs allow a comfortable standard of living. Germans can't understand this, remarking that "free time can't be paid for" (p. B1). Personal time is considered so precious in Germany that it is illegal to work more than one job during holidays, which are meant to allow people to restore themselves.

Source: Benjamin, D., & Horwitz, T. (1994, July 14). German view: "You Americans work too hard—and for what?" *Wall Street Journal*, pp. B1, B6.

to see a physician, even if you have an appointment. This carries the message that the physician's time is more valuable than ours. Professors can be late to class and students are expected to wait, but students are sometimes reprimanded if they appear after a class begins. Subordinates are expected to report punctually to meetings, but bosses are allowed to be tardy.

Chronemics express cultural attitudes toward time. In Western societies, time is valuable, so speed is highly valued (Keyes, 1992; Schwartz, 1989). Thus, we want computers, not typewriters, and we replace our programs and modems as soon as faster models hit the market. We often try to do several things at once to get more done, rely on the microwave to cook faster, and take for granted speed systems such as instant copying, photos, and so forth. Many other cultures have far more relaxed attitudes toward time and punctuality. It's not impolite in many South American countries to come late to meetings or classes, and it's not assumed people will leave when the scheduled time for ending arrives. Whether time is savored or compulsively counted and horded reflects larger cultural attitudes toward living.

The duration of time we spend with different individuals reflects our interpersonal priorities. When possible, we spend more time with people we like than with those we don't like or who bore us. Researchers report that increasing contact is one of the most important ways college students intensify relationships, and reduced time together signals decreasing interest (Baxter, 1985; Dindia, 1994; Tolhuizen, 1989).

Chronemics also involve expectations of time, which are established by cultural norms. For example, you expect a class to last fifty to seventy-five minutes. Several minutes before the end of a class period, students often close notebooks and start gathering their belongings, signaling the teacher that time is up. Similarly, we expect weekly religious services to last approximately an hour, and we might be upset if a rabbi or minister talked beyond the time we've allowed. These expectations reflect our culture's general orientation toward time, which is that it is a precious commodity that we should not give away easily.

Paralanguage

Paralanguage refers to communication that is vocal but that does not use words themselves. It includes sounds, such as murmurs and gasps, and vocal qualities, such as volume, rhythm, pitch, and inflection. Paralanguage also includes how we pronounce words, the accents we use, and the complexity of our sentences. Our voices are versatile instruments that tell others how to interpret us and what we say. Vocal cues signal others to interpret what we say as a joke, threat, statement of fact, question, and so forth.

Put It in Practice

PARALINGUISTIC CUES

Say "Oh, really" to express the following meanings:

1. I don't believe what you just said.
2. Wow! That's interesting.
3. I find your comment boring.
4. That's juicy gossip!
5. What a contemptible thing to say.

Now say "You love me" to convey these meanings:

1. You really do? I hadn't realized that.
2. That ploy won't work. I told you we're through.
3. You couldn't possibly love me after what you did!
4. Me? I'm the one you love?
5. You? I didn't think you loved anyone.

We use our voices to communicate feelings to friends and romantic partners. Whispering, for instance, signals secrecy and intimacy, while shouting conveys anger. Depending on the context, sighing may communicate empathy, boredom, or contentment. Research indicates that tone of voice is a powerful clue to feelings between marital partners. Negative paralanguage, such as sneering and ridiculing by tone of voice, are closely associated with marital dissatisfaction (Gottman, Markman, & Notarius, 1977; Noller, 1987). A derisive or sarcastic tone communicates scorn or dislike more emphatically than words. The reverse is also true: A warm voice underlines feelings of love, and a playful lilt invites frolic and fun. Tone of voice and inflection are also primary gauges for interpreting honesty.

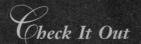

Check It Out

THE MEANING OF TIME IN WESTERN CULTURE

Cultural views of time are reflected in how we talk about time. The following everyday expressions reflect Western culture's view that time is like money—a valuable and limited resource that can be used up and must be saved.

> You're *wasting* my time.
> Mastering the computer will *save* you time.
> I don't *have* any time to *give* you.
> How do you *spend* your time?
> That mistake *cost* me three hours.
> I can't *spare* any time for that.
> I've *invested* a lot of time in this course.
> I'm *running out* of time.
> I need to learn how to *budget* my time better.
> Is this *worth* the time it will *take*?
> How much time do we *have left*?
> That guy is living on *borrowed* time.
> I *lose* a lot of time daydreaming.
> She *uses* time *profitably*.

Source: Lakoff, G., & Johnson, M. (1980). *Metaphors we live by* (pp. 7–8). Chicago: University of Chicago Press.

© E. Williamson/The Picture Cube

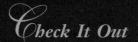

Check It Out

TO TELL THE TRUTH

Dektor Counterintelligence and Security, Inc., believes our voices reveal whether we are lying or telling the truth. Dektor invented the PSE (Psychological Stress Evaluator), a machine that measures vocal stress. Dektor claims the PSE has a 94.7% success rate in detecting lies. The PSE has been used in several court trials.

Our voices affect how others perceive us. To some extent, we control vocal cues that influence image. For instance, we can deliberately sound firm and sure of ourselves in job interviews when we want to project self-confidence. Similarly, we can consciously make ourselves sound self-righteous, seductive, and unapproachable when those images suit our purposes. In addition to the ways we intentionally use our voices to project an image, vocal qualities we don't deliberately manipulate affect how others perceive us. For instance, individuals with accents are often stereotyped. Someone with a pronounced Bronx accent may be perceived as brash, and someone with a southern drawl may be stereotyped as lazy. People with foreign accents are often falsely perceived as less intelligent than native speakers.

MELISSA

I got so much grief for my accent when I went to a junior college in New England. I never thought of myself as having an accent because everyone in Alabama talks like I do, but I guess I really stood out in Connecticut. People not only made fun of my accent, but they had all these other stereotypes about southerners being slow and unassertive. It was really hard to get anyone to judge me on my merits.

We modulate our voices to reflect our cultural heritage and to announce we are members of specific cultures. For example, African American speech has more vocal range, inflection, and tonal quality than Caucasian speech (Garner, 1994). In addition, among themselves African Americans often engage in highly rhythmical rappin' and "high talk" to craft desired identities (Ribeau et al., 1994). If you don't know what rappin', high talk, and signifying are, talk with some African Americans to find out about the special vocal patterns of their culture.

We also use paralanguage to declare gender by acting masculine or feminine. To appear masculine, men use strong volume, low pitch, and limited inflection, all of which conform to cultural prescriptions for men to be assertive and emotionally controlled. To enact femininity, women tend to use higher pitch, less volume, and more inflection, vocal features that reflect cultural views of women as deferential and polite.

We also enact class by how we pronounce words, the accents we use, and the complexity of our sentences. Class is also expressed by vocabulary (greater vocabulary is generally associated with higher education) and by grammar. In addition to paralinguistic cues, other nonverbal behaviors communicate class. For example, artifacts generally differ in the homes of working-class and upper-class people. Affluent individuals possess more books, expensive art, and valuable jewelry than do less affluent individuals.

Silence

A final type of nonverbal behavior is silence, which can communicate powerful messages. "I'm not speaking to you" actually speaks volumes. We use silence to communicate different meanings. For instance, it can symbolize contentment when intimates are so comfortable they don't need to talk. Silence can also communicate awkwardness, as you know if you've ever had trouble keeping conversation going with a new acquaintance. We feel pressured to fill the void. In some cultures, including many Native American ones, silence indicates respect and thoughtfulness.

Silence can also disconfirm others. In some families, children are disciplined by being ignored. No matter what the child says or does, parents refuse to acknowledge his or her existence. In later life, the silencing strategy may also surface. You know how disconfirming silence can be if you've ever said hello to someone and gotten no reply. Even if the other person didn't deliberately ignore us, we feel slighted. We sometimes deliberately freeze out intimates when we're angry with them. In some military academies, such as West Point, silencing is a recognized method of stripping a cadet of personhood if he or she is perceived as having broken the academy code. Similarly, the Catholic church excommunicates people who violate its canons.

GINDER

Silencing is the cruelest thing you can do to a person. That was how my parents disciplined all of us. They told us we were bad and then refused to speak to us—sometimes for several hours. I can't describe how awful it felt to get no response from them, to be a nonperson. I would have preferred physical punishment. I'll never use silencing with my kids.

In this section, we've discussed nine types of nonverbal behavior. The complex system of nonverbal communication includes face and body motions, touch, physical appearance, artifacts, environmental features, space, chronemics, paralanguage and silence. We use these nonverbal behaviors to announce our identities and to communicate how we feel about relationships with others. In the final section of this chapter, we consider guidelines for improving the effectiveness of our nonverbal communication.

Guidelines for Improving Nonverbal Communication

Nonverbal communication, like language, is symbolic and open to misinterpretation. Following two guidelines should help you avoid misunderstanding others' nonverbal behaviors and having others misperceive your actions.

© David Lissy/FPG International

Monitor Your Nonverbal Communication

The monitoring skills we have stressed in other chapters are also important for competent nonverbal communication. Self-reflection allows you to take responsibility for how you present yourself and your nonverbal messages. Think about the foregoing discussion of ways we use nonverbal behaviors to announce our identities. Are you projecting the image you desire? Do your facial and body movements represent how you see yourself and how you want others to perceive you? Do friends ever tell you that you seem uninterested or far away when they are talking to you? If so, you can monitor your nonverbal actions so that you convey greater involvement and interest in conversations.

Have you set up your spaces so that they invite the kind of interaction you prefer, or are they arranged to interfere with good communication? Paying attention to nonverbal dimensions of your world can empower you to use them more effectively to achieve your interpersonal goals.

Be Tentative When Interpreting Others' Nonverbal Communication

Although stores are filled with popular advice books that promise to show you how to read nonverbal communication, there really isn't any sure-fire formula. It's naive to think we can precisely decode something as complex and ambiguous as nonverbal communication. When we believe that we can, we risk misjudging others.

In this chapter, we've discussed findings about the meanings people attach to nonverbal behaviors. It's important to realize these are only generalizations about conclusions people draw. We have not and cannot state what any particular behavior ever means to specific individuals in a given context. For instance, we've said that satisfied couples tend to sit closer together than unhappy couples. As a general rule, this is true. However, sometimes very contented couples prefer autonomy and like to keep distance between them some of the time. In addition, someone may maintain distance because she or he has a cold and doesn't want a partner to catch it. Also, people socialized in non-Western cultures use space in different ways and have different meanings for physical closeness and distance. Because nonverbal communication is ambiguous and personal, we should not assume we can interpret it with absolute precision. You will be more effective if you qualify interpretations of nonverbal communication with awareness of personal and contextual considerations.

KINCAID

One of the most unsettling experiences of my life was trying to negotiate a deal between my company and a Japanese one. I traveled to Japan and met with a representative of the Japanese company. He wouldn't look at me when I spoke, and that made me wonder if he was being evasive. Also, he would never say "no" point blank even if he totally disagreed with something I said or if there was no way he was going to agree to terms I proposed. His style was to say, "We will have to think about that very important idea." After two days of frustrating negotiations, I met with another American business-man who explained to me that Japanese think direct eye contact is rude and that they never refuse or disagree because that would make the other person lose face. I had to learn how to read Mr. Watanabe.

Personal Qualifications   Generalizations about nonverbal behavior tell us only what is generally the case. They don't tell us about the exceptions to the rule. Nonverbal patterns that accurately describe most people may not apply to particular individuals. Although eye contact generally indicates responsiveness in Western culture, some individuals close their eyes to concentrate when listening. In such cases, it would be inaccurate to conclude a person who doesn't look at us isn't listening. Similarly, people who cross their arms and have a rigid posture are often expressing hostility or lack of interest in interaction. However, the same behaviors might mean a person is cold and trying to conserve body heat. Most people use less inflection, fewer gestures, and a slack posture when they're not really interested in what they're talking about. The same behaviors, however, are typical of any of us when we are tired.

Because nonverbal behaviors are ambiguous and vary among people, we need to be cautious about how we interpret others. A key principle to keep in mind is that nonverbal behaviors, like other symbols, have no intrinsic meaning. Meaning is something we construct and assign to behaviors. A good way to keep this distinction in mind is to rely on I-language, not you-language, which we discussed in Chapter 4. You-language might lead us to inaccurately say of someone who doesn't look at us, "You're communicating lack of interest." A more responsible statement would use I-language to say, "When you don't look at me, I feel you're not interested in what I'm saying." Using I-language reminds us to take responsibility for our judgments and feelings. In addition, it reduces the likelihood we will make others defensive by inaccurately interpreting their nonverbal behavior.

USING I-LANGUAGE ABOUT NONVERBAL BEHAVIORS

I–language makes communication about nonverbal behaviors more responsible and clear. Practice the skill of translating you–language into I–language to describe nonverbal behavior.

Example: You–language: You're staring at me.

I–language: When you look at me so intensely, I feel uneasy.

You–Language

You make me angry when
you don't clean your side
of the room.

I can tell you don't believe
me by your expression.

Don't crowd me.

Your T-shirt is offensive.

Contextual Qualifications   Like the meaning of verbal communication, the significance of nonverbal behaviors depends on the contexts in which they occur. How we act doesn't reflect only how we see ourselves and how we feel. In addition, our actions reflect the various settings we inhabit. We are more or less formal, relaxed, and open depending on context. Most people are more at ease on their own turf than someone else's, so we tend to be more friendly and outgoing in our homes than in business meetings and public spaces. We also dress according to context. Students who see me in professional clothing on campus are often surprised to find me in jeans or running clothes when they come by my home or see me in town. Like all of us, I costume myself differently for various occasions and contexts.

Immediate physical settings are not the only context that affects nonverbal communication. As we have seen, all communication, including the nonverbal dimension, reflects the values and understandings of particular cultures. We are likely to misinterpret people from other cultures when we impose the norms and rules of our own. An Arabic man who stands very close to others to talk with them is not being rude according to the standards in his culture, although he might be interpreted as pushy by Westerners. A Tibetan woman who makes little eye contact is showing respect by the norms in her country, although she might be interpreted as evasive if judged by North American rules of interaction.

MEI-LING

I often have been misinterpreted in this country. My first semester here a professor told me he wanted me to be more assertive and to speak up in class. I could not do that, I told him. He said I should put myself forward, but I have been brought up not to do that. In Taiwan, that is very rude and ugly, and all of us are taught not to speak up to teachers. Now that I have been here for three years, I sometimes speak in classes, but I am still more quiet than Americans. I know my professors think I am not so smart because I am quiet, but that is the teaching of my country.

Even within our own country we have diverse communication cultures, and each has its own rules for nonverbal behavior. We run the risk of misinterpreting men if we judge them by the norms of feminine communication culture. A man who doesn't make "listening noises" may well be listening intently according to the rules of masculine culture. Similarly, men often misperceive women as agreeing when they nod and make listening noises while another is talking. According to feminine communication cultures, ongoing feedback is a way of signaling interest, not necessarily approval. Within the understandings of African American culture, stylin' is not arrogant egotism as the same behaviors might be according to Caucasian norms. We have to adopt dual perspective when interpreting others, especially when they and we belong to different cultures.

We can become more effective nonverbal communicators if we monitor our own nonverbal behaviors and qualify our interpretation of others by keeping personal and contextual considerations in mind. Using I-language is one way to help us avoid the danger of misreading others.

SUMMARY

In this chapter, we've explored many facets of the fascinating world beyond words. We learned that nonverbal communication functions to supplement or replace verbal messages, to regulate interaction, to reflect and establish relational-level meanings, and to express cultural membership. These four principles of nonverbal behavior help us understand the complex ways in which nonverbal communication operates and what it may mean.

We discussed nine types of nonverbal communication. These are kinesics (face and body motion), proxemics (use of space), physical appearance, artifacts, environmental features, space, chronemics (use of and orientations to time), paralanguage, and silence. Each of these forms of nonverbal communication reflects cultural understandings and values and also expresses our personal identities and feelings toward others. We use nonverbal behaviors to announce and perform identities, using actions, artifacts, and contextual features to embody the rules we associate with gender, race, class, sexuality, and ethnicity. In this sense, nonverbal communication has a theatrical dimension, because it is a primary way we create and present images of ourselves.

Because nonverbal communication, like its verbal cousin, is symbolic, it has no inherent meaning that is fixed for all time. Instead, its meaning is something we construct as we notice, organize, and interpret nonverbal behaviors that we and others enact. Effectiveness requires that we learn to monitor our own nonverbal communication and to exercise caution in interpreting that of others.

KEY TERMS

Nonverbal communication   Proxemics
Kinesics   Chronemics
Artifacts

CHAPTER 6

Mindful Listening

Ben: Mom just called to tell me she and Dad are divorcing. I can't believe it—not my folks.

Mike: Your folks and half the other couples in America. Divorce isn't a big deal anymore.

Ben: It is to me. I feel like I don't have an anchor and I'm just afloat without a family anymore.

Mike: You're making too much out of this. Just forget it and get on with your life.

Ben: How can I when everything my life is based on has suddenly blown up?

Mike: They'll still pay for your last year of college, won't they?

Ben: I guess, but that's not the issue. The problem is that I don't have a home or family anymore.

Mike: Get a grip, man. You already left home when you came to college. Their divorce doesn't affect you at all. Just blow it off.

How would you describe Mike's communication in the conversation? Is he being a good communicator? Is he sensitive and responsive to Ben and his feelings?

Usually when we think about communication, we think about talking. Yet, talking is not the only or even the greatest part of communication. For people to interact and share meaning, they must also listen to one another. As obvious as this is, few of us devote as much energy to effective listening as we do to effective talking. In the example, Mike doesn't listen very well. He isn't sensitive to Ben's feelings, and he doesn't communicate support to his friend. Although most of us are probably better listeners than Mike was in this instance, few of us listen as well as we could or should.

If you think about your normal day, you'll realize that listening—or trying to—takes up about half of your waking time. Listening is the single greatest communication activity in which we engage. Studies of people, ranging from college students to professionals, indicate that the average person spends between 45 and 53% of waking time listening to others (Barker, Edwards, Gaines, Gladney, & Holley, 1981; Weaver, 1972). If we don't listen effectively, we're communicating poorly about half of the time!

Because listening is a vital and major form of communication, in this chapter we will explore what it is and how to listen effectively. First, we'll consider what's involved in listening, which is more than most of us realize. Next we'll discuss obstacles to effective listening and how we can minimize these. We'll also consider some of the forms nonlistening takes. The third section of the chapter explains different types of listening and the distinct skills required for each. To wrap up the chapter, we'll identify guidelines for improving listening effectiveness.

The Listening Process

The panel that opens this chapter represents the basic four elements of life: air, earth, fire, and water. Listening, too, involves different elements, including our ears, minds, and hearts. Although we often use the words *listening* and *hearing* as if they were synonyms, actually they are distinct. **Hearing** is a physiological activity that occurs when sound waves hit our eardrums. Listening has psychological and cognitive dimensions that mere hearing does not. **Listening** is a complex process that consists of being mindful, hearing, selecting and organizing information, interpreting communication, responding, and remembering. Listening is not just the obvious process of hearing, but also includes interpreting and responding to what others communicate. The multifaceted aspects of listening are reflected in the Chinese character in Figure 6.1, which includes the symbols for eyes, ears, and heart.

FIGURE 6.1 *The Chinese Character for the Word "Listening"*

Being Mindful

The first step in listening is making a decision to be mindful. **Mindfulness** is a concept from Zen Buddhism that refers to being fully present in the moment. To be mindful is to keep your mind on what is happening in the here and now. When we are mindful, we don't let our thoughts wander from the present situation. We don't think about what we did yesterday or plan to do this weekend, nor do we focus on our own feelings and responses. Instead, when we listen mindfully we tune in fully to another person and try to hear that person without imposing our own ideas, judgments, or feelings on him or her. Mindfulness is symbolized by paying attention, adopting an involved posture, keeping eye contact, and indicating interest in what another person says (Bolton, 1986). Mindfulness is the first step in effective listening, and it is the foundation for all other parts of the process.

Mindfulness enhances communication in two ways. First, attending fully to others allows us to understand them better than if we pay only superficial attention. Listening mindfully enables us to grasp the relational meanings of messages so that we have an idea of how another person feels about what she or he is saying. In other words, mindfulness fosters dual perspective, which is a cornerstone of effective communication. In addition, mindfulness enhances the effectiveness of another's communication. When people sense we are really listening, they tend to engage us more fully, elaborate their ideas, and express themselves in more depth.

Photo Researchers, Inc.

The inability to hear is a nuisance; the inability to communicate is a tragedy.

Lou Ann Walker

Being mindful is a choice we make. It is not a talent that some people have and others don't, nor is it something that results from what others do. Instead, it is a matter of making a personal commitment to attend fully and without diversion to another person. No amount of skill will make you a good listener if you don't choose to attend mindfully to others. Thus, your own choice of whether to be mindful is the foundation of how you listen—or fail to.

Hearing

The second process involved in listening is hearing. As we noted earlier, hearing is a physiological process in which sound waves hit our eardrums so that we become aware of noises, such as music, traffic sounds, or human voices. Unlike fully listening, hearing is a passive process: If we are present when vibrations are in the air, we will hear them. Hearing requires no attention or effort on our part.

Although hearing is not the same as listening, we have to hear in order to listen. For most of us, hearing is automatic and unhindered. However, individuals with hearing difficulties may have difficulty actually receiving oral messages. When we speak with someone who has a hearing impairment, we should face the person and check to make sure we are coming across clearly. In addition to physiological problems, hearing ability may decline when we are fatigued from concentrating on communication. You may have noticed that it's harder to pay attention in classes that run seventy-five minutes or two hours than in fifty-minute sessions. Background noise can also interfere with good hearing. If loud music is playing, a television is blaring, or others are talking in our vicinity, it's difficult to hear well. Even though this is evident, as Betsy points out, we often don't control noises that interfere with effective hearing and listening.

BETSY

My parents are so strange! To watch them, you'd think they were deliberately trying to make it impossible to hear each other. Here's what happens: Dad will turn on the radio, and then Mom will start talking. He won't hear part of what she says, and then she'll get in a huff that he ignored her. Or sometimes Mom will have the television on, and Dad will say something from the other room. When she doesn't hear him, he'll get on her case about caring more about whatever program is on than about him. They do this all the time—no wonder they can't hear each other!

Even among people who have "normal" hearing, there may be physiological differences in how we hear. Women and men seem to differ in their listening styles. As a rule, women are more attentive than men to what is happening around them. Thus, men tend to focus their hearing on specific content aspects of communication, whereas women are more likely to attend to the whole of communication, noticing details, tangents, and major themes (Weaver, 1972). Judy Pearson (1985), a prominent communication scholar, suggests this could be due to different hemispheric specialization of brains. Women usually have more developed right lobes, which govern creative and holistic thinking, whereas men typically have more developed left lobes, which control analytic and linear processing of information.

MARK

My girlfriend amazes me. We'll have a conversation, and then later one of us will bring it up again. What I remember is what we decided in the talk. She remembers that too, but she also remembers all the details about where we were and what was going on in the background and particular things one of us said in the conversation. I never notice all of that stuff, and I sure don't remember it later.

Selecting and Organizing Material

The third element of listening is selecting and organizing material. As we noted in Chapter 3, we don't perceive everything around us. Instead, we selectively attend to some messages and elements of our environments, and we disregard others. What we attend to depends on many factors, including our interests, cognitive structures, and expectations. If we realize that our own preoccupations can hamper listening, we can curb interferences. Once again, mindfulness comes into play. Choosing to be mindful doesn't necessarily mean our minds won't stray when we try to listen, but it does mean that we will bring ourselves back to the present moment. We have to remind ourselves to focus attention and concentrate on what another is saying.

We can monitor our tendencies to attend selectively by remembering that we are more likely to notice stimuli that are intense, loud, or unusual, or that otherwise stand out from the flow of communication. This implies that we may overlook communicators who speak quietly and don't call attention to themselves. Intan, an Asian American student, once told me that Caucasians often ignore what she says because she speaks in a soft voice and uses an unassertive manner. Westerners who are accustomed to outspoken, individualistic speaking styles may not attend to less bold styles. If we're aware of the tendency not to notice people who speak quietly, we can guard against it so that we don't miss out on people and messages that may be important.

Once we've selected what to notice, we then organize the stimuli to which we've attended. As you'll recall from Chapter 3, we organize our perceptions by relying on cognitive schemata, which include prototypes, personal constructs, stereotypes, and scripts. As we listen to others, we decide how to categorize them by asking which of our prototypes they most closely resemble—good friend, person in trouble, student, teacher, and so

GENDERED CLASSROOM COMMUNICATION

Research has shown that women and men communicate differently in the classroom, and that teachers respond distinctly to gendered communication styles. Because women have been socialized to be quiet, deferential, and polite, many are uncomfortable asserting themselves and their ideas and calling out answers without first being recognized by a teacher. Men, in contrast, have been taught to assert themselves, and this is evident in their classroom communication. Most men are comfortable asserting their opinions, calling attention to themselves, and competing with other students for attention in classes. Further, male students frequently voice answers or ideas without being called on and without raising their hands.

Researchers have found that teachers tend to respond to men more than to women in classes. In addition, teachers, particularly at lower grade levels, often criticize female students if they speak without raising their hands and being called on, but they accept this behavior as appropriate from males in the classroom.

Sources: Gabriel, S. L., & Smithson, I. (Eds.). (1990). *Gender in the classroom: Power and pedagogy.* Urbana, IL: University of Illinois Press. Sadker, M., & Sadker, D. (1986, March). Sexism in the classroom: From grade school to graduate school. *Phi Delta Kappan,* pp. 512–515. Spender, D. (1989). *Invisible women: The schooling scandal.* London: Women's Press.

forth. We then apply personal constructs to define in more detail others and their messages. We evaluate whether they are smart or not smart, upset or calm, reasonable or unreasonable, open to advice or closed, and so on. Based on how we construct others, we then apply stereotypes that predict what they will do. When friends are clearly distraught, as Ben was at the beginning of this chapter, we can reasonably predict they will want to ventilate and may not want advice until after they have a chance to express their feelings. Finally, we apply scripts, which specify how interaction should proceed, including how we should act.

The schemata we use to organize our perceptions help us figure out how to respond to others and what they say. When we decide someone is angry and needs to spout off, we're likely to rely on a script that tells us to back off and let the person air his or her feelings. If, on the other hand, we perceive someone as confused, we might follow a script that says we should help the person clarify her or his feelings and options. It's important to remember that *we construct others and their communication* when we use our schemata to organize perceptions. In other words, we create meaning by how we select and organize communication. This reminds us to keep perceptions tentative and open to revision. In the course of interaction, we may want to modify initial perceptions.

TONYA

I work as a volunteer counselor at the women's center, and the other day something happened that shows how wrong a script we can have. This woman came in, a student about my age, and she told me she was pregnant. She was very upset and having trouble talking, so I tried to help out by going into the discussion most pregnant women who come to the center want. I told her a lot of people have untimely pregnancies and that it doesn't have to interfere with her life. Then I said that I could recommend several doctors who could perform abortions. By then she was crying even harder, and I started trying to tell her that abortions weren't a serious medical procedure. Finally, she managed to get out that she wanted to have the baby and needed help working out that decision. Well, that's a whole different script than abortion counseling. I had misperceived her, and that led me to adopt an inappropriate script.

DOONESBURY copyright 1992 G. B. Trudeau. Reprinted with permission of Universal Press Syndicate. All rights reserved.

Interpreting Communication

The fourth part of listening is interpreting others' communication. When we interpret, we put together all that we have selected and organized in a manner that makes sense of the overall situation. The most important principle for effective interpretation is to engage in dual perspective so that you interpret others in their terms. Certainly, you won't always agree with other people and how they see themselves, others, or situations. Engaging in dual perspective doesn't require you to share another's perspective; it does, however, require you to make an earnest effort to understand others.

To interpret someone on her or his own terms is one of the greatest gifts we can give another. What we give is personal regard so deep that we open our minds to how another sees the world. A genuine effort to understand others and what things mean to them is rare and very precious. Too often we impose our meanings on others, or we try to correct or argue with them about what they feel, or we crowd out their words with our own. As listening expert Robert Bolton (1986, p. 167) has observed, good listeners "stay out of the other's way," so they can learn how the speaker views his or her situation. Because fully interpersonal communication involves recognizing others as unique individuals, we must try to grasp what their experiences mean to them. Effective listening involves trying to understand others on their terms.

BART

I'd been married and working for years when I decided I wanted to come back to school and finish my degree. When I mentioned it to the guys I worked with, they all came down hard on me. They said I was looking for an easy life as a college Joe and trying to get above them. My dad said it would be irresponsible to quit work when I had a wife and child, and he said no self-respecting man would do that. It seemed like everyone had a view of

what I was doing and why, and their views had nothing to do with mine. The only person who really listened to me was Elaine, my wife. When I told her I was thinking about going back to school, the first thing out of her mouth was "What would that mean to you?" She didn't presume she knew my reasons, and she didn't start off arguing with me. She just asked what it meant to me, then listened for a long, long time while I talked about how I felt. She focused completely on understanding me, and that made it easy to talk. Maybe that's why we're married.

© Peter L. Chapman

Responding

Effective listening also involves **responding,** which is communicating attention and interest. As we noted in Chapter 1, interpersonal communication is not a linear process in which a one person speaks at another. Rather, it is a transactive process in which we simultaneously listen and speak. Skillful listeners give outward signs that they are following and interested. In the United States, signs of responsive listening include eye contact, head nods, attentive posture, and questions and comments that invite others to elaborate. These behaviors signal that we are involved in what is happening in the moment. All of us tend to communicate more clearly and interestingly when we feel others are committed to us and our communication.

We don't respond only when others finish speaking; rather, we respond throughout interaction. This is what makes listening such an active process. As we saw earlier, we cannot avoid communication, so the issue is *what* we communicate when we are listening. Nonverbal behaviors, such as looking out a window, making notes to ourselves, and slouching, signal that we aren't involved. Disinterest is also signaled by passivity. In a book titled *Who's Listening?* the psychiatrist Franklin Ernst (1973, p. 113) remarked that "to listen is to move. To listen is to be moved. . . . The non-moving, unblinking person can reliably be estimated to be a non-listener."

Good listeners let others know they are interested during conversation. They adopt a posture of involvement, nod their heads, make eye contact, and give vocal responses such as "um hmm," "okay," and "go on." All of these nonverbal behaviors show we are attentive, interested, and ready to hear more. On the relational level of meaning, responsiveness communicates that we care about the other person and what she or he says.

Put It in Practice

RESPONSIVE LISTENING

The next time a friend starts talking with you, express disinterest by slouching, avoiding eye contact, and giving no vocal feedback. You might want to look at something else—a paper or book—while the other is talking. Note what happens as you communicate a lack of interest. How does your friend act? What happens to her or his communication? Does she or he criticize you for not listening?

Now reverse the experiment. When somebody starts talking to you, show interest. Put aside what you were doing, incline your body slightly forward, make eye contact, and give vocal feedback to indicate you are following. Note what happens as you listen responsively. Does your friend continue talking? Does she or he become more engaging?

Finally, try varying your listening style during a single conversation. Begin by listening responsively, then lapse into a passive mode that expresses disinterest. What happens when you vary your listening style?

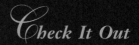

Check It Out

THE IMPACT OF RESPONSIVE LISTENING

Two researchers decided to test the impact of responsive listening on a speaker. They taught students in a college psychology course to respond with nonverbal communication cues. The professor in the class was a boring lecturer who read his notes in a monotone voice, seldom gestured, and did little to engage students. After the first few minutes of class, the students who had been trained in responsiveness began to show interest in the lecturer. They changed their postures, kept greater eye contact, nodded their interest, and so forth. Within a half a minute after the students began to respond, the lecturer started to use gestures, his speaking rate and inflection increased, and he began to interact with students visually and verbally. Then, at a prearranged signal, the students stopped responding and communicated disinterest. For a few awkward minutes the lecturer sought responses, but then he lapsed back into his monotone lecture, not engaging the students. Simply by demonstrating interest in the teacher's communication, the students were able to make him more effective and the class more exciting for everyone.

Source: Bolton, R. (1986). Listening is more than merely hearing. In J. Stewart (Ed.), *Bridges, not walls* (4th ed., pp. 159–179). New York: Random House.

Remembering

The final part of listening is **remembering,** which is the process of retaining what you have heard. According to communication scholars Ron Adler and Neil Towne (1993, p. 246), we remember less than half of a message immediately after we hear it. As time goes by, retention decreases further so that we recall only about 35% of a message eight hours after hearing it. Since we forget about two thirds of what we hear, it's important to make sure we hang on to the most important third. Effective listeners let go of a lot of details in order to retain basic ideas and general impressions (Fisher, 1987). By being selective about what to remember, we enhance our listening competence. Later in this chapter, we'll discuss more detailed strategies for retaining material to which we listen.

Effective listening is a complex process that involves being mindful, hearing, interpreting, responding, and remembering. Next we'll consider hindrances to our ability to enact the five processes that make up effective listening.

© Sepp Seitz/Woodfin Camp & Associates, Inc.

Obstacles to Effective Listening

Now that we've seen how much is involved in listening, it's easier to understand why we don't listen effectively to all of the communication in our lives. There are two broad types of obstacles to good listening—ones in communication situations and ones inside of us. (Did you notice that a series of ideas to be discussed were organized into two broad classes to aid your retention of the basic idea?)

Hindrances in Communication Situations

Much of what interferes with effective listening has to do with communication situations themselves. Although we can't always control external obstacles, knowing what situational factors hinder effective listening can help us guard against them or compensate for the noise they create.

Message Overload   The sheer amount of communication we engage in makes it difficult to listen fully all of the time. We simply aren't able to be mindful and totally involved in all of the listening we do, since it takes up 45 to 53% of our total communication activity. Instead, we screen the talk around us, much as we screen calls on our answering machines, to decide when to listen carefully.

RAYMOND

I've been married nearly thirty years, so I've figured out when I have to listen sharply to Edna and when I can just let her talk flow in one ear and out the other. She's a talker, but most of what she talks about isn't important. But if I hear code words, I know to listen up. If Edna says, "I'm really upset about such and such," or if she says, "We have a problem," my ears perk up and I listen carefully.

Message Complexity   Listening is also impeded by messages that are complex. The more detailed and complicated ideas are, the more difficult it is to follow and retain them. People for whom English is a second language often find it hard to understand complex sentences that have multiple clauses or that include slang expressions. It's tempting to tune out people who use technical vocabularies, focus on specifics, and use complex sentences. Yet we might miss interesting or important messages if we disregard complex ones. When we have to listen to messages that are dense with information, we should summon up extra energy. In addition, taking notes may help us understand and retain difficult information.

Noise   A third impediment to effective listening is noise. Sounds around us can divert our attention or even make it difficult to hear clearly. Perhaps you've been part of a crowd at a rally or a game. If so, you probably had to shout to the person next to you just to be heard. Although most noise is not as overwhelming as the roar of crowds, there is always some noise in communication situations. It might be music or television in the background, other conversations nearby, or muffled traffic sounds from outside.

GREGORY

I've been a salesman for a long time, and I know when clients are really interested and when they're not. When someone answers a phone when I'm in his or her office, I know he or she is not really focused on what I'm saying. Taking calls or leaving the door open for people to drop in communicates that they're not interested in me or the service I represent.

Gregory makes an important point by reminding us that allowing distractions communicates the relational-level meaning that we're not interested. Good listeners do what they can to create nondistracting environments. It's considerate to turn off a television or lower the volume on music if someone wants to talk with you. Professionals often instruct secretaries to hold their calls when they want to give undivided attention to a conversation with a client or business associate. It's also appropriate to suggest moving from a noisy area in order to cut down on distractions. Even if we can't always eliminate noise, we can usually reduce it or change our location to one that is more conducive to good communication.

Internal Obstacles to Effective Listening

In addition to external interferences, listening is hindered by things we do or don't do. We'll discuss four psychological obstacles to effective listening.

Preoccupation   A common hindrance to listening is preoccupation. When we are absorbed in our own thoughts and concerns, we can't focus on what someone else is saying. Perhaps you've attended a lecture right before you had a test in another class and later realized you got virtually nothing out of the lecture. That's because you were distracted by thoughts and anxieties about the upcoming test, which was of more immediate concern to you than what was being discussed in the lecture.

When we are preoccupied with our own thoughts, we can't be present for others. In other words, we're not being mindful. One method of enhancing mindfulness is to call our minds back to the present situation and the listening we want to do. It's natural for our thoughts to wander occasionally, especially if something is worrying us. However, we don't have to be passive when our thoughts roam. Instead, we may actively call our minds back by reminding ourselves to focus on the person who is speaking and the meaning of his or her message.

Prejudgments   Another reason we don't always listen effectively is that we prejudge others or their communication. Sometimes we think we already know what is being said and don't need to listen carefully. In other cases, we decide in advance that others have nothing to offer us, so we tune them out. A third kind of prejudgment occurs when we impose our preconceptions about a message on the person who is communicating. When this happens, we assume we know what another feels, thinks, and is going to say, and we then assimilate her or his message into our preconceptions. This often leads us to misunderstand what the person means, since we haven't really listened on her or his terms.

ABBIE

My boyfriend drives me crazy. He never listens, I mean really *listens, to what I am saying. He always listens through his own version of what I think and mean. Yesterday I said to him that I was having trouble with my parents about wanting to come to summer school. Before I could even explain what the trouble was, he said, "Yeah, they get real tight when you want them to pay for summer session. I've been through that one. Just keep at them and they'll come around." Well, as it so happens, money wasn't the issue at all. My parents wanted me to do an internship to get some practical experience in my field, so Jake's advice is totally irrelevant to why they are opposing me.*

Prejudgments disconfirm others, because we deny them their own voices. Instead of listening openly to them, we force their words into our own preconceived mind-set. This devalues others and their messages. When we impose our prejudgments on others' words at the relational level of meaning, we express a disregard for them and what they say.

Lack of Effort   It takes considerable effort to listen carefully, and sometimes we don't invest the necessary energy. It is hard work to be mindful—to focus closely on what others are saying, try to grasp their meanings, ask questions, and give responses so that they know we are interested and involved. In addition to these activities, we also have to control distractions inside ourselves, monitor external noise, and perhaps fight against fatigue, hunger, or other physiological conditions that can impede listening.

Because active listening requires so much effort, we're not always able or willing to do it well. Sometimes we make a decision not to listen fully, perhaps because the person or topic is not important to us. In other cases, we really want to listen, but have trouble marshaling the energy required. When this happens, an effective strategy is to ask the other person to postpone interaction until a time when you will have the energy and mindfulness to listen with care. If you explain to the other that you want to defer communication because you really are interested and want to be able to listen well, she or he is likely to appreciate your honesty and commitment to listening.

Not Recognizing Diverse Listening Styles

A final way in which we sometimes hinder our listening effectiveness is by not realizing and adjusting to different listening styles. How we listen differs for two reasons. First, different skills are required when we listen for information, to support others, and for pleasure. We'll discuss these kinds of listening later in the chapter.

A second basis for diverse listening styles is differences in what we learn about listening in our communication cultures. The more we understand about different people's rules for listening, the more effectively we can signal our attention in ways they understand. For example, Nepalese citizens give little vocal feedback when another is speaking. In that culture it would be considered rude and disrespectful to make sounds while someone else is talking. Cultures also vary in what they teach members about eye contact. In the United States, it is considered polite to make frequent, but not constant, eye contact with someone who is speaking. In other cultures, continuous eye contact is normative, and still others frown on virtually any eye contact.

Even within our country, there are differences in listening rules based on membership in gender, racial, and other communication cultures. Because feminine communication cultures regard talking as a way to form and develop relationships, responsive listening is emphasized. Thus, women, in general, make more eye contact, give more vocal and verbal feedback, and use head nodding and facial expressions to signal interest (Tannen, 1990; Wood, 1994d). Masculine culture, with its more instrumental orientation and focus on emotional control, deemphasizes obvious responsiveness. For this reason, men typically provide fewer verbal and nonverbal clues about their interest and attentiveness. If you understand these general differences between the genders, you can adapt your listening style to provide appropriate responses to both women and men.

Race also shapes differences in listening. Most Caucasians follow a communication rule that says one person shouldn't speak while another is talking, especially in formal speaking situations. Among African Americans, however, talking when another person is also talking is a form of showing interest and active participation. Thus, African Americans may signal they are listening intently by interjecting comments such as "Tell me more" or "I like what I'm hearing." Verbal responses during another's talk also occur in formal speaking within the African American community. Black churches are much more participative than Caucasian ones, and members of the congregation routinely call out responses to what a preacher is saying. When the Reverend Martin Luther King, Jr., delivered his "I Have a Dream" speech to a crowd of thousands, his words were echoed and reinforced by the listeners.

UPI/Bettmann

Injustice anywhere is a threat to justice everywhere.
MARTIN LUTHER KING, JR.

Listening competence includes being sensitive to differences in listening and speaking styles. Because others may speak and listen differently than we do, we shouldn't automatically impose our rules and interpretations on them. Instead, we should try to understand and respect their styles. By exercising dual perspective, we are more likely to listen effectively to others on their terms.

Forms of Ineffective Listening

Now that we've discussed obstacles to effective listening, let's consider forms of ineffective listening. We will discuss six types of ineffective listening. As you read about them, you may find they seem familiar, since you and others probably engage in these some of the time.

Pseudolistening   **Pseudolistening** is pretending to listen. When we pseudolisten, we appear to be attentive, but really our minds are elsewhere. We engage in pseudolistening when we want to appear conscientious, although we really aren't interested. Sometimes we pseudolisten because we don't want to hurt a friend who is sharing experiences, even though we are preoccupied with other things. We also pseudolisten when communication bores us, but we have to appear interested. Superficial talk in social situations and dull lectures are two communication situations in which we may consciously choose to pseudolisten so that we seem polite even though we really aren't involved.

RENEE

Pseudolistening should be in the training manual for flight attendants. I had that job for six years, and you wouldn't believe the kinds of things passengers told me about—everything from love affairs to family problems. At first I tried to listen, because I wanted to be a good attendant. After a year, though, I learned just to appear to be listening and to let my mind be elsewhere.

Pseduolisteners often give themselves away by revealing that they haven't been attending to communication. Common indicators of pseudolistening are responses that are tangential, irrelevant, or impervious to what was said. For example, if Martin talks to Charlotte about his interviews for a new job, she might respond tangentially by asking about the cities he visits: "Did you like New York or Atlanta better?" Although this is related to the topic of Martin's job interviews, it is tangential to the main issue. An irrelevant response would be "Where do you want to go for dinner tonight?" An impervious response such as "You're lucky to have a job that suits you" indicates that Charlotte didn't listen to what Martin said.

Monopolizing   **Monopolizing** is continuously focusing communication on ourselves instead of the person who is talking. Two tactics are typical of monopolizing. One is conversational rerouting in which a person shifts the topic of talk to himself or herself. For example, if Ellen tells her friend Marla that she's having trouble with her roommate, Marla should respond by showing interest in Ellen's problem and feelings. Instead, however, Marla might reroute the conversation by saying, "I know what you mean. My roommate is a real slob." Then Marla would go off on an extended description of her own roommate problems. Rerouting takes the conversation away from the person who is talking and focuses it on the self.

Another monopolizing tactic is interrupting to divert attention to ourselves. Interrupting can occur in combination with rerouting, so that a person interrupts and then directs the conversation to a new topic. In other cases, diversionary interrupting involves questions and challenges that are not intended to support the person who is speaking. Monopolizers may fire questions that express doubt about what a speaker says ("What makes you think that?" "How can you be sure?" "Did anyone else see what you did?") or prematurely offer advice to establish their own command of the situation and possibly to put down the other person ("What you should do is . . . " "You really blew that," "What I would have done is . . . "). Both rerouting and diversionary interrupting are techniques to monopolize a conversation. They are the antithesis of good listening.

It's important to realize that not all interruptions are attempts to monopolize communication. We also interrupt the flow of others' talk to show interest, voice support, and ask for elaboration. Interrupting for these reasons doesn't divert attention from the person speaking; instead, it affirms that person and keeps the focus on her or him. Research indicates that women tend to interrupt to show interest and support, while men interrupt to dominate conversations and capture the talk stage (Aries, 1987; Beck, 1988; Mulac, Wiemann, Widenmann, & Gibson, 1988; Stewart, Stewart, Friedley, & Cooper, 1990). Because masculine communication cultures emphasize using talk to compete for attention, men more than women engage in diversionary interrupting. Consistent with the rules of feminine communication cultures, women tend to interrupt to support and affirm others and what they are saying. Thus, women may make supportive interruptions such as "I know what you mean," "I really feel for you," or "I've had the same problem."

Selective Listening   A third form of ineffective listening is **selective listening,** which involves focusing on only particular parts of communication. We listen selectively when we screen out parts of a message that don't interest us or that we disagree with and also when we rivet attention on parts of communication that do interest us or with which we agree.

One form of selective listening focuses only on aspects of communication that interest us or correspond with our own opinions and feelings. Listeners screen out message content that doesn't interest them or correspond with their ideas. If you are worried about a storm, you will

Drabble reprinted by permission of UFS, Inc.

selectively listen to weather reports while disregarding news, talk, and music on the radio. Students often become highly attentive in classes when teachers say "This will show up on the test," because they regard information about testing as particularly important. We also listen selectively when we tune in only to topics that interest us and tune out the rest of what others say. For example, we might give only half an ear to a friend until the friend mentions spring break, and then we zero in because that topic interests us.

Selective listening also occurs when we reject communication that bores us or makes us uncomfortable. Many smokers, for instance, selectively block out reports on the dangers of smoking and of secondhand smoke. Taking in that information would be upsetting. We may also choose not to hear requests we don't want to meet. For instance, my partner, Robbie, is skillful at not taking in my requests for him to clean out the attic, and I'm equally adept at not hearing his appeals for me to increase my aerobics program. Neither of us wants to do what the other asks, so we screen out communication on those topics. Similarly, we sometimes don't listen when someone criticizes us or says something that could lead us to put ourselves down. For months I tried to suggest financial strategies to one of my friends who has no retirement savings or investments. Finally, I realized that she wasn't listening to me because the topic made her feel uncomfortable and like a failure. We all have subjects that bore or bother us, and we may selectively avoid listening to communication about them.

Defensive Listening **Defensive listening** involves perceiving personal attacks, criticisms, or hostile undertones in communication where none are intended. When we listen defensively, we assume others don't like, trust, or respect us, and we read these motives into whatever they say, no matter how innocent their communication actually is. Some individuals are generally defensive, expecting insults and criticism from all quarters. They hear threats and negative judgments in almost anything said to them. Thus, an innocent remark such as "Isn't that a new shirt?" may be perceived as a veiled suggestion that the shirt is ugly or that all the other shirts in the person's wardrobe are tacky.

In other instances, defensive listening is confined to areas where we judge ourselves as inadequate or times when we feel negative about ourselves. A man who is defensive about money may perceive phone solicitations as reproaches for his lack of earning ability; a woman who fears she is selfish may interpret offers of help as proof others don't think of her as helpful; a person who feels unattractive may hear genuine compliments as false; someone who just failed a test may hear questioning of his intelligence in benign comments.

© Ariel Skelley/The Stock Market

DAN

I was once a defensive listener. I had just gotten laid off from work—the recession, you know—and I felt like nothing. I couldn't support my family, and I couldn't stand the idea of going on unemployment. Nobody in my family ever did that. Once when my son asked me for a few bucks for a school outing, I just lit into him about how irresponsible he was about money. My wife mentioned the car needed some repair work, and I shouted at her that I wasn't a money machine. I'd never been like that before, but I was just so sensitive to being out of work that I had a chip on my shoulder. You couldn't talk to me about money without my taking it as a personal attack.

Ambushing **Ambushing** is listening carefully for the purpose of attacking a speaker. Unlike the other kinds of nonlistening we've discussed, ambushing involves very careful listening, but it isn't motivated by openness and interest in another. Instead, ambushers listen intently to gather ammunition they can use to attack a speaker. They don't mind bending or even distorting what you say in order to advance their combative goals. One of the most common instances of ambushing is public debates between political candidates. Each person listens carefully to the other for the sole purpose of later undercutting the opponent. There is no openness, no effort to understand the other's meaning, and no interest in genuine dialogue.

KRALYN

My first husband was a real ambusher. If I tried to talk to him about a dress I'd bought, he'd listen just long enough to find out what it cost and then attack me for spending money. Once I told him about a problem I was having with one of my coworkers, and he came back at me with all of the things I'd done wrong and didn't mention any of the things the other person had done. Talking to him was like setting myself up to be assaulted.

Literal Listening   The final form of ineffective listening we'll discuss is **literal listening,** which involves listening only to the content level of meaning and ignoring the relational level of meaning. As we have seen, all communication includes both content, or literal, meaning and relational meaning that pertains to the power, responsiveness, and liking between individuals. When we listen literally, we attend to only the content meaning and overlook what's being communicated about the other person or our relationship with that person. When we listen only literally, we are insensitive to others' feelings and to our connections with them.

CAMMY

My sister is a literal listener. I swear, she just doesn't get all of the meaning that is between words. The last time we were home together, Mom was talking about how bad she felt that she didn't seem to have the interest in cleaning the house as it should be and making elaborate meals. Lannie heard that, and her response to Mom was that the house wasn't clean and Mom needed to either devote more time to it or hire someone. Then Lannie told her she ought to plan the week's dinners on Sunday so that she could shop and set aside time to make nice meals. Give me a break! Mom just had a double radical mastectomy a month ago, and she's really depressed. She feels bad about losing her breasts, and she's worried that they didn't get all of the cancer. Who would feel like scrubbing floors and fixing gourmet food after going through that? What Mom needed was for us to hear that she was worried and unhappy and for us to tell her the house and fancy meals didn't matter. Anybody with an ounce of sensitivity could figure that out.

In this section, we have seen that there are many obstacles to effective listening. Ones in messages and situations include message overload, difficulty of messages, and external noise. In addition to these, there are four potential interferences inside of us: preoccupation, prejudgment, lack of effort, and failure to recognize and adapt to diverse expectations of listening. The obstacles to effective listening combine to create six types of ineffective listening. These are faking attention, ambushing speakers, monopolizing, responding defensively, attending selectively, and listening literally. Learning about hindrances to mindful listening and learning to recognize forms of nonlistening enable you to exercise greater control over how you listen and, thus, how fully you enter into relationships with other unique individuals.

Put It in Practice

IDENTIFYING YOUR INEFFECTIVE LISTENING

Apply the material we've just discussed by identifying times when you listen ineffectively.

1. Describe a situation in which you pseudolistened.
2. Describe an instance in which you monopolized communication.
3. Report on a time when you listened defensively.
4. Discuss an example of ambushing someone else.
5. Describe an instance when you listened selectively.
6. Identify a time when you listened literally.

Now repeat this exercise, but this time focus on examples of others who engage in each of the six types of ineffective listening.

Adapting Listening to Communication Goals

Now that you recognize some of the common pitfalls to effective listening, let's focus on how to listen well. The first requirement is to determine your reason for listening. We listen differently when we listen for pleasure, to gain information, and to support others about whom we care. We'll discuss the specific attitudes and skills that contribute to effective listening of each type.

Listening for Pleasure

Often the goal of listening is pleasure, or enjoyment. We don't want to learn something or understand information, and we aren't trying to support anyone else. Instead, we're listening for sheer enjoyment. Often we listen to music for pleasure. We may also listen to television shows and nightclub routines for enjoyment. Because listening for pleasure doesn't require us to remember or respond to communication, there are few guidelines for effective listening for enjoyment. The only suggestions are to be mindful and control distractions. Being mindful is important for all types of listening. Just as being mindful in lectures allows us to gain information, being mindful when listening for pleasure allows us to derive the full enjoyment from what we hear. Controlling interferences is also important when we are listening for pleasure. A beautifully rendered Mozart concerto can be wonderfully satisfying, but not if a television is on in the background.

© Chromosohm/Sohm/Stock, Boston

Informational Listening

Much of our listening has the purpose of gaining and evaluating information. We listen informationally in classes, at political debates, when important news stories are reported, and when we need guidance on everything from medical treatment to directions to a new place. In all of these cases, the primary purpose of listening is to gain and understand information in order to act appropriately or be successful. To do this, we need to use skills for critical thinking and for organizing and retaining information.

Be Mindful Our discussion of obstacles to listening suggests some important clues for how we can listen critically to information. First, it's important to make a decision to be mindful, choosing to attend carefully even if material is complex and difficult. Don't let your mind wander if information gets complicated or confusing. Instead, stay focused on your goal and take in as much as you can. Later you may want to ask questions about material that isn't clear even when you listen mindfully.

Control Obstacles You can also minimize noise in communication situations. You might shut a window to block out traffic noises or adjust a thermostat so that room temperature is comfortable. In addition, you should try to minimize psychological distractions by emptying your mind of the many concerns and ideas that can divert your attention from the communication at hand. This means you should try to let go of preoccupations as well as prejudgments that can interfere with effective listening.

Ask Questions Also important is posing questions to speakers. Asking speakers to clarify or elaborate their message allows you to gain understanding of information you didn't grasp at first and enhances insight into content that you did comprehend. "Could you explain what you meant by . . . ?" "I didn't follow your explanation of . . . " and "Can you clarify the distinction between . . . ?" are questions that allow listeners to gain further information to clarify content. Questions compliment a speaker because they indicate you are interested and want to know more.

Use Aids to Recall To understand and remember important information, we can apply the principles of perception we discussed in Chapter 3. For instance, we learned that we tend to notice and recall stimuli that are repeated. To use this principle in everyday communication, repeat important ideas to yourself immediately after hearing them. This moves the ideas from short-term to long-term memory (Estes, 1989). Repetition can save you the embarrassment of having to ask people you just met to repeat their names.

Another way to increase retention is to use mnemonic (pronounced new-monic) devices, which are memory aids that create patterns for what you've heard. You probably already do this in studying. For instance, you could create the mnemonic MASIRR, which is made up of one word for each of the six parts of listening (*M*indfulness, *A*ttending, *S*electing and organizing, *I*nterpreting, *R*esponding, *R*emembering). You can also invent mnemonics to help you recall personal information in communication. For example, KIM is a mnemonic to remember that *K*elly from *I*owa is going into *M*edicine.

Organize Information   A third technique to increase retention is to organize what you hear. When communicating informally, most people don't order their ideas carefully. The result is a flow of information that isn't coherently organized and so is hard to retain. We can impose order by regrouping what we hear. For example, suppose a friend tells you he's confused about long-range goals, then says he doesn't know what he can do with a math major, wants to locate in the Midwest, wonders if graduate school is necessary, likes small towns, needs some internships to try out different options, and wants a family eventually. You could regroup this stream of concerns into two categories: academic information (careers for math majors, graduate school, internship opportunities) and lifestyle preferences (Midwest, small town, family). Remembering those two categories allows you to retain the essence of your friend's concerns, even if you forget many of the specifics. Repetition, mnemonics to create patterns, and regrouping are ways to enhance what we remember.

Put It in Practice

IMPROVING RECALL

Apply the principles we've discussed to enhance memory.

1. The next time you meet someone, repeat his or her name to yourself three times in a row after you are introduced. Do you find you remember the name better when you do this?

2. After your next interpersonal communication class, take fifteen minutes to review your notes. Try reading them aloud so that you hear as well as see the main idea. Does this increase your retention of material covered in class?

3. Invent mnemonics to create patterns that help you remember basic information in communication.

4. Organize complex ideas by grouping them into categories. Try this first in relation to material in classes. To remember the main ideas of this chapter, you might use major subheadings to form categories: the listening process, obstacles to listening, listening goals, and guidelines. The mnemonic POGG (Process, Obstacles, Goals, Guidelines) could help you remember those categories. You can also group ideas in interpersonal interactions.

© Ariel Skelley/The Stock Market

Listening, not imitation, may be the sincerest form of flattery.

DR. JOYCE BROTHERS

By choosing to be mindful, minimizing distractions, asking questions, repeating and organizing ideas, and using mnemonic devices, we can increase our abilities to understand and remember informational communication.

Relational Listening

Listening for information focuses on the content level of meaning in communication. Yet, often we're more concerned with the relational level of meaning that has to do with another's feelings and perceptions. We engage in relational listening when we listen to a friend's worries, let a romantic partner tell us about problems in our relationship, or help someone work out a problem. Our primary interest is the other person and our relationship, rather than information. Specific attitudes and skills enhance relational listening.

Be Mindful   The first requirement for effective relational listening is to be mindful. You'll recall this was also the first step in listening for information and pleasure. When we're interested in relational-level meanings, however, a different kind of mindfulness is needed. Instead of focusing our minds on informational content, we need to concentrate on understanding feelings that may not be communicated explicitly. Thus, mindful relational listening calls on us to pay attention to what lies "between the words," the subtle clues to feelings and perceptions.

Suspend Judgment   When listening to help another person, it's important to avoid judgmental responses, at least initially. Although Western culture emphasizes evaluation, often we don't need to judge others or what they feel or do. Making judgments clutters communication by adding our evaluations to the others' experiences. When we do this, we are one step removed from them and their feelings. We've inserted something between us. To curb evaluative tendencies, we can ask whether we really need to pass judgment.

Yet there are times when it is appropriate and supportive to offer opinions and to make evaluative statements. Sometimes people we care about genuinely want our judgments, and in those cases we should be honest about how we feel. Particularly when others are confronting ethical dilemmas, they may seek the judgments of people they trust. Once my friend Cordelia was asked to work for a presidential candidate, but she had agreed to take a job at a large law firm. She talked to me about her quandary and asked me what I thought she should do. Although it was clear to me that Cordelia wanted to renege on the job and join the campaign, I couldn't honestly approve of that. I told her that I thought it would be dishonorable to go back on her word. After a long talk, Cordelia told me that I was the only friend who cared enough about her to have been so honest. Part of being a real friend in this instance was making a judgment. Yet that's appropriate only if someone invites our evaluation or if we believe another person is in danger of making a serious mistake.

Even positive evaluations ("That's a good way to approach the problem") may seem to indicate we think we have the right to pass judgment on others and their feelings. If someone asks our opinion, we should try to present it in a way that doesn't disconfirm the other person. Many times people excuse critical comments by saying, "Well you asked me to be honest" or "I mean this as constructive criticism." Too often, however, the judgments are not constructive and are more harsh than candor requires. If we are committed to helping others, we respond in ways that support them rather than tear them down.

Check It Out

LISTENING TOTALLY

Gerald Egan has studied listening extensively. Here's a paraphrase of his views on mindful relational listening:

We don't listen with just our ears, but also with our eyes and sense of touch, with our minds, hearts, and imaginations. Total listening is more than attending to another person's words. It is also listening to the meanings that are buried in the words and between the words and in the silences in communication.

Source: Egan, G. (1973). Listening as empathic support. In J. Stewart (Ed.), *Bridges, not walls*. Reading, MA: Addison-Wesley.

LOGAN

I hate the term constructive criticism. *Every time my dad says it, what follows is a put-down. By now I've learned not to go to him when I have problems or when I'm worried about something in my life. He always judges what I'm feeling and tells me what I ought to feel and do. All that does is make me feel worse than I did before.*

Understand the Other Person's Perspective   One of the most important principles for effective relational listening is to concentrate on grasping the other person's perspective. This means we have to step outside of our own point of view, at least long enough to understand another's perceptions. We can't respond feelingly to others until we understand their perspective and meanings. To do this, we must put aside preconceptions about issues and how others feel and try to focus on their words and nonverbal behaviors for clues about how they feel and think.

Paraphrasing is a method of clarifying others' meaning or needs by reflecting our interpretations of their communication back to them. For example, a friend might confide, "I think my kid brother is messing around with drugs." We could paraphrase this way: "So you're really worried that your brother's experimenting with drugs." This paraphrase allows us to clarify whether the friend has any evidence of the brother's drug involvement. The response might be, "No, I don't have any real reason to suspect him, but I just worry, since drugs are so pervasive in high schools now."

© Peter L. Chapman

This clarifies by telling us the friend's worries are more the issue than any evidence that the brother is experimenting with drugs. Paraphrasing also helps us figure out what others feel. If someone screams, "This situation is making me crazy," it's not clear whether the person is angry, hurt, upset, or going insane. We could find out which emotion prevails by saying, "You seem really angry." If anger is the emotion, the speaker could agree; if not, she or he could clarify what she or he is feeling.

Put It in Practice

LEARNING TO PARAPHRASE

Practice effective listening by paraphrasing the following statements.

1. I've got so many pressures closing in on me right now.
2. I'm worried about all of the money I've borrowed to get through school.
3. I'm nervous about telling my parents I'm gay when I see them next weekend.
4. I don't know if Kim and I can keep the relationship together once she moves away for her job.

Another strategy for increasing understanding of another's thoughts and feelings is to use **minimal encouragers.** These are communication that gently invites another person to elaborate by expressing interest in hearing more. Examples of minimal encouragers are "Tell me more," "Really?" "Go on," "I'm with you," "Then what happened?" "Yeah?" and "I see." We can also use nonverbal minimal encouragers such as a raised eyebrow to show involvement, a head motion to indicate we understand, or widened eyes to indicate we're fascinated. Minimal encouragers indicate we are listening, following, and interested. They encourage others to keep talking so that we can more fully understand what they mean. Keep in mind that these are *minimal* encouragers. They should not interrupt or take the talk stage away from another. Instead, effective minimal encouragers are very brief interjections that prompt, rather than interfere with, the flow of another's talk.

A third way to enhance understanding of what another feels or needs is to ask questions. Sometimes it's helpful to ask questions that yield insight into what a speaker thinks or feels. For instance, we might ask "How do you feel about that?" "What do you plan to do?" or "How are you working this through?" Another reason we ask questions is to find out what a person wants from us. Sometimes it isn't clear whether someone wants advice, a shoulder to cry on, or a safe place to vent feelings. If we can't figure out what's wanted, we can ask the other person. "Are you looking for advice or a sounding board?" "Do you want to talk about how to handle the situation or just air the issues?" Asking direct questions signals that we want to help and allows others to tell us how we can best do that.

Express Support   Once understanding of another's meanings and perspective is shown, relational-level listeners should focus on communicating support. This doesn't necessarily require us to agree with the other person's perspective or feelings. It does call on us to communicate support for the person, if not for the content of the person's message. To illustrate how we can support a person even if we don't agree with his or her position, consider the following dialogue between two women.

Janice: I just don't see how I can have a baby right now.

Elaine: Tell me more about what you're feeling.

Janice: I feel trapped. I mean, I've still got two years of school, and we're not ready to get married.

Elaine: So?

Janice: (silence, then) I hate the thought, but I guess I'll have to get an abortion.

Elaine: Sounds as if you don't feel very comfortable with that choice.

Janice: I'm not, but it seems like the only answer.

Elaine: What other options have you considered?

Janice: Well, I guess I really don't know of any other answers. Do you?

Elaine: You could have the baby and place it for adoption or maybe even work out an arrangement with a couple that can't have a baby of their own.

Janice: No, I really can't afford to give up nine months of my life right now. Besides, I don't think I could give away a baby after carrying it all that time. Don't you think I should have an abortion?

Elaine: Gee, I don't want to tell you what to do. I'm not comfortable endorsing abortion for myself, but you may not feel the same way.

Janice: I don't endorse abortion either, but I don't feel like I have a realistic choice.

© Mark Antman/The Image Works

There is no such thing as a worthless conversation, providing you know what to listen for.
JAMES NATHAN MILLER

Elaine: I respect you for the way you're going about making this choice. It's a good idea to talk with people like we're doing now.

Janice: I just hate the idea of having an abortion.

Elaine: It sounds like you're not very sure that's the right answer for you, either. Let's talk a little more. How do you think you'd feel if you did have an abortion?

This dialogue illustrates several principles of effective relational listening. First, notice that Elaine's first two comments are minimal encouragers, designed to nudge Janice to elaborate her perspective. Elaine's third response is a paraphrase to make sure she understands what Janice is feeling. Elaine then tries suggesting alternatives to abortion, but when Janice rejects those Elaine doesn't push her. Elaine makes her own position on abortion clear—she doesn't condone it—but she separates her personal stance from her respect for Janice and the way Janice has thought through the decision.

Particularly important in this conversation is Elaine's effort to collaborate with Janice in problem solving. By showing that she's willing to talk further and that she wants to help Janice work out the problem, Elaine acts as an active listener and a committed friend. Elaine's listening style allows Janice to talk through a very tough issue without Elaine imposing her own judgments. Sometimes it's difficult to listen openly and nonjudgmentally, particularly if we don't agree with the person speaking. However, if your goal is to support another person, then sensitive, responsive involvement including collaboration, if appropriate, is an ideal listening style.

SHERYL

I think the greatest gift my mother ever gave me was when I told her I was going to marry Bruce. He isn't Jewish, and nobody in my family has ever married out of the faith before. I could tell my mother was disappointed, and she didn't try to hide that. She asked me if I understood how that would complicate things like family relations and rearing kids. We talked for a while, and she realized I had thought through what it means to marry out of the faith. Then she sighed and said she had hoped I would find a nice Jewish man. But then she said she supported me whatever I did, and Bruce was welcome in our family. She told me she'd raised me to think for myself and that's what I was doing. I just felt so loved and accepted by how she acted.

Guidelines for Effective Listening

To develop pragmatic strategies for effectiveness, let's summarize what we've learned about listening. Three guidelines integrate and extend information already covered.

Be Mindful

By now you've read this suggestion many times. Because it is so central to effective listening, however, it bears repeated mention. Mindfulness is a choice to be wholly present in an experience. It requires that we put aside preoccupations and preconceptions in order to attend fully to what is happening in the moment. Mindful listening is a process of being totally with another person in communication. It is one of the highest compliments we can pay to others because it conveys the relational-level meaning that they matter to us. Being mindful is a choice, not a knack or a natural aptitude. It is a matter of discipline and commitment. We have to discipline our tendencies to judge others, dominate the talk stage, and let our minds wander away from what another is saying. Mindfulness also requires commitment to another person and the integrity of the interpersonal communication process. Being mindful is the first and most important principle of effective listening.

Adapt Listening Appropriately

Like all communication activities, listening varies according to goals, situations, and individuals. What we've discussed in this chapter makes it clear that there is no one best way to listen. What's effective depends on our purpose for listening, the context in which we are listening, and the needs and circumstances of the other person.

The purpose for listening is a primary influence on what skills are appropriate. When we listen for pleasure, we simply need to be mindful and minimize distractions so that we derive as much enjoyment as possible from listening. When we listen for information, a critical attitude, evaluation of material, and a focus on the content level of meaning are desirable listening behaviors. Yet, when we engage in relational listening, very different skills are needed. We want to communicate openness and caring, and the relational-level meaning is more important than the content-level meaning. Thus, we need to adapt our listening styles and attitudes to different goals.

Effective listening is also adapted to individuals. Some people need considerable prompting and encouraging to express themselves, while others need only for us to be silent and attentive. Paraphrasing helps some individuals clarify what they think or feel, whereas others don't need that kind of assistance. Because people respond to different kinds of listening, we need to be skillful in using a variety of listening behaviors and to know when each is appropriate. You may recall that in Chapter 1 we identified ability to employ a range of skills and knowledge of when each is called for as two of the foundations of effective interpersonal communication.

Although fully interpersonal communication requires us to interact with others as unique individuals, there are some generalizations that can guide our choices of how to listen. We've noted, for instance, that men and women have generally different listening styles. As a rule, women provide a good deal of vocal and visual response to speakers to indicate that they are interested and following. Men generally make fewer listening noises, providing less overt feedback on their involvement and their feelings about what is being said. Because our listening styles reflect the rules we learned in our communication cultures, they also reflect our expectations of how others should listen to us. Knowing this, we might remind ourselves to give more overt responses when listening to women than when listening to men. Conversely, if we have feminine listening inclinations, we might want to curb some of our responsiveness. In masculine communication cultures, nodding and saying "yes" or "um hmm" are interpreted to mean agreement, not just involvement, so a feminine listening style can be misinterpreted by a masculine speaker. Of course, there are exceptions to these generalizations. Some women don't provide a great deal of feedback, and some men do. Thus, our best bet is to treat generalizations as hypotheses, not truths. This allows us to act on the basis of what is generally appropriate, but at the same time to stay open to the possibility that we may need to revise our behaviors in particular cases.

Listen Actively

We've seen that effective listening is an active process that requires substantial effort. When we realize all that's involved in listening, we appreciate how active an effort it is. Hearing is a physiological process that is passive; we don't have to do anything but be in the vicinity of sound waves to hear. Listening, however, is a highly active process. To do it effectively, we have to be willing to focus our minds, organize and interpret others' ideas and feelings, generate responses that signal our interest and that enhance both content and relational levels of meaning, and retain what we have learned in the process of listening. In some situations, we also become active partners by listening collaboratively and engaging in problem solving. Doing all of this is hard work! Recognizing that genuine listening is an active process prepares us to invest the amount of effort required to do it effectively.

SUMMARY

Zeno of Citium was an ancient philosopher who once remarked that "we have been given two ears and but a single mouth, in order that we may hear more and talk less." Thousands of years later, there is still wisdom in that comment. Listening is a major and vital part of communication, yet too often we don't consider it as important as talking. In this chapter, we've explored the complex and demanding process of listening.

We began by distinguishing hearing and listening. Hearing is a straightforward physiological process that doesn't require effort on our part. Listening, in contrast, is a complicated process involving hearing, attending, selecting and organizing, interpreting, responding, and remembering. Doing it well requires commitment and skill.

To understand what interferes with effective listening, we discussed both hindrances in situations and messages and obstacles in ourselves. Listening is complicated by message overload, complexity of material, and external noise in communication contexts. In addition, listening can be hampered by our preoccupations and prejudgments, by a lack of effort, and by our not recognizing differences in listening styles. These obstacles to careful listening give rise to various types of ineffective listening, including pseudolistening, monopolizing, selective listening, defensive listening, ambushing, and literal listening. Each of these forms of inept listening signals that we aren't fully present in interaction.

We also discussed different purposes for listening and identified the skills and attitudes that advance each. Listening for pleasure is supported by mindfulness and efforts to minimize distractions and noise. Informational listening requires us to adopt a mindful attitude and to think critically, organize and evaluate information, clarify understanding through asking questions, and develop aids for retention of complex material. Relational listening also requires mindfulness, but it calls for different listening skills. Suspending judgment, paraphrasing, giving minimal encouragers, and expressing support enhance the effectiveness of relational listening.

The ideas we've discussed yield three guidelines for improving listening effectiveness. First, we need to be mindful—to be fully present in communication and focused on what is happening between us and others. Second, we should adapt our listening skills and style to accommodate differences in listening purpose and individuals. Finally, a summary suggestion is to remember that listening is an active process and to be prepared to invest energy and effort in doing it skillfully. Because listening is important in all communication contexts, we will revisit some of the ideas covered here as we discuss dynamics in relationships in the next three chapters.

KEY TERMS

Hearing	Selective listening
Listening	Defensive listening
Mindfulness	Ambushing
Responding	Literal listening
Remembering	Paraphrasing
Pseudolistening	Minimal encouragers
Monopolizing	

PART TWO

Weaving Communication into Relationships

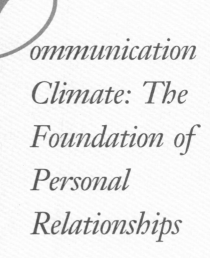

CHAPTER 7

Communication Climate: The Foundation of Personal Relationships

*D*o you feel foggy-headed or down when the sky is overcast and upbeat when it's sunny? Does your mood ever shift as the weather changes? Most of us do respond to the climate. We feel more or less positive depending on the conditions around us. In much the same way that we react to physical weather, we also respond to the climates in personal relationships.

In the wallhanging shown on the preceding page, the clouds and sky establish the feeling of the scene. In the same way, **interpersonal climate** is the overall feeling, or emotional mood, of a relationship. Interpersonal climate is not something we can see or measure objectively, and it's not made up of things people do together. Instead, climate is the dominant feeling between people who are involved with each other. Two couples might live in the same apartment complex, have similar jobs, and distribute responsibilities for cleaning, cooking, and shopping in the same way. Yet in one of the relationships there is constant tension, marked by short and sometimes cutting remarks and frequent flares of temper. In the other relationship the pervasive feeling is comfortable and friendly. Although the two couples do similar things, the climates of their relationships differ dramatically.

Because interpersonal climate concerns the overall feeling between people, it is the foundation of personal relationships. Both friendships and romantic relationships develop climates that reflect and establish emotional moods. In this chapter, we focus on climate as a cornerstone of satisfying interpersonal relationships. We'll begin by discussing the elements of healthy interpersonal relationships. Next, we'll examine two general types of climates and the kinds of communication that foster each. The third section of the chapter identifies guidelines for creating and sustaining healthy interpersonal climates.

This chapter inaugurates a focus on personal relationships, which will occupy our attention for the final four chapters in this book. Impressive research by communication scholars in recent years provides a wealth of information about communication skills and perspectives that influence the quality of close relationships. Drawing on that research, we'll extend our discussion of climate with Chapter 8, which focuses on conflict as a natural process in close relationships. In that chapter, we will learn that a healthy relationship climate and good communication skills can help us realize the constructive potential of conflict. The final two chapters explore links between ideas and skills discussed in the first eight chapters to communication between friends and romantic partners.

Elements of Satisfying Personal Relationships

Personal relationships are basic to our lives. As we saw in Chapter 1, we relate to others to fulfill human needs for survival, safety, belonging, esteem, self-actualization, and diversity. People who lack friends are more depressed and have lower self-esteem than people who have satisfying friendships (Hojat, 1982; Jones & Moore, 1989). Most recently, communication scholars report that some lonely people are locked into a "negativity cycle" in which they focus on negative aspects of interaction and discount positive aspects. This leads them to feel more pessimistic about their relationships and themselves, which, in turn, heightens their awareness of negative features (Duck, Pond, & Leatham, 1994). The converse is also true: When we are involved in satisfying relationships, we feel more positive about ourselves and life. Researchers have shown that people who fall in love see the world through "rose-colored glasses" (Hendrick & Hendrick, 1988).

© Catherine Karnow/Woodfin Camp & Associates, Inc.

NAVITA

The worst time in my whole life was my first semester here. I felt so lonely being away from my family and all my friends at home. Back there we were really close, and there was always somebody to be with and talk to, but I didn't know anybody on this campus. I felt all alone and like nobody cared about me. I became depressed and almost left school, but then I started seeing a guy and I made a couple of friends. Everything got better once I had some people to talk to and be with.

Many people feel as Navita does. Research indicates that loneliness during the first year of college depends more on whether a person has friends than on good family ties and romantic relationships (Cutrona, 1982). It seems that we look primarily to friends to satisfy our needs for belonging and acceptance.

Because personal relationships make such a difference in our lives, we need to understand what makes relationships healthy and gratifying. In a book on personal relationships, I reviewed over 700 articles and books on intimacy (Wood, 1995c). I concluded that four features characterize satisfying close relationships: investment, commitment, trust, and comfort with relational dialectics. Members of different cultures may have distinct rules for what each feature is and how it is communicated. For example, in general, Westerners rely heavily on verbal disclosures to build trust, whereas most Asians are less verbally revealing and depend on actions to build trust. Caucasians tend to regard commitment as a tie between two people while Asians, Hispanics, and African Americans see commitment more as a broad tie that links families and communities (Gaines, 1995). Although people may experience and express these four features in diverse ways, they appear to be cornerstones of closeness for most humans. Taken together, these four features create a strong nucleus for a relationship and confirm the value of each partner.

© Bachmann/Photo Researchers, Inc.

Investments

Good relationships grow out of **investments**, which are what we put into relationships that we could not retrieve if the relationship were to end. Investments are not just ideas in our heads. Rather, they must be communicated through words and actions between partners. When we care about another person, we invest time, energy, thought, and feelings into interaction. In doing this, we invest *ourselves* in others. Investments are powerful because they are personal choices. Further, investments cannot be recovered, so the only way to make good on them is to stick with a relationship (Brehm, 1992). We can't get back the time, feelings, and energy we invest in a relationship. We cannot recover the history we have shared with another person. Thus, to leave is to suffer a loss of investments made.

Put It in Practice

YOUR INVESTMENTS IN RELATIONSHIPS

What have you invested in your closest friendship and romantic relationship?

1. How much time have you spent?
2. How many decisions have you made to accommodate your friend? Your romantic partner?
3. How much money have you spent?
4. How much is your history entwined with that of your friend? Your romantic partner?
5. How much trust have you given each intimate?
6. How much support have you given each intimate?
7. Do your partners' investments roughly equal yours?

Finally, explain what would be lost if these relationships ended. Could you recover your investments?

Perceived equality of partners' investments affects satisfaction with relationships. Researchers report that in the happiest dating and married couples, partners feel they invest equally (Fletcher, Fincham, Cramer, & Heron, 1987; Hecht, Marston, & Larkey, 1994). When we feel we are investing more than a partner, we tend to be dissatisfied and resentful. When it seems our partner is investing more than we are, we may feel guilty. Because imbalance of either sort is disconfirming, perceived inequity erodes satisfaction (Brehm, 1992). Not surprisingly, communication is affected by perceived inequity. Partners who feel they are investing unequally tend to communicate limited support to one another and to minimize major disclosures (Brehm, 1992).

SIBBY

I dated this one guy for a long time before I finally had to cut my losses. He said he loved me, but he wouldn't put anything in the relationship. I gave so much—always accommodating him, doing things for him, loving him, but there just wasn't any reciprocity. It was a one-way street with him, and I felt like he didn't value me very much at all.

Commitment

Closely related to investments is **commitment,** which is a decision to remain with a relationship. The hallmark of commitment is the assumption of a future. In committed relationships, partners assume they will continue together. Unlike passion or attraction, which exist in the present, commitment links partners to the future. Because partners in committed relationships view their connection as a given, they are unlikely to bail out during the inevitable rough times. Instead, they weather those, confident that they will stay together. Communication between committed partners reflects the assumed continuity of the relationship. Problems and tensions that inevitably arise aren't seen as reasons to end a relationship. Instead, partners try to work through their conflicts. We'll discuss ways to manage conflicts in detail in Chapter 8.

Whereas love is a feeling we can't necessarily control, commitment is a decision. It is a personal choice to maintain a relationship. Partners who make this choice strive for dual perspective and commit to listening and speaking effectively to one another. Aaron Beck (1988), a counselor, believes that the decision to commit injects responsibility into relationships. When partners make a commitment, they take responsibility for continuing to invest in and care for their bond. Without responsibility, relationships

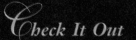

LOVE AND COMMITMENT: DIFFERENT MATTERS

To find out what holds a relationship together, Mary Lund studied 129 heterosexual college seniors. She measured their commitment and love for partners in February and in the summer following graduation. She found that the continuation of relationships depended more on commitment than love. Couples who had high levels of love but low commitment to a shared future were less likely to remain together than couples who were highly committed to a joint future. Thus, the *intention* to stay together is a more powerful glue than positive feelings between partners.

Lund's study also showed that commitment is more strongly linked to making investments than to perceptions that a relationship is rewarding or that love exists. Investments increase commitment because they are personal choices, while loving and being loved are not acts of will.

Summarizing her findings, Lund said that although love usually accompanies commitment, commitment and investments have more to do with whether a relationship lasts than do love and rewards.

Source: Lund, M. (1985). The development of investment and commitment scales for predicting continuity of personal relationships. *Journal of Social and Personal Relationships, 2,* 3–23

This is such a dumb time, Jack, to start talking about whether or not something is written in stone.

Keeping Up by William Hamilton is reprinted by permission of Chronicle Features, San Francisco, CA.

DIFFERENT MODES OF CLOSENESS

Research indicates that women generally disclose more frequently and more deeply than men. Until recently, this difference was interpreted to mean that men are less interested in or comfortable with intimacy. However, recent work suggests that the sexes may not differ in how much they value closeness, but they create it in different ways.

Feminine communication cultures emphasize using personal talk to create and sustain closeness. Thus, in general, women learn to disclose personal thoughts and feelings as a primary way of enhancing intimacy. This is called *closeness in dialogue.*

Because masculine communication cultures place less emphasis on personal talk, men typically don't regard intimate conversation and self-disclosure as a path to closeness. Instead, they usually learn to bond with others through doing things together. Their mode is called *closeness in the doing.*

The two ways of expressing and experiencing closeness are equally valid, and both should be respected.

Source: Wood, J. T., & Inman, C. C. (1993). In a different mode: Masculine styles of communicating closeness. *Journal of Applied Communication Research, 21,* 279–295.

are subject to the whims of feeling and fortune, which are hardly a stable basis for enduring intimacy.

Trust

A third cornerstone of healthy personal relationships is a high degree of **trust** between partners. Trust involves believing in another's reliability (he or she will do what is promised) and emotionally relying on another to care about and protect our welfare (Brehm, 1992). Individuals earn each other's trust by communicating honestly and by honoring each other's perspective. When we trust someone, we count on her or him to be loving and respectful. These feelings allow us to feel psychologically safe.

One reason that trust is so important to close friendships and romantic relationships is that it allows us to take risks with others. For intimacy to grow, we have to risk ourselves. We must be able to confide in others and trust them to care about us and our feelings. Trust develops as people do what they say they will and as they provide support and safety to each other.

Self-Disclosure One clear influence on trust is self-disclosure, which can both build and reflect trust between people. **Self-disclosure** is revealing personal information about ourselves that others are unlikely to discover in other ways. According to researchers who have studied communication between intimates, self-disclosure is a key gauge of closeness, at least among Westerners (Derlega & Berg, 1987; Hansen & Schuldt, 1984). Self-disclosure should take place gradually and with appropriate caution. It's unwise to tell anyone too much about ourselves too quickly, especially if revelations could be used against us. We begin by disclosing relatively superficial information ("I'm from a small town," "I love Mexican food," "I'm afraid of heights"). If a person responds with empathy to early and limited disclosures, we're likely to reveal progressively intimate information ("My father served time in prison," "I am lesbian," "I go through periods of real depression"). If these disclosures are also met with understanding and confidentiality, trust continues to grow.

In the early stages of relationship development, reciprocity of disclosures seems important. An individual is willing to keep disclosing only so long as the other person is also revealing personal information (Cunningham, Strassberg, & Haan, 1986). The need to match disclosures recedes in importance once trust is established. Partners in stable relationships don't feel the need to reciprocate disclosures immediately. Unlike beginning acquaintances, they have the time to reciprocate on a more leisurely schedule. Thus, disclosure between established intimates is more likely to be greeted with a response to what has been revealed than with an equivalent disclosure. Of course, there are exceptions to these general patterns. People vary in how much they want to self-disclose, so an absolute amount of disclosure is not a surefire measure of closeness. Also, people vary in their perceptions of the link between disclosure and intimacy, so we need to respect individual differences.

Although self-disclosing is important early in relationships, it is not a primary communication dynamic over the long haul. When we're first getting to know another, we have to reveal ourselves and learn about the other, so disclosures are necessary and desirable. In relationships that endure, however, disclosures make up very little of the total communication between partners. Although disclosure wanes over time, partners continue to reap the benefits of the trust and depth of personal knowledge created by early disclosures. Also, partners do continue to disclose new experiences and insights to one another; however, there is less disclosure as a relationship matures. Decreased frequency and depth of disclosures, other than explosions of negative feelings, are key signals of trouble in a relationship (Baxter, 1987). We are reluctant to entrust others with our secrets and personal emotions when intimacy is fading or gone.

CRAIG

I think what first clued me in that Shelby was losing interest was that she stopped telling me private stuff about herself. For the first couple of months we dated, she shared so much about her dreams, plans, and fears. The more she told me about herself and the more I told her, the closer I felt. But then she seemed to withdraw and not want to share her private thoughts. That was really the start of the end.

Comfort with Relational Dialectics

A final quality of healthy relationships is understanding and being comfortable with **relational dialectics.** These are opposing forces, or tensions, that are normal parts of all relationships. Leslie Baxter, a scholar of interpersonal communication, has identified three dialectics of relationships (Baxter, 1988, 1990, 1993; Baxter & Simon, 1993). We'll discuss the three to clarify how they operate as normal, productive processes in relational life.

Autonomy/Connection　All close friends and romantic partners experience tension between wanting to be autonomous, or individual, and wanting to be close, or connected. Because we want to be deeply linked to others, we seek intimacy and sharing. Friends and lovers want to spend time

© Lawrence Migdale/Stock, Boston

I love you,
Not only for what you are,
But for what I am
When I am with you.
ROY CROFT

with each other, have joint interests, and talk personally. At the same time, each of us needs a sense of independent identity. We want to know that our individuality is not swallowed up by relationships. We need our own space, so we seek distance even from our intimates.

Relationship counselors agree that the most central and continuous friction in most close relationships arises from the contradictory impulses for autonomy and connection (Beck, 1988; Scarf, 1987). When Robbie and I take vacations, we are intensely together for a week or more. We travel together, eat all meals together, and sleep and interact in confined spaces where privacy is limited.

Typically, when we return home after a vacation, we interact very little for several days. Having been immersed in togetherness, we both seek distance to reestablish our autonomous identities. Both autonomy and closeness are natural human needs. The challenge is to preserve individuality while also creating unity in a relationship.

KEN

Dialectics explains something that has really confused me. I've never understood how I could want so much to be with Ashley for a while and then feel suffocated and need to get away. I've worried that it means I don't love her anymore or there is something wrong between us. But now I see how both needs are normal and okay.

Novelty/Predictability   The second dialectic is the tension between wanting routine, or familiarity, and wanting novelty in a relationship. All of us like a certain amount of routine to provide security and predictability to our lives. For example, my friend Nancy and I long ago agreed to get together every Sunday for brunch and visiting. We count on that as a steady, habitual time to see each other. Yet too much routine becomes boring, so it's also natural to seek novel experiences. Every so often Nancy and I decide to explore a new restaurant or make a day trip just to introduce variety into our customary routine.

Openness/Closedness   The third dialectic is a tension between wanting open communication and needing a degree of privacy, even with intimates. With our closest partners, we want to share our inner selves and be open with no holds barred. Even so, we also desire a zone of privacy, and we want our partners to respect that. Some partners agree not to talk about certain topics, such as money or religion. Although they are open about other matters, these topics are respected as off-limits. It's also normal to be temporarily closed after we have revealed something highly personal.

Although intimate relationships are sometimes idealized as totally open and honest, in reality completely unbridled expressiveness would be intolerable (Baxter, 1993; Petronio, 1991). There is nothing wrong when we seek privacy; it doesn't mean a relationship is in trouble. It means only that we need both openness and closedness in our lives.

The three dialectics create ongoing tensions in healthy relationships. This is a problem only if partners don't understand that dialectics and the tension they generate are natural parts of relational life. If we think it's wrong to be closed at times or not to want togetherness always, then we'll misinterpret our feelings and what they mean. Once we realize that dialectics are normal in all relationships, we can accept and grow from the tensions they generate.

Dialectics do not operate in isolation. Instead, they interact and affect one another within the overall system of a relationship. Thus, friends who are highly open are also likely to be very connected, whereas a more closed couple tends to favor greater autonomy (Aries, 1987). Relational dialectics also interact with other facets of interpersonal communication. For instance, partners who prefer a high amount of individuality tend to create more individual spaces and fewer common ones in their homes than do partners who favor greater connection (Fitzpatrick, 1988; Fitzpatrick & Best, 1979). Frequent and in-depth disclosures are most likely in relationships that are highly open and connected. Like all aspects of interpersonal communication, relational dialectics operate systemically.

Responding to Dialectics   There is no single correct method of responding to relational dialectics. Baxter (1990) has identified four ways partners deal with the tension generated by opposing needs. One response, called neutralization, is to negotiate a balance between the two poles of a dialectic. This involves striking a compromise in which each need is met to an extent, but neither is fully satisfied. A couple that does this might have a fairly consistent equilibrium between the amount of novelty and the amount of routine in their relationship.

A second response is to give priority to one of the needs in a dialectic and neglect the other. For example, friends might focus on novelty and suppress their needs for ritual and routine. Some partners cycle between competing poles of dialectics, so that they favor each one alternately. A couple could be open and continuously together for a period and then be autonomous and closed for a time.

BEVERLY

My folks are so funny. They plod along in the same old rut for ages and ages, and my sister and I can't get them to do anything different. Mom won't try a new recipe for chicken because "we like ours like I always fix it." Dad won't try a new style of shirt because "that's not the kind of shirt I wear." Dynamite wouldn't blow them out of their ruts. But then all of a sudden they'll do a whole bunch of unusual things. Like once they went out to three movies in a day, and the next day they went for a picnic at the zoo. This kind of zaniness goes on for a while, then it's back to humdrum for months and months. I guess they get all of their novelty in occasional bursts.

A third way to manage dialectics is to let each dialectical need apply to certain spheres, issues, or times. For instance, friends might be open about many topics, but respect each other's privacy in one or two areas. A couple might have rigid daily schedules and patterns of socializing, but be very spontaneous on vacations. Many dual-career couples are autonomous about their work, relying little on each other for advice, although they are very connected about family, collaborating and being close in that area.

The final method of dealing with dialectics is called reframing. This is a complex and transformative strategy in which partners redefine contradictory needs as not in opposition. In other words, they reframe their perceptions by redefining what is happening. My colleagues and I found an example of this in a recent study of differences between intimate partners (Wood et al., 1994). Some partners transcended the opposition between autonomy and connection by defining differences and disagreements as enhancing intimacy. Another example of reframing is deciding that novelty and predictability are not opposites, but allies. A couple I know regards routine and spontaneity as supporting each other. Their routines make novelty interesting, and novelty makes routines comforting.

Put It in Practice

APPLYING RELATIONAL DIALECTICS

How do relational dialectics operate in your life? To find out, select three of your relationships. One should be a very close friendship, one a current or past romantic relationship, and one a friendly but not really intimate relationship. For each relationship answer these questions:

1. How are needs for autonomy expressed and satisfied?
2. How are needs for connection expressed and met?
3. How are needs for novelty expressed and met?
4. How are needs for predictability expressed and met?
5. How are needs for openness expressed and satisfied?
6. How are needs for closedness expressed and met?

Now think about how you manage the tension between opposing needs in each dialectic. When do you rely on separation, neutralization, segmentation, and reframing? How satisfied are you with your responses? Experiment with new ways of managing dialectical tensions.

Dialectics can be effectively managed in a variety of ways. However, research indicates that, in general, the least effective and least satisfying response is to honor one need and repress the opposing one (Baxter, 1990). Squelching any natural human impulse diminishes us. The challenge is to find ways to accommodate all of our needs, even when they seem contradictory.

Healthy relationships exist when partners create a climate in which each feels valued and comfortable with the other. This tends to happen when partners make commitments and investments, build trust, and effectively manage dialectical tensions. Underlying all of the elements we've discussed is confirmation, which is at the heart of fulfilling interpersonal relationships. Because confirmation is so important to relationships, the next section of the chapter explores how communication influences confirming climates.

Confirming and Disconfirming Climates

The philosopher Martin Buber (1957) believed that each of us needs confirmation to be healthy and to grow. Buber also emphasized that full humanness can develop only when people confirm others and are confirmed by them. The essence of confirmation is valuing. We all want to feel we are valued, especially by our intimates. When others confirm us, we feel cherished and respected. When they disconfirm us, we feel discounted and less good about ourselves.

FIGURE 7.1 *Continuum of Interpersonal Climates*

Interpersonal climates exist on a continuum from confirming to disconfirming (Figure 7.1). Of course, few relationships are purely confirming or disconfirming. In reality, most fall in between the two end points of the continuum. In these, some communication is confirming while other messages are disconfirming, or communication cycles between being basically confirming and basically disconfirming.

Levels of Confirmation and Disconfirmation

Building on Buber's ideas, as well as those of psychiatrist R. D. Laing (1961), communication scholars have extended insight into confirming and disconfirming climates (Cissna & Sieburg, 1986). They have identified specific kinds of communication that confirm or disconfirm others on three levels. The most basic form of confirmation is recognizing that another person exists. We do this with nonverbal behaviors (a smile, hug, or touch) and verbal communication ("Hello," "Good to meet you," "I see you're home"). We disconfirm others at a fundamental level when we don't acknowledge their existence. For example, you might not speak to or look at a person when you enter a room. Not responding to someone's question also disconfirms their presence. Parents who punish a child by refusing to speak to her or him disconfirm the child's existence. A person who uses "the silent treatment" disconfirms another's existence.

REGGIE

Any African American knows what it means to have your existence denied. The law may forbid segregation now, but it still exists. When I go to an upscale restaurant, sometimes people just look away. They ignore me, like I'm not there. I've even been ignored by waitstaff in restaurants. This is especially true in the south where a lot of whites still don't want us in their clubs and schools.

© Peter L. Chapman

Freedom . . . is characterized by a constantly renewed obligation to remake the Self.

JEAN-PAUL SARTRE

A second and more positive level of confirmation is acknowledgment of what another feels, thinks, or says. Nonverbally we acknowledge others by nodding our heads or by making strong eye contact to indicate we are listening. Verbal acknowledgments are direct responses to others' communication. If a friend says, "I'm really worried that I blew the LSAT exam," you could acknowledge that by responding, "So you're scared that you didn't test well on it, huh?" This paraphrasing response acknowledges both the thoughts and the feelings of the other person.

We disconfirm others when we don't acknowledge their feelings or thoughts. For instance, if you respond to your friend's statement about blowing the LSAT by saying, "Want to go out and shoot some darts tonight?" that would be an irrelevant response that ignores the friend's comment. It also disconfirms another when we deny their feelings and communication: "You did fine on the LSAT."

LORI

You'd be amazed by how often people refuse to acknowledge what differently abled people say. A hundred times I've been walking across campus and someone has come up and offered to guide me. I tell them I know the way and don't need help, and they still put an arm under my elbow to guide me. I may be blind, but there's nothing wrong with my mind. I know if I need help. Why won't others acknowledge that?

Lori makes an important point. We shouldn't assume we know what others will perceive as confirming. You may recall that in Chapter 4 we emphasized that we shouldn't presume to speak for others. It is fundamentally disconfirming to be made voiceless when others ignore what we say and think. Especially when we deal with people who differ from us in im-

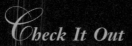
GUIDELINES FOR COMMUNICATING WITH PERSONS WITH DISABILITIES

1. When talking with someone who has a disability, speak directly to the person, not to a companion or interpreter.

2. When introduced to a person with a disability, offer to shake hands. People who have limited hand use or who have artificial limbs can usually shake.

3. When meeting a person with a visual impairment, identify yourself and anyone who is with you. If a person with a visual impairment is part of a group, preface comments to him or her with a name.

4. You may offer assistance, but don't provide it unless your offer is accepted. Then ask the person how you can best assist (ask for instructions).

5. Treat adults as adults. Don't patronize people in wheelchairs by patting them on the shoulder or head; don't use childish language when speaking to individuals who have no mental disability.

6. Respect the personal space of persons with disabilities. It is rude to lean on a wheelchair, since that is part of an individual's personal territory.

7. Listen mindfully when talking with someone who has difficulty speaking. Don't interrupt or supply words to others. Just be patient and let them finish. Don't pretend to understand if you don't. Instead, explain what you didn't understand and ask the person to respond.

8. When you talk with persons who use a wheelchair or crutches, try to position yourself at their eye level and in front of them to allow good eye contact.

9. It is appropriate to wave your hand or tap the shoulder of persons with hearing impairments as a way to get their attention. Look directly at the person and speak clearly, slowly, and expressively. Face those who lip-read, place yourself in a good light source, and keep hands, cigarettes, and gum away from your mouth.

10. Relax. Don't be afraid to use common expressions such as "See you later" to someone with a visual impairment or "Did you hear the news?" to someone with a hearing difficulty. They're unlikely to be offended and may turn the irony into a joke.

Source: Adapted from AXIS Center for Public Awareness of People with Disabilities, 4550 Indianola Avenue, Columbus, OH 43214.

portant ways, we should take time to learn what they perceive as confirming and disconfirming.

The final level of confirmation is endorsement. Endorsement involves accepting another's feelings or thoughts as valid. In the foregoing example, you could endorse by saying, "It's natural to be worried about the LSAT when you have so much riding on it." We disconfirm others when we don't accept their thoughts and feelings. If you respond to the friend by saying, "That's crazy" or "How can you worry about the LSAT when people are starving in Rwanda?" you reject the validity of the expressed feelings.

Table 7.1 illustrates the different levels on which confirmation and disconfirmation occur. The most essential confirmation we can give is to recognize another exists. Conversely, the most basic kind of disconfirmation is to deny someone exists. When we don't speak to others or when we look away when they approach us, we disconfirm their existence. We say, "You

TABLE 7.1 Confirming and Disconfirming Messages

	Confirming Messages	Disconfirming Messages
Recognition	You exist.	You don't exist.
	"Hello."	Silence
Acknowledgment	You matter to me.	You don't matter.
	We have a relationship.	We are not a team.
	"I'm sorry you're hurt."	"You'll get over it."
Endorsement	What you think is true.	You are wrong.
	What you feel is okay.	You shouldn't feel what you do.
	"I feel the same way."	"Your feeling doesn't make sense."

aren't there." On the second level, we confirm others by acknowledging their ideas and feelings, which carries the relational-level meaning that they matter to us. In essence, we say "I am paying attention because your feelings and ideas matter to me." We disconfirm others on this level when we communicate that they don't matter to us, that we don't care what they feel or think. The highest form of confirmation is acceptance of others and what they communicate. We feel validated when others accept us as we are and accept what we think and feel. Disconfirmation is not mere disagreement. Disagreements, after all, can be productive and healthy, and they imply that people matter enough to each other to argue. What is disconfirming is to be told that we or our ideas are crazy, wrong, stupid, or deviant.

WAYNE

I've gotten a lot of disconfirmation since I came out. When I told my parents I was gay, Mom said, "No, you're not." I told her I was, and she and Dad both said I was just confused, but I wasn't gay. They refuse to acknowledge I'm gay, which means they reject who I am. My older brother isn't any better. His view is that I'm sinful and headed for hell. Now what could be more disconfirming than that?

When we understand that confirmation is basic for all of us and that it is given or withheld on different levels, we gain insight into relationships. If you think about what we've discussed, you'll probably find that the relationships in which you feel most valued and comfortable are ones with a high degree of confirmation.

Put It in Practice

ANALYZE YOUR RELATIONSHIPS

Think about two relationships in your life. One should be a relationship in which you feel good about yourself and safe in the connection. The second relationship should be one in which you feel disregarded or not valued. Identify instances of each level of confirmation in the satisfying relationship, and instances of each level of disconfirmation in the unpleasant one. Recognizing confirming and disconfirming communication should give you insight into why these relationships are so different.

Confirming and disconfirming messages are important influences on the climate of personal relationships. In addition, other kinds of communication contribute to the overall feeling of a relationship. We'll now consider specific forms of communication that shape the interpersonal atmosphere between friends and romantic partners.

Defensive and Supportive Climates

Communication researcher Jack Gibb (1961, 1964, 1970) studied the relationship between communication and interpersonal climates. He began by noting that in some relationships we feel defensive and on guard, while in others we feel safe and supported. To understand how communication contributes to these two interpersonal climates, Gibb identified six types of communication that promote defensive climates and six that foster supportive ones.

"Dennis, I would like to talk to you for a minute—off line."
Drawing by Mort Gerberg. © 1994 The New Yorker Magazine, Inc.

Evaluation Versus Description   We tend to become defensive when we feel that others are evaluating us. Few of us feel what Gibb called "psychologically safe" when we are the targets of judgments. Other communication researchers report that evaluative communication evokes defensiveness (Eadie, 1982; Stephenson & D'Angelo, 1973). It's not surprising that Wayne in the last commentary felt judged by his family when he told them he was gay. His parents and brother made evaluations—very negative ones of him and of gayness. As we noted in Chapter 6, even positive evaluations can sometimes make us defensive, since they carry the relational meaning that another person feels entitled to judge us. Here are several examples of evaluative statements: "You have no discipline," "It's dumb to feel that way," "You shouldn't have done that," "You did the right thing," "That's a stupid idea."

Descriptive communication doesn't evaluate others or what they think and feel. Instead, it describes behaviors without passing judgment. I-language, which we learned about in Chapter 4, describes what the person speaking feels or thinks, but it doesn't evaluate another (you-language does evaluate). For example, "I wish you hadn't done that" describes your feelings, whereas "You shouldn't have done that" evaluates another's behavior. Descriptive language may also refer to another, but it does so by describing, not evaluating, the other's behavior. For example: "You seem to be sleeping more lately" (versus "You're sleeping too much"). "You've lost

RELATIONSHIP TIP # 42: TRY TO SEE THE BEAUTY IN LIFE'S LITTLE IRONIES.

SELF-CENTERED? MOI? HOW DO YOU THINK THAT MAKES ME FEEL?

Reprinted by permission of Jennifer Berman.

your temper three times today" (versus "Quit flying off the handle"). "You are running late" (versus "You shouldn't have kept me waiting").

Put It in Practice

USING DESCRIPTIVE LANGUAGE

To develop skill in supportive communication, translate the following evaluative statements into descriptive ones.

Example: Evaluative:

This report is poorly done.

Descriptive:

This report doesn't include background information.

Evaluative

You're lazy.

I hate the way you dominate conversations with me.

Stop obsessing about the problem.

You're too involved.

Certainty Versus Provisionalism Certainty language is absolute and often dogmatic. It suggests there is one and only one answer, valid point of view, or reasonable course of action. Because communication laced with certainty proclaims an absolutely correct position, it slams the door on further discussion. There's no point in talking with people whose minds are made up and who demean any point of view other than theirs. Sometimes certainty is expressed by restating a position over and over, instead of responding to alternate ideas from others (Alexander, 1979).

One form of certainty communication is **ethnocentrism,** which is the assumption that our culture and its norms are *the* only right ones. For instance, someone who says "It is just plain rude to call out during a sermon" doesn't understand the meaning of the call-response pattern in African culture. The speaker instead assumes that Western Anglo communication styles are the only correct ones. Dogmatically asserting "It's disrespectful to be late" reveals a lack of awareness of cultures that are less obsessed with speed and efficiency than the United States. Additional examples of certainty statements are "This is the only idea that makes sense," "My mind can't be changed because I'm right," and "Only a fool would vote for that person."

MONIKA

My father is a classic case of closed-mindedness. He has his ideas and every-thing else is crazy. I told him I was majoring in communication studies, and he hit the roof. He said there was no future in learning to write speeches, and he told me I should go into business so that I could get a good job. He never even asked me what communication studies is. If he had, I would have told him it's a lot more than speech writing. He starts off sure that he knows everything about whatever is being discussed. He has no interest in other points of view or learning something new. He just locks his mind and throws away the key. We've all learned just to keep our ideas to ourselves around him—there's no communication.

An alternative to certainty is provisionalism, which communicates openness to other points of view. When we speak provisionally, or tenta-tively, we suggest we have a point of view, yet our minds aren't sealed. We signal we're willing to consider alternative positions, and this encourages others to voice their ideas. Provisional communication includes statements such as "The way I tend to see the issue is . . . ," "One way to look at this is . . . ," and "Probably what I would do in that situation is . . ." Notice how each of these comments signals that the speaker realizes there could be other positions that are also reasonable. Tentativeness signals an open mind, which is why it invites continued communication.

Strategy Versus Spontaneity   Most of us feel on guard when we think others are manipulating us or being less than up-front about what's on their minds. Defensiveness is a natural response to feeling that others are using strategies in an effort to control us. Strategic communication doesn't allow openness between people, because one person is keeping something from another (Eadie, 1982). An example of strategic communication is this: "Would you do something for me if I told you it really matters?" If the speaker doesn't tell us what we're expected to do, it feels like a setup.

We're also likely to feel that another is trying to manipulate us with a comment such as "Remember when I helped you with your math last term and when I did your chores last week because you were busy?" With a pre-amble like that, we know a trap of some sort is being set. We also get de-fensive when we suspect others of using openness to manipulate how we feel about them. For instance, people who disclose intimate personal infor-mation early in a relationship may be trying to win our trust and to trick us into revealing details of our own personal life. Nonverbal behaviors may also convey strategy, as when a person pauses a long time before answering or refuses to look at us when he or she speaks. A sense of deception pol-lutes the communication climate.

MAJA

A guy I dated last year was a real con artist, but it took me a while to figure that out. He would look me straight in the eye and tell me he really felt he could trust me. Then he'd say he was going to tell me something he'd never told anyone else in his life, and he'd tell me about fights with his father or how he didn't make the soccer team in high school. The stuff wasn't really that personal, but the way he said it made it seem that way. So I found my-self telling him a lot more than I usually disclose and a lot more than I should have. He started using some of the information against me, which was when I started getting wise to him. Later on, I found out he ran through the same song and dance with every girl he dated. It was quite an act!

Spontaneity is the counterpoint to strategy. Spontaneous communication feels open, honest, and unpremeditated. "I really need your help with this computer glitch" is a more spontaneous comment than "Would you do something for me if I told you it really matters?" Likewise, it is more spontaneous to ask for a favor in a straightforward way ("Would you help me?") than to preface a request with a recitation of all we've done for someone else. Whereas strategic communication comes across as contrived and devious, spontaneous interaction feels authentic and natural.

Control Versus Problem Orientation   Controlling communication is also likely to trigger defensiveness. Similar to strategies, controlling communication more overtly attempts to manipulate others. A common in-stance of controlling communication is when a person insists her or his solution or preference should prevail. Whether the issue is trivial (what movie to see) or serious (where to locate after college), controllers try to impose their point of view on others. This disconfirms and disrespects others.

Defensiveness arises because the relational meaning is that the person exerting control thinks she or he has greater power, rights, or intelligence than others. It's disconfirming to be told our opinions are wrong, our pref-erences don't matter, or we aren't smart enough to have good ideas. Con-trolling communication is particularly objectionable when it combines with strategies. For example, a husband who earns a higher salary might say to his wife, "Well, I like the Honda more than the Ford you want, and it's my money that's going to pay for it." The speaker not only pushes his prefer-ence, but also tells his wife that he has more power than she does because he makes more money.

Problem-oriented communication is less likely than control to gener-ate defensiveness. Rather than imposing a preference, problem-oriented communication focuses on finding answers that satisfy everyone. The goal is to come up with a solution that all parties find acceptable. Here's an ex-ample of problem-oriented communication: "It seems that we have really different ideas about how to spend our vacation. Let's talk through what each of us wants and see if there's a way for both of us to have a good vacation." Notice how this statement invites collaboration and emphasizes the goal of meeting both people's needs. According to communication researchers, problem-oriented behaviors tend to reduce conflict and keep lines of communication open (Alexander, 1979; Civickly, Pace, & Krause, 1977). One of the strengths of focusing on problems is that the relational level of meaning emphasizes the importance of the relationship between communicators. In contrast, controlling behaviors aim for one person to triumph over the other, an outcome that undercuts interpersonal harmony.

Neutrality Versus Empathy   Gibb's (1961, 1964, 1970) observations of group interaction revealed that people tend to become defensive when others act in a neutral, or detached, manner. It's easy to understand why we might feel uneasy with people who seem distant and removed, especially if we are talking about personal matters. Research on interview climates indicates that defensiveness arises when an interviewer appears withdrawn and distant (Civickly et al., 1977). Neutral communication implies a lack of regard and caring for others. Consequently, it disconfirms their worth.

© Steven Peters/Tony Stone Images, Inc.

In contrast to neutrality, expressed empathy confirms the worth of others and our concern for their thoughts and feelings. Empathic communication is illustrated by these examples: "I can understand why you feel that way," "It sounds like you really feel uncomfortable with your job," "You seem to feel very secure in the relationship." Gibb stressed that empathy doesn't necessarily mean agreement; instead, it conveys acceptance of other people and recognition of their perspectives. Especially when we don't agree with others, it's important to communicate that we respect them as persons. Doing so fosters a supportive communication climate, even if differences exist.

Superiority Versus Equality   The final pair of behaviors affecting climate concerns the relationship between people that is communicated at the relational level of meaning. We feel understandably on guard when talking with people who act as if they are better than we are. Obviously, this disconfirms our worth by making us feel inadequate in their eyes. Consider several messages that convey superiority: "I know a lot more about this than you," "You just don't have my experience," "Is this the best you could do?" "You really should go to my hairdresser." Each of these messages clearly says, "You aren't as good (smart, savvy, competent, attractive) as I am." Predictably, the result is that we protect our self-esteem by defensively shutting out the people and messages that belittle us.

We feel more relaxed and comfortable when communicating with people who treat us as equals. At the relational level of meaning, expressed equality communicates respect and equivalent status between people. This promotes an open, unguarded climate in which interaction flows freely. Communicating equality has less to do with actual skills and abilities, which may differ between people, than with interpersonal attitudes. We can have outstanding experience or ability in certain areas and still show regard for others and what they have to contribute to interaction. Creating a climate of equality allows everyone to be involved without fear of being judged inadequate.

Put It in Practice

ASSESSING COMMUNICATION CLIMATE

Use the behaviors we've discussed as a checklist for assessing communication climates. The next time you feel defensive, ask whether others are communicating superiority, control, strategy, certainty, neutrality, or evaluation. Chances are one or more of these are present in communication.

For a communication climate you find supportive and open, check to see whether the following behaviors are present: spontaneity, equality, provisionalism, problem orientation, empathy, and description.

To improve defensive climates, try modeling supportive communication. Resist the normal tendencies to respond defensively when a climate feels disconfirming. Instead, focus on being empathic, descriptive, and spontaneous; showing equality and tentativeness; and solving problems.

We've seen that confirmation, which may include recognizing, acknowledging, and endorsing others, is the basis of healthy communication climates. Our discussion of defensive and supportive forms of communication enlightens us about the specific behaviors that tend to make us feel confirmed or disconfirmed. Now that we understand how communication creates interpersonal climates, we're ready to consider guidelines for communicating to create healthy, positive climates for your relationships.

Guidelines for Creating and Sustaining Healthy Climates

We've seen that communication plays a vital role in creating the climate of relationships. To translate what we've learned into pragmatic information, we'll discuss five guidelines for building and sustaining healthy climates.

Actively Use Communication to Shape Climates

The first principle is to use what you've learned in this chapter to enhance climates in your relationships. Now that you know what generates defensive and supportive climates, you can monitor your communication to make sure it contributes to open, positive interaction. You can identify and stifle disconfirming patterns of talk such as evaluation and superiority. In addition, you can actively work to use supportive communication such as problem orientation and tentativeness.

Active management of communication climate also involves accepting and growing from the tension generated by relational dialectics. Although friction between contradictory needs can naturally make us uncomfortable, we should recognize its constructive potential. Communication scholars who have studied dialectics point out that they generate growth and change in relationships (Baxter, 1990, 1993; Wood et al., 1994).

The discomfort of tension pushes us to transform our relationships by changing the dynamics in them. When a couple feels bored, they are motivated to inject novelty into their relationship; when there is too much innovation, they crave rituals and find ways to increase predictability. Our growth as individuals and as partners in relationships depends on honoring our needs for both autonomy and connection, both novelty and routine, and both openness and closedness. When any of these needs is not met, we experience tension that leads to change. Thus, the friction of dialectics keeps us aware of our multiple needs and the importance of fulfilling each of them.

Accept and Confirm Others

Throughout this chapter, we've seen that confirmation is a cornerstone of healthy climates and fulfilling relationships. Although we can understand how important confirmation is, it isn't always easy to give it. Sometimes we disagree with others or don't like certain things they do. Being honest with others is important, since it enhances trust between people. Communication research indicates that, in fact, people expect real friends to be sources of honest feedback, even if it isn't always pleasant to hear (Rawlins, 1994). This implies we should express honest misgivings about our friends' behaviors or other aspects of their identity. False friends tell us only what we want to hear. Deceit, no matter how well intentioned, diminishes personal growth and trust between people. We can offer honest feedback within a context that assures others we value and respect them, as Houston's commentary explains.

HOUSTON

The best thing my friend Jack ever did for me was to light into me about experimenting with drugs. He told me it was stupid to play with my mind and to risk my health just for kicks, and he kept at me until I tapered off.

© Rhoda Sidney/PhotoEdit

What made it work was that Jack was clear that he thought too much of me to stand by when I was hurting myself. A lot of my other so-called friends just stood by and said nothing. Jack is the only one who was a real friend.

It can be difficult to accept and affirm others when we find their needs taxing or discover conflicts between our preferences and those of others. It's not unusual for one partner to desire more closeness than another or for partners to differ in the paths they travel to achieve closeness. These are common problems, and partners need to discuss them in order to work out mutually agreeable solutions.

For a relationship to work, both partners must be confirmed. Confirmation begins with accepting others and the validity of their needs and preferences. This doesn't mean that you feel the same way or that you defer your own needs. Instead, the point is to recognize and respect others' needs just as you wish them to respect yours. Dual perspective is a primary tool for accepting others because it calls on us to consider them on their own terms. Although intimate talk may be what makes you feel most close to another person, you should also realize that a partner may experience greater closeness by doing things together. To meet both of your needs, you could take turns honoring each other's preferred paths to closeness. Alternatively, you might combine the two styles of intimacy by doing things together that invite conversation. For example, backpacking is an activity in which talking naturally occurs.

Affirm and Assert Yourself

It is just as important to affirm and accept yourself as to do that for others. You are no less valuable; your needs are no less important; your preferences are no less valid. It is a misunderstanding to think interpersonal communication principles we've discussed concern only how we behave toward others. Equally, they pertain to how we should treat ourselves. Thus, the principle of confirming people's worth applies equally to others and yourself. Likewise, we should respect and honor both our own and others' needs, preferences, and ways of creating intimacy.

Although we can't always meet the needs of all parties in relationships, it is possible and desirable to give voice to everyone, including yourself. If your partner favors greater autonomy than you do, you need to recognize that preference and also assert your own. If you don't express your feelings, there's no way others can confirm you. Thus, you should assert your feelings and preferences while simultaneously honoring different ones in others.

LAQUANDA

It took me a long time to learn to look out for myself as well as I look out for others. I was always taught to put others first, probably because I'm a girl. I mean neither of my brothers had that drilled into them. But I did, and for years I would just muffle my needs and whatever I wanted. I concentrated on pleasing others. I thought I was taking care of relationships, but really I was hurting them, because I felt neglected and I resented that. What I'm working on now is learning to take care of myself and others at the same time.

TABLE 7.2 Aggression, Assertion, and Deference

Aggressive	Assertive	Deferential
We're going to spend time together.	I'd like to create more time for us.	It's okay with me not to spend time with each other.
Tell me what you're feeling, I insist.	I would like to understand more of how you feel.	If you don't want to talk about how you feel, okay.
I don't care what you want; I'm not going to a movie.	I'm really not up for a movie tonight.	It's fine with me to go to a movie if you want to.

Unlike aggression, assertion doesn't involve putting your needs above those of others. But, unlike deference, assertion doesn't subordinate your needs to those of others. Assertion is a matter of clearly and nonjudgmentally stating what you feel, need, or want (see Table 7.2). This should be done without disparaging others and what they want. You should simply make your feelings known in an open, descriptive manner.

Because relationships include more than one person, they must involve acceptance and affirmation of more than one. Good relationships develop when partners understand and respect each other. The first requirement for this to happen is for each person to communicate honestly how she or he thinks and feels and what she or he wants and needs. A second requirement is for each person to communicate respect for the other's feelings and needs.

We should remember that the meaning of assertion varies among different cultures. For instance, openly asserting your own ideas is considered disrespectful in Korea and parts of China. Even if Koreans or Chinese don't want to do something, they seldom directly turn down another's request. Thus, people with diverse cultural backgrounds may have different ways of affirming and asserting themselves. To communicate effectively with others, we need to learn how they affirm themselves and how they express their feelings in direct or indirect ways.

We can tolerate sometimes not getting what we want without feeling personally devalued. However, it is far more disconfirming to have our needs go unacknowledged. Even when partners disagree or have conflicting needs, each person can state his or her feelings and express awareness of the other's perspective. Usually there are ways to acknowledge both viewpoints, as Eleanor illustrates.

ELEANOR

About a year after George and I married, he was offered a promotion if he'd move to Virginia. We were living in Pennsylvania at the time, and that's where our families and friends were. I didn't want to move, because I was rooted with my people, but we could both see how important the move was to George's career. The week before we moved, George gave me the greatest present of our lives. He handed me two tickets—one for a round-trip flight from Virginia to Pennsylvania so that I could visit my family, and a copy of a second ticket he'd gotten for my best friend so that she could visit me after we moved. I felt he really understood me and had found a way to take care of my needs. I still have the ticket stubs in my box of special memories.

Self-Disclose When Appropriate

As we noted earlier, self-disclosure allows people to know each other in greater depth. For this reason, it's an important communication skill, especially in the early stages of relationships. Research indicates that appropriate self-disclosure tends to increase trust and feelings of closeness (Cosby, 1973). In addition, self-disclosure can enhance self-esteem and security in relationships because we feel that others accept the most private parts of us. Finally, self-disclosure is an important way to learn about ourselves. As we reveal our hopes, fears, dreams, and feelings, we get responses from others that give us new perspectives on who we are. In addition, we gain insight into ourselves by seeing how we interact with others in new situations.

Although self-disclosure has many potential values, it is not always advisable. As we have seen, self-disclosure necessarily involves risks—the risk that others will not accept what we reveal or that they might use it against us. Appropriate self-disclosure minimizes these risks by proceeding slowly and in climates where sufficient trust has been proved. It's wise to "test the waters" gradually before plunging into major self-disclosures. Begin by revealing information that is personal but not highly intimate or able to damage you if exploited. Before disclosing further, observe how the other person responds to your communication and what she or he does with it. You might also pay attention to whether the other person reciprocates by disclosing personal information to you. Because self-disclosures involve risk, we need to be cautious about when and to whom we reveal ourselves. When trust exists and we want to intensify a relationship, self-disclosure is one of many communication practices that can be healthy.

A number of years ago, Joseph Luft and Harry Ingham created a model of different sorts of knowledge that affect self-development. They called the model the Johari Window (Figure 7.2), which is a combination of their first names, Joe and Harry.

Four types of information are relevant to the self. Open, or public, information is known to both us and others. Your name, height, major, and tastes in music are probably free information that you share easily with others. The blind area contains information that others know about us, but we don't know about ourselves. For example, others may see that we are insecure even though we think we've hidden that well. Others may also recognize needs or feelings that we've not acknowledged to ourselves. The third area includes hidden information, which we know about ourselves but choose not to reveal to most others. You might not tell many people about your vulnerabilities or about traumas in your past because you consider this private information. The unknown area is made up of information about ourselves that neither we nor others know. This consists of your untapped resources, your untried talents, and your reactions to experiences you've never had. You don't know how you will manage a crisis until you've been in one, and you can't tell what kind of parent you would be unless you've had a child.

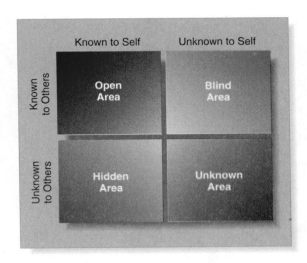

FIGURE 7.2 *The Johari Window*

Since a healthy self-concept requires knowledge of ourselves, it's important to gain access to information in our blind and unknown areas. One way to do this is to expand our experiences by entering unfamiliar situations, trying novel things, and experimenting with new kinds of communication. Another way to increase self-knowledge is to interact with others to learn how they see us. We can gain insight into ourselves by reflecting on their perceptions.

Respect Diversity in Relationships

Just as individuals differ, so do relationships. There is tremendous variety in what people find comfortable, affirming, and satisfying in interpersonal interaction. It's counterproductive to try to force all people and relationships to fit into a single mode. For example, you might have one friend who enjoys a lot of verbal disclosure and another who prefers less. There's no reason to try to persuade the first friend to disclose less or the second one to be more revealing. Similarly, you may be comfortable with greater closeness in some of your relationships and more autonomy in others. The differences between people create a rich diversity of relationships we can experience.

© Gary A. Conner/PhotoEdit

DORZIUS

Communication has a lot to do with climate in work relationships too. When I first came here from Haiti, I had many job interviews. People would say to me, "We've never hired one of you," like Haitians are not normal people. They also would say I would have to work hard and was I ready to do that, which told me they assumed I was lazy. When I did get a job, my supervisor watched me much more closely than he watched nonforeign workers. He was always judging.

Even a single relationship varies over time, and we should accept this as normal. Because dialectics generate constant tension, partners continuously shift their patterns and ways of honoring contradictory needs. It's natural to want more closeness at some times and more distance at others in the life of a relationship. It's also advisable to experiment with different responses to dialectical tensions. You may find it's effective to compromise between closeness and autonomy and to satisfy your desire for openness by sharing certain topics while meeting your need for privacy by not discussing other topics.

Because people and relationships are diverse, we should strive to respect a range of communicative choices and relationship patterns. In addition, we should be cautious about imposing our meaning on others' communication. People from various cultures, including ones within the United States, have learned different communication styles. What Westerners consider openness and healthy self-disclosure may feel offensively intrusive to people from some Asian societies. The dramatic, assertive speaking style of many African Americans can be misinterpreted as abrasive within a Western Caucasian perspective. The best way to understand what other's behavior means is to ask. This conveys the relational message that they matter to you, and it allows you to gain insight into the interesting diversity among us.

The guidelines we've discussed combine respect for self, others, and relationships into communication that fosters healthy, affirming climates for connections with others. We can transform our relationships when we take responsibility for shaping interpersonal climates and when we develop the knowledge and communication skills to do so.

SUMMARY

In this chapter, we've explored personal relationships and the communication climates that make them more or less satisfying. Four elements of healthy interpersonal connections are investments, commitment, trust, and comfort with relational dialectics. Even though love is important for intimacy, it alone is insufficient. To it we must add personal choices to invest ourselves, make enduring commitments to remain with others even in hard times, develop trust, and learn to manage the ongoing dialectical tensions that promote change and growth.

Perhaps the most basic requirement for healthy communication climates is confirmation. Each of us wants to feel valued, especially by those for whom we care most deeply. When partners recognize, acknowledge, and endorse each other, they give the important gift of confirmation. They communicate, "You matter to me." We discussed particular kinds of communication that foster supportive and defensive climates in relationships. Defensiveness is bred by evaluation, certainty, superiority, strategies, control, and neutrality. More supportive climates arise from communication that is descriptive, provisional, equal, spontaneous, empathic, and problem-oriented.

To close the chapter, we considered five guidelines for building healthy communication climates. The first one is to assume responsibility for communicating in ways that actively enhance the mood of a relationship. Second, we should accept and confirm our friends and romantic partners, communicating that we respect them, even though we may not always agree with them or feel the same as they do. The third guideline is a companion to the second one: We should accept and confirm ourselves just as fully as we do for others. Each of us is entitled to assert our own thoughts, feelings, and needs. Doing so allows us to honor ourselves and to help our partners understand us. A fourth guideline is to self-disclose when appropriate so that we increase our security in relationships and so that we add to the information we have about ourselves. Finally, we should embrace diversity in relationships as a source of personal and interpersonal growth. People vary widely, as do the relationship patterns and forms they prefer. By respecting differences among us, we all expand our insights into the fascinating array of ways that humans form and sustain intimate relations.

In the next three chapters, we'll look in greater detail at personal relationships. Chapter 8 extends our discussion of climate by examining how we can create constructive relationship contexts for dealing effectively with tensions. Chapter 9 discusses friendships, and Chapter 10 considers romantic relationships. In each chapter, we consider what these relationships are, how communication affects them, and how we might cope with some of the inevitable problems and challenges of sustaining close relationships over time. What we have learned about climate, as well as what we've learned about other facets of interpersonal communication in earlier chapters, will serve as a foundation for a more in-depth look at the dynamics of close relationships.

KEY TERMS

Interpersonal climate

Investments

Commitment

Trust

Self-disclosure

Relational dialectics

Ethnocentrism

CHAPTER 8

Managing Conflict in Relationships

Dave: You made me so angry when you flirted with other guys at the party last night.

Pam: Yeah, well you made me angry when you got drunk.

Dave: I wouldn't have to drink so much if you paid more attention to me.

Pam: Maybe I would if you'd clean up your act. For instance, why don't you get serious about graduate school and start acting responsible?

Dave: I'll do that right after you quit smoking and spend some time with me instead of always burying yourself in readings for your classes.

Pam: You just say that because you're jealous that I am succeeding in *my* graduate program.

Dave: Succeeding, hah. Social work isn't a real career.

Pam: At least it's *a* career. That's more than you have.

Dave: You never do anything but complain, complain, complain. You really are a drag.

Clearly Dave and Pam are having trouble. The real problem isn't the issues they're discussing, but how they manage conflict. Dave and Pam are not communicating constructively. What we've learned in previous chapters helps us understand how negative communication fuels discord between them. For example, Dave launched the conversation with you-language. Instead of owning his anger, he blamed Pam for it. In turn, she didn't own her anger. Also, each of them disconfirmed the other with personal attacks. Further, neither of them really recognized and acknowledged the other's point of view. Each of them listened defensively and engaged in ambushing the other. Pam and Dave pursued their individual agendas and failed to connect with each other. The result is that Pam and Dave clash, much like the squares in the crazy quilt that opens this chapter.

Let's start the conversation over and see how more positive communication might improve what happens.

Dave: I felt hurt when you flirted with other guys at the party last night. *[Dave owns his feelings.]*

Pam: I can understand that. I know you don't like for me to pay attention to other men. *[She acknowledges Dave's feelings.]* I got upset when you drank too much, and I want you to understand how I feel about that. *[Pam owns her feelings and asserts her needs in the situation.]*

Dave: You're right. *[He acknowledges and endorses her concern.]* I guess I was feeling kind of angry because you're so focused on your graduate program, and I can't seem to get started. *[Because an affirming climate has been created, Dave can disclose his deeper worries to Pam.]*

Pam: I know you feel discouraged right now. *[She again acknowledges his feelings.]* I would too. *[She shows empathy.]* But you're so smart, and you'll do great once you settle on a course of action. *[She shows she believes in him.]* Why don't we put our heads together to sort through some of the options and try to figure out how you can proceed. *[She offers support and shows commitment to his welfare.]*

Dave: That would really help me. I just need to talk through a lot of possibilities. *[He acknowledges her offer of help.]* I'd really like to get your perspective on some ideas I've got. *[He shows he values her viewpoint.]*

© Bob Daemmrich/The Image Works

The conflict proceeded very differently in the second instance. Both Pam and Dave owned their feelings and confirmed each other by acknowledging expressed concerns. The supportive climate they established enabled Dave to reveal deeper worries that lay below his opening complaint about flirting. Pam and Dave worked together to solve a problem that mattered to both of them. Probably the relationship was strengthened by how they managed their conflict.

Not all conflicts can be turned around as effectively as this one. There is no magic bullet for handling conflict constructively. Even skillful communication is not a remedy for all of the tensions that come up in relationships. However, communication is one of the most important influences on how conflict affects relationships. Skillful speaking and listening help us manage conflict, regardless of the difficulties we face. Research shows that communication problems contribute to relational dissatisfaction and breakup (Dindia & Fitzpatrick, 1985). We also know that positive communication is one of the strongest influences on long-term satisfaction (Markman, 1981). Communication powerfully sculpts conflict and its consequences.

In this chapter, we'll explore how communication and conflict weave together in interpersonal relationships. We'll begin by considering principles about conflict so that we understand what it is and the roles it plays in our relationships. Second, we'll consider basic orientations to conflict, and the ways in which gender affects our approach to conflict. The third section of the chapter focuses on specific communication patterns that enhance or impede constructive management of conflict. We'll conclude by identifying guidelines for communicating effectively when engaging in conflict.

Principles of Conflict

We've all experienced conflict in our relationships, so we have a general idea of what it is. We can say **conflict** exists when individuals who depend on each other express different views, interests, or goals and perceive their views as incompatible or oppositional.

Conflict is more than just having differences. We disagree with many people about many things, but this doesn't invariably lead to conflict. For example, I don't like the way my neighbors landscaped their yard, my in-laws don't like large dogs like our Labrador, and Robbie and I don't see eye to eye on money matters. None of these disagreements, however, sparks conflict. I realize that my neighbors have a right to fix their yard as they please; my mother-in-law and father-in-law tolerate our Labrador, and we accept their Boston bulldog; and Robbie and I long ago decided to keep our finances separate. In these cases, the disagreements don't negatively affect the relationships.

Conflict is expressed disagreement, struggle, or discord. We communicate differences both verbally and nonverbally. Shooting daggers with your eyes communicates anger and discord every bit as clearly as saying "I'm angry with you." Walking out on a conversation and slamming a door express hostility, as does refusing to talk to someone. When individuals are involved in conflict, they recognize they have differences and they express them in some manner.

Conflict can occur only between people who depend on each other. Differences don't have to be resolved between people who don't affect each other. I have no stake in my neighbors' yard, and they don't need my approval to landscape as they wish. The differing preferences in dogs that my in-laws and we have don't interfere with our relationship as long as we each leave our dog home when we visit. If Robbie and I disagreed on pets, then there might be conflict, since we live together and the pets we own affect both of us. We may disagree with others and even make negative judgments of them, but conflict exists only when it is expressed by individuals who affect one another. Lenore, a twenty-year-old student, explains that conflict assumes connection.

LENORE

It's kind of strange, but you really don't fight with people who don't matter. With a lot of guys I dated, if I didn't like something they did, I just let it go because they weren't important enough for the hassle. But Rod and I argue a lot, because we do affect each other. Maybe fighting is a sign that people care about each other.

Four principles of conflict expand our understanding.

Conflict Is a Natural Process in All Relationships

Conflict is a normal, inevitable part of all interpersonal relationships. When people matter to each other and affect each other, disagreements are unavoidable. You like meat and your friend is a strict vegetarian. You prefer to rent a condo and avoid the hassles of home ownership, but your mate's fondest dream is to own a home. You believe money should be enjoyed, and your partner lives by the philosophy of saving for a rainy day. You want to move where there's a great job for you, but the location has no career prospects for your partner. You prefer to bring work home rather than staying late at the office, but your partner resents it when you work at home. Again and again, we find ourselves seemingly at odds with people who matter to us. When this happens, we have to resolve the differences, preferably in a way that doesn't harm the relationship.

The presence of conflict does not indicate a relationship is unhealthy or in trouble, although how partners manage conflict does influence relational health. Actually, conflict indicates that individuals are involved with each other. If they weren't, there would be no need to resolve differences. This is a good point to keep in mind when conflicts arise because it reminds us that a strong connection underlies even disagreement.

RON

It sounds funny, but the biggest thing my fiancée and I fight about is whether it's okay to fight. I was brought up not to argue and to think that conflict is bad. In her family, people did argue a lot, and she thinks it is healthy. What I'm coming to realize is that there is a lot of conflict in my family but it's hidden, so it never gets dealt with very well. I've seen her and her parents really go at it, but, I have to admit, they work through their differences and people in my family don't.

Ron's insight is important. He has realized that conflict is an undercurrent in his family, but it remains unresolved because people won't discuss tensions. Most of us have attitudes about conflict that reflect scripts we learned in our families. Like Ron, some of us were taught that conflict is bad and should be avoided, while others of us learned that airing differences is healthy.

Put It in Practice

UNDERSTANDING YOUR CONFLICT SCRIPT

What conflict script did you learn in your family? Think back to your childhood and adolescence and try to remember what implicit rules for conflict your family modeled and perhaps taught.

1. Did people disagree openly with each other?
2. What was said when disagreements surfaced? Did your parents suggest it was rude or bad manners to argue? Did they encourage open discussion of differences?
3. How do you currently reflect your family's conflict script? Now that you can edit family scripts and author your own, how would you like to deal with conflict?

Read on in this chapter to consider ways you might write a conflict script that is constructive and reflects your values.

Although conflict itself is inevitable, how we manage it is not. We can deal with differences more or less effectively, and our choices have personal and relational impact.

Conflict May Be Overt or Covert

Conflict may be expressed openly or covertly. Overt conflict exists when individuals deal with their differences in a straightforward manner. They might calmly discuss their disagreement, intensely argue about ideas, or engage in a shouting match. Overt conflict may also involve physical attacks, although of course that's not recommended!

Yet, much conflict isn't overt. Covert conflict exists when partners camouflage disagreements and express their feelings indirectly. When angry, a person may deliberately do something to hurt or upset a partner. For instance, Janet is annoyed because her roommate Myra has cleaned up Janet's half of the apartment, so when Myra is studying, Janet turns the stereo on at high volume. Knowing that Elliott hates to be kept waiting, his wife intentionally arrives twenty minutes late for a dinner date. These individuals expressed their anger indirectly and conflict was covert.

A common form of covert conflict is **games,** which Eric Berne (1964) cataloged in a fascinating book titled *Games People Play.* According to Berne, games are interactions in which the real conflicts are hidden or denied and a counterfeit excuse is created for arguing or criticizing. In a game called "Blemish," one person pretends to be complimentary but actually puts another down. If Ann asks her friend if she looks okay for an important interview, the friend could respond, "Gee you look really great with the new suit and hair style. There's just this one little thing. You seem to be kind of overweight lately. Your stomach and hips look big, and that suit doesn't hide the extra pounds." The friend is playing "Blemish," because she focuses on one thing that is wrong and downplays all that is right. Her unexpressed anger or resentment surfaces covertly.

Another game is "NIGYYSOB" ("Now I've Got You You Son of a Bitch"). In this one, an individual deliberately sets another person up for a fall. Knowing that her husband has poor taste in furniture, Nina asks him to pick out a new chair for their home. When it arrives and predictably is ugly, Nina criticizes her husband. She worked to find a way to make him fail and then pounced on him when he did. Another game is "Mine Is Worse Than Yours." Suppose you tell a friend that you are overloaded with two tests and a paper due next week, and your friend says, "You think that's bad? Listen to this: I have two tests, three papers, and an oral report all due in the next two weeks." Your friend expressed no concern for your plight; rather, he told you that his situation is worse. In this game, people try to monopolize rather than listening and responding to each other.

CHUCK

My parents specialize in games. Dad likes to set Mom up by asking her to take care of some financial business or get the car fixed. Then he explodes about what she does. I think he is just trying to find excuses for blessing her out. Mom also plays games. Her favorite is Blemish. She always finds something wrong with an idea or a paper I've written or a vacation or whatever. Then she just harps and harps on the defect. Sometimes being around them is like being in a mine field.

"Yes, but" is a game in which a person pretends to be asking for help, but then refuses all help that's offered. Doing this allows the player to make the other person feel inadequate for being unable to help. Lorna asks her boyfriend to help her figure out how to better manage her money. When he suggests she should spend less, Lorna says, "Yes, but I don't buy anything I don't need." When he suggests she might work extra hours at her job, she responds, "Yes, but that would cut into my free time." When he mentions she could get a job that pays more per hour, Lorna says, "Yes, but I really like the people where I work now." When he points out that she could save a lot by packing lunches instead of buying them, she replies, "Yes, but I'd have to get up earlier." "Yes, but" continues until the person trying to help finally gives up in defeat. Then the initiator of the game can complain "You didn't help me."

Games and covert aggression are generally ineffective ways to manage conflict. Both approaches are dishonest, because they camouflage the real issues behind counterfeit communication. Thus, it's virtually impossible for friends and romantic partners to resolve the real problems.

Put It in Practice

IDENTIFYING GAMES IN YOUR COMMUNICATION

Apply what you've read about covert conflict to your own life. Describe an example of when you or someone you have a relationship with played each of these games:

Blemish

NIGYYSOB

Mine Is Worse Than Yours

Yes, but

What was accomplished by playing the game? Were the real conflicts addressed?

©1994 Cathy Guisewite. Reprinted by permission of Universal Press Syndicate. All rights reserved.

Conflict Can Be Managed Well or Poorly

The third principle is that conflict can be managed more or less constructively. Because conflict is natural and inevitable, we need to learn to deal with it in ways that benefit us as individuals and our relationships. People respond to conflict in a variety of ways, ranging from physical attack to verbal aggression to reflective problem solving. Although each method may resolve differences, some are clearly preferable to others. Depending on how we handle disagreements, conflict can either promote continuing attachment or split a relationship apart.

Communication skills are especially important when dealing with differences. We need to know how particular behaviors affect interpersonal conflict so that we can make intelligent decisions about how to act. Without a base of good information about communication and conflict, we can only follow scripts that we have learned from previous interactions and observations. Unfortunately, not all of us have learned constructive scripts for managing conflict. Later in this chapter, we'll identify specific kinds of communication that foster healthy and unhealthy conflict. Some forms of communication can actually enhance relationships as well as resolving disagreements effectively, while other communication can erode trust, climate, and the self-esteem of partners. Learning how different kinds of communication affect relationships, individuals, and resolution of conflict empowers you to make informed choices about how to deal with conflict in your relationships.

Conflict Can Be Good for Individuals and Relationships

Although we tend to think of conflict negatively, actually it can be beneficial in a number of ways. When managed constructively, conflict can help us grow as individuals and strengthen our relationships. We can enlarge our perspectives by engaging conflict to propel personal growth and learning. We deepen insight into our ideas and feelings when we have to express them and consider critical responses. Sometimes this supports our own identity by clarifying how we differ from others. In a study I co-authored, romantic partners indicated that one value of differences was strengthening awareness of partners' individuality (Wood et al., 1994).

Differences can also prompt personal growth by helping us see when it's appropriate to change our minds. Conflict allows us to consider points of view different from our own. Based on what we learn, we may change our opinions, behaviors, or goals. As Jaleh points out, conflict can enhance understanding and spur positive personal growth.

© Audrey Gottlieb/Monkmeyer

Sometimes it's worse to win a fight than to lose.
BILLIE HOLIDAY

JALEH

A while back I was arguing with a buddy of mine about quotas. I've always supported them because I think that's the only way African Americans have a chance of getting the education and jobs they deserve. Without quotas, people of color will still be shut out no matter how skilled or smart or achieving they are. But the guy I was debating is against quotas because he thinks they hurt us. He said that as long as quotas are used, any African American in a good school or with a status job will be regarded as there because of quota not merit. What really made me think was when he said that quotas can be used against blacks—like if a school has a quota for 10% minorities, it can refuse to admit more than 10% minorities even if more are qualified. Arguing with him has pushed me to rethink my position.

Conflict can also benefit relationships. In fact, a book titled *The Intimate Enemy: How to Fight Fair in Love and Marriage* states that verbal conflict between intimates is highly constructive and desirable if it is managed constructively (Bach & Wyden, 1973). One potential relational benefit of conflict is its ability to expand partners' understandings of each other. What begins as a discussion of some particular issue usually winds up providing broader information about why partners feel as they do and what meanings they attach to the issue. In the example that opened this chapter, the original complaint about Pam's flirting led to the discovery that Dave felt insecure about his identity and Pam's respect for him, since she was succeeding in graduate work and he wasn't. Once his concern emerged, the couple could address the *real* issue.

Ron Arnett (1986), a scholar of communication ethics, points out that lack of conflict isn't necessarily a symptom of a healthy relationship. It's at least as likely that low levels of conflict reflect lack of emotional depth between partners or repression of disagreements. Researchers report that there is no association between the number of arguments spouses have and marital happiness (Howard & Dawes, 1976). Some of the respondents in the study I mentioned previously (Wood et al., 1994) said differences energized their relationships by providing zest and excitement. This may explain the interesting finding that sexual activity and arguments are positively related. It seems that partners who argue more also have livelier sex lives (Howard & Dawes, 1976). One group of researchers refers to this as "keeping a positive balance in the marital bank account" (Gottman et al., 1976b). When conflict is managed well, it can be constructive for both individuals and relationships.

To review, we've discussed four basic principles about conflict. First, we noted that conflict is both natural and inevitable in interpersonal relationships. Second, we discovered that conflict may be overtly displayed or covertly expressed through indirect communication or games that camouflage real issues. The third principle is that how we manage conflict influences its resolution and its impact on interpersonal climates. Finally, we saw that conflict can be constructive for both individuals and relationships. We can now build on these principles by discussing diverse ways people think about and respond to conflict.

Dealing with Conflict

We've noted that conflict can be managed in various ways, some more effective than others. We now want to look at two influences on how individuals deal with conflict.

Views of Conflict

How we perceive conflict affects how we deal with it. One of the greatest influences on our views of conflict is our cultural background. In societies such as the United States, conflict and assertive competition are accepted and even encouraged. In other societies, individuals are taught to avoid conflict and to seek harmony with others. We'll discuss cultural variations in conflict later in the chapter. Based on cultural learnings and personal experiences, individuals adopt one of three views of conflict. Each of these is appropriate in some situations; the challenge is to know when a particular view is constructive.

Lose–Lose   A lose–lose orientation assumes that conflict results in losses for everyone. A wife might feel that conflicts over money hurt her, her husband, and the marriage. Similarly, a person may not argue with a friend, believing the result would be wounded pride for both of them. The lose–lose view presumes that conflict cannot produce winners or benefits. Although this perspective is not usually beneficial in dealing with interpersonal conflicts, it has merit in other circumstances. One obvious value of this approach is that it prompts us to ask whether we want or need to engage in conflict. Some issues aren't worth the energy and the discomfort that conflict arouses. For instance, Robbie and I have very different ideas about the appropriate timetable for airline travel. He prefers to get to the airport at least 90 minutes before a flight, whereas I prefer to arrive just a few minutes in advance. For the first years of our marriage this was a source of discord that yielded no benefits for either of us. Finally, I decided that the schedule was a dumb thing to argue about, and I simply planned to leave when Robbie preferred. We also disagree on cars, but Robbie defers to my preference, since cars matter more to me than to him. Neither cars nor flight schedules are worth conflict. We might also have a more peaceful planet if national leaders believed that war only produces losers, regardless of whether one side officially "wins."

© Ron Chapple/FPG International

Win–Lose Win–lose orientations assume one person wins at the expense of the other. A person who sees conflict as a win–lose matter thinks disagreements are battles that can have only one victor. What one person gains is at the other's loss; what one person loses benefits the other. Partners who disagree about whether to move to a new location might lock into a yes–no mode, in which only two alternatives are seen. They make no effort to find a mutually acceptable solution, such as moving to a third place that meets both partners' needs or having a long-distance relationship so that each person can have the best individual location. The more person A argues for moving, the more person B argues for not moving. Eventually one of them "wins," but at the cost of the other and the relationship. A win–lose orientation toward conflict tends to undermine relationships, because someone has to lose. There is no possibility that both can win, much less that the relationship can.

Before you dismiss win–lose as a totally unconstructive view of conflict, let's consider when it might be effective. Win–lose can be appropriate when we have low commitment to a relationship and little desire to take care of the person with whom we disagree. When you're buying a car, for instance, you want the best deal you can get, and you have little concern for the dealer's profit. I adopted a win–lose approach to conflict with doctors when my father was dying. The doctors weren't doing all they could to help him, because they saw little value in investing time in someone who was dying, but I wanted them to do everything possible to help my father. We had opposing views, and I cared less about whether the doctors were happy and liked me than about "winning" the best medical care for my father.

Win–Win Win–win orientations assume there are usually ways to resolve differences so that everyone gains. For people who view conflict as win–win, the goal is to come up with a resolution that everyone involved can accept. A person is willing to make some accommodations in order to build a solution that lets others win also. When partners adopt win–win views of conflict, they often discover solutions that neither had thought of previously. This happens because they are committed to their own and the other's satisfaction. Sometimes win–win attitudes result in compromises that satisfy enough of each person's needs to provide confirmation and to protect the health of the relationship.

TESS

One of the roughest issues for Jerry and me was when he started working most nights. The time after dinner had always been "our time." When Jerry took the new job, he had to stay in constant contact with the California office. Jerry and I used to do something together at 6 P.M., but because of the time difference, it's only 3 P.M. on the West Coast and the business day is still going. I was hurt that he no longer had time for us, and he was angry that I wanted time he needed for business. We kept talking and came up with the idea of spending a day together each weekend, which we'd never done. Although my ideal would still be to share evenings, this solution keeps us in touch with each other.

Lose–lose, win–lose, and win–win are basic ways individuals think about conflict. What we learned in Chapter 3 reminds us that how we perceive something has a powerful impact on what it means to us and on the possibilities of resolution that we imagine. Remember how you couldn't solve the nine dots problem in Chapter 3 if you perceived it as a square? In a similar way, we're unlikely to find a win–win solution when we conceive conflict as win–lose or lose–lose.

Put It in Practice

YOUR VIEW OF CONFLICT

Could you identify your perception of conflict from this discussion? To check, answer these questions:

1. When conflict seems about to occur, do you:
   a. marshal arguments for your solution
   b. feel everyone is going to get hurt
   c. feel there's probably a way to satisfy everyone

2. When involved in conflict, do you:

    a. feel competitive urges

    b. feel resigned that everyone will lose

    c. feel committed to finding a mutual solution

3. When you disagree with another person, do you:

    a. assume the other person is wrong

    b. assume neither of you is right

    c. assume there are good reasons for what each of you thinks and feels

Key: (a) answers indicate a win–lose view of conflict; (b) answers suggest a lose–lose view; (c) answers reflect a win–win view.

Responses to Conflict

In addition to having basic views of what conflict is, most individuals have fairly consistent patterns for responding to conflict. A series of studies identified four distinct ways North Americans respond to relational distress (Rusbult, 1987; Rusbult, Johnson, & Morrow, 1986; Rusbult & Zembrodt, 1983; Rusbult, Zembrodt, & Iwaniszek, 1986). These are represented in Figure 8.1. According to this model, responses to conflict can be either active or passive, depending on how emphatically they address problems. Responses can also be constructive or destructive in their capacity to resolve tension and to preserve relationships.

The exit response involves leaving a relationship either by walking out or by psychologically withdrawing. Refusing to talk about a problem is an example of psychological exit. Ending a relationship rather than deal with a conflict is an example of literal exit. Because exit doesn't address problems, it is destructive. Because it is forceful in evading conflict, it is active.

The neglect response occurs when an individual denies or minimizes problems. Individuals communicate that they prefer to neglect conflicts by making statements such as "There isn't a problem," "You're creating a problem where none exists," or "You're making a mountain out of a molehill." These statements either deny a problem exists or deny that a problem is important. Neglect is generally destructive, since it evades difficulties, and it is passive because it avoids discussion. In some specific situations, however, neglect may be an effective response to conflict. For instance, if an issue can't be resolved, discussing it may further harm a relationship. Also, if a conflict isn't important to you, it may be appropriate not to deal with it.

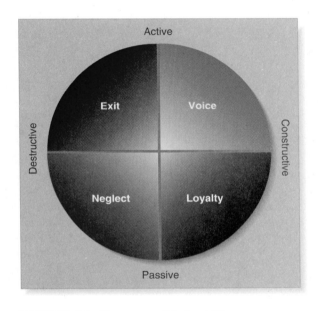

FIGURE 8.1 *Responses to Relational Distress*

WIN–WIN ATHLETICS

Americans view sports as competitions in which one person or team wins and the other loses. This perspective is in dramatic contrast to the Japanese attitude toward athletics. In baseball, for instance, the goal is not for one team to win, but for a tie to be achieved. The Japanese play for ties because that way nobody loses face. Everyone plays hard and competitively, yet nobody loses—no face is lost. That's a perfect game!

When the Japanese win a championship they try to win by only slim margins. One team may be ahead by many games at a point in the season, but by the end of the season that team will have trimmed its lead to one or two games. This preserves the face of the other teams, since they don't lose by an embarrassing degree.

Source: American games, Japanese rules. (1988). Frontline documentary. National Public Television. Cited in Ferrante, J. (1992). *Sociology: A global perspective* (p. 102). Belmont, CA: Wadsworth.

The loyalty response is staying committed to a relationship despite differences. Often this involves deferring to another in order to preserve a relationship. In other cases, loyalty is enacted by focusing on what is good and desirable about the relationship and by deemphasizing problems in it. Loyalty is silent allegiance that doesn't actively address conflict, so it is a passive response. Since it doesn't end a relationship and it preserves the option of addressing tension later, loyalty is constructive.

ZONDOMONI

In South Africa, the tradition is for women not to speak out against their husbands. Women are supposed to support whatever the husband says or does. A woman who speaks out or who disagrees with her husband or any male relative is considered bad; she is behaving inappropriately.

But some of us are now challenging this custom. I disagreed with my father about my marriage, and he did not speak to me for many months after. Now he speaks to me again. I also sometimes disagree with my husband. Life is changing in South Africa.

Finally, voice is an active, constructive strategy that responds to conflict by talking about problems and trying to fix them. Individuals who respond with voice identify problems or tensions and assert a desire to deal with them. Voice implies that people care enough about a relationship to notice when something is wrong and to want to do something to improve the situation. Thus, voice is often the most constructive strategy for enduring intimate relationships.

Although each of us has developed a preferred response, we can become skillful in other responses if we choose. Constructive strategies (voice and loyalty) are advisable for relationships that matter to you and that you want to maintain. Of those two, voice is stronger, because it actively intervenes to resolve conflict. Loyalty may be useful as an interim strategy when partners need time to reflect or cool off before dealing with tension directly.

Variations on a Theme

How we view and respond to conflict reflects our personal and social identities. Thus, factors such as cultural background, gender, and sexual orientation may affect how we perceive and manage conflict in our lives.

Cultural Background   A major influence on how we deal with conflict is cultural teachings. In the United States, assertiveness and individuality are emphasized, so native citizens tend to be more active and competitive in responding to conflict. More than many peoples, Westerners adopt an exchange view of relationships in which each person expects (and sometimes demands) to get "my fair share." As a people, we are reluctant to give in, defer, or be passive.

In more communal societies such as the Netherlands, people have less individualistic perspectives and are less likely to focus on winning at conflict (Vanyperen & Buunk, 1991). Similarly, in Japan and many other Asian cultures, open disagreement is strongly condemned. Japanese society teaches people to accommodate or appear to do so and not to express disagreement openly. This explains why Ting-Toomey (1991), a communication professor, reported that Japanese persons tend to favor the exit approach to conflict.

© Anne Dowie

VALAYA

One of the hardest adjustments for me has been how Americans assert themselves. I was very surprised that students argue with their teachers. We would never do that in Taiwan. It would be extremely disrespectful. I also see friends argue, sometimes very much. I understand this is a cultural difference, but I have trouble accepting it. I learned that disagreements hurt relationships.

Gender   Women and men differ in how they respond to conflict. In general, women are more likely to enact loyalty and voice, both of which have constructive implications for relationships. Men, on the other hand, respond more often with exit and neglect. These differences in response tendencies make sense in light of what we know about gendered socialization. As we noted in Chapter 4, women are taught to place a priority on relationships and to use talk to create and sustain closeness. Thus, it's natural for women to want to talk about problems. Women are also more likely than men to defer and compromise, which reflects gendered prescriptions for women to accommodate others (Wood 1986, 1992).

NICK

My girlfriend drives me crazy. She thinks anytime the slightest thing is wrong in our relationship, we have to have a long, drawn-out analysis of it. I just don't want to spend all that time dissecting the relationship.

GINA

My boyfriend is a world-class avoider. When something is wrong between us, I naturally want to talk about it and get things right again. But he will evade, tell me everything's fine when it's not, say the problem is too minor to talk about, and use any other tactic he can come up with to avoid facing the problems. He seems to think if you don't deal with problems they somehow solve themselves.

Masculine socialization places less emphasis on talk as a means to intimacy, so as a group, men are less likely than women to see discussion as a good way to handle conflict in personal relationships. In professional situations and athletics, however, men may be very vocal in dealing with conflict. Yet in their personal lives, men often deny or minimize problems rather than deal openly with them. However, research indicates that in Western relationships, avoiding discussion seldom helps matters and it often compounds tension between partners in a relationship. Long-term studies of marriage indicate that husbands are more inclined than wives to withdraw from conflict and that stonewalling by husbands is a strong predictor of divorce (Bass, 1993). The other response preferred by men, exit, is a unilateral show of power, which is part of masculine socialization. Men, more than women, use coercive tactics, both verbal and physical, to avoid discussing problems and to force their resolutions on others (Snell, Hawkins, & Belk, 1988; White, 1989).

Put It in Practice

GENDERED STYLES OF CONFLICT

Reflect on responses to conflict used by you and two women and two men you know well. Do your observations indicate that women are more likely than men to defer and accommodate and to want to talk about problems? Do the men you observe tend to avoid problems or exit when they arise?

Sexual Preference Do gays and lesbians respond to conflict differently than heterosexuals? Actually, sexual preference doesn't seem to be a major influence on how individuals see and deal with conflict. Rusbult and her colleagues (1986) found that gay men were much like heterosexual men, and lesbians were similar to heterosexual women, in their responses to conflict. Similarly, a major national study reported that gender explains far more of the differences between partners than does affectional preference (Blumstein & Schwartz, 1983). I drew the same conclusion from my research on how gay, lesbian, and heterosexual couples manage relationship crises (Wood, 1986, 1994b).

At first this finding seems surprising, since sexual orientation is such a core part of identity. On closer examination, however, it makes sense that gays and lesbians don't approach conflict differently than heterosexuals. The majority of children, regardless of affectional orientation, are socialized on the basis of their sex. Thus, boys, both gay and straight, tend to learn masculine orientations toward interaction, whereas lesbian and straight girls are socialized toward feminine styles of interaction.

Although gays, lesbians, and heterosexuals seem similar in how they think about and respond to conflict, affectional preference is linked to some differences in relationship tensions. First, gays and lesbians appear to have fewer sexual conflicts and to talk more openly about sexual issues than heterosexuals (Masters & Johnson, 1979). This can be significant, since sexual tensions can poison overall satisfaction with a relationship (Cupach & Comstock, 1990).

© Thelma Shumsky/The Image Works

The aim of argument, or discussion, should not be victory, but progress.

JOSEPH JOUBERT

On the whole, gay and lesbian couples may have less overall conflict than heterosexuals. It's possible that gay and lesbian partners have an intragender empathy that heterosexual couples lack (Masters & Johnson, 1979). Because most homosexual partners were socialized in the same gender culture, they often share views of the importance of talk and activities in relationships. Of all couples, lesbians most often rely on voice to talk through tensions. Because both partners usually view communication as the primary path to intimacy, they are similarly inclined to engage in process talk. Gay male couples, in contrast, talk less about relationship issues than other couples and are more likely than other partners to exit when problems arise (Wood, 1994b). Heterosexual couples talk more than gays and less than lesbians about their relationship, reflecting a combination of gendered socialization.

In this section, we've seen that people differ in how they view and respond to conflict. Although lose–lose and win–lose perceptions of conflict are appropriate in situations where there is low commitment to relationships and others, the win–win view is generally ideal when partners care about each other and want to stay together.

TABLE 8.1 Summary of Constructive and Unproductive Communication

Constructive	Unproductive
Validations of each other	Disconfirmation of each other
Sensitive listening	Poor listening
Dual perspective	Preoccupation with self
Recognize other's concerns	Cross-complaining
Asking for clarification	Hostile mindreading
Infrequent interruptions	Frequent interruptions
Focus on specific issues	Kitchensinking
Compromises and contracts	Counterproposals
Useful metacommunication	Excessive metacommunication
Summarizing the concerns of both partners	Self-summarizing

People respond to conflict either actively (voice, exit) or passively (neglect, loyalty) and in ways that either help (voice, loyalty) or harm (exit, neglect) relationships. How we think about and respond to conflict is learned, not innate. It reflects our cultural background, gender, and affectional preference. The fact that conflict orientations are learned suggests that we can develop skills for managing tension constructively. In the next section, we discuss specific communication behaviors that affect the process of conflict and its impact on relationships.

Communication Patterns During Conflict

Marriage counselors have particularly keen insight into how conflict dynamics affect relationships. Communication scholar Anita Vangelisti (1993) reports that counselors stress communication training for couples who manage conflict unproductively. Therapeutic training teaches partners to recognize destructive and constructive patterns of communication and to use constructive patterns in their relationships. In this section, we discuss specific kinds of communication that foster or impede effective conflict (Gottman, 1979, 1993; Gottman et al., 1976a, 1976b).

Unproductive Communication Patterns

Ineffective communication can have serious consequences. It damages efforts to resolve problems, harms individuals, and jeopardizes relational health. The communication that creates unproductive patterns in conflict reflects a preoccupation with self and a disregard for the other. This is not genuine interpersonal communication, since partners don't recognize and engage each other as unique individuals.

Specific communication behaviors make up the syndrome of destructive conflict communication. Table 8.1 identifies behaviors in early, middle, and late stages in the process of unproductive conflict (Gottman et al., 1976a).

Early Stages   The foundation for destructive conflict is established by communication that fails to confirm individuals. If John says, "I want us to spend more time together," Shelly may reply, "That's unreasonable." This disconfirms John's feeling and request. Shelly could also disconfirm him by not replying at all, which would be a refusal to acknowledge him. During

© Peter L. Chapman

early stages, partners tend not to listen well. They may listen selectively, taking in only what they expect or want to believe. In addition, partners display little mindfulness. They don't show that they are interested in what the other is saying. Instead, they may give feedback that disconfirms the other. For instance, Shelly could roll her eyes to tell John his request is outrageous, or she might shrug and turn away to signal she doesn't care what he wants. Poor listening is also demonstrated when partners don't respond to each other.

Cross-complaining occurs when one person's complaint is met by a countercomplaint. Shelly could respond to John's request for more time by saying, "Yeah, well what I want is a little more respect for what I do." That response doesn't address John's concern; it is an attempt to divert the conversation and to switch the fault from Shelly to John. Poor listening and disconfirmation establish a climate in which dual perspective is low and defensiveness is high.

Negative climates tend to build on themselves. As partners continue to talk, mindreading is likely. Instead of asking John to clarify or explain his feelings, Shelly assumes she knows his motives. Perhaps she thinks he wants to divert her from her work so that she doesn't succeed. If Shelly makes this assumption, she discounts what John wants. Mindreading in distressed relationships has a distinctively negative tone. Partners assume the worst motives and feelings of each other. The negative assumptions they make fuel hostility and mistrust.

Middle Stages   Once a negative climate has been set, it is stoked by other unconstructive communication. Focusing on specific issues is one of the clearest differences between partners who resolve conflicts constructively and those who don't. In unproductive conflict interaction, partners engage in **kitchensinking,** in which everything except the kitchen sink is thrown into the argument. John may add to his original complaint by recalling all sorts of other real and imagined slights from Shelly. In turn, she may reciprocate by hauling out her own laundry list of gripes. The result is such a mass of grievances that partners are overwhelmed. They can't solve all of the problems they've dragged into the discussion, and they may well forget what the original issue was. Kitchensinking is particularly likely to occur when partners have a host of concerns they've repressed for some time. Once a conflict begins, everything that has been stored up is thrown in.

The middle stages of unproductive conflict are also marked by frequent interruptions that disrupt the flow of talk. These interruptions aren't efforts to clarify ideas or feelings. Instead, they are objections to what a partner says: "How dare you say I don't know how to manage money?"

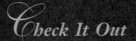

HOW TO FIGHT

Rules for Fighting Dirty

1. Apologize prematurely.
2. Refuse to take the fight seriously.
3. Chain-react by piling on all the issues and gripes (kitchensinking).
4. Hit below the belt. Use intimate knowledge to humiliate the other person.
5. Withdraw and avoid confrontation: walk out, be silent.
6. Withhold affection, approval, recognition, or material things.
7. Encourage others to side with you against your partner.
8. Play demolition derby with your partner's character—tell her or him what's wrong with her or him, what she or he thinks, feels, means, and so on (mindreading).
9. Demand more—nothing is ever enough. Push to have everything your way
10. Attack a person, activity, value, or idea that your partner holds dear.

Rules for Fighting Clean

1. Fully express your positive and negative feelings.
2. Define your out-of-bounds areas of vulnerability.
3. Paraphrase the other's arguments in your own words and allow the other to do likewise.
4. Think *before* fighting, not after fighting. Try not to let your feelings undermine reason and fair play.
5. Consider the merit of the other person's opinions of you before rejecting or accepting them.
6. Focus on the other person's behavior and ideas.
7. Define what the fight is about and stay within limits.
8. Look for where you and your partner agree, as well as where you disagree.
9. Decide how each of you can help the other resolve the issue in a way that satisfies her or him.
10. Avoid discussing a problem or conflict when you are emotionally raw.

Source: Adapted from Bach, G. R., & Wyden, P. (1973). *The intimate enemy: How to fight fair in love and marriage.* New York: Avon.

Interruptions may also be attempts to derail a partner's issues and reroute discussion: "I have no interest in talking about time together. What I'd like to discuss is your responsibility for this house." Cross-complaining frequently continues in this middle stage of the syndrome. Because neither partner is allowed to develop thoughts fully (or even to finish a sentence), discussion never focuses on any topic long enough to make headway in resolving it.

Later Stages Even if partners make little progress in solving their problems, limited time and energy guarantee an end to an episode of conflict. Solutions become the focus in the final stage of unproductive conflict. Unfortunately, preceding stages didn't lay the groundwork for effective discussion of solutions. As a result, each person's proposals are met with counterproposals. The self-preoccupation that first surfaced in the early phase persists now so that each person is more interested in pushing his or her solution than in considering that of the other. John proposes, "Maybe we could spend two nights together each week." Shelly counterproposes, "Maybe you could assume responsibility for half of the chores around here." Her counterproposal fails to recognize and acknowledge his suggestion. Compounding self-preoccupation is self-summarizing, which is when a person keeps repeating what she or he has said. This is egocentric communication. It is not genuine interpersonal communication, since it ignores the other person and simply reiterates the speaker's feelings and perspective.

A final form of negative communication in the middle and later phases of unproductive conflict is excessive metacommunication. **Metacommunication** is communication about communication. For example, John might say, "I think maybe we're getting sidetracked in this discussion," or Shelly might say, "I think we're avoiding talking about the real issue here." Both of these are comments about the communication that is happening. Gottman and his associates (1976a, b, 1977) have found that both distressed and satisfied couples engage in metacommunication. However, they do so in very different ways. Couples who manage conflict effectively use metacommunication to keep discussion on track, and then they return to the topics at hand. For instance, during a disagreement, Aaron might comment that Norma doesn't seem to be expressing her feelings and invite her to do so. Then he and Norma would return to their discussion. In contrast, couples who manage conflict ineffectively often become embroiled in metacommunication and can't get back to the issues. For example, Norma and Aaron might get into an extended argument about whether she's expressing feelings and not return to the original topic of conflict. Excessive metacommunication is more likely to block partners than to resolve tensions cooperatively.

These forms of communication that make up the unproductive conflict syndrome reflect egocentrism and dogmatism. They also promote egocentrism and dogmatism, since negative communication tends to be self-perpetuating. Unproductive conflict doesn't involve dual perspective, and it seals off awareness of common grounds as well as potential avenues of compromise.

You may recall that in Chapter 1, we described interpersonal communication as systemic, because all aspects of communication interact and affect each other. This is clearly the case in the unproductive conflict syndrome. Egocentrism leads to poor listening, which promotes disconfirmation, which fuels defensiveness, which stokes dogmatism, which leads to hostile mindreading and kitchensinking, which pave the way for self-summarizing. Each negative form of communication feeds into the overall negative system. Unproductive communication fosters a defensive, negative climate, which makes it virtually impossible to resolve conflicts. When egocentrism prevails, each partner is more interested in getting his or her own way than in creating a solution that both can accept. In addition, unconstructive communication is so disconfirming that it damages individual partners and the long-term health of the relationship.

Constructive Communication Patterns

According to relationship counselors, healthy, constructive communication during conflict is open, nonjudgmental, confirming, and nonstrategic. In addition, it reflects dual perspective by focusing on both partners and the relationship even when tension is high. Constructive communication creates a supportive, positive climate that increases the possibility of resolving conflict without harming the relationship. Let's look at how constructive communication plays out in the three phases of the conflict syndrome.

Early Stages The foundation for constructive management of conflict is laid early in interaction. To establish a good climate, partners confirm each other by recognizing and acknowledging each other's concerns and feelings. Returning to our example, when John says, "I want us to spend more time together," Shelly could confirm him by replying, "I wish we could too. It's nice that you want us to have more time together." That simple

© Peter L. Chapman

The most powerful stimulus for
changing minds is not a chemical.
Or a baseball bat. It is a word.
GEORGE MILLER

act on Shelly's part communicates to John that she is listening and that she cares about his concerns and about him. After she says that, a different conversation unfolds. It might go like this:

John: Yeah, it just seems that we used to spend a lot more time together, and we felt closer then. I miss that.

Shelly: I do too. It sounds as if what's really on your mind is how close we are, not specifically the amount of time we spend together. Is that right?

John: Yeah, I guess that is more what's bothering me, but I kind of think they're connected, don't you?

Shelly: I see what you mean. But we won't feel closer just by spending more time together. I think we also need some shared interests like we used to have.

John: I'd like that. Do you have any ideas?

Let's highlight several things in this conversation. First, notice that when Shelly began by reflecting John's opening statement, he elaborated and clarified what was troubling him. Instead of time per se, the issue is closeness. Listening sensitively, Shelly picks up on this and refocuses their conversation on closeness. We should also notice that Shelly doesn't mindread; instead, she asks John whether she understood what he meant. When he asks Shelly whether she thinks time and closeness are related, John shows openness to her perceptions; thus, he confirms her and doesn't mindread. The openness they create clears the way for effective discussion of how to increase closeness. Once a supportive climate is established, the couple can proceed to the middle stages of conflict knowing they are not fighting each other, but working together to solve a problem.

Middle Stages   The positive groundwork laid in the early phase of conflict supports what happens as partners dig into issues. The middle stages of constructive conflict are marked by what Gottman (1993) calls "agenda building," which involves staying focused on the main issues. Kitchensinking is unlikely to derail discussion, since partners keep communication on target. It's not that other issues might not come up as they do in unproductive conflict. However, partners who have learned to communicate effectively control digressions. One useful technique is **bracketing,** which is noting that an issue that comes up in the course of conflict is important and needs to be discussed at a later time. Bracketing allows partners to stay effectively focused on a specific issue at one time, but to agree to deal with other issues later. Bracketing confirms partners' feelings that issues brought up are important by promising to deal with them later. Yet by bracketing topics that are peripheral to the current discussion, partners are able to stay on track and make progress in resolving the immediate issue.

During the middle stage of constructive conflict, partners continue to show respect for each other by interrupting infrequently. Any interruptions that occur are to clarify meanings ("Before you go on, could you explain what you mean by closeness?") or to check perceptions ("So you think time together leads to closeness?"). Unlike disruptive interruptions, ones that clarify ideas and check perceptions confirm the person speaking by showing that the listener wants to understand the meaning. In this stage, partners continue to recognize and acknowledge each other's points of view. Rather than the cross-complaining that characterizes unproductive conflict, partners acknowledge each other's feelings, thoughts, and concerns. This doesn't mean they don't put their own concerns on the table. Constructive conflict requires that we assert our own feelings and needs as part of engaging in honest dialogue. There is no conflict between honoring ourselves and others, and doing both is the essence of good interpersonal communication.

Final Stages   The opening phase of constructive conflict establishes a supportive climate for discussion. The focus of the middle stages is to elaborate issues and feelings so that partners understand all that is involved. In the culminating phase, attention shifts to resolving the tension between partners. Whereas in unproductive conflict this involves meeting proposals with counterproposals, in constructive conflict partners continue to operate cooperatively. Keeping in mind that they share a relationship, they continue using dual perspective to remain aware of both individuals' perspectives. Instead of countering each other's proposals, partners engage in **contracting,** which is building a solution through negotiation and acceptance of parts of proposals. The difference between counterproposals and contracting is illustrated in this example:

Counterproposals

John: I want us to spend three nights a week doing things together.

Shelly: I can't do that right now, because we're short-handed at work and I am filling in nights. Get a hobby so you aren't bored nights.

John: Not being bored isn't the same as our being close. I want us to spend time together again.

Shelly: I told you, I can't do that. Don't be so selfish.

John: Aren't we as important as your job?

Shelly: That's a stupid question. I can't take three nights off. Let's take more vacations.

Contracting

John: I want us to spend three nights a week doing things together.

Shelly: I'm all for that, but right now we're short-handed at work. How about if we use your idea but adjust it to my job. Maybe we could start with one night each week and expand that later.

© Paul Barton/The Stock Market

John: Okay, that's a start, but could we also reserve some weekend time for us?

Shelly: That's a good idea. Let's plan on that. I just can't be sure how much I'll have to work on weekends until we hire some new people. What if we promise to give ourselves an extra week's vacation to spend together when we have full staff?

John: Okay, that's a good back-up plan, but can we take weekend time when you don't work?

Shelly: Absolutely. How about a picnic this Sunday?

In the counterproposal scenario, John and Shelly were competing to get their own ways. Neither tried to identify workable parts of the other's proposals or to find common grounds. Because each adopts a win–lose view of the conflict, it's likely that both of them and the relationship will be losers. A very different tone shows up in the contracting scenario. In it, both partners look for ways to agree with each other, while also asserting their own concerns. Neither partner represses personal needs, but each is committed to finding what might be workable in the other's proposals.

BETTINA

My son and I used to argue all the time, and we never got anywhere because we were each trying to get our own way and we weren't paying attention to the other. Then we went into family counseling, and we learned how to make our arguments more productive. The most important thing I learned was to be looking for ways to respond to what my son says and wants. Once I started focusing on him and trying to satisfy him, he was more willing to listen to my point of view and to think about solutions that would satisfy me. We still argue a lot—I guess we always will—but now it's more like we're working things through together instead of trying to tear each other down.

Specific differences between unproductive and productive conflict can be summarized as the difference between confirming and disconfirming communication. The particular kinds of communication that generate unproductive conflict share the quality of disconfirming the partner and/or the relationship. On the other hand, the communication in constructive conflict consistently confirms both partners and the relationship. This reminds us of the importance of supportive, confirming climates, which we explored in Chapter 7. The climate, or emotional mood, of interpersonal relationships is created by communication. Our discussion of specific skills highlights communication that fosters affirming climates in which conflicts can be productively resolved without damage to relationships.

Guidelines for Communicating Effectively During Conflict

Our study of conflict, along with many of the ideas we've considered in previous chapters, suggests four guidelines for dealing with conflict. Following these should increase your ability to handle conflicts effectively.

Focus on the Overall Communication System

Conflict does not occur in a vacuum. Instead, it takes place in the context of relationships and the overall communication climate established over time. As we noted in Chapter 1, communication is systemic, which means it occurs in contexts, and it is composed of many interacting parts. Applying the principle of systems to conflict, we can see that how we deal with conflict is shaped by factors beyond an immediate disagreement. This means that we must attend to the overall systems of relationships and communication if we wish to make conflict constructive.

Couples who have developed negative interpersonal climates cannot argue constructively simply by practicing "good conflict techniques" such as focusing talk and not interrupting. Those techniques occur within larger contexts that affect how they are interpreted. Partners who have learned to be generally defensive and distrustful are unlikely to respond openly to even the best conflict methods. By the same reasoning, in climates that are generally supportive and confirming, even unconstructive conflict communication is unlikely to derail relationships. Conflict, like all interaction, is affected by its contexts.

To make conflict more constructive in your relationships you should apply the information and guidelines discussed throughout this book. These will allow you to create positive, affirming interpersonal climates in which conflict can be managed most constructively. Engaging in mindful listening, which we discussed in Chapter 6, is essential to effective management of conflict. Also important is creating confirming climates, which we examined in Chapter 7. In addition, it's a good idea to apply the guidelines for effective verbal and nonverbal communication that we considered in Chapters 4 and 5. What you've learned about self-concept and perception should also help you control the multiple factors that influence how you deal with conflict in your relationships. In other words, conflict is part of a larger whole, and we must make that whole healthy in order to create a context in which conflict can be resolved without jeopardizing partners or relationships.

Time Conflict Effectively

Timing affects how we communicate about conflicts. There are three ways to use chronemics so that conflicts are most likely to be effective. First, try not to engage in serious conflict discussions at times when one or both people will not be fully present psychologically. Most of us are more irritable when we are sick or stressed. We're also less attentive and less mindful listeners when we are tired. It's generally more productive to discuss problems in private rather than in public settings. If time is limited or we are rushing, we're less likely to take the time to deal constructively with differences. It's impossible to listen well, develop ideas, and respond thoughtfully when a stopwatch is ticking in our minds. One guideline to keep in mind, then, is to time when you have conflicts.

A second guideline for timing is to be flexible about when you deal with differences. Constructive conflict is most likely when everyone's needs are accommodated. If one partner feels ready to talk about a problem, but the other doesn't, it's probably wise to delay discussion. This only works, of course, if the person who isn't ready agrees to talk about the issue at a later time. Since research indicates that men are more likely than women to avoid relationship conflicts, they may be especially reluctant to talk about disagreements without first gaining some distance (Beck, 1988; Rusbult, 1987). Some individuals prefer to tackle problems as soon as they arise, whereas other people need time to percolate privately before interacting.

STEPHANIE

I have a really hot temper, so I can cut someone to pieces if I argue when I'm mad. I have hurt a lot of friends by attacking them before I cooled off, and I hate myself when I act like that. I have finally figured out that I can handle fights constructively if I cool down. Now when I'm hot, I tell my friends or my boyfriend that I can't discuss it right then. Later, when I'm calm, I can talk without saying things that hurt them and that I feel bad about.

A third way to use chronemics to promote positive conflict is bracketing, which we discussed earlier in this chapter. It is natural that a variety of issues needing attention come up in the course of conflict. If we try to deal with all the sideline problems that arise, however, we can't focus on the immediate problem. Bracketing other concerns for later discussion lets us keep conflict focused productively. Keep in mind, however, that bracketing works only if partners return to the issues they set aside.

Honor Yourself, Your Partner, and the Relationship

Throughout this book we've emphasized the importance of honoring yourself, others, and relationships. It's important to keep all three in balance, especially when conflicts arise. Just as it is ineffective to disregard others' concerns, it is also unwise to muffle your own. For conflicts to be resolved in truly satisfying ways, each person must put her or his ideas, feelings, and needs on the table. Only then can partners engage in informed, open efforts to generate workable solutions to their problems.

In addition to attending to ourselves and our friends and romantic partners, we must remember that relationships are affected by how we handle conflict. For this reason, win–lose orientations toward conflict should really be called win–lose–lose, since when one person wins, both the other person and the relationship lose. Win–win orientations and constructive forms of communication make it possible for both individuals and the relationship to be winners.

Show Grace When Appropriate

Finally, an important principle to keep in mind during conflict is that **grace** is sometimes appropriate. Although the idea of grace has not traditionally been discussed in communication texts, it is very much a part of spiritual and philosophical thinking, which should influence how we interact with others. You don't have to be religious to show grace, nor do you have to have a knowledge of philosophy. All that's required is a willingness to sometimes excuse someone who has no formal right to expect your compassion.

© David Bitters/The Picture Cube, Inc.

By definition, grace is granting forgiveness or putting aside our own needs when there is no standard that says we should or must do so. Rather than being prompted by rules or expectations, grace springs from a generosity of personal spirit. Grace is not forgiving when we *should*—for instance, excusing people who aren't responsible for their actions. Also, grace isn't allowing others to have their way when we have no choice. Instead, grace is unearned and unnecessary kindness. For instance, two roommates agree to split chores and one doesn't do her share because she has three tests in a week. Her roommate might do all the chores even though there is no agreement or expectation of this generosity. This is an act of grace. It's also an act of grace to defer to another person's preference when you could hold out for your own. Similarly, when someone hurts us and has no right to expect forgiveness, we may choose to forgive anyway. We do so not because we *have* to, but because we want to. Grace is a matter of choice.

Grace involves the Zen concept of **letting go,** which is to free ourselves of anger, blame, and judgments about another and what she or he did. When we let go of these feelings, we release both ourselves and others from their consequences. Sometimes we tell a friend we forgive him for some offense, but then later we remind him of it. We might say we'll forget a transgression by our romantic partner, but later hold it against her. When we continue to hang on to blame and judgment, we haven't really let go, so we have not really shown grace. There's no grace when we blackmail others for kindness or hang onto hostile feelings. An act of

"Look, instead of constantly grading one another, let's make this a simple pass/fail relationship."

Reprinted from *The Chronicle of Higher Education* with the permission of Carole Cable.

grace must also be done gracefully. It is not grace if we yield to a friend and snap, "Okay, have it your own darned way." Grace doesn't create feelings of debt in others. Grace involves letting go of hostile feelings with a style that is as graceful as what we actually do.

Grace is given without strings. We show kindness, defer our needs, or forgive a wrong *without any expectation of reward.* Grace isn't doing something nice to make a friend feel grateful or indebted to us. It's also not acting in grace when we do something with the expectation of a payback. To do a favor for your partner because you want a reciprocal favor is a matter of bargaining, not grace. For an act to be one of grace, it must be done without conditions or expectations of return.

Grace is not always appropriate, and it can be exploited by individuals who take advantage of kindness. Some people repeatedly abuse and hurt others, confident that pardons will be granted. When grace is extended and then exploited, it may be unwise to extend it again. However, if you show grace in good faith and another takes advantage, you should not fault yourself. Kindness and a willingness to forgive are worthy moral precepts. Those who abuse grace, not those who offer it, are blameworthy.

Because Western culture emphasizes assertion and protection of self-interests, grace is not widely practiced or esteemed. We are told to stand up for ourselves, not let others walk on us, not put up with being hurt, and not tolerate transgressions. It is important to honor and assert ourselves, as we've emphasized throughout this book. However, self-interest and self-assertion alone are insufficient principles for creating rich interpersonal relationships.

None of us is perfect. We all make mistakes, hurt others with thoughtless acts, and occasionally do things we know are wrong. Sometimes there is no *reason* others should forgive us when we wrong them; we have no right to expect exoneration. Yet, in human relations there has to be some room for redemption, for the extension of grace when it is not required or earned. Clearly we should not always forgive others if they betray or hurt us, and certainly we should be cautious of granting grace repeatedly to someone who exploits it. At the same time, the richest relationships allow some room for grace in occasional moments.

SUMMARY

This chapter focused on conflict as a natural, inevitable, and potentially constructive aspect of interpersonal life. Because conflicts are normal and unavoidable in any relationship of real depth, the challenge is to learn to manage conflicts effectively. Patterns of conflict are shaped by how individuals view conflict. We discussed lose–lose, win–lose, and win–win approaches to conflict, and explored how each affects interaction. In addition, conflict patterns are influenced by how individuals respond to tension. Inclinations to exit, neglect, show loyalty, or voice conflict vary in how actively they deal with tension and how constructive they are for relationships. In most cases, voice is the preferred response because only it allows partners to intervene actively and constructively when conflicts arise.

Communication is particularly important in influencing the process of interpersonal conflict. Research by communication scholars as well as clinicians indicates that patterns of interaction that promote constructive management of conflict include being mindful, confirming others, showing dual perspective, listening sensitively, focusing discussion, contracting solutions, and avoiding mindreading, interrupting, self-summarizing, and cross-complaining.

Finally, we considered four guidelines for increasing the constructiveness of interpersonal conflict. First, we need to remember that conflicts occur within overall systems of communication and relationships. To be constructive, conflict must take place within supportive, confirming climates in which good interpersonal communication is practiced. Second, it's important to time conflicts so that all individuals have the time they need for private reflection and for productive discussion. A third principle is to balance commitments to yourself, others, and relationships when conflict arises. It is unwise to squelch any of these three, since all are affected by how we manage disagreements. Finally, we saw that it is sometimes appropriate to show grace in our personal relationships. Although grace can be exploited, it can also infuse relationships with kindness and make room for inevitable human errors. It's important to balance the tensions inherent in the notion of grace so that we recognize both its potential values and its dangers.

In the next two chapters, we'll explore the worlds of friendship and romance. As we do so, we'll carry forward the information and guidelines we've considered in this chapter, since how we manage conflicts affects the health of our friendships and romantic relationships.

KEY TERMS

Conflict	Bracketing
Games	Contracting
Kitchensinking	Grace
Metacommunication	Letting go

CHAPTER 9

Friendships in Our Lives

*T*he friendship sampler shown on the preceding page portrays the variation and beauty of friendships. Like this quilt, the design of our lives is made richer by the friendships that thread through them. Friends help us pass time, grow personally, celebrate moments of joy, and get us through the trials and tribulations of everyday life. Each new friend we weave into our lives enriches us and our interpersonal world.

Put It in Practice

WHAT IS FRIENDSHIP?

Think about your close friends, and respond to the six questions below.

	Very	Somewhat	Not Very
1. How important are friends in your life?	_____	_____	_____
2. How important is it for friends to accept each other?	_____	_____	_____
3. How important is it for friends to trust each other?	_____	_____	_____
4. How important is it for friends to feel emotionally close to each other?	_____	_____	_____
5. How important is it for friends to provide companionship in doing activities?	_____	_____	_____
6. How important is it for friends to help each other with practical assistance?	_____	_____	_____

The six questions you just answered focus on primary expectations of friendship. If you are like most people, you responded that friendship is very important in your life and that most or all of items 2–6 are very important to you. Across differences in race, gender, class, and sexual preference, most of us expect friends to provide intimacy, acceptance, trust, practical assistance, and support. These are common threads in diverse friendships. However, people differ in how they express trust, intimacy, acceptance, and support in friendship.

In this chapter, we will explore what friendships are, how they work, and how they differ among us. To launch our discussion, we'll identify common features of friendship as well as variations that result from diverse cultural backgrounds. Second, we'll explore the development and rules of friendships. Next, we'll consider pressures on friendship and how we can deal with these. Guidelines for effective communication between friends conclude the chapter.

The Nature of Friendship

Friendship is a unique relationship. In contrast to most relationships, friendship is voluntary. Biology or legal procedures establish relationships among family members, and proximity defines neighbors and coworkers. Friends, however, come together voluntarily. Friendships are also unique in lacking institutionalized structure or guidelines. There are legal and religious ceremonies for marriage and social and legal rules that govern marital relationships. We have no parallel ceremonies to recognize friendships and no formal standards to guide interaction between friends. The lack of social standards and recognition makes friendship a particularly challenging and exciting relationship.

Even though there are no formal standards for friendship, we seem to have generated some fairly consistent ideas about what a friend is and what happens between friends. Regardless of race, affectional preference, gender, age, and class, Westerners share some basic expectations of what friends do and what friendship is.

Willingness to Invest

Most people assume friendships require personal investments (Duck & Wright, 1993; Monsour, 1992). We expect to invest time, effort, energy, thought, and feeling in our friendships. Women and men of both homosexual and heterosexual orientations report that having friends is important for a fulfilling life (Mazur, 1989; Nardi & Sherrod, 1994; Sherrod, 1989). Although people differ in how they build and experience friendship, it seems we agree it's important.

LAKISHA

I don't know what I'd do without my friends. More than once they've held me together when I had a fight with my mom or broke up with a guy. When something good happens, it's not quite real until I share it with my friends. I don't think I could be happy without friends.

DENNIS

I really count on my buddies to be there for me. Sometimes we talk or do stuff, but a lot of times we just hang out together. That might not sound important, but it is. Hanging out with friends is a big part of my life.

© Mark Antman/The Image Works

Each friend represents a world in us, a world possibly not born until they arrive.

ANAÏS NIN

Intimacy

We also expect emotional closeness with friends. We want our friends to know our inner selves and to let us know theirs. In addition, intimacy implies that friends like or love each other and care about each other's happiness. Yet the shared view that friendship includes intimacy isn't paralleled by shared ideas about what intimacy is. Research on friendship suggests that how we experience and express intimacy with friends depends on our backgrounds.

Closeness Through Dialogue   One way to build and express intimacy is through communication. For many people, communication is the centerpiece of intimate friendship. This is especially true for people socialized in feminine culture, which emphasizes talk as a primary path to intimacy. In general, women see talking and listening as the main activities that create and sustain feelings of closeness (Aries, 1987; Becker, 1987; Rubin, 1985). Talk between women friends tends to be disclosive and emotionally expressive. Women discuss not only major events and issues, but also day-to-day activities. This "small talk" isn't really small at all, since it allows friends to understand the rhythms of each other's life. Intimacy is created as friends talk about themselves and their relationships and as they reveal personal feelings and information. Out of intimate conversation friends weave their separate worlds into a shared mosaic. This builds a strong and deep sense of connection.

A majority of women expect to know and be known by close friends. This is also true of androgynous men, who incorporate both feminine and masculine values into their identities (Jones & Dembo, 1989; Williams, 1985). Communication is a primary path to rich, personal knowledge, so women friends talk in depth about personal feelings and information. They want friends to know and understand their deepest selves and they want to know their friends in emotional depth. Because it is disclosive and personal, communication between women friends is highly expressive (Brehm, 1992).

LORI ANN

My girlfriends and I know everything about each other. We tell all our feelings and don't hold anything back. I mean it's total knowledge. We give updates on each new episode in relationships with guys, and we talk about what it means. There's just nothing I wouldn't tell my friends.

Reflecting the rules of feminine culture, communication between women friends is typically responsive and supportive (Wright & Scanlon, 1991). Friends use facial expressions and head movements to show involvement. In addition, they ask questions and give feedback that signals they are following and want to know more. Women friends also offer generous emotional support to one another. They do this by accepting each other's feelings and staying involved in each other's dreams, problems, and lives.

Closeness Through Doing   A second way to create and express closeness is by sharing activities. Friends enjoy doing things together and doing things for one another. Activities and companionship are the center of friendship for some individuals. Closeness through doing is often the rule in men's friendships (Swain, 1989; Wood & Inman, 1993). As we have seen in previous chapters, masculine cultures pivot on activities such as sports. This may be why men, in general, find it more natural to build intimacy through doing things than through talking. Sharing activities and working toward common goals (winning the game or battle) build a sense of camaraderie (Sherrod, 1989).

© Mark Antman/The Image Works

JOSH

The thing I like about my buddies is that we can just do stuff together without a lot of talk. Our wives expect us to talk about every feeling we have as if that's required to be real. I'm tight with my buddies, but we don't have to talk about feelings all the time. You learn a lot about someone when you hunt together or coach the Little League.

Josh has a good insight. We do reveal ourselves and learn about others in the process of doing things together. In the course of playing football or soccer, teammates learn a lot about each other's courage, reliability, willingness to take risks, and security. Soldiers who fight together also discover each other's strengths and weaknesses. Strong emotional bonds and personal knowledge can develop without verbal interaction (Rubin, 1985).

Intimacy through doing also involves expressing care by doing things for friends. Swain (1989) says men's friendships typically involve a give and take of favors. Jake helps Matt move into his new apartment, and Matt later assists Jake with a glitch in his computer. As a rule, men place more value than women on giving and receiving practical help. Perhaps because masculine socialization emphasizes instrumental activities, men are more likely than women to see doing things for others as a primary way to say they care. Sometimes this leads to misunderstandings between women and men. If Myra sees intimate talk as the crux of closeness, she may not interpret Ed's practical help in fixing her computer as indicating that he cares about her.

KAYA

My husband's life centers on doing things for me and our kids. He looks for things to do for us. Like when our son came home over break, he tuned up his car and replaced a tire. I hadn't even noticed the tire was bad. When I wanted to return to school, he took a second job to make more money. One day he came home with a microwave to make cooking easier for me. All the things he does for us are his way of expressing love.

It would be a mistake to conclude that women and men are completely distinct in how they create intimacy. Actually, they are more alike than we often think. Recent studies reveal that the sexes are not as different as they are sometimes stereotyped to be (Duck & Wright, 1993). Although women generally place a special priority on communication, men obviously talk with their friends. Like women, men disclose personal feelings and vulnerabilities. They simply do it less, as a rule, than women. Similarly, although men's friendships may be more instrumental, women friends also do things with and for each other and count these as important in friendship (Duck & Wright, 1993). Many of the differences between how women and men create and express intimacy are matters of degree, not absolute contrasts.

Put It in Practice

YOUR STYLE OF INTIMACY

Do gendered dynamics operate in your friendships? Find out by considering the activities below in terms of how often you do each thing with your closest friends of the same sex.

1. Talk about family problems
2. Exchange favors (provide transportation, lend money)
3. Engage in sports, including shooting hoops and so forth
4. Try to take their minds off problems with diversions
5. Disclose your personal anxieties and fears
6. Talk about your romantic relationships
7. Do things together (camping, going to a game, shopping)
8. Confide secrets you wouldn't want others to know
9. Just hang out without a lot of conversation
10. Talk about small events in your day-to-day life
11. Provide practical assistance to help friends
12. Talk explicitly about your feelings for each other
13. Discuss and work through tensions in your friendship
14. Physically embrace or touch to show affection
15. Ignore or work around problems in the friendship

Items 1, 5, 6, 8, 10, 12, 13, and 14 have been found to be more prominent in women's friendships; items 2, 3, 4, 7, 9, 11, and 15 tend to be more pronounced in men's friendships.

Reprinted by permission of Johnny Hart and Creators Syndicate, Inc.

Acceptance

A third common expectation of friends is that they will accept us. We expect friends to like us for who we are and to accept us, warts and all. Each of us has shortcomings and vices, but we count on friends to accept us in spite of these. With friends we feel we shouldn't have to put up false fronts. If we feel low, we can act that way instead of faking cheerfulness. If we are unhappy, we can express our feelings openly without fear of being rejected. If we are upset, we don't have to hide it. We expect friends to accept us as we are and as we change over time.

The essence of acceptance is feeling that we are okay as human beings. As we saw with Maslow's hierarchy of human needs in Chapter 1, being accepted by others is important to our sense of self-worth. Most of us are fortunate enough to gain acceptance from family as well as friends. However, this is not always true for lesbians and gays. Sadly, some parents reject sons and daughters who are homosexual. They refuse to validate the basic worth of a child who isn't heterosexual. Parental rejection echoes Western culture's general hostility to homosexuality. Because social and familial acceptance is sometimes lacking for them, gays and lesbians may count on friends for acceptance even more than heterosexuals do (Nardi & Sherrod, 1994). Friendships may have heightened importance because they often substitute for families. This is why a recent book on gay and lesbian relationships is titled *Families We Choose* (Weston, 1991).

DOUG

About a year ago, I came out to my parents, and they acted like I was from another planet. It was like once I said I was gay, nothing else about me mattered. Just being gay made me less than human. They shouted and cried and threatened and begged me to get therapy. The only thing they didn't do was consider that maybe I didn't need therapy—maybe it's okay to be gay. The gay community became my family. They are the people who accept me and support who I am. I still hope Mom and Dad will come around one day, but in the meantime I've made another family for myself.

Notice in Doug's commentary that he felt judged by his parents, which probably made him feel defensive. Doug's experience also illustrates the damage done by totalizing others by focusing on a single aspect of their identity and ignoring many others. Doug is still a student, a loving son, a whole person with dreams, ambitions, hopes, and fears. Yet, he feels that his parents see only his sexual orientation and disregard everything else about him.

Although lesbians and gays may depend more heavily than heterosexuals on friends for acceptance, there are few other differences in how their friendships operate. Like heterosexuals, gays and lesbians value friendship and distinguish among casual, close, and best friends. Also like heterosexuals, gays and lesbians rely on both communication and activities as paths to intimacy.

Trust

A key component of close friendships is trust, which has two dimensions. First, trust involves confidence in others to be dependable. We count on them to do what they say and to not do what they promise not to. Second, trust assumes emotional reliability, which is the belief that a friend cares about us and our welfare. When we feel both dimensions of trust, we don't need to preface private information with warnings not to tell anyone, and we don't have to have detailed knowledge about what our friends do and who they talk with to believe that they will not hurt us.

SARINI

Trust is the bottom line for friends. It's the single most important thing. It takes me a long time to really trust someone, but when I do, it's complete. I was so hurt when a friend told another person something I told her in confidence. We still get together, but the trust is gone. I don't tell her private things, so there's no depth.

Like most qualities of friendship, trust is something that develops gradually and in degrees. We learn to trust people over time as we interact with them and discover they do what they say and don't betray us. As trust develops, friends increasingly reveal themselves to one another. As each new disclosure is accepted and kept confidential, trust continues to grow. When a high level of trust develops, friends are free from the uncertainty and insecurity that is natural in early stages of relationships (Boon, 1994).

How much trust develops between friends depends on a number of factors. First, our individual histories influence our capacity to trust others. Recalling the discussion of attachment styles in Chapter 2, you'll remember that early interactions with caregivers shape our beliefs about others. For those of us who got consistently loving and good care, trusting others is not especially difficult. On the other hand, some children receive care that isn't loving and reliable—sometimes people are there when we need them, and at other times they aren't. If caring is either absent or inconsistent, the capacity to trust others withers. Researchers think the tendency to trust or not trust others is relatively enduring unless later experiences reverse the early lessons about relationships (Bartholomew, 1993).

JAMES

It's tough for me to really trust anybody, even my closest friends or my girlfriend. It's not that they aren't trustworthy. The problem's in me. I just have trouble putting full faith in anyone. When my parents had me, Dad was on the bottle, and Mom was thinking about divorce. He got in Alcoholics Anonymous and they stayed together, but I wonder if what was happening between them meant they weren't there for me. Maybe I learned from the start that I couldn't count on others.

Family scripts also influence how much and how quickly we trust others. Some of us were taught that people are good and we should count on them, whereas others of us learned that people are untrustworthy and we shouldn't ever turn our back on anyone. Basic scripts like these, although not irrevocable, affect the ease and extent of our ability to trust.

Willingness to take risks also influences trust in relationships. There is considerable risk in trusting a friend with our secrets, fears, and flaws. The friend could always use the information against us or share our most private disclosures with others (Boon, 1994). We can never *know* for sure what friends will do with private information, but we trust them not to use it to exploit or expose us. In this sense, trust is a leap into the unknown. To emphasize the risk in trusting, it has been said that "trust begins where knowledge ends" (Lewis & Weigert, 1985, p. 462). The risk involved may explain why we trust only selected people.

Support

Communication scholars Brant Burleson and Wendy Samter (1994) report that support is a basic expectation of friendship. We expect friends to support us in times of personal stress. Once individuals leave home for college, friends often become the primary people to whom they turn for help and comfort (Adelman, Parks, & Albrecht, 1987).

There are many ways to show support. What is common among the various types of support is the relational message "I care about you." Often we support friends by listening to their problems. The more mindfully we listen, the more support we provide. How we respond also shows support. For example, it's supportive to offer to help a friend with a problem or to talk through options. Another way we support friends is by letting them

© Zigy Kaluzny/Tony Stone Images, Inc.

know they're not alone. When we say "I've felt that way too" or "I had the same problem," we signal that we understand their feelings. Having the grace to accept friends when they err or hurt us is also a way to show support. To comfort friends in difficult times, we can validate their worth and help them place problems in a larger perspective that includes positive outlooks (Burleson, 1984).

Another important form of support is being available. Sometimes we can't do or say much to ease a friend's unhappiness. Breaking up with a partner, losing a parent, or being rejected by a graduate program are not matters we can change by our words or deeds. However, we can offer ourselves. We show we care by standing by friends so that at least they have company in their sadness. In one study, young adults said the essence of real friendship was "being there for each other" (Secklin, 1991). It is a great comfort to know someone is there for us no matter what.

JOSÉ

Last year my father died back in Mexico, and I wasn't with him when he died. I felt terrible. My friend Alex spent a lot of time with me after my father died. Alex didn't do anything special, and we didn't even really talk much about my father or how I felt. But he was there for me, and that meant everything. I knew he cared even though he never said that.

Women and men tend to differ somewhat in how they support friends. Because feminine socialization emphasizes personal communication, women generally exceed men in providing verbal emotional support (Aries, 1987; Becker, 1987; Duck & Wright, 1993). They are likely to talk in detail about feelings, dimensions of emotional issues, and fears that accompany distress. By talking in depth about emotional troubles, women help each other identify and ventilate feelings. In addition, intimate talk weaves friends closely together. This exemplifies closeness through dialogue.

Men rely less than women on emotional talk to support friends. Instead, they typically engage in "covert intimacy," a term Scott Swain (1989) coined to describe the indirect ways men support one another. Instead of an intense hug, which a woman might use to support a hurting friend, men are more likely to clasp a shoulder or playfully punch an arm. Instead of engaging in direct and sustained emotional talk, men tend to communicate support more instrumentally. This could mean giving advice on how to solve a problem or offering assistance, such as a loan or transportation. Finally, men are more likely than women to support friends by coming up with diversions (Cancian, 1987; Tavris, 1992). If you can't make a problem any better, at least you can take a friend's mind off it. "Let's go throw some darts," or "Let's check out the new movie" are offers to support a friend by providing diversions. These ways of supporting others are consistent with the masculine mode of closeness.

RICH

Girls and guys help each other out in different ways. If I don't want to think about some problem, I want to be with a guy friend. He'll take my mind off the hassle. If I'm with a girl, she'll want to talk about the problem and wallow in it, and that just makes it worse sometimes. But when I really need to talk or get something off my chest, I need a girl friend. Guys don't talk about personal stuff.

In Western society, there are fairly common expectations of friends. We expect friends to invest in friendship and to provide intimacy, acceptance, trust, and support. As a result of gender, race, class, age, and sexual orientation, we may differ in how we experience and express friendship. However, it seems that these five common expectations transcend differences among us. Yet, it's not enough for friends to have these feelings; they must also communicate them. Skills in verbal and nonverbal communication, listening, building climate, and managing conflict contribute to our ability to express friendship in ways that we and others feel.

The Development and Rules of Friendships

The ways friendship grows and operates are not random. Although we're usually not aware of patterns, friendships tend to follow rules in how they develop and function.

The Developmental Course of Friendship

Most friendships develop over time in fairly patterned ways. Although intense bonds are sometimes formed quickly in unusual circumstances such as crises, the majority of friends work out their relationship in a series of stages. Bill Rawlins (1981), an interpersonal communication researcher who focuses on communication between friends, developed a six-stage model of how friendships develop (Figure 9.1).

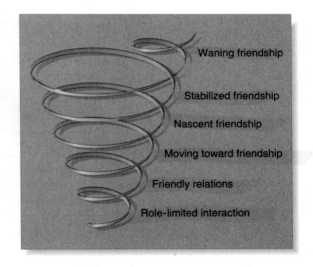

FIGURE 9.1 *The Developmental Course of Friendship*

Role-Limited Interaction Friendships begin with an encounter in two individuals' social circle. We might meet a new person at work, through membership on athletic teams, in clubs, or by chance in an airport, store,

© Bob Daemmrich/Tony Stone Images, Inc.

or class. The initial meeting is the first stage of interaction and, possibly, friendship. During this stage, we tend to rely on standard social rules and roles. We are polite, and we are less than fully open and disclosive, because we aren't ready to reveal our private selves. In early meetings, people don't have enough personal knowledge of each other to engage in dual perspective. Instead, they rely on more general scripts and stereotypes. Also, early interactions are often awkward and laced with uncertainty, since individuals haven't worked out their own patterns for relating to each other.

Friendly Relations   The second stage of friendship is friendly relations, in which individuals check the other out to see whether common ground and interests exist. Jean tries to start a conversation with Paula by commenting on the teacher in a class they share. If Paula responds with her impressions of the teacher, she conveys the relational-level message that she's interested in interacting. A business person may joke or engage in small talk to see if an associate wants to move beyond the acquaintance level of relating. Although friendly exchanges are not dramatic, they are useful. Through them, we explore the potential for a more personal relationship with another person.

Moving Toward Friendship   During the third stage of interaction, we start making serious moves to create a friendship. Until this stage, we stick pretty closely to social rules and norms and we interact in contexts where we naturally meet. Moving toward friendship involves stepping beyond social roles. We might make a small self-disclosure or comment that we're angry about something to signal we'd like to personalize the relationship. We also move toward friendship when we meet outside of contexts that naturally occur. Emily might ask her associate Sam if he wants to stop at a bar for a drink before leaving for the day. Ben might ask his classmate Drew if he wants to get together to study. Sometimes we involve others to lessen the potential awkwardness of being with someone we don't yet know well. For instance, Amy might invite Stuart to a party where others will be present. As we interact more personally with others, we begin to talk about feelings, values, interests, and attitudes. This personal knowledge forms the initial foundation of friendship.

Nascent Friendship   If individuals continue to interact and to like what they discover in each other, they begin to think of themselves as friends or as becoming friends. This is the stage of nascent, or embryonic, friendship. At this point, social rules and standards become less important, and friends begin to work out their own private rules for regulating interaction. When my friend Nancy and I were in this stage, we agreed to reserve Sunday brunch for each other every week. This was a private rule we generated to accommodate our schedules and preferences. Some friends settle into patterns of getting together for specific things (watching games, shopping, racquetball, going to movies) and don't ever expand those boundaries. Other friends share a wider range of times and activities. Although friends are working out rules for their relationship during the nascent stage, often they aren't aware of the rules until later. The milestones of this stage are that individuals begin to think of themselves as friends and to work out their own patterns for interaction.

Stabilized Friendship   When friends feel established in each other's life, the friendship is stabilized. A key benchmark of this stage is the assumption of continuity. Whereas in earlier stages, individuals didn't count on getting together unless they made a specific plan, stabilized friends assume they'll continue to see each other. We no longer have to ask if a friend wants to get together again. We take future encounters for granted because we consider the relationship ongoing.

Ꮯheck It Out

MAINTAINING FRIENDSHIPS

Do we spend more time with casual or best friends? The answer might surprise you. A recent study indicates that frequent interaction is more important for casual than close or best friendships. When casual friends don't see each other, they aren't sure the friendship still exists.

Lack of interaction doesn't appear to threaten relationships between best friends. Close and best friendships depend more on assurances of affection, though these need not be frequent. The best explanation is that close and best friends feel more secure in their connection than do casual friends. Because they assume they're continuing parts of each other's life, best friends don't need regular interaction.

Source: Based on a study by Rose, S., & Serafica, F. (1986). Keeping and ending casual, close and best friendships. *Journal of Social and Personal Relationships, 3,* 275–288.

Another criterion of this stage is trust, which stabilizes the friendship. Throughout earlier stages of interaction, individuals make limited disclosures to build and test trust. A close friendship is unlikely to stabilize until there is a mutually high level of trust. Once friends have earned each other's trust, many of the barriers to fully interpersonal communication disintegrate. It now feels safe to share intimate information and to reveal vulnerabilities that we normally conceal from others. As we communicate more openly, our friendships become more honest and personal. We remove social masks we wear with most people and enter into I–Thou relationships by engaging friends in their unique individuality. Stabilized friendships may continue indefinitely, in some cases lasting a lifetime.

MARLENE

Martha and I go way, way back—all the way to childhood when we lived in the same housing complex. As kids we made mudpies and ran a lemonade stand together. In high school, we double-dated and planned our lives together. Then we both got married and stayed in touch, even when Martha moved away. We still sent each other pictures of our children, and we called a lot. When my last child entered college, I decided it was time for me to do that too, so I enrolled in college. Before I did that, though, I had to talk to Martha and get her perspective on whether I was nuts to go to college in my thirties. She thought it was a great idea, and she's thinking about that for herself now. For nearly forty years we've shared everything in our lives.

© Tom & Dee Ann McCarthy/The Stock Market

All human beings have an innate need to hear and tell stories and to have a story to live by.

HARVEY COX

Waning Friendship   As we have seen, a common expectation of friendship is investment. When one or both individuals stop investing in a friendship, it is likely to wane. Sometimes friends drift apart because each is pulled in different directions by career and family demands. In other cases, friendships deteriorate because they've run their natural course and become boring. A third reason friendships end is violations of trust or other rules friends establish for themselves. Saying "I don't have time for you now" may violate friends' tacit agreement to always make room for each other. Criticizing a friend or not sharing confidences may also breach unspoken rules between friends. When friendships deteriorate or suffer serious violations, communication changes in predictable ways. Defensiveness and uncertainty rise, causing individuals to be more guarded, less spontaneous, and less disclosive than they were in the stage of stabilized friendship. Communication may also become more controlling and strategic as waning friends try to protect themselves from further exposure and hurt.

Even when serious violations occur between friends, relationships can sometimes be repaired. For this to happen, however, both friends must be committed to rebuilding trust and intimacy. They must be willing to work through their feelings in open, constructive discussion.

Rules of Friendship

Friendships are governed by **relationship rules** that specify what is expected and what is not allowed. Relationship rules are usually unspoken understandings that regulate how partners interact. For instance, most friends have a tacit understanding that they can be a little late, but they won't keep each other waiting long. A delay of five minutes is within the rules, but a forty-minute delay is a violation.

Many rules concern what friends want and expect of each other, such as support, time, and acceptance. Equally important are "shalt not" rules that define what won't be tolerated. For example, most Westerners would consider it a betrayal if a friend slept with their romantic partner.

JUANITA

Celia and I had been friends for three years before we decided to share an apartment. After a while I noticed that my best pair of earrings was missing, and then a gold necklace my father gave me disappeared. Money I was sure I had in my wallet was gone a couple of times. I thought this was strange, but it never occurred to me that Celia would steal from me. Then one day, I needed one of Celia's purses that went with my outfit. She wasn't there, but since we borrowed each other's clothes all the time, I didn't think anything about getting it from her closet. When I opened the purse, I saw my earrings and necklace. I never felt so betrayed in all my life. I asked her to move out that day.

Rules regulate both trivial and important aspects of interaction. Not interrupting may be a rule, but breaking it probably won't destroy a good friendship. On the other hand, stealing money, jewelry, or romantic partners may be the death knell of a friendship.

In addition to private rules that friends develop to reflect their individual styles and preferences, Westerners have a number of common rules about what friendship is—and is not.

As you may have noticed, many shalt nots for friendship are inverted forms of the rules for sustaining good friendships. Although friends may never explicitly discuss their rules, the rules matter, as we discover if we violate one!

The typical pattern through which friendships develop and the rules that guide them explain how friendships form and operate. In the next section, we consider some of the pressures and complications that sometimes jeopardize even very close and satisfying friendships.

Pressures on Friendships

Like all human relationships, friendships experience pressures that range from mild to severe. To understand the strains friends face, we'll consider internal tensions and external constraints that tug at friendships.

Internal Tensions

Friendships, like all personal connections, are vulnerable to tensions inherent in being close. **Internal tensions** are relationship stresses that grow out of individuals and their interaction. We'll consider three of these.

Relational Dialectics In earlier chapters, we discussed relational dialectics, which are opposing human needs that create tension and propel change in close relationships. The three dialectics are tension between connection and autonomy, openness and privacy, and novelty and

Check It Out

THE RULES OF FRIENDSHIP

When researchers asked people to describe their ideas about what is needed to maintain a good friendship, they found high consistency on a number of rules for keeping friendship intact:

1. Stand up for a friend when she or he isn't around.
2. Share your successes and how you feel about them.
3. Give emotional support.
4. Trust and confide in each other.
5. Help a friend when he or she is needy.
6. Respect a friend's privacy.
7. Try to make friends feel good when you are together.

People were just as consistent in what they described as "antirules," or ways to end a friendship:

1. Fail to tolerate your friend's friends.
2. Criticize a friend in front of others.
3. Share a friend's confidences with other people.
4. Fail to show a friend you like him or her.
5. Fail to support a friend.
6. Nag a friend, or get on his or her case.
7. Fail to confide in a friend.
8. Fail to help a friend when she or he is needy.
9. Act jealous or critical of friend's other friends.

Source: Argyle, M., & Henderson, M. (1985). The rules of relationships. In S. W. Duck & D. Perlman (Eds.), *Understanding personal relationships: An interdisciplinary approach* (pp. 63–84). Beverly Hills, CA: Sage.

"When I was your age, 'your mother wears combat boots' was an insult."

From *The Wall Street Journal.*
Reprinted by permission of Cartoon Features Syndicate.

familiarity. These three dialectics punctuate friendship, prompting us to adjust continuously to natural, yet contradictory needs.

Dialectics may strain friendships when individuals differ in their needs. For instance, there could be tension if Joe is bored and needing novelty, but his friend Andy is overstimulated and seeking calming routines. Similarly, if Andy has just broken up with a woman, he may seek greater closeness with Joe right at the time that Joe has a strong need to feel independent of others. When needs collide, friends should talk. It's important to be up-front about what you need and to be sensitive to what your friend needs. Doing this simultaneously honors yourself, your friend, and the relationship. The goal is for friends to express themselves honestly and to engage in dual perspective and sensitive listening within a supportive communication climate. When this occurs, friends can usually work out ways to meet each person's needs or at least to understand that differing needs don't reflect unequal commitment to the friendship.

LANA

My girlfriends and I are so often in different places that it's hard to take care of each other. If one of my friends isn't seeing anyone special, she wants more time with me and wants to do things together. If I'm in a relationship with a guy, her needs feel demanding. But when I've just broken up, I really need my friends to fill time and talk with. So I try to remember how I feel and use that to help me accept it when my friends need my time.

Lana highlights the importance of dual perspective in dealing with tensions caused by relational dialectics. She draws on her own experience of breakups to understand her friends' perspective when they've broken up. This motivates Lana to make time to be with her friends. If she communicates her understanding and acceptance, her friends will feel she supports and cares about them.

Relational dialectics are natural and constructive forces in friendship. They keep us aware of multiple, sometimes clashing needs. In addition, because we find tension uncomfortable, dialectics motivate us to fine-tune friendships continuously. The strains dialectics spark can be managed by revising friendships and by accepting dialectical tensions as normal, ongoing relational processes.

Diverse Communication Styles Friendships may also be strained when friends misinterpret each other's communication. The potential for misunderstanding mushrooms as our society becomes increasingly diverse, making it more likely that some of our friends will have cultural backgrounds different from our own. Because how we communicate reflects the understandings and rules of our culture, misinterpretations are likely between friends from different cultures (Wood, 1995a). For instance, in many Asian societies, individuals are socialized to be unassuming and modest, while the United States encourages assertion and celebrating ourselves. Thus, a native Japanese might perceive a friend from Milwaukee as arrogant for saying, "Let's go out to celebrate my acceptance to law school." A Thai woman might not get the support she wants from a friend from Brooklyn because she was taught not to assert her needs and the Brooklyn friend was taught that people should speak up for themselves.

Misunderstandings also arise from differences within cultures in the United States. Aaron, who is white, might feel hurt if Markus, an African American friend, turns down an invitation to a concert in order to go home to care for an ailing aunt. Aaron might interpret this as a rejection by Markus, since he perceives that Markus is using the aunt as an excuse to avoid going out with him. Aaron would interpret Markus differently if he realized that, as a rule, African Americans are more communal than European Americans, so taking care of extended family members is a priority (Gaines, 1995). Ellen may feel that her friend Jed isn't being supportive when instead of empathizing with her problems, he offers advice or suggests they go out to take her mind off her troubles. Yet, he *is* showing support according to masculine rules of communication. Jed, on the other hand, may feel that Ellen is intruding on his autonomy when she pushes him to talk about his feelings. According to feminine rules of communication, however, Ellen *is* showing interest and concern.

Differences themselves aren't usually the cause of problems in friendship. Instead, how we interpret and judge others' communication is the root of tension and hurt. What Jed and Ellen did wasn't the source of their frustrations. Jed interpreted Ellen according to his communication rules, not hers, and she interpreted Jed according to her communication rules, not his. Notice that the misunderstandings result from our interpretations of others' behaviors, not the behaviors themselves. This reminds us of the need to distinguish between fact and inferences.

Check It Out

JAPANESE FRIENDSHIPS

The Japanese distinguish between two types of friendships. *Tsukiai* are friendships based on social obligation. These usually involve neighbors or work associates and tend to have limited life spans. Friendships based on affection and common interests usually last a lifetime: Personal friendship is serious business. The number of personal friends is very small and stable, in contrast to friendship patterns in the United States. Friendships between women and men are rare in Japan. Prior to marriage, only 20% of Japanese say they have close friends of the opposite sex.

Sources: Based on studies by Atsumi, R. (1980). Patterns of personal relationships. *Social Analysis, 5,* 63–78. Mochizuki, T. (1981). Changing patterns of mate selection. *Journal of Comparative Family Studies, 12,* 318–328.

Sexual Attraction   Sexual attraction can also cause difficulty between friends. Friendships between heterosexual men and women, or gay men, or lesbians often include sexual tensions. Because Western culture so strongly emphasizes gender and sex, it's difficult not to perceive people in sexual terms (Johnson, Stockdale, & Saal, 1991; O'Meara, 1989). Even if there is no sexual activity between friends, sexual undertones may ripple beneath the surface of their friendships.

SHASHA

It is so hard to be just friends with guys. When I try to be friends with a guy, he'll hit on me at some point. I tell guys if friendship is all I'm interested in and they agree, but they hit on me anyway. It's happened so much that by now I feel on guard with guys even before they start anything.

Sexual attraction or invitations can be a problem between friends who have agreed not to have a sexual relationship. Tension over sexuality can be present in friendships between heterosexual women and men (West, Anderson, & Duck, 1996) as well as in friendships between lesbians and between gay men (Nardi & Sherrod, 1994). Trust may be damaged if someone we consider a friend makes a pass. Further, once a friend transgresses the agreed-on boundaries of the friendship, it's hard to know how to act with each other or to feel completely comfortable.

Relational dialectics, misinterpretations of different communication styles, and sexual attraction are sources of internal tension in many friendships. Usually straightforward communication, although not always easy, is the best way to deal with these problems and restore comfortableness. Guidelines for effective communication that we've discussed in other chapters apply here. For example, it's important to be clear when stating your own needs and preferences. Also, it's wise to rely on I-language so that you communicate what you feel and want without assuming what your friend wants and feels. Sensitive listening and supportive communication are also helpful in keeping a friendship intact while partners address sexual tensions.

External Constraints

In addition to internal tensions, friendships may encounter pressures from outside sources. Three of these are competing demands, changes, and geographic distance.

Competing Demands   Friendships exist within larger social systems that affect how they function (Allan, 1994). Because our lives are complex, we continuously struggle to balance competing demands for our time and energy. Since friendships are voluntary and not governed by formal rules, they can be neglected more easily than careers or marriages. Our work and our romantic relationships tend to be woven into our everyday lives, ensuring they will get daily attention. Time with friends, however, isn't reserved in what we must do each day. We have to make room in our lives, plan meetings, and set aside time to interact. When all that we *must* do overwhelms us, we may not get to what we *want* to do.

We may also neglect friends because of other relationships. When a new romance is taking off, we may be totally immersed in it. The excitement of getting to know a new person can absorb all of our time and thoughts. Friends may also be neglected when other important relationships in our lives are in crisis. If one of our parents is ill or another friend is having trouble, we may need all of our energy to cope with the acute situation. When we are wrapped up in other relationships in happy or anxious ways, we have little of ourselves left to give to friends. To avoid hurting friends, we should let them know when we need a "leave of absence from the friendship" to deal with immediate priorities. If we don't explain our inattention to friends, they may feel hurt or rejected (Wood, 1995c).

Personal Changes   Our friendships change as our lives do. Although a few friendships are lifelong, most persist for shorter periods. If you think about your experiences, you'll realize that many of your friends changed as you made major transitions in your life (Allan, 1994). The people you spent time with and counted as friends shifted when you started high school, entered college, or moved to a new town. They'll change again when you leave college, move for career or family reasons, and perhaps have children. Since one base of friendship is common interests, established friends may not be able to share new interests we develop.

RUTH

Sandi and I had been friends for years when I had my first baby. Gradually, we saw less of each other and couldn't find much to talk about when we did get together. She was still doing the singles scene, and I was totally absorbed in mothering. I got to know other mothers in the neighborhood, and soon I thought of them as my friends. What's funny is that last year Sandi had a baby, and it was so good to get together and talk. We reconnected with each other.

Even if our interests don't change or our friends' interests change with ours, friendships often wither because we don't have time to take care of them (Duck, Rutt, Hurst, & Strejc, 1991). If we or members of our family have serious health problems, friendships may be neglected. Similarly, the early stages of a career require enormous amounts of energy and time. There may not be enough time or energy left to maintain friendships, even ones that matter to us. Each new context we enter realigns our friendship circles.

Lee West, Jennifer Anderson, and Steve Duck (1996), who study communication in personal relationships, point out that friendships also vary across the life span. In grammar school and high school, peer friendships

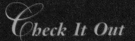

FRIENDSHIP IN A MOBILE SOCIETY

In 1992, the U.S. Census Bureau reported that 41.4 million people in the United States moved in the previous year. Although many of those who moved stayed within the same state, 14 million citizens moved to new states. Of course, the impact of moves on relationships is significant. Each move affects everyone in the mover's social network who is left behind.

are very important to most of us. During the twenties, many people are starting careers and families, and they have less time and energy to devote to friends. Later in life it seems that friends again ascend in importance as people once again have more time to develop and invest in friendships.

We're most likely to become friends with people we see regularly, so where we live and work influences our choice of friends (Wellman, 1985). Similarly, unemployment alters friendships because it isolates people from their usual social networks (Allen, Waton, Purcell, & Wood, 1986). Social class affects friendships because it shapes our interests and tastes in everything from music to lifestyle. In addition, class constrains where people live and work, as well as how much money they have for socializing with friends (O'Connor, 1992). Gay and lesbian communities allow friendships to crystallize around shared interests, concerns, and political goals. Similarly, communities for older citizens and kindergarten for younger ones are contexts in which friendships form on the basis of similarities in life stage and interests. Our friends change over the course of life as we and our interests continuously evolve.

Geographic Distance   Who are your closest friends? How often do you see them? What will happen when you locate in different parts of the country? Most friendships face the challenge of distance, and many won't survive it. Currently, as many as 90% of North Americans have at least one long-distance friendship (Rohlfing, 1995). In our highly mobile society, friendships are continuously in flux.

Whether distance ends friendship depends on several factors. Perhaps the most obvious influence is how much individuals care about continuing to be friends. The greater the commitment, the more likely a friendship will persist in spite of separation. Geographic distance is the reason the majority of high school friendships dissolve when individuals begin college (Rose, 1984). Yet, the likelihood of sustaining a long-distance friendship also depends on other factors, such as socioeconomic class and gender.

Because socioeconomic class profoundly affects who we are and how we live, it's not surprising that it influences the prospect that long-distance friendships will endure. The reason is simple: money. Friendships that survive distance involve frequent phone calls and letters and visits every so often. It takes money to finance trips and long-distance calls. Thus, friends with greater economic resources are better able to maintain their relationships than are friends with less discretionary income (Willmott, 1987).

Thus, people in middle and upper socioeconomic classes have a greater chance of bridging distance with friends. A second way in which socioeconomic class affects the endurance of long-distance friendships is flexibility in managing work and family. Middle- and upper-class individuals usually have generous vacations and flexibility in work schedules, so they can make time to travel. Working-class citizens tend to have less personal control over when they work and how much vacation time they get. Income also affects our ability to pay for babysitters who may make it possible for a parent to visit a friend for a weekend.

Put It in Practice

MAINTAINING FRIENDSHIP AT A DISTANCE

Do you have a long-distance friendship? If so, which of the following strategies do you use to maintain it?

Call at least once a week.

Call at least once a month.

Communicate by electronic mail at least weekly.

Call once or twice a year.

Write letters.

Visit weekly.

Visit monthly.

Visit occasionally.

Have conversations in your head with the friend.

Now identify three ways you might strengthen the closeness between you and your friend.

Gender also affects the endurance of long-distance friendships. There appear to be two reasons why women are more likely than men to sustain ties with friends who live at a distance. First, the sexes differ in how much they value same-sex friendships and how much they give to and get from them. Compared to women, men place less value on their same-sex relationships and invest less in them (Duck & Wright, 1993). This is especially true of married men who often name their wives as their best friends (Rubin, 1985). Women are also more willing than men to adjust schedules and priorities to make time for friends (Rubin, 1985), and they are more willing to tolerate less than ideal circumstances for being with friends.

For example, mothers who sustain long-distance friendships report that when they visit, they are seldom alone, since their children need attention and care. Even though these mothers say they miss the intimacy of uninterrupted conversations, they value each other enough to sustain friendships under the terms that are possible (Rohlfing, 1995). Women also report getting more out of their friendships with women than men report getting from their friendships with men (Duck & Wright, 1993). For women more than men, friendships are a primary and important thread woven through their lives.

CASS

My parents are so different from each other in their approaches to friendship. When I was growing up, Dad was on a career roll, so we were always moving to better neighborhoods or new towns. Each time we moved, he'd make a whole new set of friends. Even if his old friends lived nearby, he would want to be with the people he called his new peers. Mom is 180 degrees different. She still talks with her best friend in the town where I was born. She has stayed close to all of her good friends, and they don't change with the season like Dad's do. Once I asked him if he missed his old friends, and he said that friends were people you share common interests with so they change as your job does. That doesn't make sense to me.

Another reason women and men differ in commitment to maintaining long-distance friendships is that the sexes diverge somewhat in what they regard as the nucleus of closeness. As we've seen previously, shared interests and emotional involvement are the crux of closeness for women. Both of these are achieved primarily through communication, especially personal talk (Aries, 1987; Becker, 1987). The focus of men's friendships tends to be activities, which can't be shared when friends are apart (Swain, 1989; Wood & Inman, 1993). Women can and do sustain ties with important friends by talking on the phone and writing. Men, on the other hand, are more likely to replace friends who move with others who can share activities they enjoy (Rohlfing, 1995). Rubin's (1985) studies led her to say that women tend to develop "friends of the heart," whereas men often develop "friends of the road," that change as they move. It is easier to replace a friend who was a tennis partner than one with whom we shared intimate feelings and details of our life.

Like all relationships, friendships confront pressures and challenges from both inside and outside. Internal tensions in friendship involve relational dialectics, diverse communication styles, and sexual attraction. External challenges to friendship include competing demands, personal changes, and distance. How we respond to these pressures and how they affect our friendships depend on many factors, including personal qualities, commitment to friends, socioeconomic class, age, and gender.

Guidelines for Communication Between Friends

To conclude this chapter, we'll consider guidelines for communicating effectively with friends. Before discussing specific guidelines, however, we should realize that the principles for healthy communication with friends echo the basic principles of good interpersonal communication that we've discussed in preceding chapters. You should be aware that your self-concept and your perceptions influence how you interpret interaction with friends. It's also important to create a confirming climate by being open, spontaneous, empathic, equal, and nonevaluative. In addition, you should keep in mind what you have learned about using verbal and nonverbal communication effectively. Finally, managing conflict constructively is impor-

© Manuello Paganelli/Woodfin Camp & Associates, Inc.

tant in friendships, as in all relationships. In addition to these general principles, we can identify three specific guidelines for satisfying communication between friends.

Dual Perspective

As in all interpersonal relationships, dual perspective is important in friendship. To be a good friend we must understand and accept our friends' perspectives, thoughts, and feelings. As we've noted before, accepting another person's perspective is not the same as agreeing with it. The point is to understand what friends feel and think and to accept that as their reality. Dual perspective helps us to understand others on *their* terms, not ours.

To exercise dual perspective, we distinguish between our judgments and perceptions, on the one hand, and what friends say and do, on the other. It's important to remember the abstraction ladder we discussed in Chapter 3. When we feel hurt or offended by something a friend says, we should keep in mind that our perceptions and inferences do not equal their behavior. A friend acts, we perceive the action selectively, we then interpret and evaluate what happened, and finally we assign meaning to it and make inferences from what we've labeled. Notice how far from the original act we move in the process of trying to make sense of it. There's lots of room for slippage as we ascend the abstraction ladder. For example, when Shereen tells her friend Kyle that she's upset and needs support, she shouldn't assume he's uninterested if he suggests they go out for the evening. As we have learned, men often support friends by trying to divert them from problems.

© Lori Adamski Peek/Tony Stone Images, Inc.

It's all in the ear of the beholder.
TOM HAYDEN

Two communication principles help us avoid misinterpreting our friends. First, it's useful to ask questions to find out what others mean. Shereen might ask Kyle, "Why would you want to go out when I said I needed support?" This would allow Kyle to explain that he was trying to support her in his own way. Consequently, Shereen could grasp his meaning and interpret what he did in that light. Second, we should explain, or translate, our own feelings and needs. Shereen could say, "What would help me most right now is to have a sympathetic ear. Could we just stay in and talk about the problem?" If we make our needs clear, we're more likely to get the kind of support we value.

Communicate Honestly

A few years ago, a close friend named Gayle asked me for advice. Several months earlier she had agreed to give the keynote speech at a professional conference, and now she had an opportunity to travel to Italy with her partner at the time of the conference. She wanted to accompany her partner to Italy, but wondered if it was ethical to renege on her agreement to give the keynote address. Following principles we've discussed in this book, I first asked a number of questions to find out how Gayle felt and what her perspective was. It became clear she really wanted me to tell her it was okay to retract her agreement to give the speech. Because I love Gayle, I wanted to support her preference and to encourage her to do what she wanted. Yet, I didn't think it would be right for her to go back on her word, and I didn't think Gayle would respect herself in the long term if she welshed on a commitment.

I took a deep breath and told her three things: First, I said that her personal integrity was the issue and that she shouldn't withdraw her acceptance. Second, I told her I would support her and love her whatever she decided to do. And, third, I suggested there might be more than two options. At first she was quiet, clearly disappointed that I hadn't enthusiastically endorsed her dream. As we talked, we came up with the idea of her making the keynote speech and then joining her partner who would already be in Italy. Even with this plan, Gayle was dejected when she left, and I felt I'd let her down by not supporting her dream. Later that night she called to thank me for being the only friend who was really honest with her. After we'd talked, she'd realized it went against her own values to renege on her word, and nobody else had reminded her of that. Every other friend had told her to go to Italy and enjoy the trip.

Honesty is one of the most important gifts friends can give each other. Even when honesty is less than pleasant or not what we think we want to hear, we count on it from friends. In fact, people believe that honest feedback is what sets "real friends" apart from others (Burleson & Samter, 1994). Sometimes it's difficult to be honest with friends, as it was for me with Gayle. Yet, if we can't count on our friends for honest feedback, then where can we turn for truthfulness?

Many people make the mistake of confusing support with saying only nice things that others want to hear. Yet, this is not the essence of support. The key is caring enough about a person to look out for her or his welfare. Parents discipline children and set limits because they care about their children's long-term welfare. Colleagues who want to help each other give honest, often critical, feedback on work so that others can improve. Romantic partners who are committed tell each other when they perceive problems or when the other isn't being his or her best self. We can be supportive and loving while being honest, but to be less than honest is to betray trust placed in us. Honesty is part of what it means to care genuinely about another. Although it may be easier to tell friends what they want to hear or only nice things, genuine friendship includes honest feedback and candid talk.

Openness to Differences

A third principle for forming rich friendships is to be open to diversity in people. As we learned in Chapter 4, Western culture encourages polarized thinking. We have been socialized to think in either-or terms: Either she's like me or not; either he acts like I do or he's wrong; either they support me as I want to be supported or they're not real friends. The problem with this either-or thinking is that it sharply limits interpersonal growth.

Egocentric mind-sets and either-or thinking limit our horizons. We can't learn and grow if we reject what and who is different simply because they're different. Most of us tend to choose friends who are like us. We feel more immediately comfortable with friends who share our values, attitudes, backgrounds, and communication rules. But if we restrict our friends to people like us, we miss out on the fascinating variety of people and relationships that are possible. It does take more time and effort to understand and become comfortable with individuals who differ from us, but the dividends of doing so can be exceptional. Forming friendships with diverse people facilitates both your growth as an individual and the richness of your interpersonal world.

Check It Out

EXPERIENCING THE WORLD'S ABUNDANCE

If we are to have any chance at all of experiencing the world's abundance, we first need to change our thinking about the kind of world we live in. We need to change our habitual way of constructing what we think of as real. Most of us have been conditioned to think in either-or terms, to divide our world up into bits and pieces and parts . . . in-group and out-group. . . .

In relationships, according to the either-or mind set, we have your needs and my needs, your way of doing or seeing things and mine. . . . Most of us were taught that *either* your way *or* my way is valid. We rarely consider the possibility that *both* may be!

Source: Campbell, S. M. (1986, p. 263). From either-or to both-and relationships. In J. Stewart (Ed.), *Bridges, not walls* (4th ed.). New York: Random House.

SUMMARY

Friends are important in our lives. In this chapter, we learned how friendships form and how they function and change over time. We began by considering common expectations for friends, including investment, intimacy, acceptance, and support. Into our discussion of these common themes we wove insights about differences among us. We discovered there are some differences in how women and men create and express intimacy, invest in friendships, and show support. We also saw that gay and lesbian friendships largely parallel heterosexual ones in style and importance.

Friendships are ordered by developmental stages and rules. Friendships evolve gradually, moving from role-governed interactions to stable friendship and, sometimes, to waning friendship. Both social rules and private ones generated by friends provide regularity and predictability to interaction so that friends know what to expect from each other.

Like all relationships, friendships encounter challenges and tensions that stem from the relationship itself and from causes beyond it. Internal tensions of friendship include managing relational dialectics and misunderstandings and dealing with sexual attraction. External pressures on friendship are competing demands, changing personal needs and interests of friends, and geographic distance. Principles of interpersonal communication covered throughout this book suggest how we can manage these pressures, as well as the day-to-day dynamics of close friendships. In addition, communication between friends is especially enhanced by engaging in dual perspective, being honest, and being open to diversity and the growth it can prompt in all of us.

KEY TERMS

Relationship rules
Internal tensions

CHAPTER 10

Committed Romantic Relationships

PERSONALS

SBF, age 22, seeking responsible 22–30 year old S/DBM who enjoys dancing, quiet conversations, walks on beaches, and independent women. Friendship is necessary, romance possible. Send letter to Box 1234.

Successful, professional DWM looking for petite, blonde 18–25 yo who enjoys biking, travel, movies, and sailing. Should be 5'2" to 5'4", 100–105 pounds, blue eyes preferred. Send letter and photo to Box 3121

Mature, but not old: Fifty-something widow looking for companion to share movies, travel, and time together. Send letter to Box 2131.

Personal ads are a phenomenon of our era. From small towns to bustling cities, newspapers have column after column of ads written by people who are looking for someone to love. We want to build a life with someone and travel with that special person through the years ahead. If we weave love carefully, it may endure and retain its beauty over the years, just as the Indian silk weaving shown on the preceding page.

In this chapter, we will explore communication dynamics in committed romantic relationships. We'll begin by defining committed romantic relationships and the different styles of loving that individuals bring to romance. Next we discuss how romantic relationships evolve over time and how partners create a private culture for their intimacy. Third, we'll consider challenges that complicate and sometimes dissolve romantic bonds. Finally, we'll identify guidelines for effective communication in committed romance.

Committed Romantic Relationships

Committed romantic relationships are voluntary relationships that we assume will be primary and continuing parts of our lives. Unlike many relationships, enduring romantic ones are voluntary, at least in Western culture. We don't pick our relatives, neighbors, or work associates. Our romantic intimates, however, are people we choose.

Committed romantic relationships are unique in two ways. First, they involve romantic or sexual feelings in addition to the sort of love we feel for friends and family. Another distinctive quality of romantic relationships is that they are considered primary and permanent in our society. We expect to move away from friends and family, but we assume we'll be permanently connected to a romantic partner. Current divorce rates indicate that roughly half of those who marry will separate. Even so, we think of romantic commitment (though not every romantic relationship) as permanent, and this makes romance unique.

Cultural Shaping of Romantic Ties

Views of romantic relationships vary across cultures. In some countries, marriages are arranged by families, and spouses may get to know each other only after the wedding ceremony. In other cultures, including some fundamentalist Mormon communities in the United States, polygamy is practiced—though only men have multiple mates (Werner, Altman, Brown, & Ginat, 1993). In Western societies, marriage is an autonomous choice of two individuals who live relatively independent of families. In many other societies, however, marriage joins two families, and couples are intricately connected to both families.

© James Wilson/Woodfin Camp & Associates, Inc.

Imagination continually frustrates tradition; that is its function.
JOHN PFEIFFER

MANSOORA

I find it very odd that Americans marry only each other and not whole families. In South Africa, people marry into families. The parents must approve of the choice or marriage does not happen. After marriage, the wife moves in with the husband's family. To me this is stronger than a marriage of only two people.

Even within a single country, views of committed romantic relationships vary over time. Whereas traditional marriage once was the only socially recognized form of romantic commitment, today we have a smorgasbord of relationship forms. Commuter marriages are increasingly common (Rohlfing, 1995) as are cohabiting arrangements (Cunningham & Antill, 1995). In the 1990s, the Census Bureau invented a formal category for cohabiting couples: POSSLQ, which is an acronym for Persons of the Opposite Sex Sharing Living Quarters. Approximately 25% of people in the United States who are nineteen or older are cohabiting or have cohabited at some time in their lives (Cunningham & Antill, 1995). The popularity of cohabitation is also rising in other countries, including Australia, Canada, and France.

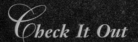

DIVORCE AND DISOBEDIENCE

In China, the family has traditionally been considered sacred, and divorces occurred only if a spouse denounced ancestors or killed someone in his mate's family. Marriages were regarded as enduring social ties that did not depend on love. Wang Wanli encountered the strong pressure not to divorce when he sought to end his marriage in 1981. Chinese traditions often require an individual to get the approval of the work unit for a divorce. In Mr. Wang's case, his unit didn't approve; in fact, they reassigned him to work in the village where he and his wife had grown up in the hope that the community would fortify the marriage. When Wang refused to work there, he was dismissed for disobeying orders.

In the 1980s, the Chinese marriage law was amended to state that love is the most important element for marriage and that the demise of love is justification for divorce. In response to that change, divorces skyrocketed. Between 1980 and 1990, divorces more than doubled, rising from 341,000 to 800,000.

Source: WuDunn, S. (1991, April 17). Romance, a novel idea, rocks marriages in China. *New York Times*, pp. B1, B12.

Every society recognizes and gives privileges to relationships of which it approves and withholds legitimacy from those of which it disapproves. Currently, the United States approves of marriage between heterosexual men and women, and there is increasing toleration of cohabiting heterosexuals. Social acceptance of divorce, remarriage, and single-parent families has also increased. The traditional Western ideal of the family consisted of a male breadwinner, a female homemaker, and 2.4 children (I've often wondered what that .4 child was like!). That solitary ideal has given way to multiple family forms. We have dual-earner couples with children, child-free marriages, single-parent families, and couples in which men are homemakers and women are the primary or sole wage earners. A collage of romantic relationships makes up the contemporary scene.

Despite some changes in social attitudes, commitments between gays and lesbians are not yet widely accepted. The cultural bias against homosexual relationships is enforced by denying gays and lesbians privileges that heterosexual couples enjoy. In 1994, for instance, all 50 states still denied legal status to homosexual relationships. Thus, gays and lesbians can't file joint tax returns, have next-of-kin visiting privileges, insure each other as family, or will each other tax-free property. In addition, discrimination often faces homosexual couples who wish to rent or buy property or raise children (Issacson, 1989; Weston, 1991).

PEGGY

I get so burned up about how society treats gay and lesbian couples. My mom and Adrienne have lived together since Mom and Daddy divorced when I was two. We've always been a family. We eat together, work out problems together, vacation together, make decisions together—everything a heterosexual family does. But my mom and Adrienne aren't accepted as a legitimate couple. We've had to move several times because they were "queers," which is what a neighbor called them. Mom's insurance company won't cover Adrienne, so they have to pay for two policies. It goes on and on. I'll tell you, though, I don't know many heterosexual couples as close or stable as Adrienne and Mom.

Reprinted by permission of Doug Marlette and Creators Syndicate.

Dimensions of Committed Romantic Relationships

For years, researchers have struggled to define what romantic commitment is. As a result of their work, we now believe that romantic love consists of three dimensions: intimacy, commitment, and passion. Although we can think about these dimensions separately, actually they overlap and interact in the overall system of romantic relationships (Acker & Davis, 1992; Hendrick & Hendrick, 1989). One scholar who has studied enduring romantic relationships arranges these three dimensions to form a triangle (Figure 10.1), which represents the different facets of love (Sternberg, 1986).

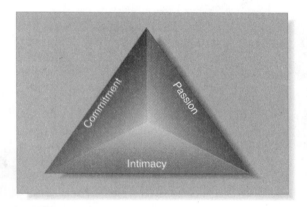

FIGURE 10.1
The Triangle of Love

Passion   For most of us, passion is what first springs to mind when we think about romance. **Passion** is intensely positive feelings and desires for another person. Passion is not equivalent to sexual or sensual emotions, although these are types of passion. In addition to erotic feelings, passion may involve intense emotional, spiritual, and intellectual attraction. The sparks and emotional high of being in love stem from passion. It's why we feel "butterflies in the stomach" and fall "head over heels."

As much fun as passion is, it isn't the primary foundation for enduring romance. In fact, research consistently shows that passion is less central to how we think about love than intimacy and commitment. This makes sense when we realize that passion can seldom be sustained for a lifetime. Like other intense feelings, it ebbs and flows. Since passion comes and goes and is largely beyond our will, it isn't a strong basis for long-term relationships. In other words, passion may set romance apart from other relationships, but it isn't what holds romance together. To build a lasting relationship, we need something more durable.

© David Young Wolff/Tony Stone Images, Inc.

Chains do not hold a marriage together. It is threads, hundreds of tiny threads which sew people together through the years.

SIMONE SIGNORET

Commitment   The something else needed is commitment, the second dimension of romantic relationships. Commitment is an intention to remain with a relationship. As we noted earlier, commitment is not the same thing as love. Love is a feeling based on rewards we get from being involved with a person. Commitment, in contrast, is a decision based on investments we put into a relationship (Lund, 1985). We choose to entwine our life and future with another person's.

THERESA

I'm sick of guys who say they love me, but run if I try to talk about the future. They're allergic to the C-word. If you truly love someone, how can you not be committed?

In an important study of American values, Robert Bellah and his colleagues (1985) found that most Westerners want both passion and commitment in long-term romantic relationships. We desire the euphoria of passion, but we know that it won't weather rough times or ensure compatibility and comfort on a day-in, day-out basis. We also want commitment as a stable foundation for a life together. Commitment is a determination to stay together *in spite* of trouble, disappointments, sporadic restlessness, and lulls in passion. Commitment involves responsibility, not just feeling (Beck, 1988). The responsibilities of commitment are to make a relationship a priority and to invest continuously in it.

WADE

I've been married for fifteen years, and we would have split a dozen times if love was all that held us together. A marriage simply can't survive on love alone. You can't count on feeling in love or passionate all the time. Lucy and I have gone through spells where we were bored with each other or where we wanted to walk away from our problems. We didn't because we made a promise to stay together "for better or for worse." Believe me, a marriage has both.

Passion happens without effort—sometimes even in spite of our efforts! Commitment is an act of will. Passion is a feeling; commitment is a choice. Passion may fade in the face of disappointments and troubles; commitment remains steadfast. Passion has to do with the present moment; commitment is tied to the future. Without commitment, romantic relationships are subject to the whims of transient feelings and circumstances. This is fine for the short term, but it can't sustain romance over the long haul.

Put It in Practice

MEASURING LOVE AND COMMITMENT

Think of a current or past romance to answer these questions:

1. Do you think your relationship will be permanent?

2. Do you feel you can confide in your partner about virtually anything?

3. Are you attracted to other potential partners or to a single lifestyle?

4. Would you be miserable if you couldn't be with your partner?

5. Would you find it personally difficult to end your relationship?

6. If you felt lonely, would your first thought be to seek your partner?

7. Do you feel obligated to continue this relationship?

8. Would you forgive your partner for virtually anything?

9. In your opinion, do you think your partner intends to continue this relationship?

10. Is one of your primary concerns your partner's welfare?

Commitment is measured by odd-numbered items; love is measured by even-numbered items. Based on Lund, M. (1985). The development of investment and commitment scales for predicting continuity of personal relationships. *Journal of Social and Personal Relationships, 2,* 15.

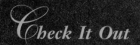

Check It Out

THE PROTOTYPE OF LOVE

It appears that Westerners have a fairly specific prototype of what love is. Research repeatedly reveals that we regard feeling valued by and comfortable with another as more important than passion. Love is typified by feelings such as closeness, caring, and friendship, and by commitment, as defined by features such as trust and respect. Intimacy and commitment eclipse passion in importance. Even when people are asked what's most important for "being in love," companionate features have priority.

Do women and men differ in how important they consider the dimensions of love? Although women and men don't differ significantly in what they consider typical of love in general, they do diverge in their personal ideals for love. For both sexes, passion is less salient than companionate features. However, features linked to intimacy and commitment are even more prominent in women's personal ideals of love than in men's. The only feature that men rate higher than women is fantasy. No differences have been found among heterosexuals, gays, and lesbians.

Sources: Button, C. M., & Collier, D. R. (1991, June). *A comparison of people's concepts of love and romantic love.* Paper presented at the Canadian Psychological Association Conference, Calgary, Alberta. Fehr, B. (1993). How do I love thee: Let me consult my prototype. In S. W. Duck (Ed.), *Understanding relationship processes, 1: Individuals in relationships* (pp. 87–122). Newbury Park, CA: Sage. Luby, V., & Aron, A. (1990, July). *A prototype structuring of love, like, and being in-love.* Paper presented at the Fifth International Conference on Personal Relationships, Oxford, UK. Rousar, E. E. III, & Aron, A. (1990, July). *Valuing, altruism, and the concept of love.* Paper presented at the Fifth International Conference on Personal Relationships, Oxford, UK.

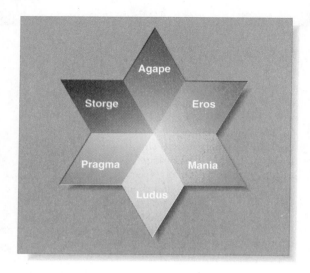

FIGURE 10.2
The Colors of Love

Intimacy   The third dimension of romantic relationships is intimacy. **Intimacy** includes feelings of closeness, connection, and tenderness. Unlike passion and commitment, which are distinct dimensions of romance, intimacy seems to underlie passion and commitment, being part of both (Acker & Davis, 1992). Intimacy is related to passion because both dimensions involve feelings. The link between intimacy and commitment is connectedness, which joins partners not only in the present, but through the past and into the future.

Intimacy is abiding affection and warm feelings for another person. It is why partners are comfortable with each other and enjoy being together even when fireworks aren't exploding. When asked to evaluate various features of love, people consistently rate companionate features such as getting along and friendship as most important. Although passionate feelings also matter, they are less central to perceptions of love than caring, honesty, respect, friendship, and trust (Fehr, 1993; Luby & Aron, 1990).

Romantic relationships are complex combinations of passion, commitment, and intimacy, and these dimensions interact. To add to our understanding of romance, let's now consider the different styles of loving that individuals have.

Styles of Loving

Does real love grow out of long friendship?
Should you love someone whose background is similar to yours?
Would you rather suffer yourself than have someone you love suffer?
Is love at first sight possible?

Is the real fun of love getting someone to fall for you rather than becoming seriously involved?

If you were to survey everyone in your class, you'd discover different answers to the above questions. For every person who thinks love grows out of friendship, someone else believes love at first sight is possible. For each of us who considers love the most important focus of life, another person views love as a game.

Although we accept varied tastes in everything from clothes to lifestyle, we seem less open-minded about diversity in love. Whatever we have experienced as love is what we consider "real love." Anything else we discount as "just infatuation," "a sexual fling," or "being a doormat." Yet, it appears people differ in how they love (Lee, 1973, 1988).

Just as there are three primary colors, there are three primary styles of loving. In addition, just as purple is created by blending the primary colors of blue and red, secondary love styles are made by blending primary ones. Secondary styles are as vibrant as primary ones, just as purple is as lovely as red or blue. Figure 10.2 illustrates the colors of love.

Primary Styles of Love The three primary styles of love are eros, storge, and ludus. **Eros** is a powerful, passionate style of love that blazes to life suddenly and dramatically. It is an intense kind of love that may include sexual, spiritual, intellectual, or emotional attraction. Erotic love is the most intuitive and spontaneous of all styles, and it is also the fastest moving. Erotic lovers are likely to self-disclose early in a relationship, be very sentimental, and fall in love hard and fast. Although folk wisdom claims women are more romantic than men, research indicates that men are more likely than women to be erotic lovers (Hendrick & Hendrick, 1996).

© Michael Kevin Daly/The Stock Market

ROSA

When I fall for someone, I fall all the way—like, I mean total and all that. I can't love halfway, and I can't go gradually, though my mother is always warning me to slow down. That's just not how I love. It's fast and furious for me.

Storge (pronounced store-gay) is a comfortable, even-keeled kind of love based on friendship. Storgic love tends to grow gradually and to be peaceful and stable. In most cases, it grows out of common interests, values, and life goals (Lasswell & Lobsenz, 1980). Storgic relationships don't have the great highs of erotic love, but neither do they have the fiery conflict and anger that erotic people often experience. Steadiness is storge's standard mood.

STEPHEN

Lisa and I have been together for fifteen years now, and it's been easy and steady between us from the start. I don't remember even falling in love way back when. Maybe I never did fall in love with Lisa. I just gradually grew into loving her and feeling we belonged to each other.

The final primary style of love is **ludus,** which is playful love. Ludic lovers see love as a game. It's a lighthearted adventure full of challenges, puzzles, and fun, but love is not to be taken seriously. For ludics, commitment is poison. Instead, they like to play the field and enjoy falling in love; they don't seek commitment. Many people go through ludic periods but are not true ludics. After ending a long-term relationship, it's natural and healthy to avoid serious involvement for a while. Dating casually and steering clear of heavy entanglement may be wise and fun. Ludic loving may also suit people who enjoy romance but aren't ready to settle down. Research indicates that more men than women have ludic inclinations when it comes to love (Hendrick & Hendrick, 1996).

"It turns out there was a computer error—
we weren't made for each other after all."
© 1994 by Sidney Harris. *The Wall Street Journal.*

VIJAY

I'm not ready to settle down, and I may not ever be. I really like dating and seeing if I can get a girl to fall for me, but I'm not out for anything permanent. To me, the fun is in the chase. Once somebody falls for me, I kind of lose interest. It's just not challenging anymore.

Secondary Styles of Love   There are three secondary styles of love: pragma, mania, and agape. **Pragma,** as the name suggests, is pragmatic or practical love. Pragma blends the conscious strategies of ludus with the stable, secure love of storge. Pragmatic lovers have clear criteria for partners such as religious affiliation, career, and family background. Although many people dismiss pragma as coldly practical and not really love, this is a mistake. Pragmatic lovers aren't necessarily unfeeling or unloving at all. For them, though, practical considerations are the foundation of enduring commitments, so these must be satisfied before they let themselves fall in love. Pragmatic considerations also guide arranged marriages in which families match children for economic and social reasons.

RANCHANA

I have to think carefully about who to marry. I must go to graduate school, and I must support my family with what I earn when I finish. I cannot marry someone who is poor, who will not help me get through school, or who won't support my family. For me, these are very basic matters.

Mania derives its name from the Greek term *theia mania*, which means "madness from the gods" (Lee, 1973). Manic lovers have the passion of eros, but they play by ludic rules with results that can be disturbing to them and those they love. Typically unsure that others really love them, manics may devise tests and games to evaluate a partner's commitment. They may also think obsessively about a relationship and be unable to think about anyone or anything else. In addition, manic lovers often experience emotional extremes, ranging from euphoric ecstasy to bottomless despair.

PAT

I never feel sure of myself when I'm in love. I always wonder when it will end, when my boyfriend will walk away, when he will lose interest. Sometimes I play games to see how interested a guy is, but then I get all upset if the game doesn't work out right. Then I just wallow in my insecurities, and they get worse the more I think about them.

The final style of love is **agape,** which is a blend of storge and eros. The term *agape* comes from St. Paul's admonition that we should love others without expectation of personal gain or return. Agapic lovers feel the intense passion of eros and the constancy of storge. Generous and selfless, agapic lovers will put a loved one's happiness ahead of their own without any expectation of reciprocity. For them, loving and giving to another is its own reward. Many of my students comment that agapic love sounds more possible for saints than for mere mortals. Research bears out this insight, since the original studies of love styles found no individuals who were purely agapic. However, many people have agapic tendencies in their style of loving.

KEENAN

My mother is agapic. She has moved more times than I can count because my father needed to relocate to advance. She agreed to the house he wanted and went on the vacations he wanted, even when she had other ideas. There's nothing she wouldn't do for him. I used to think she was a patsy, but I've come to see her way of loving as very strong.

In thinking about styles of love, you should keep several points in mind. First, most of us have a combination of styles (Hendrick, Hendrick, Foote, & Slapion-Foote, 1984). So you might be primarily storgic with strong agapic inclinations or mainly erotic with an undertone of ludic mischief. Second, your style of love is not necessarily permanent. Recent studies indicate we learn how to love (Maugh, 1994), so our style of loving may change as we have more experiences in loving. Third, remember that your love style is part of an overall interpersonal system, so it is affected by all other aspects of your relationship (Hendrick & Hendrick, 1996). Your partner's style of love may influence your own. If you are primarily erotic

© Chuck Savage/The Stock Market

and in love with a strong ludic, it's possible manic tendencies will be evoked. Finally, we should realize that individual styles of love are not good or bad in an absolute sense; what matters is how partners' styles fit together. An erotic partner's intensity might overwhelm a calm storgic; an agapic person might be exploited by a true ludic; the extremes of mania would clash with the serene steadiness of storge.

Although passion is important in romantic relationships, intimacy and commitment are necessary to sustain them for the long term. We've also discussed different styles of loving, which are one influence on how individuals experience and express romantic intimacy. To add to the knowledge we've gained, we'll now consider how committed romantic relationships develop and function.

The Organization of Romantic Relationships

Like friendships, romantic relationships tend to follow a developmental course. Initially, scholars thought relationships move through stages as a result of objective activities such as self-disclosing. More recently, however, we have realized that romance progresses based on how we perceive interaction, not on interaction itself (Honeycutt, 1993). For example, if Terry discloses personal information to Janet, then the relationship will escalate if Janet and Terry interpret self-disclosure as a move toward greater intimacy. If Janet doesn't perceive Terry's disclosure as personal, she's unlikely to feel he has made a move toward greater closeness. It is the meaning they assign to self-disclosing, not the actual act of self-disclosing, that determines how they perceive their level of intimacy.

As we learned in Chapter 3, perceiving is an active process in which we notice, organize, and interpret what goes on around us. We use cognitive schematas and information from past experiences to decide what things mean. The meanings we assign to romance, however, are not entirely individualistic. They also reflect broad cultural beliefs that we internalize as we are socialized. Because members of a society share many views, there are strong consistencies in how we perceive what happens in romantic relationships. Research shows that Western college students agree on the script for first dates (Pryor & Merluzzi, 1985). They also share ideas about how men and women should act. The majority of college students think men should initiate and plan dates and make decisions about most activities, but women control sexual activity (Rose & Frieze, 1989). In other cultures, different rules prevail. For example, in India, marriages are often arranged by parents and love is understood to be something couples develop after they wed. In Nepal, ritualistic dancing and celebrations are an important part of courtship. Although views of romantic relationships vary among cultures, every culture has shared understandings of what love is and how love develops.

Developmental Phases

Research on the evolution of romantic relationships has focused on Western society, so we know little about the developmental course of romance in other cultures. The research tells us that Westerners perceive romantic relationships as escalating, navigating, or deteriorating. Within these three broad categories, we distinguish a number of more specific stages (Figure 10.3).

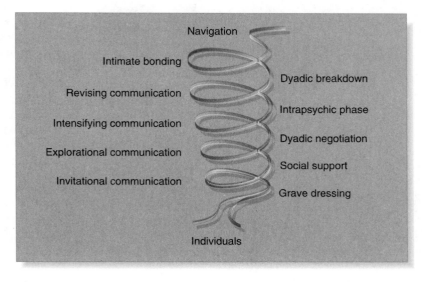

FIGURE 10.3
Developmental Phases in Romantic Relationships

Escalating   In moving toward romantic commitment, we recognize six stages of interaction. The first is individuals who aren't interacting. We are aware of ourselves as individuals with particular needs, goals, love styles, and qualities that affect what we look for in relationships.

E D N A

It's funny how things change as we age. When I was first dating in my teens, the topics for small talk early in the relationship were your major, career plans, and background. Now I'm forty-seven, divorced, and dating again, and the opening topics tend to be about career achievements, past marriages, and finances.

The second stage is **invitational communication** in which individuals signal they are interested in interacting and respond to invitations from others. "Want to dance?" "Where are you from?" "I love this kind of music," "Hi, my name's Shelby" are examples of bids for interaction. Invitational communication usually follows a conventional script for initial interaction. The meaning of invitational communication is found on the relational level, not the content level. "I love this kind of music" literally means a person likes the music. On the relational level of meaning, however, the message is "I'm available and interested. Are you?"

BASES OF ROMANTIC ATTRACTION

Gay men tend to desire very specific physical characteristics, including an extremely attractive face, a slim and well-conditioned body, and good grooming. In addition, they want partners who are self-sufficient and have prestigious careers that yield good incomes.

Straight men also state that physical attractiveness is very important to them in romantic partners. They report looking for women who are slim and beautiful. Intelligence, status, and personality matter less than physical beauty.

Lesbians generally stress emotional and personal qualities in partners and care little about physical appearance or dress. Although some lesbians admire a "butch" look, others prefer traditional feminine beauty. Lesbians value economic independence in partners, though less so than gays.

Straight women emphasize personal qualities in romantic partners. Warmth, honesty, kindness, and personal integrity are among the qualities straight women consider important. They also value ambition and status in partners.

Sources: Based on Huston, M., & Schwartz, P. (1995). Relationships of lesbians and gay men. In J. T. Wood & S. W. Duck (Eds.), *Understanding relationship processes, 6: Off the beaten track: Understudied relationships*, pp. 89–121. Thousand Oaks, CA: Sage. Sprecher, S. (1989). The importance to males and females of physical attractiveness, earning potential, and expressiveness in initial attraction. *Sex Roles, 21*, 591–607.

RELATIONAL MEANINGS OF INVITATIONS

Go to a place where people are likely to meet for the first time. Observe how individuals extend and respond to invitations for interaction.

What are the content meanings of invitations and responses?

What do you perceive as the relational meaning of invitations and responses?

Of all the people we meet, we are attracted to only a few. The three greatest influences on initial attraction are self-concept, proximity, and similarity. How we see ourselves affects the people we consider candidates for romance. Heterosexuals, lesbians, bisexuals, and gays seek romance with others who share their affectional preference. Social class also influences whom we notice and consider appropriate for us. The myth that the United States is color-blind and classless is disproved by the fact that most people pair with others of their race and social class. Even with all of the attention to diversity in our era, research indicates that people still seek others who are similar to them. In fact, social prestige influences dating patterns now more than in the 1950s (Whitbeck & Hoyt, 1994). Most college students seek to date people who share their social and class backgrounds.

In addition to personal identity, proximity and similarity influence initial attraction. We can interact only with people we meet, so where we live, work, and socialize affects the possibilities for relationships. Nearness to others, however, doesn't necessarily increase liking. **Environmental spoiling** describes situations in which proximity breeds ill will. This happens when we're forced to be around others whose values, lifestyles, or behaviors conflict with our own. For the most part, we seek romantic partners who are like us. "Birds of a feather" seems more true than "opposites attract." In general, we are attracted to people whose values, attitudes, and lifestyles are similar to ours. Similarity of personality is also linked to long-term marital happiness (Caspi & Harbener, 1990).

Explorational communication is the third stage in relational escalation, and it involves exchanging information to explore the possibilities for a relationship. We use communication to announce our identities and to learn about others. In this stage, individuals fish for common interests and grounds for interaction: Are you from the south? Do you like jazz? What kind of family did you come from? Have you been following the political debates? As we continue to interact with others, both breadth and depth of information increase. Because we perceive self-disclosure as a sign of trust, it tends to escalate intimacy (Berger & Bell, 1988). At this early stage of interaction, reciprocity of disclosure is expected so that one person isn't more vulnerable than the other (Duck, 1992; Miell & Duck, 1986).

If early interaction increases attraction, then individuals may dramatically escalate the relationship. **Intensifying communication** increases the depth of a relationship by increasing personal knowledge and allowing a couple to begin creating a private culture. My students nicknamed this stage "euphoria" to emphasize the intensity and happiness it embodies. During this phase, partners spend more and more time together, and they rely less on external structures such as movies or parties. Instead, they immerse themselves in the budding relationship and may feel they can't be together enough. Further disclosures are exchanged, personal biographies are filled in, and partners increasingly learn how each other feels and thinks. As personal knowledge expands, dual perspective is possible.

SUSAN

I fell in love this year after being alone for eight years after my husband died. Sometimes I think I'm crazy because I'll miss Ben at night after spending the whole day with him. We call each other several times a day just to say hello. I feel as giddy as a teenager.

Also characteristic of the intensifying stage are idealizing and personalized communication. Idealizing involves seeing a relationship and a partner as more wonderful, exciting, and perfect than they really are (Hendrick & Hendrick, 1988). During euphoria, partners often exaggerate each other's virtues, downplay or fail to perceive vices, and overlook problems in the

THE MATCHING GAME

Do people look for great physical attractiveness in picking friends, dates, and life partners? At first, it might seem that each of us would want the most attractive intimates we could find. It seems, however, that others' attractiveness is only one factor. The other is how attractive we consider ourselves.

In general, people tend to match themselves with others who are about as physically attractive as they are. We may fantasize about relationships with people who are breathtaking, but when reality settles in we're likely to pass them by for someone more at our level of attractiveness.

© Francie Manning/The Picture Cube, Inc.

Exploration is really the essence of the human spirit.
FRANK BORMAN

relationship. It is also during euphoria that partners begin to develop relationship vocabularies made up of nicknames and private codes. Most relationship vocabularies include terms that symbolize important experiences partners have shared. Sometimes I say "namaste" to Robbie. This is a Nepali greeting that means "I honor the spirit that is in you and the oneness of us all." Saying "namaste" reminds us of the month we spent trekking in the mountains of Nepal. Relationship vocabularies both reflect and fuel intimacy.

Put It in Practice

INTIMATE TALK

Do you and your partner have a private language in your relationship?

1. Do you have special nicknames for each other that others don't have and use?

2. Do you have special words that you made up to describe experiences, activities, and feelings?

3. Do you have codes that allow you and your partner to send messages in public that other people don't understand?

4. How does your special relationship language reflect your relationship? How does it affect the bond?

Revising communication, although not part of escalation in all romantic relationships, is important. During this stage, partners come down out of the clouds to look at their relationship more realistically than they had. Problems and dissatisfactions are recognized as partners evaluate the relationship's potential to survive. With the rush of euphoria over, partners consider whether this relationship is one they want for the long term. If it is, they work through obstacles to long-term viability. Many couples that fall in love and move through the intensifying stage choose not to stay together. It is entirely possible to love a person with whom we don't want to share our life or to decide that it's better to stay together without formalizing the relationship. Some older couples make this choice, since marrying can decrease their social security payments.

THELMA

Breaking up with Ted was the hardest thing I ever did. I really loved him, and he loved me, but I just couldn't see myself living with a Christian. My whole heritage is Jewish— it's who I am. I celebrate Hanukkah, not Christmas. Seder, Passover, and Yom Kippur are very important to me. Those aren't part of Ted's heritage, and he wouldn't convert. I loved him, but we couldn't have made a life together.

Commitment is a decision to stay with a relationship permanently. This decision transforms a romantic relationship from one based on past and present experiences and feelings into one with a future. Prior to making a commitment, partners don't view the relationship as continuing forever. With commitment, the relationship becomes a given, around which they arrange other aspects of their lives.

Navigating **Navigating** is a long-term process. Ideally a relationship stabilizes in navigating once a commitment has been made. Navigating is the ongoing process of staying committed and living a life together. Although we hope to stabilize in navigating, the stage itself is full of movement. Couples continuously adjust, work through new problems, revisit old ones, and accommodate to changes in their individual and relational lives. In relationships that do endure, ongoing navigation helps partners avoid dangerous shoals and keep their intimacy on a good course. To use an automotive analogy, navigating involves both preventive maintenance and periodic repairs (Canary & Stafford, 1994). The goals of navigating are to keep intimacy satisfying and healthy and to remedy any serious problems that arise. To understand the navigating stage, we'll discuss relational culture, place-making, and everyday interaction.

The nucleus of intimacy is **relational culture,** which is a private world of rules, understandings, meanings, and patterns of acting and interpreting that partners create for their relationship (Wood, 1982, 1995c). Relational culture includes how a couple manages relational dialectics. Jan and Byron may negotiate a lot of autonomy and little togetherness, whereas Louise and Teresa emphasize connectedness and minimize autonomy. Bobby and Cassandra are very open and expressive, while Mike and Zelda preserve more individual privacy in their marriage. There are not right and wrong ways to manage dialectics, since individuals and couples differ in what they need. What is most important is for couples to agree on how to deal with tensions between autonomy and connection, openness and privacy, and novelty and routine (Fitzpatrick & Best, 1979; Wood, 1995c).

Relational culture includes communication rules that partners work out. Couples develop agreements, usually unspoken, about how to signal anger, love, sexual interest, and so forth. They also develop routines for contact. Robbie and I catch up while we're fixing dinner each day. Other couples reserve weekends for staying in touch.

Check It Out

THE CHEMISTRY OF LOVE

People often say they have chemistry or don't have chemistry with others. Recent research suggests there may be a factual, biological basis to the idea that there is chemistry between people. Consider:

The *cuddle chemical* is oxytocin, which is stimulated by either physical or emotional cues. Oxytocin is released when babies nurse, making mothers nuzzle and cuddle them. Oxytocin also pours out during sexual arousal and lovemaking, making lovers want to caress and cuddle one another.

The *infatuation chemical* is phenylethylamine (PEA). Like amphetamines, PEA makes our bodies tremble when we're attracted to someone and makes us feel euphoric, happy, and energetic when we're in love.

The *attachment chemical* is really a group of morphinelike opiates that calm us and create feelings of relaxed comfort. This allows couples to form more peaceful, steady relationships than the speedlike PEA does. Opiates of the mind promote abiding commitment.

Source: Ackerman, D. (1994). *A natural history of love.* New York: Random House.

© Alexandra Boulat/Material World

© Michael Major/Envision

© David Bartruff/Artistry International

© Guglielmo Micheli/Material World

Placemaking is the process of creating a personal environment that is comfortable and that reflects the values, experiences, and tastes of a couple (Werner et al., 1993). In our home, Robbie and I have symbols of our travels: Tibetan carpets, a batik from Thailand, ancient masks from Nepal, and a wood carving from Mexico. We also have photographs of friends and family members who matter to us. Our CDs include much jazz, lots of Mozart, and a number of crossover artists, and we have built-in bookshelves, all overloaded, in most rooms of our home. The books, photos, music, and travel souvenirs make the house into a home that reflects who we are and what we've done together.

An especially important dimension of relational culture is everyday interaction. Partners weave the basic fabric of their relationship in day-to-day conversations that realize their togetherness. Most conversations between intimates aren't dramatic or noteworthy; actually, the majority of interaction is fairly routine and mundane. Yet everyday talk is more important than major celebrations and big crises in creating and sustaining intimacy (Duck, 1994b; Spencer, 1994). Ordinary talk between partners nourishes their interpersonal climate by continuously recognizing and affirming each other.

Deterioration   Steve Duck, a scholar of communication in personal relationships, proposed a five-phase model of relational decline. **Dyadic breakdown** is the first stage, and it involves degeneration of established patterns, understandings, and routines that make up a relational culture. Partners may stop talking after dinner, no longer bother to call when they are running late, and in other ways neglect the "little" things that tie them together. As the fabric of intimacy weakens, dissatisfaction intensifies.

There are general gender differences in the causes of dyadic breakdown. For women, unhappiness with a relationship most often arises when communication declines in quality and/or quantity. Men are more likely to be dissatisfied by specific behaviors. For instance, men report being dissatisfied when their partners don't greet them at the door and make special meals (Riessman, 1990). For many men, dissatisfaction also arises if they have domestic responsibilities, which they feel aren't a man's job (Gottman & Carrère, 1994). Many women feel a relationship is breaking down if "we don't really communicate with each other anymore," whereas men tend to feel dissatisfied if "we don't do fun things together anymore." Another gender difference is in who notices problems in a relationship. As a rule, women are more likely than men to perceive declines in intimacy. Since women are socialized to take care of relationships, they are more likely than men to notice tensions and early symptoms of problems (Cancian, 1989; Tavris, 1992).

The **intrapsychic phase** involves brooding about problems in the relationship and dissatisfactions with a partner (Duck, 1992). Women's brooding about languishing relationships tends to focus on perceived declines in closeness and intimate communication, while men's reflections more often center on lapses in joint activities and acts of consideration between partners. It's easy for the intrapsychic phase to become a self-fulfilling prophecy: As gloomy thoughts snowball and awareness of positive features of the relationship ebb, partners may actually bring about the failure of their relationship. During the intrapsychic phase, partners may begin to think about alternatives to the relationship.

Dyadic negotiation, the third phase in relational decline, doesn't always occur (Duck, 1992). As we saw in Chapter 8, women are more likely to respond to conflict by initiating discussion of problems, and men often deny problems or exit rather than talk about them. Communication scholars report that many people avoid talking about problems, refuse to return calls from partners, and in other ways evade confronting difficulties (Baxter, 1984; Metts, Cupach, & Bejlovec, 1989). Although this is understandable, since it is painful to talk about the decline of intimacy, avoiding problems does nothing to resolve them and may, in fact, make them worse. In formal relationships such as marriage, partners must negotiate matters such as division of property and child custody, but they may choose to talk through lawyers rather than directly to each other. What happens in the negotiation phase depends on how committed partners are, whether they perceive attractive alternatives to the relationship, and whether they have the communication skills to work through problems constructively.

If partners lack commitment and/or communication skills needed to resuscitate intimacy, they enter the **social phase** of disintegration, which involves figuring out how to tell outsiders they are parting. Either sepa-

Check It Out

ABSENCE MAKES THE WORDS GROW FONDER

© Frank Siteman/The Picture Cube, Inc.

Couples who have long-distance or commuter relationships face many challenges. Yet what long-distance partners say is most difficult is the loss of daily routines and conversation about everyday matters. What they miss most is sharing trivial details of their lives and "small talk."

Source: Gerstel, N., & Gross, H. (1985). *Commuter marriage.* New York: Guilford.

rately or in collaboration, partners decide how to explain their breakup to friends, children, in-laws, and social acquaintances. When partners don't cooperatively craft a joint explanation for breaking up, friends may take sides, gossip, and disparage one or the other partner as the "bad guy" (La Gaipa, 1982).

Social support is a phase in which partners look to friends and family for support during the breakup. Others can provide support by being available and by listening mindfully. Partners may give self-serving accounts of the breakup in order to save face and secure sympathy and support from others. Thus, Beth may portray Janine as at fault and herself as the innocent party in a breakup. During this phase, partners often criticize their exes and expect friends to take their side (Duck, 1992). Although self-serving explanations of breakups are common, they aren't necessarily constructive. It's a good idea to monitor communication during this period so that we don't say things we'll later regret.

SAMANTHA

I really hate it when couples in our social circle divorce. It never fails that we lose one of the two of them as a friend, because each of them wants us to take sides. They each blame the other and expect us to help them do that, and you can't do it for both spouses. One of them won't be a friend any more.

Grave dressing is the final phase in relational decline, and it involves burying the relationship and accepting its end. Like individuals, relationships deserve a proper burial (Duck, 1992). During grave dressing, we work to make sense of the relationship—what it meant, why it failed, and how it affected them. Usually, individuals need to mourn intimacy that has died. Even if we initiate a breakup, we are sad about the failure to realize what seemed possible at one time. Grave dressing completes the process of relational dissolution by putting the relationship to rest so that partners can get on with their individual lives.

The stages we have discussed describe how most people perceive the course of romance. However, not all couples follow the standard pattern. Some partners skip one or more stages in the typical sequences of escalation or deterioration, and many of us cycle more than once through certain stages. For example, a couple might soar through euphoria, work out some tough issues in revising, then go through euphoria a second time. It's also normal for long-term partners to depart navigation periodically to experience both euphoric seasons and intervals of dyadic breakdown. Further, because relationships are embedded in larger systems, it's likely that romantic intimacy follows different developmental paths in other cultures.

Now that we understand the basic anatomy of romantic relationships, we're ready to consider some of the special challenges to sustaining them over the long term.

Sally Forth   By Greg Howard

© 1992. Reprinted with special permission of King Features Syndicate.

Challenges to Sustaining Romantic Relationships

Enduring romantic relationships face a number of difficulties. Many of the challenges are natural, even inevitable in all forms of intimacy. All couples have to deal continuously with the tensions of relational dialectics, gendered dynamics, and conflicts that are sometimes severe. In addition to the generic problems of relationships, romantic partners may encounter four special complications.

Ensuring Equity

Perceived equity is very important in committed romantic relationships. **Equity** means fairness, based on the perception that both partners invest relatively equally in a relationship and benefit similarly from their investments. We all want to feel that our partners are as committed as we are and that we gain equally from being together. Although few partners demand moment-to-moment equality, most of us want our relationships to be equitable over time. Inequity tends to breed unhappiness, which lessens satisfaction and commitment and sometimes prompts affairs (Walster, Traupmann, & Walster, 1978).

Equity has multiple dimensions. We may evaluate the fairness of financial, emotional, physical, and other contributions to a relationship. One area that strongly affects relational quality is perceived equity in housework and child care. Inequitable division of domestic obligations fuels dissatisfaction and resentment, both of which harm intimacy (Gottman & Carrère, 1994). Marital stability is more closely linked to perceptions of equitable divisions of child care and housework than to income or sex life (Fowers, 1991; Suitor, 1991).

THE SECOND SHIFT

© Michael Newman/PhotoEdit

In 80% of dual-worker families, men work one job and women work two—the second shift begins when they come home. Not only do women do more domestic work than men, but they do work that is less satisfying and more stressful. Women tend to do the day-in, day-out jobs such as cooking, shopping, and helping children with homework. Men more often do domestic work that they can schedule to suit themselves. Mowing the lawn can be scheduled flexibly, whereas fixing meals must be done on a tight timetable. Men also are more likely to take care of occasional and fun child-care activities, such as visiting the zoo, while women manage the daily grind of bathing, dressing, and feeding children.

As a rule, women assume **psychological responsibility,** which involves remembering, planning, and coordinating domestic activities. Parents may alternate who takes children to the doctor, but it is usually the mother who remembers when checkups are needed, makes appointments, and reminds the father to take the child. Birthday cards and gifts are signed by both partners, but women typically assume the psychological responsibility for remembering when birthdays are and for buying cards and gifts.

Source: Based on Hochschild, A., with Manchung, A. (1989). *The second shift.* New York: Viking Press.

Beginning with the Industrial Revolution, men were assigned responsibility for earning income and women for caring for children and a home. A gendered division of labor no longer makes sense, since more than 83% of marriages today include two wage earners (Wilkie, 1991). Unfortunately, divisions of family and home responsibilities have not changed in response to changing employment patterns. Even when both partners in heterosexual relationships work outside the home, the vast majority of child care and homemaking is done by women (Nussbaum, 1992; Okin, 1989). In only 20% of dual-worker families do men assume equal domestic responsibilities (Hochschild with Manchung, 1989). Although many men with partners who work outside the home do contribute, they do less than a fair share. Since the 1950s, the amount of housework and child care that husbands do has risen a scant 10%—from 20 to 30% (Pleck, 1987).

CORA MAY

I said, "Either things are going to change around here or I'm leaving." He didn't believe me, but I stood my ground. For twenty years I had done all of the housework, the cooking, and the child care, while he did none of these. Walter just went to his job each day and came back home for me to wait on him. Well, I went to my job each day too. I worked hard, and I was tired when I got home. You'd think he could figure that out, wouldn't you? It got really bad when I started taking night courses. I need to study at night, not fix meals and do laundry, so I asked him to help out. You'd think he'd been stung by a bee. He said no, so I just quit fixing his meals and left his laundry when I washed my clothes. Finally, he got with the program.

How are domestic responsibilities managed when both partners are the same sex? Lesbian couples create more egalitarian relationships than either heterosexuals or gays. More than any other type of couple, lesbians are likely to share decision making and domestic work (Huston &

Schwartz, 1995). Consequently, lesbians are least likely to perceive inequity in contributions to homelife (Kurdek, 1993). Gay men, like their heterosexual brothers, use the power derived from income to authorize inequitable contributions to domestic life. In gay couples, the man who makes more money has and uses more power, both in making decisions that affect the relationship and in avoiding housework (Huston & Schwartz, 1995). This suggests that power is the basis of gendered divisions of labor and that men, more than women, seek the privileges of power, including evasion of domestic work.

The perception of inequity damages romantic relationships. It creates resentment and anger and erodes love. As resentment eclipses positive feelings, dissatisfaction mushrooms. In addition, there are health consequences. Women who work a second shift are stressed, starved for sleep, and susceptible to illness because they are continuously doing double duty (Hochschild with Manchung, 1989). Successful long-term relationships in our era require more equitable divisions of home responsibilities than have been traditional.

Illustration by Jean-Philippe Delhomme/Based on a campaign created by Mullen Advertising for the AIDS Action Committee of Massachusetts, Inc.

Negotiating Safer Sex

In the HIV/AIDS era, sexual activities pose serious, even deadly, threats to romantic relationships. The World Health Organization estimates that currently 17 million people are HIV positive, and 3 million people around the world were infected with HIV in 1993 ("Three Million," 1994). Looking ahead, the statistics are even more grim: It's estimated that 40 million people will be diagnosed as having HIV by the year 2000 ("Death Toll," 1991). Despite vigorous public education campaigns, many individuals still don't practice safer sex, which includes practicing abstinence, restricting sexual activity to a single partner who has been tested for HIV, and/or using latex condoms (Reel & Thompson, 1994). In a recent nationwide survey, only 48% of men and 32% of women reported using condoms (Clements, 1994). Not practicing safer sex puts both partners at grave risk for early death.

Why don't people who know about HIV/AIDS consistently follow safer sex techniques? Communication scholars have discovered two primary reasons. First, many individuals find it more embarrassing to talk

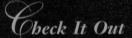

Check It Out

REASONS GOOD ENOUGH TO DIE FOR?

When students and members of singles organizations were asked about their sexual activities, these were the top five reasons they reported for not practicing safer sex:

1. I knew my partner. We'd discussed our past sexual experiences.
2. I use another form of birth control.
3. A condom wasn't available at the time.
4. Things happened too fast.
5. I didn't feel I was at risk.

Source: Based on Reel, B. W., & Thompson, T. L. (1994). A test of the effectiveness of strategies for talking about AIDS and condom use. *Journal of Applied Communication Research, 22,* 127–141.

about sex than to engage in it. They find it awkward to ask direct questions of partners ("Have you been tested for HIV?" "Are you having sex with anyone else?") or to make direct requests of partners ("I want you to wear a condom," "I would like for you to be tested for HIV before we have sex"). Naturally, it's difficult to talk explicitly about sex and the dangers of HIV/AIDS. However, it is far more difficult to live with HIV or the knowledge you infected a lover.

A second reason people sometimes fail to practice safer sex is that their rational thought and control are debilitated by drugs and/or alcohol. In a series of studies of college students' sexual activities, communication researchers Sheryl Bowen and Paula Michal-Johnson (1995) found that safer sex precautions are often neglected when individuals drink heavily. The National Council on Alcoholism and Drug Dependence reports that sexually active teens are less likely to use condoms after drinking ("What Teens Say," 1994). Alcohol and other drugs loosen inhibitions, including appropriate concerns about personal safety.

Discussing and practicing safer sex may be embarrassing, but there is no other sensible option. Principles of effective interpersonal communication we've discussed help ease the discomfort of negotiating safer sex. I–language that owns your feelings is especially important. It is more constructive to say "I feel unsafe having unprotected sex" than to say "Without a condom, you could give me HIV." A positive interpersonal climate is fostered by relational language, such as "we," "us," and "our relationship," to talk about sex (Reel & Thompson, 1994). Individuals who care about themselves and their partners are honest about their sexual histories and careful in their sex practices.

Violence and Abuse

Although we like to think of romantic relationships as loving, many are not. Violence and abuse are unfortunately common between romantic partners, and they cut across lines of class, race, and ethnicity (French, 1992; West, 1995). Violence is high not only in heterosexual marriage, but also in heterosexual cohabitation. In fact, cohabiting couples have the highest incidence of violence of all couples (Cunningham & Antill, 1995;

White & Bondurant, 1996). Cohabiting women suffer one and one half to two times more physical abuse than married women, perhaps because their partners are less committed than husbands (Ellis, 1989).

© Thelma Shumsky/The Image Works

The majority of detected violence and abuse in intimacy seems to be committed by men against women. Currently in the United States, a woman is beaten every twelve seconds by a husband or intimate, and four women a day are beaten to death (Brock-Utne, 1989). Rape and date rape are escalating, especially when individuals have been drinking ("What Teens Say," 1994). Verbal and emotional abuse cause deep and lasting scars (Vachss, 1994). And dysfunctional relationships, often called toxic connections, seem to be rising (Wright & Wright, 1995). Mental health counselors who specialize in violence have come to the conclusion that relationships in which men abuse women are not rare, but exemplify in extreme form the traditional power dynamics that structure relationships between women and men (Goldner, Penn, Sheinberg, & Walker, 1990). Men are taught to use power to assert themselves and to compete with others, whereas women are socialized to defer and preserve relationships. When these internalized patterns combine in heterosexual relationships, a foundation exists for men to abuse and batter women and for women to tolerate it, rather than be disloyal (West, 1995).

KATRINA

It's hard for me to believe now, but I was in an abusive relationship, and it took me a long time to get out of it. The first time Ray hit me, I was so surprised I didn't know what to do, so I didn't do anything. The next time, I told him to stop or I'd leave. He said how sorry he was and promised never to hit me again, and then he was real sweet for a long time. I felt like he really did love me, and I felt I should stand by him. And then it happened again. I went to talk to my minister, and he told me my Christian duty was to honor the marriage vows I made before God, so I went back again. Each time Ray beat up on me, he'd follow it with being romantic and sweet, so I'd get sucked back in. I didn't finally leave him until he threw me down some stairs and dislocated my shoulder.

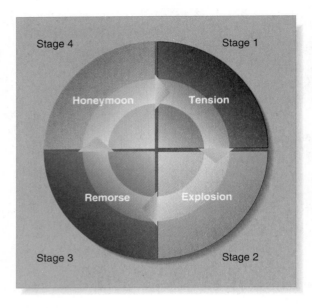

FIGURE 10.4
The Cycle of Abuse

Violence seldom stops without intervention. Instead it follows a predictable cycle just as Katrina described: Tension mounts in the abuser, the abuser explodes by being violent, the abuser then is remorseful and loving, the victim feels loved and that the relationship is working, and then tension mounts up and the cycle begins again (Figure 10.4).

Being loyal in the face of abuse, a response to conflict that we discussed in Chapter 8, is inappropriate, since it doesn't protect a victim's safety. Relationships that are violent and abusive are unhealthy for everyone involved. They obviously jeopardize the comfort, health, and sometimes the survival of victims of violence. Less obvious is the damage experienced by abusers. Using physical force against others is a sign of weakness—an admission that a person can't exercise power in intellectual or emotional ways and must resort to the most crude and unimaginative methods of influence. Further, abusers can destroy relationships that they need and want.

Put It in Practice

RESISTING VIOLENCE

No one should tolerate violence, especially from a person who claims to love her or him. If you are being abused, seek counseling to discover and think through your options. If you suspect someone you care about is being abused, be a real friend and talk with the person. Too often signs of abuse are ignored because we find it awkward to talk about violence between intimates. However, standing by and doing nothing is a kind of abuse in itself. If you are abusing someone you care about, get professional help.

Surviving Distance

In Chapter 9, we discussed the challenges distance poses for friendship. Geographic separation can be even more difficult for romantic couples because Western culture teaches us to expect to live with our partners. The assumption of living together permanently, however, isn't universal. Some Asians and Hispanics come to the United States alone and work several years before bringing spouses and children to join them. In Nepal, many

Tamong men who live in the southern hill country move to the city of Kathmandu for six months of each year, and they serve as guides, cooks, and porters for treks into the Himalayas. Westerners facing long-distance relationships might take heart from the fact that couples in other cultures manage to stay together despite long periods of living apart.

Many of us will be involved in long-distance romantic relationships, since they are increasingly common (U.S. Bureau of the Census, 1992). Fully 70% of college students are or have been in long-distance romances (Rohlfing, 1995). The number of long-distance romantic relationships will increase further as more partners pursue independent careers and as extended travel becomes part of more people's jobs. In 1994, my partner, Robbie, was on the road more than 120 days, and I was gone from our home for nearly 100!

Perhaps the two greatest problems are the lack of daily sharing of small events and unrealistic expectations about time together. First, not being able to share small talk and daily routines is a major loss. As we have seen, sharing the ordinary comings and goings of days helps partners keep their lives woven together. The routine conversations that romantic partners have form the basic fabric of their relationship. The second outstanding problem is unrealistic expectations for time together. Because partners have so little time together, they often believe every moment must be perfect. They feel that there should be no harsh words or conflict and that they should be happily focused on each other for all of the time they have together. Yet, this is an unrealistic expectation. Conflict and needs for autonomy are natural and inevitable in all romantic relationships. They may be even more likely in reunions of long-distance couples, since partners are used to living alone and have established independent rhythms that may not mesh well.

The good news is that these problems don't necessarily sabotage long-distance romance. Most researchers report that partners

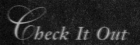

DIFFICULTIES IN LONG-DISTANCE ROMANCE

© Peter L. Chapman

Partners involved in long-distance romantic relationships in the United States report the following challenges:

1. It takes money to maintain long-distance relationships.
2. It's hard for partners to negotiate comfortable rules for each partner's in-town relationships.
3. Partners are hyperconscious about the limited time they do have together. Expectations for good sharing and no rough spots can be unrealistic.
4. It's hard to assess relationships when you aren't with your partner.
5. You miss many nonverbal cues in phone calls.
6. You can't share daily news about your lives.

Sources: Gross, H. E. (1980). Couples who live apart: Time/place disjunctions and their consequence. *Symbolic Interaction, 3,* 69–82. Rohlfing, M. (1995). Doesn't anybody stay in one place anymore? An exploration of the understudied phenomenon of long-distance relationships. In J. T. Wood & S. W. Duck (Eds.), *Understanding relationship processes, 6: Off the beaten track: Understudied relationships,* pp. 173–196. Thousand Oaks, CA: Sage.

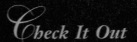
COPING WITH GEOGRAPHIC SEPARATION

College students report nine coping strategies they use to sustain intimacy across long distances.

1. Recognize that long-distance relationships are common; you're not alone.

2. Create more social support systems (friends) while separated from a romantic partner.

3. Communicate creatively—send video- and audiotapes.

4. Before separating, work out ground rules for going out with friends, phoning, visiting, and writing.

5. Use time together "wisely" to be affectionate and to have fun together. Being serious all the time isn't constructive.

6. Maintain honesty. Especially when partners live apart, they need to be straight with each other.

7. Build an open, supportive communication climate so that you can talk about issues and feelings.

8. Maintain trust by abiding by ground rules that were agreed on, phoning when you say you will, and keeping lines of communication open.

9. Focus on the positive aspects of separation.

Source: Westefield, J. S., & Liddell, D. (1982). Coping with long-distance relationships. *Journal of College Student Personnel, 23*, 550–551.

can maintain satisfying commitments in spite of geographic separation (Rohlfing, 1995). To overcome the difficulties of long-distance love, many couples engage in creative communication to sustain intimacy.

The strategies devised by college students are sound guidelines for sustaining intimacy across distance. Notice that these strategies reflect many of the communication principles we've discussed in this and previous chapters. Because partners don't have the comfort of everyday interaction, it is especially important to build climates that are trusting, open, and honest in long-distance relationships. It's also critical that couples who live apart focus on what is positive and good about the relationship and even the separation. One important advantage of living apart is that each partner can concentrate more fully on work, school, or other priorities (Gross, 1980). This may allow partners to advance in their careers so that when they are reunited they have secure jobs and better than average resources.

Romantic relationships experience many of the pressures that beset all personal relationships. Three problems that pose special difficulty for romantic partners are achieving equity, negotiating safer sex, and managing the strains of separation. Commitment, flexibility, and effective interpersonal communication help partners meet the challenges of keeping romance healthy and satisfying over the long term.

Guidelines for Communication Between Romantic Partners

Enduring romantic relationships are important sources of personal growth and happiness. Keeping love and commitment alive for a lifetime is one of the greatest challenges we all face. To meet the challenge of sustaining intimacy over the long term, practice the interpersonal communication skills we've discussed throughout this book. Build supportive climates, listen mindfully, engage in dual perspective, and deal constructively with conflicts. In addition, two specific guidelines apply to intimate communication.

Show Respect and Consideration

For romantic intimacy to remain healthy and satisfying, partners need to demonstrate continuously that they value and respect one another. As obvious as this guideline seems, many couples don't follow it. Sometimes we treat strangers with more respect and kindness than we offer romantic partners. It's easy to take for granted a person who is a continuing part of our life and to be less loving, respectful, and considerate than we should be.

JACKSON

One of the things I love most about Meleika is the way she starts each day. Before getting out of bed, she reaches over and kisses my cheek. Then she gets up and showers while I sneak a little more shut-eye. When I get up, the first thing she always says is "morning love." That is such a great way to start each day. Even after five years of marriage she starts each day by letting me know I matter.

Consideration and respect don't magically infuse relationships just because we know about interpersonal communication skills, such as those we've discussed in this book. For a respectful, confirming climate to exist, partners must *practice* effective interpersonal communication in the relationship. We should be as mindful of good communication when we enter a dialogue with established romantic partners as when we talk with casual acquaintances.

They should be respectful of one another, particularly when discussing problems and complaints. Disagreement is natural and often constructive, but how we disagree with a partner is critical. Studies of marriages reveal differences between how satisfied and dissatisfied spouses talk about complaints and problems. Satisfied couples assert grievances and express anger and disagreement. Dissatisfied couples, however, communicate criticism, contempt, and sometimes disgust (Gottman & Carrère, 1994). It would be appropriate for Mary to tell Simon "I feel angry when you smoke in the house because the smell bothers me." However, it would be personally disrespectful for Mary to say, "Smoking is a filthy, repulsive habit. Every time you light a cigarette you look revolting." The first statement is a civil complaint about a behavior; the second statement is a vicious attack on John's personal worth.

Both our relationships and our self-respect are at stake in how we act toward intimate partners. As we learned in Chapter 1, communication is irreversible. Harsh words and personal insults cannot be taken back once we've said them. Neither can we retract sneers, scowls and other nonverbal behaviors that express contempt. Because we cannot undo communication or its impact, we need to be mindful about what we say and how we say it.

Make Daily Choices That Enhance Intimacy

Perhaps the most important guideline for sustaining romantic relationships is to be aware that they are creative projects that reflect the choices partners make. Relationships are not things we enter, but processes we create and continuously refine. Realizing that we are choice makers enables us to take responsibility for our choices and how they chart the course of intimacy.

The romantic relationships we create reflect a series of personal choices. Although we are not always aware that we are making choices, we continuously choose who we will be and what kind of relationships we will fashion. Intimate partners choose to sustain closeness or let it wither, to build climates that are open or closed and defensive, to rely on constructive or destructive communication to deal with conflict, to fulfill or betray trust, and to enhance or diminish each other's self-concept.

Too often we focus on large choices such as whether to commit, how to manage a serious conflict, or how to celebrate an anniversary. As important as major choices are, they don't make up the basic fabric of a relationship (Wood, 1995c). Instead, undramatic, day-to-day choices sculpt the quality of intimacy. Do you listen mindfully to a partner when you are tired? Do you continue to invest in intimacy after the initial euphoria has waned? Do you care enough about a relationship to work through crises and conflicts? Do you neglect your partner when you've had a rough day? Do you exert the effort to use dual perspective so that you can understand your partner on her or his terms? Seemingly small choices like these shape the quality of intimacy and the individuals in it. Although they appear small and insignificant, our ordinary, daily choices weave the basic fabric of our romantic relationships. By being aware of the impact of our "small" choices, we can make ones that continuously enhance the quality of intimacy.

SUMMARY

In this chapter, we focused on the dynamics of romantic relationships. We have seen that they are complex blends of intimacy, commitment, and passion. Although passion may be the most dramatic dimension of romantic relationships, it is not necessarily the most important for long-term stability and happiness. Commitment, or the intention to stay together, and intimacy, or feelings of warmth and connection, are also critical for love that lasts. Love, however, comes in many forms, and we considered six distinct styles of loving and how they might combine in romantic relationships.

The typical developmental course of romance begins with an escalation phase in which communication concentrates on gaining personal knowledge and building a private culture for the relationship. If individuals decide to stay together permanently, they commit to a future of intimacy. At that point they enter the extended phase of navigating in which they continuously adjust to small and large changes in their individual and joint lives. If a romantic bond falters, partners follow a path of deterioration, moving from dissatisfaction to negotiation to grave dressing in which they lay the relationship to rest.

In addition to the normal challenges that all relationships face, romantic bonds experience unique pressures and problems. Among these are achieving equity between partners, negotiating safer sex, responding to violence and abuse, and managing love at a distance. These and other difficulties are best handled by practicing good interpersonal communication, showing respect for partners, and recognizing the impact of so-called small choices on the quality of a relationship. Following these guidelines, as well as others identified in previous chapters, should enhance your ability to create satisfying romantic relationships that can stand the test of time.

KEY TERMS

Committed romantic
  relationships
Passion
Intimacy
Eros
Storge
Ludus
Pragma
Mania
Agape
Invitational
  communication
Environmental spoiling
Explorational
  communication

Intensifying
  communication
Revising communication
Navigating
Relational culture
Placemaking
Dyadic breakdown
Intrapsychic phase
Dyadic negotiation
Social phase
Social support
Grave dressing
Equity
Psychological
  responsibility

Continuing the Conversation

Although *Everyday Encounters* is drawing to a close, the conversation we've launched in these pages will continue. Interpersonal communication will be central to your life in the years ahead. As I reflect on what we've discussed, I perceive three threads that weave through the entire book.

Communication Creates and Reflects Identity

Communication is both an important source of personal identity and a primary means by which we express who we are. Our sense of personal identity grows directly out of interpersonal communication. We enter the world without any clear sense of self, and we look to others to tell us who we are. Parents, siblings, and others who are significant in the first years of our life provide us with reflected appraisals that express how they see us and our value. As we venture beyond the confines of family, we continue to see ourselves through the eyes of others. Peers, teachers, friends, and romantic partners communicate their views of us, and those become part of how we see ourselves and how we define our paths of personal growth.

Identity not only grows out of interpersonal communication but also is expressed in communication. How we communicate expresses who we are. Verbally and nonverbally, we announce that we are dominant or deferential, outgoing or introverted, caring or indifferent, egotistical or interested in others, assertive or passive, accepting or judgmental, and so forth.

Interpersonal Communication Is Central to Relationships

Communication is the heart of personal relationships. The health and endurance of personal relationships depend in large measure on our ability to communicate effectively. For relationships to be satisfying, we need to know how to express our own feelings, needs, and ideas in ways that others can understand. We also need to know how to listen sensitively and responsively to our intimates and how to create climates that are supportive and affirming. Communication is the basis of meaning in human relationships, and it is the primary way we build, refine, sustain, and transform close connections with others.

Interpersonal Communication Occurs in a Diverse World

A third theme of this book is that social diversity shapes and is reflected in communication. We've seen that our social standpoints affect how we communicate and how we interpret the communication of others. What is normal or desirable in one social group may be offensive or odd in other communities. Once we understand that standpoints shape communication, we are able to see that there are no absolutely right or wrong styles of communicating. Our ways of communicating, then, reflect not just our individual identities, but also standpoints that are shaped by the social groups to which we belong.

Diverse cultures and the communication styles they cultivate offer rich opportunities to learn about others and ourselves. The more we interact with people whose backgrounds, beliefs, and communication styles differ from our own, the more we will grow as individuals and as members of a common world.

What you've studied about interpersonal communication should give you insight into how each of these themes applies in your current life. Let's now consider how they pertain to our personal and collective future.

The Road Ahead

Interpersonal communication will be as much a part of your everyday life in the future as it is today, although it may assume different forms and functions in the years ahead. The skills and perspectives we've discussed in this book will serve you well in meeting the challenges that will accompany changes in yourself, relationships, and society.

In the coming years, your interpersonal relationships will change both in ways you anticipate and in ways that surprise you. Some of the friends you have today will still be close in years to come, while others will fade away. Some romances of the moment will flourish and endure, and others will wither. New people will come into your life, and familiar ones will leave. Each person who enters or exits your life will affect your personal identity.

There will also be changes and surprises in *how* people go about the process of forming and sustaining relationships. The trend toward long-distance romances and friendships will grow as more individuals who care about each other find they cannot live and work in the same location. Technology will also alter how we communicate with friends and romantic partners. Increasingly, we will rely on electronic forms of communication to sustain important personal relationships. Currently, I use e-mail to stay in daily contact with a man who has been my friend for twenty years, and I am looking forward to meeting in person a woman with whom I've become friendly through electronic communication. In the future, friends, romantic partners, and family members will make increasing use of the Internet to stay in touch.

Finally, interpersonal communication and relationships will evolve in response to changes in the larger society. Medical advances will stretch the average life span further, so that a promise to stay together "'til death do us part" will involve a greater time commitment than it does today. Longer lives will also increase the number of older people in society and the opportunities for them to be part of our friendships and families. Relationship forms that are not recognized or approved today may be accepted in the future. Interaction with an increasing diversity of people will change our perspective on what relationships are and how to sustain them. In addition, the broadened horizons diversity fosters will alter the options we recognize for creating our own relationships.

Neither you nor I can foresee what lies ahead for us and for our world. However, we can predict with assurance that there will be changes in us, others, and cultural life. Whatever changes we experience, we can be sure that interpersonal communication will continue to be central to our happiness and effectiveness.

In *Everyday Encounters* and the course it accompanies, you have learned a good deal about interpersonal communication. I hope that the understandings you've gained and the skills you've acquired will be valuable to you in the years ahead. If you commit to practicing and continuously enlarging the principles and skills introduced in this book, then you are on the threshold of a lifelong journey that will enrich you and your relationships with others. I wish all of that for you, and more.

Abstract Removed from concrete reality. Symbols are abstract because they are inferences and generalizations abstracted from a total reality.

Agape A secondary style of loving that is selfless and based on giving to others, not receiving rewards or returns from them. Agape is a blend of eros and storge.

Ambiguous Unclear meaning. Symbols are ambiguous because their meanings vary from person to person, context to context, and so forth.

Ambushing Listening carefully for the purpose of attacking a speaker.

Anxious/resistant attachment style This style tends to develop when a caregiver behaves inconsistently toward a child—sometimes being loving, and other times being rejecting or neglectful.

Arbitrary Random or unnecessary. Symbols are arbitrary because there is no necessary reason for any particular symbol to stand for a particular referent.

Artifacts Personal objects we use to announce our identities and personalize our environments.

Attachment styles Patterns of parenting that teach children who they are, who others are, and how to approach relationships.

Attributions Causal accounts that explain why things happen and why people act as they do.

Bracketing Noting an important issue that comes up in the course of discussing other matters and that needs to be discussed at a later time. Bracketing allows partners to stay effectively focused on a specific issue at one time, but to agree to deal with other issues later.

Chronemics A type of nonverbal communication concerned with how we perceive and use time to define identities and interaction.

Cognitive complexity Determined by the number of constructs used, how abstract they are, and how elaborately they interact to create perceptions.

Commitment A decision to remain with a relationship. Commitment is one of three dimensions of enduring romantic relationships, and it has more impact on relational continuity than does love alone. It is also an advanced stage in the process of escalation in romantic relationships.

Committed romantic relationships Voluntary connections we presume will be primary and continuing parts of our lives. Committed romantic relationships include three dimensions: intimacy, passion, and commitment.

Communication rules Shared understandings of what communication means and what behaviors are appropriate in various situations.

Conflict Exists when individuals who depend on each other express different views, interests, or goals and perceive their differences as incompatible or as opposed by the other.

Constitutive rules Communication rules that define what communication means by specifying how certain communicative acts are to be counted.

Constructivism Theory that states that we organize and interpret experience by applying cognitive structures called schemata.

Content level of meaning Refers to the content or denotative information in communication. Content-level meanings are literal.

Contracting Building a solution through negotiation and acceptance of parts of proposals for resolution. Contracting is usually present in the later stages of constructive conflict.

Culture Beliefs, understandings, practices, and ways of interpreting experience that are shared by a number of people.

Defensive listening Perceiving personal attacks, criticisms, or hostile undertones in communication when none are intended.

Direct definition Communication that explicitly tells us who we are by specifically labeling us and reacting to our behaviors. Direct definition usually occurs first in families, and also in interaction with peers and others.

Dismissive attachment style Promoted by caregivers who are disinterested, rejecting, or abusive toward children. Unlike people who develop fearful attachment styles, those with a dismissive style do not accept the caregiver's view of them as unlovable. Instead, they dismiss others as unworthy and thus do not seek close relationships.

Downers People who communicate negatively about us and reflect negative appraisals of our self-worth.

Dual perspective The ability to understand both your own and another person's perspective, beliefs, thoughts, and/or feelings.

Dyadic breakdown The first stage of relational decay. Dyadic breakdown involves degeneration of established patterns, understandings, and routines that make up a relational culture and that sustain intimacy on a day-to-day basis.

Dyadic negotiation Stage of relational deterioration that involves brooding about dissatisfaction.

Ego boundaries Define where an individual stops and the rest of the world begins.

Empathy Ability to feel with another person—to feel what she or he feels in a situation.

Environmental spoiling Process by which proximity breeds ill will.

Equity Fairness, based on the perception that both partners invest relatively equally in a relationship and benefit similarly from their investments. Perceived equity is a primary influence on satisfaction with relationships.

Eros A powerful, passionate style of love that blazes to life suddenly and dramatically. Eros is one of the three primary styles of loving.

Ethnocentrism The assumption that our culture and its norms are the only right ones. Ethnocentric communication reflects certainty, which tends to create defensive communication climates.

Explorational communication The third stage in relational escalation, which involves exchanges of information to check out the possibilities of a relationship.

Fearful attachment style Cultivated when the caregiver in the first bond communicates in consistently negative, rejecting, or even abusive ways to a child.

Games Interactions in which the real conflicts are hidden or denied and a counterfeit excuse is created for arguing or put-downs.

Grace Granting forgiveness or putting aside personal needs when it is not required or expected. Grace reflects generosity of spirit.

Grave dressing The final phase in relational decline, it involves burying the relationship and putting it to rest.

Hearing A physiological activity that occurs when sound waves hit our eardrums. Unlike listening, hearing is a passive process.

Identity scripts Guides to action based on rules for living and identity. Initially communicated in families, scripts define our roles, how we are to play them, and basic elements in the plot of our lives.

I–It communication Impersonal communication in which individuals are treated as objects or instruments for our purposes.

Intensifying communication Stage in the escalation of romantic relationships that increases the depth of a relationship by increasing personal knowledge and allowing a couple to begin creating a private culture. Also called euphoria.

Internal tensions Relationship stresses that grow out of individuals and their interaction.

Interpersonal climate The overall feeling, or emotional mood, of a relationship.

Interpersonal communication A selective, systemic, ongoing process in which unique individuals interact to reflect and build personal knowledge and to create meanings.

Interpersonal communication competence Communication that is interpersonally effective and appropriate. Competence includes abilities to monitor oneself, engage in dual perspective, enact a range of communication skills, and adapt communication appropriately.

Interpretation The subjective process of evaluating and explaining perceptions.

Intimacy Includes feelings of closeness, connection, and tenderness between lovers. Intimacy is one of three dimensions of committed romantic relationships.

Intrapsychic phase The second phase in disintegration of romantic relationships, this involves brooding about problems in the relationship and dissatisfactions with a partner.

Investment Something put into a relationship that cannot be recovered should the relationship end. Investments, more than rewards and love, increase commitment.

Invitational communication The second stage in the escalation phase of romantic relationships. In this stage, individuals signal they are interested in interacting and respond to invitations from others.

I–Thou communication Fully interpersonal communication in which individuals acknowledge and deal with each other as unique individuals who meet fully in dialogue.

I–You communication Interaction that is midway between impersonal and interpersonal communication. In I–You relationships, communicators acknowledge one another as human beings, but do not know and act toward each other as unique individuals in their totalities.

Kinesics Body position and body motions, including those of the face.

Kitchensinking Unproductive form of conflict communication in which everything except the kitchen sink is thrown into the argument.

Letting go To free ourselves of anger, blame, and judgments about another and what she or he did. Letting go of these feelings is part of showing grace.

Listening A complex process that consists of being mindful; hearing, selecting, and organizing information; interpreting communication; responding; and remembering.

Literal listening Listening only to the content level of meaning and ignoring the relational level of meaning.

Loaded language An extreme form of evaluative language that relies on words that strongly slant perceptions and, thus, meanings.

Ludus One of three primary styles of love. Ludus is playful love in which the goal is not commitment, but to have fun at love as a game or a series of challenges and maneuvers.

Mania One of three secondary styles of loving made up of eros and ludus. Mania is passionate, sometimes obsessive love that includes emotional extremes.

Metacommunication Communication about communication. When excessive, as in unproductive conflict interaction, metacommunication becomes self-absorbing and diverts partners from the issues causing conflict.

Mindfulness A concept from Zen Buddhism that refers to being fully present in the moment. Being mindful is the first step of listening and the foundation for all others.

Mindreading Assuming we understand what another person thinks or how another person perceives something.

Minimal encouragers Communication that gently invites another person to elaborate by expressing interest in hearing more.

Monitoring The capacity to observe and regulate your own communication.

Monopolizing Continuously focusing communication on ourselves instead of on the person who is talking.

Navigating After relationships have escalated to commitment, partners navigate to continuously adjust and rework interaction to keep a relationship satisfying and healthy. Ideally, this stage lasts a lifetime.

Noise Anything that distorts communication so that it is more difficult for individuals to understand one another.

Nonverbal communication All forms of communication other than words themselves. Nonverbal communication includes inflection and other vocal qualities as well as several other behaviors.

Paraphrasing A method of clarifying another's meaning by reflecting our interpretations of his or her communication back to him or her.

Particular others One source of social perspectives that individuals use to define themselves and guide how they think, act, and feel. The perspectives of particular others are the viewpoints of specific individuals who are significant to the self.

Passion Intensely positive feelings and desires for another person. Passion is based on rewards from involvement and is not equivalent to commitment. It is one of three dimensions of enduring romantic relationships.

Perception An active process of selecting, organizing, and interpreting people, objects, events, situations, and activities.

Personal constructs Bipolar "mental yardsticks" that allow us to measure people and situations along specific dimensions of judgment.

Person-centered communication Ability to adapt messages effectively to particular others.

Person-perception The ability to perceive another as a unique and distinct individual apart from social roles and generalizations.

Perspective of the generalized other The collection of rules, roles, and attitudes endorsed by the whole social community in which we live.

Placemaking Process of creating a personal environment that is comfortable and that reflects the values, experiences, and tastes of individuals.

Physical environment is part of relational culture, which is the nucleus of intimacy.

Pragma A secondary style of loving that is pragmatic or practical in nature. Pragma is a blend of storge and ludus.

Process An ongoing, continuous dynamic flow that has no clear-cut beginnings or endings and that is always evolving and changing. Interpersonal communication is a process.

Prototypes Knowledge structures that define the clearest or most representative examples of some category.

Proxemics A type of nonverbal communication that includes space and how we use it.

Pseudolistening Pretending to listen.

Psychological responsibility Responsibility to remember, plan, and coordinate domestic work and child care. In general, women assume psychological responsibility for child care and housework, even if both partners share in the actual tasks.

Punctuation Defining the beginning and ending of interaction or interaction episodes.

Reflected appraisal Process of seeing and thinking about ourselves in terms of the appraisals of us that others reflect.

Regulative rules Communication rules that regulate interaction by specifying when, how, where, and with whom to talk about certain things.

Relational culture A private world of rules, understandings, and patterns of acting and interpreting that partners create to give meaning to their relationship. Relational culture is the nucleus of intimacy.

Relational dialectics Opposing forces, or tensions, that are normal parts of all relationships. The three relational dialectics are autonomy/intimacy, novelty/routine, and openness/closedness.

Relational level of meaning Refers to what communication expresses about the relationship between communicators. Three dimensions of relational-level meanings are liking or disliking, responsiveness, and power (control).

Relationship rules Guidelines that friends or romantic partners have for their relationships. Usually relationship rules are not explicit, but tacit, understandings.

Remembering The process of recalling what you have heard. This is the sixth part of listening.

Responding Symbolizing your interest in what is being said with observable feedback to speakers during the process of interaction. This is the fifth of six elements in listening.

Revising communication A stage in the escalation of romantic relationships that many, but not all, couples experience. Revising involves evaluating a relationship and working out any obstacles or problems before commiting for the long term.

Scripts One of four cognitive schemata. Scripts define expected or appropriate sequences of action in particular settings.

Secure attachment style The most common and the most positive attachment style. This style develops when the caregiver responds in a consistently attentive and loving way to a child.

Selective listening Focusing on only selected parts of communication. We listen selectively when we screen out parts of a message that don't interest us or with which we disagree, and also when we rivet attention on parts of communication

that do interest us or with which we agree.

Self A multidimensional process that involves forming and acting from social perspectives that arise and evolve in communication with others and ourselves.

Self-disclosure Revealing personal information about ourselves that others are unlikely to discover in other ways.

Self-fulfilling prophecy Acting in ways that bring about our expectations or judgments of ourselves.

Self-sabotage Self-talk that communicates we are no good, we can't do something, we can't change, and so forth. Self-sabotaging communication undermines belief in ourselves and motivation to change and grow.

Self-serving bias Tendency to attribute our positive actions and successes to stable, global, internal influences that we control, and to attribute negative actions and failures to unstable, specific, external influences beyond our control.

Social comparison Involves comparing ourselves with others to form judgments of our own talents, abilities, qualities, and so forth.

Social phase Part of relational disintegration in which partners figure out how to inform outsiders that the relationship is ending.

Social support Phase of relational decline in which partners look to friends and family for support during the trauma of breaking up.

Standpoint theory Claims that a culture includes a number of social groups that differently shape the perceptions, identities, and opportunities of members of those groups.

Static evaluation Assessments that suggest something is unchanging. "Bob is impatient" is a static evaluation.

Stereotypes Predictive generalizations about people and situations.

Storge A comfortable, friendly kind of love, often likened to friendship. It is one of three primary styles of loving.

Symbols Abstract, arbitrary, and ambiguous representations of other phenomena, including feelings, events, ideas, relationships, situations, and individuals.

Systemic A quality of interpersonal communication that means it takes place within multiple systems that influence what is communicated and what meanings are constructed. Examples of systems affecting communication are physical context, culture, personal histories, and previous interactions between people.

Totalizing Responding to a person as if one aspect of him or her is the total of who he or she is.

Trust Entails two factors: (1) belief in another's reliability (he or she will do what is promised); (2) emotional reliance on another to care about and protect our welfare. Trust is believing that private information about us is safe with another person because she or he cares for us and will look out for our welfare.

Uppers People who communicate positively about us and who reflect positive appraisals of our self-worth.

Vultures An extreme form of downers. They not only communicate negative images of us, but actually attack our self-concepts.

Acitelli, L. (1988). When spouses talk to each other about their relationship. *Journal of Social and Personal Relationships, 5,* 185–199.

Acitelli, L. (1993). You, me, and us: Perspectives on relationship awareness. In S. W. Duck (Ed.), *Understanding relationship processes, 1: Individuals in relationships* (pp. 144–174). Newbury Park, CA: Sage.

Acker, M., & Davis, M. H. (1992). Intimacy, passion and commitment in adult romantic relationships: A test of the triangular theory of love. *Journal of Social and Personal Relationships, 9,* 21–51.

Ackerman, D. (1994). *A natural history of love.* New York: Random House.

Adelman, M. B., Parks, M. R., & Albrecht, T. L. (1987). Supporting friends in need. In T. L. Albrecht, M. B. Adelman & Associates (Eds.), *Communicating social support* (pp. 105–125). Beverly Hills, CA: Sage.

Adler, R., & Towne, N. (1993). *Looking out/looking in* (7th ed.). Fort Worth, TX: Harcourt Brace Jovanovich.

Ainsworth, M. D. S., Blehar, M. C., Waters, E., & Wall, S. (1978). *Patterns of attachment: A psychological study of the strange situation.* Hillsdale, NJ: Lawrence Erlbaum.

Alexander, E. R., III. (1979). The reduction of cognitive conflict: Effects of various types of communication. *Journal of Conflict Resolution, 23,* 120–138.

Allan, G. (1994). Social structure and relationships. In S. W. Duck (Ed.), *Understanding relationship processes, 3: Social context and relationships* (pp. 1–25). Newbury Park, CA: Sage.

Allen, S., Waton, A., Purcell, K., & Wood, S. (1986). *The experience of unemployment.* Basingstoke: Macmillan.

American games, Japanese rules. (1988). Frontline documentary. National Public Television. Cited in Ferrante, J. (1992). *Sociology: A global perspective* (p. 102). Belmont, CA: Wadsworth.

Andersen, M. L., & Collins, P. H. (Eds.). (1992). *Race, class, and gender: An anthology.* Belmont, CA: Wadsworth.

Argyle, M., & Henderson, M. (1984). The rules of friendship. *Journal of Social and Personal Relationships, 1,* 211–237.

Argyle, M., & Henderson, M. (1985). The rules of relationships. In S. W. Duck & D. Perlman (Eds.), *Understanding personal relationships: An interdisciplinary approach* (pp. 63–84). Beverly Hills, CA: Sage.

Aries, E. (1987). Gender and communication. In P. Shaver (Ed.), *Sex and gender* (pp. 149–176). Newbury Park, CA: Sage.

Arnett, R. C. (1986). The inevitable conflict and confronting in dialogue. In J. Stewart (Ed.), *Bridges, not walls* (4th ed., pp. 272–279). New York: Random House.

Atsumi, R. (1980). Patterns of personal relationships. *Social Analysis, 5,* 63–78.

Bach, G. R., & Wyden, P. (1973). *The intimate enemy: How to fight fair in love and marriage.* New York: Avon.

Baine, D. (1986). *Memory and instruction.* Englewood Cliffs, NJ: Educational Technology Publications.

Barker, L., Edwards, R., Gaines, C., Gladney, K., & Holley, F. (1981). An investigation of proportional time spent in various communication activities by college students. *Journal of Applied Communication Research, 8,* 101–109.

Bartholomew, K. (1993). From childhood to adult relationships: Attachment theory and research. In S. W. Duck (Ed.), *Understanding relationship processes, 2: Learning about relationships* (pp. 30–62). Newbury Park, CA: Sage.

Bartholomew K., & Horowitz, L. M. (1991). Attachment styles among young adults: A test of a four-category model. *Journal of Personality and Social Psychology, 61,* 226–244.

Bass, A. (1993, December 5). Behavior that can wreck a marriage. *Raleigh News and Observer,* p. 8E.

Bates, E. (1994, fall). Beyond black and white. *Southern Exposure,* pp. 11–15.

Bateson, M. C. (1990). *Composing a life.* New York: Penguin/Plume.

Baxter, L. A. (1984). Trajectories of relationship disengagement. *Journal of Social and Personal Relationships, 7,* 141–178.

Baxter, L. A. (1985). Accomplishing relational disengagement. In S. Duck & D. Perlman (Eds.), *Understanding personal relationships: An interdisciplinary approach* (pp. 243–265). Beverly Hills, CA: Sage.

Baxter, L. A. (1987). Self-disclosure and relationship disengagement. In V. Derlega & J. H. Berg (Eds.), *Self-disclosure: Theory, research, and therapy* (pp. 155–174). New York: Plenum.

Baxter, L. A. (1988). A dialectical perspective on communication strategies in relationship development. In S. W. Duck, D. F. Hay, S. E. Hobvoll, W. Iches, & B. Montgomery (Eds.), *Handbook of personal relationships* (pp. 257–273). London: John Wiley.

Baxter, L. A. (1990). Dialectical contradictions in relational development. *Journal of Social and Personal Relationships, 7,* 69–88.

Baxter, L. A. (1993). The social side of personal relationships: A dialectical perspective. In S. Duck (Ed.), *Understanding relationship processes, 3: Social context and relationships* (pp. 139–165). Newbury Park, CA: Sage.

Baxter, L. A., & Simon, E. P. (1993). Relationship maintenance strategies and dialectical contradictions in personal relationships. *Journal of Social and Personal Relationships, 10,* 225–242.

Be civil. (1994, July 5). *Wall Street Journal,* p. A1.

Beck, A. (1988). *Love is never enough.* New York: Harper & Row.

Becker, C. S. (1987). Friendship between women: A phenomenological study of best friends. *Journal of Phenomenological Psychology, 18,* 59–72.

Bellah, R., Madsen, R., Sullivan, W., Swindler, A., & Tipton, S. (1985). *Habits of the heart: Individualism and commitment in American life.* Berkeley, CA: University of California Press.

Belsky, J., & Pensky, E. (1988). Developmental history, personality, and family relationships: Toward an emergent family system. In R. A. Hinde & J. Stevenson-Hinde (Eds.), *Relationships within families: Mutual influences* (pp. 193–217). Oxford, UK: Clarendon.

Benjamin, D., & Horwitz, T. (1994, July 14). German view: "You Americans work too hard—and for what?" *Wall Street Journal,* pp. B1, B6.

Berg, J. H. (1987). Responsiveness and self-disclosure. In V. J. Derlega & J. H. Berg (Eds.), *Self-disclosure: Theory, research, and therapy.* New York: Plenum.

Berger, C. R., & Bell, R. A. (1988). Plans and the initiation of social relationships. *Human Communication Research, 15,* 217–235.

Bergner, R. M., & Bergner, L. L. (1990). Sexual misunderstanding: A descriptive and pragmatic formulation. *Psychotherapy, 27,* 464–467.

Berne, E. (1964). *Games people play.* New York: Grove.

Bernstein, B. (Ed.). (1973). *Class, codes, and control* (Vol. 2). London: Routledge and Kegan Paul.

Bernstein, B. (1974). *Class, codes, and control: Theoretical studies toward a sociology of language* (rev. ed.). New York: Shocken Books.

Birdwhistell, R. (1970). *Kinesics and context.* Philadelphia: University of Pennsylvania Press.

Blumer, H. (1969). *Symbolic interaction: Perspective and method.* Englewood Cliffs, NJ: Prentice-Hall.

Blumstein, P., & Schwartz, P. (1983). *American couples: Money, work, and sex.* New York: William Morrow.

Bolton, R. (1986). Listening is more than merely hearing. In J. Stewart (Ed.), *Bridges, not walls* (4th ed., pp. 159–179). New York: Random House.

Boon, S. (1994). Dispelling doubt and uncertainty: Trust in romantic relationships. In S. W. Duck (Ed.), *Understanding relationship processes, 4: Dynamics of relationships* (pp. 86–111). Thousand Oaks, CA: Sage.

Bowen, S. P., & Michal-Johnson, P. (1995). Sexuality in the AIDS era. In S. W. Duck & J. T. Wood (Eds.), *Understanding relationship processes, 5: Relationship challenges* (pp. 150–180). Thousand Oaks, CA: Sage.

Bowlby, J. (1973). *Separation: Attachment and loss* (Vol. 2). New York: Basic Books.

Bowlby, J. (1988). *A secure base: Parent–child attachment and healthy human development.* New York: Basic Books.

Bozzi, V. (1986, February). Eat to the beat. *Psychology Today,* p. 16.

Bradbury, T. N., & Fincham, F. D. (1990). Attributions in marriage: Review and critique. *Psychological Bulletin, 107,* 3–33.

Brehm, S. (1992). *Intimate relations* (2nd ed.). New York: McGraw-Hill.

Brock-Utne, B. (1989). *Feminist perspectives on peace and peace education.* New York: Pergamon Press.

Buber, M. (1957). Distance and relation. *Psychiatry, 20,* 97–104.

Buber, M. (1970). *I and thou* (Walter Kaufmann, Trans.). New York: Scribner.

Burgoon, J. K., Buller, D. B., Hale, J. L., & deTurck, M. A. (1984). Relational messages associated with nonverbal behaviors. *Human Communication Research, 10,* 351–378.

Burgoon, J. K., Buller, D. B., & Woodhall, G. W. (1989). *Nonverbal communication: The unspoken dialogue.* New York: Harper & Row.

Burleson, B. R. (1984). Comforting communication. In H. E. Sypher & J. L. Applegate (Eds.), *Communication by children and adults: Social cognitive and strategic processes* (pp. 63–104). Beverly Hills, CA: Sage.

Burleson, B. R. (1987). Cognitive complexity. In J. C. McCroskey & J. A. Daly (Eds.), *Personality and interpersonal communication* (pp. 305–349). Newbury Park, CA: Sage.

Burleson, B. R., & Samter, W. (1994). A social skills approach to relationship maintenance: How individual differences in communication skills affect the achievement of relationship functions. In D. J. Canary & L. Stafford (Eds.), *Communication and relational maintenance*. Orlando, FL: Academic Press.

Button, C. M., & Collier, D. R. (1991, June). *A comparison of people's concepts of love and romantic love*. Paper presented at the Canadian Psychological Association Conference, Calgary, Alberta.

Caldera, Y. M., Huston, A. C., & O'Brien, M. (1989): Social interactions and play patterns of parents and toddlers with feminine, masculine, and neutral toys. *Child Development, 60,* 70–76.

Campbell, S. M. (1986). From either-or to both-and relationships. In J. Stewart (Ed.), *Bridges, not walls* (4th ed., pp. 262–270). New York: Random House.

Canary, D., & Stafford, L. (Eds.). (1994). *Communication and relational maintenance*. New York: Academic Press.

Cancian, F. (1987). *Love in America*. Cambridge, MA: Cambridge University Press.

Cancian, F. (1989). Love and the rise of capitalism. In B. Risman & P. Schwartz (Eds.), *Gender in intimate relationships* (pp. 12–25). Belmont, CA: Wadsworth.

Capella, J. N. (1991). The biological origins of automated patterns of human interaction. *Communication Theory, 1,* 4–35.

Carnes, J. (1994, spring). An uncommon language. *Teaching Tolerance,* pp. 56–63.

Caspi, A., & Harbener, E. S. (1990). Continuity and change: Assortive marriage and the consistency of personality in adulthood. *Journal of Personality and Social Psychology, 58,* 250–258.

Cassirer, E. (1944). *An essay on man.* New Haven: Yale University Press.

Chodorow, N. (1989). *Feminism and psychoanalytic theory.* New Haven: Yale University Press.

Christensen, A., & Heavey, C. (1990). Gender and social structure in the demand/withdraw pattern in marital conflict. *Journal of Personality and Social Psychology, 59,* 73–81.

Cissna, K. N. L., & Sieburg, E. (1986). Patterns of interactional confirmation and disconfirmation. In J. Stewart (Ed.), *Bridges, not walls* (4th ed., pp. 230–239). New York: Random House.

Civickly, J. M., Pace, R. W., & Krause, R. M. (1977). Interviewer and client behaviors in supportive and defensive interviews. In B. D. Ruben (Ed.), *Communication yearbook, 1* (pp. 347–362). New Brunswick, NJ: Transaction Books.

Clements, M. (1994, August 7). Sex in America today. *Parade,* pp. 4–6.

Cloven, D. H., & Roloff, M. E. (1991). Sense-making activities and interpersonal conflict: Communicative cures for the mulling blues. *Western Journal of Speech Communication, 55,* 134–158.

Coates, J., & Cameron, D. (1989). *Women in their speech communities: New perspectives on language and sex.* London: Longman.

Condry, S. M., Condry, J. C., & Pogatshnik, L. W. (1983). Sex differences: A study of the ear of the beholder. *Sex Roles, 9,* 697–704.

Cooley, C. H. (1912). *Human nature and the social order.* New York: Scribner.

Cosby, P. (1973). Self-disclosure: A literature review. *Psychological Bulletin, 79,* 73–91.

Crockett, W. (1965). Cognitive complexity and impression formation. In B. A. Maher (Ed.), *Progress in experimental personality research, 2.* New York: Academic Press.

Cronen, V., Pearce, W. B., & Snavely, L. (1979). A theory of rule-structure and types of episodes and a study of perceived enmeshment in undersired repetitive patterns ("URPs"). In D. Nimmo (Ed.), *Communication yearbook, 3.* New Brunswick, NJ: Transaction Books.

Cunningham, J. A., Strassberg, D. S., & Haan, B. (1986). Effects of intimacy and sex-role congruency on self-disclosure. *Journal of Social and Clinical Psychology, 4,* 393–401.

Cunningham, J. D., & Antill, J. K. (1995). Current trends in nonmarital cohabitation: The great POSSLQ hunt continues. In J. T. Wood & S. W. Duck (Eds.), *Understanding relationship processes, 6: Off the beaten track: Understudied relationships* (pp. 148–172). Thousand Oaks, CA: Sage.

Cupach, W. R., & Comstock, J. (1990). Satisfaction with sexual communication in marriage: Links to sexual satisfaction and dyadic adjustment. *Journal of Social and Personal Relationships, 7,* 179–182.

Cutrona, C. E. (1982). Transitions to college: Loneliness and the process of social adjustment. In L. A. Peplau & D. Perlman (Eds.), *Loneliness: A sourcebook of* current theory, research, and therapy (pp. 291–309). New York: Wiley Interscience.

Death toll from AIDS escalating. (1991, January 21). *Dayton Daily News*, p. 4A.

DeFrancisco, V. (1991). The sounds of silence: How men silence women in marital relations. *Discourse and Society, 2*, 413–423.

Delia, J., Clark, R. A., & Switzer, D. (1974). Cognitive complexity and impression formation in informal social interaction. *Speech Monographs, 41*, 299–308.

Derlega, V. J., & Berg, J. H. (1987). *Self-disclosure: Research, theory, and therapy.* New York: Plenum.

Dindia, K. (1994). A multiphasic view of relationship maintenance strategies. In D. Canary & L. Stafford (Eds.), *Communication and relational maintenance* (pp. 91–112). New York: Academic Press.

Dindia, K., & Fitzpatrick, M. A. (1985). Marital communication: Three approaches compared. In S. Duck & D. Perlman (Eds.), *Understanding personal relationships: An interdisciplinary approach* (pp. 137–157). Newbury Park, CA: Sage.

Dixson M., & Duck, S. W. (1993). Understanding relationship processes: Uncovering the human search for meaning. In S. W. Duck (Ed.), *Understanding relationship processes, 1: Individuals in relationships* (pp. 175–206). Newbury Park, CA: Sage.

Duck, S. W. (1985). Social and personal relationships. In M. L. Knapp & G. R. Miller (Eds.), *Handbook of interpersonal communication* (pp. 655–686). Beverly Hills, CA: Sage.

Duck, S. W. (1990). Relationships as unfinished business: Out of the frying pan and into the 1990s. *Journal of Social and Personal Relationships, 7*, 5–24.

Duck, S. W. (1992). *Human relationships* (2nd ed.). Newbury Park, CA: Sage.

Duck, S. W. (1994a). *Meaningful relationships.* Thousand Oaks, CA: Sage.

Duck, S. W. (1994b). Steady as (s)he goes: Relational maintenance as a shared meaning system. In D. Canary & L. Stafford (Eds.), *Communication and relational maintenance* (pp. 45–60). New York: Academic Press.

Duck, S. W., Pond, K., & Leatham, G. (1994). Loneliness and the evaluation of relational events. *Journal of Social and Personal Relationships, 11*, 253–276.

Duck, S. W., Rutt, D. J., Hurst, M. H., & Strejc, H. (1991). Some evident truths about conversation in everyday relationships: All communications are not created equal. *Human Communication Research, 18*, 228–267.

Duck, S. W., & Wright, P. H. (1993). Reexamining gender differences in same-gender friendships: A close look at two kinds of data. *Sex Roles, 28*, 709–727.

Eadie, W. F. (1982). Defensive communication revisited: A critical examination of Gibb's theory. *Southern Speech Communication Journal, 47*, 163–177.

Eckman, P., Friesen, W., & Ellsworth, P. (1971). *Emotion in the human face: Guidelines for research and an integration of findings.* Elmsford, NY: Pergamon Press.

Egan, G. (1973). Listening as empathic support. In J. Stewart (Ed.), *Bridges, not walls.* Reading, MA: Addison-Wesley.

Ellis, D. (1989). Male abuse of a marriage or cohabiting female partner. *Violence and Victims, 4*, 235–255.

Eloy, S. V., Guerrero, L. K., Andersen, P. A., & Spitzberg, B. H. (1992, May). *Coping with the green-eyed monster: Relational satisfaction and communicative reactions to jealousy.* Paper presented at the annual meeting of the International Communication Association, Miami, FL.

Ernst, F., Jr. (1973). *Who's listening? A handbook of the transactional analysis of the listening function.* Vallejo, CA: Addresso'set.

Estes, W. K. (1989). Learning theory. In A. Lessold & R. Glaser (Eds.), *Foundations for a psychology of education.* Hillsdale, NJ: Lawrence Erlbaum.

Faludi, S. (1991). *Backlash: The undeclared war against American women.* New York: Crown.

Fehr, B. (1993). How do I love thee: Let me consult my prototype. In S. W. Duck (Ed.), *Understanding relationship processes, 1: Individuals in relationships* (pp. 87–122). Newbury Park, CA: Sage.

Fehr, B., & Russell, J. A. (1991). Concept of love viewed from a prototype perspective. *Journal of Personality and Social Psychology, 60*, 425–438.

Ferrante, J. (1992). *Sociology: A global perspective.* Belmont, CA: Wadsworth.

Fincham, F. D., & Bradbury, T. N. (1987). The impact of attributions in marriage: A longitudinal analysis. *Journal of Personality and Social Psychology, 53*, 510–517.

Fisher, B. A. (1987). *Interpersonal communication: The pragmatics of human relationships.* New York: Random House.

Fisher, J. D., & Byrne, D. (1975). Too close for comfort: Sex differences in response to invasions of personal space. *Journal of Personal and Social Psychology, 32*, 15–21.

Fitzpatrick, M. A. (1988). *Between husbands and wives: Communication in marriage.* Newbury Park, CA: Sage.

Fitzpatrick, M. A., & Best, P. (1979). Dyadic adjustment in relational types: Consensus, cohesion, affectional expression and satisfaction in enduring relationships. *Communication Monographs, 46,* 167–178.

Fletcher, G. J., & Fincham, F. D. (1991). Attribution in close relationships. In G. J. Fletcher & F. D. Fincham (Eds.), *Cognition in close relationships* (pp. 7–35). Hillsdale, NJ: Lawrence Erlbaum.

Fletcher, G. J., Fincham, F. D., Cramer, L., & Heron, N. (1987). The role of attributions in the development of dating relationships. *Journal of Personality and Social Psychology, 51,* 875–884.

Fletcher, G. J., & Fitness, J. (1990). Occurrent social cognition in close relationship interaction: The role of proximal and distal variables. *Journal of Personality and Social Psychology, 59,* 464–474.

Fowers, B. J. (1991). His and her marriage: A multivariate study of gender and marital satisfaction. *Sex Roles, 24,* 209–221.

Fox-Genovese, E. (1991). *Feminism without illusions.* Chapel Hill, NC: University of North Carolina Press.

French, M. (1992). *The war against women.* New York: Summit.

Gabriel, S. L., & Smithson, I. (Eds.). (1990). *Gender in the classroom: Power and pedagogy.* Urbana, IL: University of Illinois Press.

Gaines, S., Jr. (1995). Relationships among members of cultural minorities. In J. T. Wood & S. W. Duck (Eds.), *Understanding relationship processes, 6: Off the beaten track: Understudied relationships* (pp. 51–88). Thousand Oaks, CA: Sage.

Garner, T. (1994). Oral rhetorical practice in African American culture. In A. González, M. Houston, & V. Chen (Eds.), *Our voices:* *Essays in culture, ethnicity, and communication* (pp. 81–91). Los Angeles: Roxbury.

Gergen, K. (1991). *The saturated self: Dilemmas of identity in contemporary life.* New York: Basic Books.

Gerstel, N., & Gross, H. (1985). *Commuter marriage.* New York: Guilford.

Gibb, J. (1961). Defensive communication. *Journal of Communication, 11,* 141–148.

Gibb, J. R. (1964). Climate for trust formation. In L. Bradford, J. Gibb, & K. Benne (Eds.), *T-group theory and laboratory method* (pp. 279–309). New York: John Wiley.

Gibb, J. R. (1970). Sensitivity training as a medium for personal growth and improved interpersonal relationships. *Interpersonal Development, 1,* 6–31.

Gibbs, J. T. (1992). Young black males in America: Endangered, embittered, and embattled. In M. L. Andersen & P. H. Collins (Eds.), *Race, class, and gender: An anthology* (pp. 267–276). Belmont, CA: Wadsworth.

Goldner, V., Penn, P., Sheinberg, M., & Walker, G. (1990). Love and violence: Gender paradoxes in volatile attachments. *Family Process, 19,* 343–364.

Gottman, J. (1979). *Marital interaction: Experimental investigations.* New York: Academic Press.

Gottman, J. (1993). The roles of conflict engagement, escalation or avoidance in marital interaction: A longitudinal view of five types of couples. *Journal of Consulting and Clinical Psychology, 61,* 6–15.

Gottman, J., & Carrère, S. (1994). Why can't men and women get along? Developmental roots and marital inequities. In D. J. Canary & L. Stafford (Eds.), *Communication and relational maintenance* (pp. 203–229). New York: Academic Press.

Gottman, J., Markman, H. J., & Notarius, C. (1977). The topography of marital conflict: A sequential analysis of verbal and nonverbal behavior. *Journal of Marriage and the Family, 39,* 461–477.

Gottman, J., Notarius, C., Gonso, J., & Markman, H. J. (1976a). *A couple's guide to communication.* Champaign, IL: Research Press.

Gottman, J., Notarius, C., Markman, H., Banks, S., Yoppi, B., & Rubin, M. E. (1976b). Behavior exchange theory and marital decision making. *Journal of Experimental Social Psychology, 34,* 14–23.

Gross, H. E. (1980). Couples who live apart: Time/place disjunctions and their consequence. *Symbolic Interaction, 3,* 69–82.

Hall, E. T. (1959). *The silent language.* New York: Doubleday.

Hall, E. T. (1966). *The hidden dimension.* New York: Anchor.

Hall, E. T. (1968). Proxemics. *Current Anthropology, 9,* 83–108.

Hall, J. A. (1978). Gender effects in decoding nonverbal cues. *Psychological Bulletin, 85,* 845–857.

Hall, J. A. (1987). On explaining gender differences: The case of nonverbal communication. In P. Shaver & C. Hendricks (Eds.), *Sex and gender* (pp. 177–200). Newbury Park, CA: Sage.

Hamachek, D. (1992). *Encounters with the self* (3rd ed.). Fort Worth: Harcourt Brace Jovanovich.

Hansen, J. E., & Schuldt, W. J. (1984). Marital self-disclosure and marital satisfaction. *Journal of Marriage and the Family, 46,* 923–926.

Haraway, D. (1988). Situated knowledges: The science question in feminism and the privilege of partial perspective. *Signs, 14,* 575–599.

Harding, S. (1991). *Whose science? Whose knowledge? Thinking from women's lives.* Ithaca, NY: Cornell University Press.

Harris, T. J. (1969). *I'm OK, you're OK.* New York: Harper & Row.

Hayakawa, S. I. (1962). *The use and misuse of language.* New York: Fawcett Publications.

Hayakawa, S. I. (1964). *Language in thought and action* (2nd ed.). New York: Harcourt, Brace & World.

Hecht, M. L., Marston, P. J., & Larkey, L. K. (1994). Love ways and relationship quality in heterosexual relationships. *Journal of Social and Personal Relationships, 11,* 25–44.

Hegel, G. W. F. (1807). *Phenomenology of mind* (J. B. Baillie, Trans.). Germany: Wurzburg & Bamburg.

Heider, F. (1958). *The psychology of interpersonal relations.* New York: John Wiley.

Hendrick, C., & Hendrick, S. (1988). Lovers wear rose colored glasses. *Journal of Social and Personal Relationships, 5,* 161–184.

Hendrick, C., & Hendrick, S. (1989). Research on love: Does it measure up? *Journal of Personality and Social Psychology, 56,* 784–794.

Hendrick, C., & Hendrick, S. (1996). Gender and the experience of heterosexual love. In J. T. Wood (Ed.), *Gendered relationships.* Mountain View, CA: Mayfield.

Hendrick, C., Hendrick, S., Foote, F. H., & Slapion-Foote, M. J. (1984). Do men and women love differently? *Journal of Social and Personal Relationships, 2,* 177–196.

Henley, N. M. (1977). *Body politics: Power, sex and nonverbal communication.* Englewood Cliffs, NJ: Prentice-Hall.

Higginbotham, E. (1992). We were never on a pedestal: Women of color continue to struggle with poverty, racism, and sexism. In M. L. Andersen & P. H. Collins (Eds.), *Race, class, and gender: An anthology* (pp. 183–190). Belmont, CA: Wadsworth.

Hochschild, A., with Manchung, A. (1989). *The second shift.* New York: Viking Press.

Hojat, M. (1982). Loneliness as a function of selected personality variables. *Journal of Clinical Psychology, 38,* 136–141.

Honeycutt, J. M. (1993). Memory structures for the rise and fall of personal relationships. In S. W. Duck (Ed.), *Understanding relationship processes, 1: Individuals in relationships* (pp. 30–59). Newbury Park, CA: Sage.

Honeycutt, J. M., Woods, B., & Fontenot, K. (1993). The endorsement of communication conflict rules as a function of engagement, marriage and marital ideology. *Journal of Social and Personal Relationships, 10,* 285–304.

Houston, M. (1994). When black women talk with white women: Why dialogues are difficult. In A. González, M. Houston, & V. Chen (Eds.), *Our voices: Essays in culture, ethnicity, and communication* (pp. 133–139). Los Angeles: Roxbury.

Howard, J. W., & Dawes, R. M. (1976). Linear prediction of marital happiness. *Personality and Social Psychology Bulletin, 2,* 478–480.

Huston, M., & Schwartz, P. (1995). Relationships of lesbians and gay men. In J. T. Wood & S. W. Duck (Eds.), *Understanding relationship processes, 6: Off the beaten track: Understudied relationships* (pp. 89–121). Thousand Oaks, CA: Sage.

Huston, T. L., McHale, S. M., & Crouter, A. C. (1985). When the honeymoon is over: Changes in the marriage relationship over the first year. In R. Gilmour & S. Duck (Eds.), *The emerging field of personal relationships* (pp. 109–132). Hillsdale, NJ: Lawrence Erlbaum.

Issacson, W. (1989, November 20). Should gays have marriage rights? *Time,* pp. 101–102.

James, K. (1989). When twos are really threes: The triangular dance in couple conflict. *Australian and New Zealand Journal of Family Therapy, 10,* 179–186.

Jeffries, V. (1994). Virtue and attraction: Validation of a measure of love. *Journal of Social and Personal Relationships, 10,* 99–117.

Johnson, C. B., Stockdale, M. S., & Saal, F. E. (1991). Persistence of men's misperceptions of friendly cues across a variety of interpersonal encounters. *Psychology of Women Quarterly, 15,* 463–465.

Johnson, F. L. (1989). Women's culture and communication: An analytic perspective. In C. M. Lont & S. A. Friedley (Eds.), *Beyond the boundaries: Sex and gender diversity in communication* (pp. 301–316). Fairfax, VA: George Mason University Press.

Jones, E., & Gallois, C. (1989). Spouses' impressions of rules for communication in public and private marital conflicts. *Journal of Marriage and the Family, 51,* 957–967.

Jones, G. P., & Dembo, M. H. (1989). Age and sex role differences in intimate friendships during childhood and adolescence. *Merrill-Palmer Quarterly of Behavior and Development, 35,* 445–462.

Jones, W. H., & Moore, T. L. (1989). Loneliness and social support. In M. Hojat & R. Crandall (Eds.), *Loneliness: Theory, research, and applications* (pp. 145–156). Newbury Park, CA: Sage.

Kaye, L. W., & Applegate, J. S. (1990). Men as elder caregivers: A response to changing families. *American Journal of Orthopsychiatry, 60,* 86–95.

Keeley, M. P., & Hart, A. J. (1994). Nonverbal behavior in dyadic interaction. In S. W. Duck (Ed.), *Understanding relationship processes, 4: Dynamics of relationships* (pp. 135–162). Thousand Oaks, CA: Sage.

Kelley, H. H. (1967). Attribution theory in social psychology. In D. Levine (Ed.), *Nebraska symposium on motivation* (Vol. 15, pp. 192–238). Lincoln: University of Nebraska Press.

Kelly, C., Huston, T. L., & Cate, R. M. (1985). Premarital relationship correlates of the erosion of satisfaction in marriage. *Journal of Social and Personal Relationships, 2,* 167–178.

Kelly, G. A. (1955). *The psychology of personal constructs.* New York: W. W. Norton.

Keyes, R. (1992, February 22). Do you have the time? *Parade,* pp. 22–25.

Knapp, M. L. (1972). *Nonverbal communication in human interaction.* New York: Holt, Rinehart & Winston.

Kohlberg, L. (1958). *The development of modes of thinking and moral choice in the years 10 to 16.* Unpublished doctoral dissertation, University of Chicago, Chicago, IL.

Korzybski, A. (1958). *Science and sanity* (4th ed.). Lakeville, CT: International Non-Aristotelian Library Publishing Company.

Kurdek, L. A. (1993). The allocation of household labor in gay, lesbian, and heterosexual married couples. *Journal of Social Issues, 49,* 127–139.

Labor letter. (1994, July 16). *Wall Street Journal,* p. A1.

Labov, W. (1972). *Sociolinguistic patterns.* Philadelphia: University of Pennsylvania Press.

La Gaipa, J. J. (1982). Rituals of disengagement. In S. W. Duck (Ed.), *Personal relationships, 4: Dissolving personal relationships.* London: Academic Press.

Laing, R. D. (1961). *The self and others.* New York: Pantheon.

Lakoff, G., & Johnson, M. (1980). *Metaphors we live by.* Chicago: University of Chicago Press.

Langer, S. (1953). *Feeling and form: A theory of art.* New York: Scribner.

Langer, S. (1979). *Philosophy in a new key: A study in the symbolism of reason, rite, and art* (3rd ed.). Cambridge, MA: Harvard University Press.

Langston, D. (1992). Tired of playing monopoly? In M. L. Andersen & P. H. Collins (Eds.), *Race, class, and gender: An anthology* (pp. 110–119). Belmont, CA: Wadsworth.

Lasswell, M., & Lobsenz, N. M. (1980). *Styles of loving.* New York: Doubleday.

Leathers, D. G. (1976). *Nonverbal communication systems.* Boston: Allyn & Bacon.

Leathers, D. G. (1986). *Successful nonverbal communication: Principles and applications.* New York: Macmillan.

Lee, J. A. (1973). *The colours of love: An exploration of the ways of loving.* Don Mills, Ontario, Canada: New Press.

Lee, J. A. (1988). Love-styles. In R. J. Sternberg & M. L. Barnes (Eds.), *The psychology of love* (pp. 38–67). New Haven: Yale University Press.

Lee, R. (1994, November 3). Housing for the non-discriminating buyer. *Wall Street Journal,* p. A18.

Lee, W. S. (1994). On not missing the boat: A processual method for intercultural understanding of idioms and lifeworld. *Journal of Applied Communication Research, 22,* 141–161.

Le Poire, B. A., Burgoon, J. K., & Parrott, R. (1992). Status and privacy restoring communication in the workplace. *Journal of Applied Communication Research, 4,* 419–436.

Levine, R. (1988). The pace of life across cultures. In J. E. McGrath (Ed.), *The social psychology of time.* Newbury Park, CA: Sage.

Lewis, J. D., & Weigert, A. J. (1985). Social atomism, holism and trust. *Sociological Quarterly, 26,* 455–471.

Lorde, A. (1992). Age, race, class, and sex: Women redefining difference. In M. L. Andersen & P. H. Collins (Eds.), *Race, class, and gender: An anthology* (pp. 495–502). Belmont, CA: Wadsworth.

Luby, V., & Aron, A. (1990, July). *A prototype structuring of love, like, and being in-love.* Paper presented at the Fifth International Conference on Personal Relationships, Oxford, UK.

Lund, M. (1985). The development of investment and commitment scales for predicting continuity of personal relationships. *Journal of Social and Personal Relationships, 2,* 3–23.

Lytton, H., & Romney, D. M. (1991). Parents' differential socialization of boys and girls: A meta-analysis. *Psychological Bulletin, 109,* 267–296.

Mahjubah: The Magazine for Moslem Women. (1984). Cited in Ferrante, J. (1992). *Sociology: A global perspective* (p. 418). Belmont, CA: Wadsworth.

Main, M. (1981). Avoidance in the service of attachment. In K. Immelmann, G. Barlow, L. Petrenovich, & M. Main (Eds.), *Behavioral development: The Beilfield interdisciplinary project.* New York: Cambridge University Press.

Major, B., Schmidlin, A. M., & Williams, L. (1990). Gender patterns in social touch: The impact of setting and age. In C. Mayo & N. M. Henley (Eds.), *Gender and nonverbal behavior* (pp. 3–37). New York: Springer-Verlag.

Malandro, L. A., & Barker, L. L. (1983). *Nonverbal communication.* Reading, MA: Addison-Wesley.

Maltz, D. N., & Borker, R. (1982). A cultural approach to male–female miscommunication. In J. J. Gumpertz (Ed.), *Language and social identity* (pp. 196–216). Cambridge: Cambridge University Press.

Markman, H. J. (1981). Prediction of marital distress: A 5–year follow-up. *Journal of Consulting and Clinical Psychology, 49,* 760–762.

Maslow, A. H. (1968). *Toward a psychology of being.* New York: Van Nostrand Reinhold.

Masters, W. H., & Johnson, V. E. (1979). *Homosexuality in perspective.* Boston: Little, Brown.

Maugh, T., II. (1994, November 26). Romantics seem to be bred, not born. *Raleigh News and Observer,* pp. 1A, 4A.

Mazur, E. (1989). Predicting gender differences in same-sex friendships from affiliation motive and value. *Psychology of Women Quarterly, 13,* 277–291.

McGee-Cooper, A., with Trammel, D., & Lau, B. (1992). *You don't have to go home from work exhausted.* New York: Bantam.

Mead, G. H. (1934). *Mind, self, and society.* Chicago: University of Chicago Press.

Mehrabian, A. (1976). *Public places, private spaces.* New York: Basic Books.

Mehrabian, A. (1981). *Silent messages: Implicit communication of emotion and attitudes* (2nd ed.). Belmont, CA: Wadsworth.

Metts, S., Cupach, W. R., & Bejlovec, R. A. (1989). "I love you too much to ever start liking you": Redefining romantic relationships. *Journal of Social and Personal Relationships, 6,* 259–274.

Miell, D. E., & Duck, S. W. (1986). Strategies in developing friendship. In V. J. Derlega & B. A. Winstead (Eds.), *Friendship and social interaction* (pp. 129–143). New York: Springer-Verlag.

Miller, G. R., & Parks, M. R. (1982). Communication in dissolving relationships. In S. W. Duck (Ed.), *Personal relationships 4: Dissolving personal relationships* (pp. 127–154). London: Academic Press.

Miller, J. B. (1993). Learning from early relationship experience. In S. W. Duck (Ed.), *Understanding relationship processes, 2: Learning about relationships* (pp. 1–29). Newbury Park, CA: Sage.

Mochizuki, T. (1981). Changing patterns of mate selection. *Journal of Comparative Family Studies, 12,* 318–328.

Monsour, M. (1992). Meanings of intimacy in cross- and same-sex friendships. *Journal of Social and Personal Relationships, 9,* 277–295.

Montgomery, B. M. (1988). Quality communication in personal relationships. In S. W. Duck (Ed.), *Handbook of personal relationships* (pp. 343–366). New York: John Wiley.

Mulac, A., Wiemann, J. M., Widenmann, S. J., & Gibson, T. W. (1988). Male/female language differences and effects in same-sex and mixed-sex dyads: The gender-linked language effect. *Communication Monographs, 55,* 315–335.

Nardi, P. M., & Sherrod, D. (1994). Friendship in the lives of gay men and lesbians. *Journal of Social and Personal Relationships, 11,* 185–199.

Narem, T. R. (1980). Try a little TLC. *Science, 80,* 15.

Nelson, M. B. (1994, June 23). Violence from the locker room. *Raleigh News and Observer,* p. 13A.

New York Public Library Desk Reference. (1989). New York: Simon & Schuster/Songstone Press, pp. 189–191.

Noller, P. (1986). Sex differences in nonverbal communication: Advantage lost or supremacy regained? *Australian Journal of Psychology, 38,* 23–32.

Noller, P. (1987). Nonverbal communication in marriage. In D. Perlman & S. Duck (Eds.), *Intimate relationships: Development, dynamics, and deterioration* (pp. 149–176). Newbury Park, CA: Sage.

Nussbaum, J. E. (1992, October 18). Justice for women! *New York Review of Books,* pp. 43–48.

O'Connor, P. (1992). *Friendships between women.* London: Harvester Wheatsheaf.

Okin, S. M. (1989). *Gender, justice, and the family.* New York: Basic Books.

Olien, M. (1978). *The human myth.* New York: Harper & Row.

O'Meara, J. D. (1989). Cross-sex friendship: Four basic challenges of an ignored relationship. *Sex Roles, 21,* 525–543.

Patterson, M. L. (1992). A functional approach to nonverbal exchange. In R. S. Feldman & B. Rime (Eds.), *Fundamentals of nonverbal behavior* (pp. 458–495). New York: Cambridge University Press.

Patton, B. R., & Ritter, K. (1976). *Living together . . . female/male communication.* Columbus, OH: Charles E. Merrill.

Pearce, W. B., Cronen, V. E., & Conklin, F. (1979). On what to look at when analyzing communication: A hierarchical model of actors' meanings. *Communication, 4,* 195–220.

Pearson, J. C. (1985). *Gender and communication.* Dubuque, IA: William C. Brown.

Petronio, S. (1991). Communication boundary management: A theoretical model of managing disclosure of private information between married couples. *Communication Theory, 1,* 311–335.

Pettigrew, T. F. (1967). Social evaluation theory: Consequences and applications. In D. Levine (Ed.), *Nebraska symposium on motivation* (pp. 241–311). Lincoln: University of Nebraska Press.

Phillips G. M., & Wood, J. T. (1983). *Communication and human relationships.* New York: Macmillan.

Piaget, J. (1932/1965). *The moral judgment of the child.* New York: Free Press.

Pleck, J. H. (1987). American fathering in historical perspective. In M. S. Kimmel (Ed.), *Changing men: New directions in research on men and masculinity* (pp. 83–97). Englewood Cliffs, NJ: Prentice-Hall.

Pomerleau, A., Bolduc, D., Malcuit, G., & Cossette, L. (1990). Pink or blue: Environmental stereotypes in the first two years of life. *Sex Roles, 22,* 359–367.

Pryor, J. B., & Merluzzi, T. V. (1985). The role of expertise in processing social interaction scripts. *Journal of Experimental Social Psychology, 21,* 362–379.

Public pillow talk. (1987, October). *Psychology Today,* p. 18.

Raspberry, W. (1994, July 5). Major gains in minorities' grades at Tech. *Raleigh News and Observer,* p. 9A.

Rawlins, W. K. (1981). *Friendship as a communicative achievement: A theory and an interpretive analysis of verbal reports.* Doctoral dissertation, Temple University, Philadelphia, PA.

Rawlins, W. K. (1994). Being there and growing apart: Sustaining friendships during adulthood. In D. Canary & L. Stafford (Eds.), *Communication and relational maintenance* (pp. 275–294). New York: Academic Press.

Reel, B. W., & Thompson, T. L. (1994). A test of the effectiveness of strategies for talking about AIDS and condom use. *Journal of Applied Communication Research, 22,* 127–141.

Reis, H. T., Senchak, M., & Solomon, B. (1985). Sex differences in the intimacy of social interaction: Further examination of potential explanations. *Journal of Personality and Social Psychology, 48,* 1204–1217.

Ribeau, S. A., Baldwin, J. R., & Hecht, M. L. (1994). An African-American communication perspective. In L. Samovar & R. Porter (Eds.), *Intercultural communication: A reader* (7th ed., pp. 140–147). Belmont, CA: Wadsworth.

Riessman, C. (1990). *Divorce talk: Women and men make sense of personal relationships.* New Brunswick, NJ: Rutgers University Press.

Rohlfing, M. (1995). Doesn't anybody stay in one place anymore? An exploration of the understudied phenomenon of long-distance relationships. In J. T. Wood & S. W. Duck (Eds.), *Understanding relationship processes, 6: Off the beaten track: Understudied relationships* (pp. 173–196). Thousand Oaks, CA: Sage.

Root, M. P. P. (1990). Disordered eating habits in women of color. *Sex Roles, 22,* 525–536.

Rose, S. M. (1984). How friendships end: Patterns among young adults. *Journal of Social and Personal Relationships, 1,* 267–277.

Rose, S., & Frieze, I. H. (1989). Young singles' scripts for a first date. *Gender and Society, 3,* 258–268.

Rose, S., & Serafica, F. (1986). Keeping and ending casual, close and best friendships. *Journal of Social and Personal Relationships, 3,* 275–288.

Rosenberg, M. (1979). *Conceiving the self.* New York: Basic Books.

Rousar, E. E., III, & Aron, A. (1990, July). *Valuing, altrusim, and the concept of love.* Paper presented at the Fifth International Conference on Personal Relationships, Oxford, UK.

Ruberman, T. R. (1992, January 22–29). Psychosocial influences on mortality of patients with coronary heart disease. *Journal of the American Medical Association 267,* pp. 559–560.

Rubin, L. (1985). *Just friends: The role of friendship in our lives.* New York: Harper & Row.

Ruddick, S. (1989). *Maternal thinking: Towards a politics of peace.* Boston: Beacon Press.

Rusbult, C. (1987). Responses to dissatisfaction in close relationships: The exit–voice–loyalty–neglect model. In D. Perlman & S. W. Duck (Eds.), *Intimate relationships: Development, dynamics, and deterioration* (pp. 109–238). London: Sage.

Rusbult, C. E., Johnson, D. J., & Morrow, G. D. (1986). Impact of couple patterns of problem solving on distress and nondistress in dating relationships. *Journal of Personality and Social Psychology, 50,* 744–753.

Rusbult, C. E., & Zembrodt, I. M. (1983). Responses to dissatisfaction in romantic involvement: A multidimensional scaling analysis. *Journal of Experimental Social Psychology, 19,* 274–293.

Rusbult, C. E., Zembrodt, I. M., & Iwaniszek, J. (1986). The impact of gender and sex-role orientation on responses to dissatisfaction in close relationships. *Sex Roles, 15,* 1–20.

Rusk, T., & Rusk, N. (1988). *Mindtraps: Change your mind, change your life.* Los Angeles: Price, Stern, Sloan.

Sadker, M., & Sadker, D. (1986, March). Sexism in the classroom: From grade school to graduate school. *Phi Delta Kappan*, pp. 512–515.

Sallinen-Kuparinen, A. (1992). Teacher communicator style. *Communication Education, 41,* 153–166.

Samovar, L., & Porter, R. (Eds.). (1994). *Intercultural communication: A reader* (7th ed.). Belmont, CA: Wadsworth.

Scarf, M. (1987). *Intimate partners.* New York: Random House.

Schiminoff, S. B. (1980). *Communication rules: Theory and research.* Newbury Park, CA: Sage.

Schwartz, T. (1989, January/February). Acceleration syndrome: Does everyone live in the fast lane nowadays? *Utne Reader,* pp. 36–43.

Sebeok, T. A., & Rosenthal, R. (Eds.). (1981). *The Clever Hans phenomenon: Communication with horses, whales, apes and people.* New York: New York Academy of Sciences.

Secklin, P. (1991, November). *Being there: A qualitative study of young adults' descriptions of friendship.* Paper presented at the Speech Communication Association Convention, Atlanta, GA.

Secord, P. F., Bevan, W., & Katz, B. (1956). The Negro stereotype and perceptual accentuation. *Journal of Abnormal and Social Psychology, 54,* 78–83.

Shattuck, T. R. (1980). *The forbidden experiment: The story of the wild boy of Aveyron.* New York: Farrar, Straus & Giroux.

Sherrod, D. (1989). The influence of gender on same-sex friendships. In C. Hendrick (Ed.), *Close relationships* (pp. 164–186). Newbury Park, CA: Sage.

Shotter, J. (1993). *Conversational realities: The construction of life through language.* Newbury Park, CA: Sage.

Simon, S. B. (1977). *Vulture: A modern allegory on the art of putting oneself down.* Niles, IL: Argus Communications.

Smitherman, G. (1994). *Black talk: Words and phrases from the hood to the amen corner.* Boston: Houghton Mifflin.

Snell, W. E., Jr., Hawkins, R. C., II, & Belk, S. S. (1988). Stereotypes about male sexuality and the use of social influence strategies in intimate relationships. *Journal of Clinical and Social Psychology, 7,* 42–48.

Spain, D. (1992). *Gendered spaces.* Chapel Hill, NC: University of North Carolina Press.

Spencer, T. (1994). Transforming relationships through ordinary talk. In S. W. Duck (Ed.), *Understanding relationship processes, 4: Dynamics of relationships* (pp. 58–85). Thousand Oaks, CA: Sage.

Spender, D. (1989). *Invisible women: The schooling scandal.* London: Women's Press.

Spitz, R. (1965). *The first year of life.* New York: International Universities Press.

Spitzack, C. (1990). *Confessing excess.* Albany, NY: State University of New York Press.

Spitzack, C. (1993). The spectacle of anorexia nervosa. *Text and Performance Quarterly, 13,* 1–21.

Sprecher, S. (1989). The importance to males and females of physical attractiveness, earning potential, and expressiveness in initial attraction. *Sex Roles, 21,* 591–607.

Stephenson, S. J., & D'Angelo, G. (1973). *The effects of evaluative/empathic listening and self-esteem on defensive reactions in dyads.* Paper presented to the International Communication Association. Montreal, Quebec, Canada.

Sternberg, R. J. (1986). A triangular theory of love. *Psychological Review, 93,* 119–135.

Stewart, J. (1986). *Bridges, not walls* (4th ed.). New York: Random House.

Stewart, L. P., Stewart, A. D., Friedley, S. A., & Cooper, P. J. (1990). *Communication between the sexes: Sex differences and sex role stereotypes* (2nd ed.). Scottsdale, AZ: Gorsuch Scarisbrick.

Stone, R. (1992). The feminization of poverty among the elderly. In M. L. Andersen & P. H. Collins (Eds.), *Race, class, and gender: An anthology* (pp. 201–214). Belmont, CA: Wadsworth.

Suitor, J. J. (1991). Marital quality and satisfaction with the division of household labor across the family life cycle. *Journal of Marriage and the Family, 53,* 221–230.

Swain, S. (1989). Covert intimacy: Closeness in men's friendships. In B. Risman & P. Schwartz (Ed.), *Gender and intimate relationships* (pp. 71–86). Belmont, CA: Wadsworth.

Sypher, B. (1984). Seeing ourselves as others see us. *Communication Research, 11,* 97–115.

Tannen, D. (1990). *You just don't understand: Women and men in conversation.* New York: William Morrow.

Tavris, C. (1992). *The mismeasure of woman.* New York: Simon & Schuster.

Templin, N. (1994, October 17). Wanted: Six bedrooms, seven baths for empty nesters. *Wall Street Journal,* pp. B1, B7.

Thomas, V. G. (1989). Body-image satisfaction among black women. *Journal of Social Psychology, 129,* 107–112.

Three million around the world contracted AIDS in last year. (1994, August 9). *Raleigh News and Observer,* p. 5A.

Ting-Toomey, S. (1991). Intimacy expressions in three cultures: France, Japan, and the United States. *International Journal of Intercultural Relations, 15,* 29–46.

Toffler, A. (1970). *Future shock.* New York: William Morrow.

Toffler, A. (1980). *The third wave.* New York: William Morrow.

Tolhuizen, J. H. (1989). Communication strategies for intensifying dating relationships: Identification, use, and structure. *Journal of Social and Personal Relationships, 6,* 413–434.

Treichler, P. A., & Kramarae, C. (1983). Women's talk in the ivory tower. *Communication Quarterly, 31,* 118–132.

Trotter, R. J. (1975, October 25). The truth, the whole truth, and nothing but . . . *Science News, 108,* 269.

Ueland, B. (1992, November/December). Tell me more: On the fine art of listening. *Utne Reader,* pp. 104–109.

U.S. Bureau of the Census. (1992). *Current population reports, geographical mobility* (pp. 20–463). Washington, DC: U.S. Government Printing Office.

Vachss, A. (1994, August 28). You carry the cure in your own heart. *Parade,* pp. 4–6.

Vangelisti, A. (1993). Couples' communication problems: The counselor's perspective. *Journal of Applied Communication Research, 22,* 106–126.

Vanyperen, N. W., & Buunk, B. P. (1991). Equity theory and exchange and communal orientation from a cross-national perspective. *Journal of Social Psychology, 131,* 5–20.

Villarosa, L. (1994, January). Dangerous eating. *Essence,* pp. 19–21, 87.

Walker, M. B., & Trimboli, A. (1989). Communicating affect: The role of verbal and nonverbal content. *Journal of Language and Social Psychology, 8,* 229–248.

Walster, E., Traupmann, J., & Walster, G. W. (1978). Equity and extramarital sexuality. *Archives of Sexual Behavior, 7,* 127–141.

Watzlawick, P., Beavin, J., & Jackson, D. D. (1967). *Pragmatics of human communication.* New York: W. W. Norton.

Weaver, C. (1972). *Human listening: Processes and behavior.* Indianapolis: Bobbs-Merrill.

Weber, S. N. (1994). The need to be: The socio-cultural significance of black language. In L. Samovar & R. Porter (Eds.), *Intercultural communication: A reader* (7th ed., pp. 221–226). Belmont, CA: Wadsworth.

Wellman, B. (1985). Domestic work, paid work, and net work. In S. W. Duck & D. Perlman (Eds.), *Understanding personal relationships.* Beverly Hills, CA: Sage.

Wells, W., & Siegel, B. (1961). Stereotyped somatypes. *Psychological Reports, 8,* 77–78.

Werner, C. M., Altman, I., Brown, B. B., & Ginat, J. (1993). Celebrations in personal relationships: A transactional/dialectical perspective. In S. W. Duck (Ed.), *Understanding relational processes, 3: Social context and relationships* (pp. 109–138). Newbury Park, CA: Sage.

Werner, C., Altman, I., & Oxley, D. (1985). Temporal aspects of homes: A transactional perspective. In I. Altman & C. M. Werner (Eds.), *Home environments: Vol. 8. Human behavior and environment: Advances in theory and research* (pp. 1–32). Beverly Hills, CA: Sage.

Werner, C. M., & Haggard, I. M. (1985). Temporal qualities of interpersonal relationships. In G. R. Miller & M. L. Knapp (Eds.), *Handbook of interpersonal communication* (pp. 59–99). Beverly Hills, CA: Sage.

West, C., & Zimmerman, D. H. (1987). Doing gender. *Gender and Society, 1,* 125–151.

West, J. (1995). Understanding how the dynamics of ideology influence violence between intimates. In S. W. Duck & J. T. Wood (Eds.), *Understanding relationship processes, 5: Confronting relationship challenges* (pp. 129–149). Thousand Oaks, CA: Sage.

West, L., Anderson, J., & Duck, S. (1996). Crossing the barriers to friendship between men and women. In J. T. Wood (Ed.), *Gendered relationships.* Mountain View, CA: Mayfield.

Westefield, J. S., & Liddell, D. (1982). Coping with long-distance relationships. *Journal of College Student Personnel, 23,* 550–551.

Weston, K. (1991). *Families we choose: Lesbian, gays, kinship.* New York: Columbia University Press.

Wexner, L. B. (1954). The degree to which colors (hues) are associated with mood-tones. *Journal of Applied Psychology, 38,* 432–435.

What teens say about drinking. (1994, August 7). *Parade,* p. 9.

Whitbeck, L. B., & Hoyt, D. R. (1994). Social prestige and assortive mating: A comparison of students from 1956 and 1988. *Journal of Social and Personal Relationships, 11,* 137–145.

White, B. (1989). Gender differences in marital communication patterns. *Family Process, 28,* 89–106.

White, J., & Bondurant, B. (1996). Gendered violence in intimate relationships. In J. T. Wood (Ed.), *Gendered relationships.* Mountain View, CA: Mayfield.

Whorf, B. (1956). *Language, thought, and reality.* New York: MIT Press/John Wiley.

Wiemann, J. M., & Harrison, R. P. (Eds). (1983). *Nonverbal interaction.* Beverly Hills, CA: Sage.

Wilkie, J. R. (1991). The decline in men's labor force participation and income and the changing structure of family economic support. *Journal of Marriage and the Family, 53,* 111–122.

Williams, D. G. (1985). Gender, masculinity–femininity, and emotional intimacy in same-sex friendship. *Sex Roles, 12,* 587–600.

Willmott, P. (1987). *Friendship networks and social support.* London: Policy Studies Institute.

Wilson, J. A. R., Robick, M. C., & Michael, W. B. (1974). *Psychological foundations of learning and teaching* (2nd ed.). New York: McGraw-Hill.

Wolf, N. (1991). *The beauty myth.* New York: William Morrow.

Wood, J. T. (1982). Communication and relational culture: Bases for the study of human relationships. *Communication Quarterly, 30,* 75–84.

Wood, J. T. (1986). Different voices in relationship crises: An extension of Gilligan's theory. *American Behavioral Scientist, 29,* 273–301.

Wood, J. T. (1992). *Spinning the symbolic web.* Norwood, NJ: Ablex.

Wood, J. T. (1993). Engendered relations: Interaction, caring, power, and responsibility in intimacy. In S. W. Duck (Ed.), *Understanding relationship processes, 3: Social context and relationships* (pp. 26–54). Newbury Park, CA: Sage.

Wood, J. T. (1994a). Engendered identities: Shaping voice and mind through gender. In D. Vocate (Ed.), *Intrapersonal communication: Different voices, different minds* (pp. 145–167). Hillsdale, NJ: Lawrence Erlbaum.

Wood, J. T. (1994b). Gender and relationship crises: Contrasting reasons, responses, and relational orientations. In J. Ringer (Ed.), *Queer words, queer images: The construction of homosexuality* (pp. 238–265). New York: New York University Press.

Wood, J. T. (1994c). Gender, communication, and culture. In L. Samovar & R. Porter (Eds.), *Intercultural communication: A reader* (7th ed., pp. 155–164). Belmont, CA: Wadsworth.

Wood, J. T. (1994d). *Gendered lives: Communication, gender, and culture.* Belmont, CA: Wadsworth.

Wood, J. T. (1994e). *Who cares? Women, care, and culture.* Carbondale, IL: University of Southern Illinois Press.

Wood, J. T. (1995a). Diversity in dialogue: Communication between friends. In J. Makau & R. Arnett (Eds.), *Ethics of communication in an age of diversity.* Urbana: University of Illinois Press.

Wood, J. T. (1995b). Feminist scholarship and research on relationships. *Journal of Social and Personal Relationships, 12,* 103–120.

Wood, J. T. (1995c). *Relational communication.* Belmont, CA: Wadsworth.

Wood, J. T. (Ed.). (1996). *Gendered relationships.* Mountain View, CA: Mayfield.

Wood, J. T., Dendy, L., Dordek, E., Germany, M., & Varallo, S. (1994). Dialectic of difference: A thematic analysis of intimates' meanings for differences. In K. Carter & M. Presnell (Eds.), *Interpretive approaches to interpersonal communication* (pp. 115–136). New York: State University of New York Press.

Wood, J. T., & Inman, C. C. (1993). In a different mode: Masculine styles of communicating closeness. *Journal of Applied Communication Research, 21,* 279–295.

Wren, C. S. (1990, October 16). A South Africa color bar falls quietly. *New York Times,* pp. Y1, Y10.

Wright, P. H., & Scanlon, M. B. (1991). Gender role orientations and friendship: Some attenuation but gender differences still abound. *Sex Roles, 24,* 551–566.

Wright, P. H., & Wright, K. (1995). Codependency: Personality syndrome or relationship process? In S. Duck & J. T. Wood (Eds.), *Understanding relationship processes, 5: Confronting relationship challenges* (pp. 109–128). Thousand Oaks, CA: Sage.

WuDunn, S. (1991, April 17). Romance, a novel idea, rocks marriages in China. *New York Times,* pp. B1, B12.

Yerby, J., Buerkel-Rothfuss, N., & Bochner, A. (1990). *Understanding family communication.* Scottsdale, AZ: Gorsuch Scarisbrick.

Zorn, T. (1995). Bosses and buddies: Constructing and performing simultaneously hierarchical and loose friendship relationships. In J. T. Wood & S. W. Duck (Eds.), *Understanding relationship processes, 6: Off the beaten track: Understudied relationships* (pp. 122–147). Thousand Oaks, CA: Sage.

Frontmatter photographs: p. ix: © Goldberg/Monkmeyer; p. x: © A. Sieveking/Petit/Photo Researchers, Inc.; p. xi: © James Holland/Stock, Boston; p. xii: © Donna Binder/Impact Visuals; p. xiii: © Anne Dowie; p. xiv: © LeDuc/Monkmeyer; p. xv: © Mark Antman/The Image Works; p. xvi: © Audrey Gottlieb/Monkmeyer; p. xvii: © Catherine Karnow/Woodfin Camp & Associates; p. xviii: © Rhoda Sidney/PhotoEdit.

All photographs of quilts and embroidery, with the exception of those on pages 41, 93, 177, 207, and 237, are reproduced with the kind permission of the Embroiderers' Guild Collection, London.

p. 1: Patchwork bedcover, English, late nineteenth century. Woven silk, 6′1¼″ × 6′7½″. Given by Mrs. G. Foxton and Mrs. M. Hodge. Photograph by Julia Hedgecoe.

p. 3: Red silk breast scarf, Greece, eighteenth century, 1′3¼″ × 1′3½″. Photograph by Julie Hedgecoe. Inset: © David Young-Wolff, PhotoEdit.

p. 11: Two William Morris hangings, late nineteenth century. Cotton, linen, and silk, 1′8¼″ × 4′3½″ and 3′ × 1′11″. Given by Lady Studholme. Pho-

tograph by Julia Hedgecoe. Inset: © David M. Grossman/Photo Researchers, Inc.

p. 41: Barbara Lee Smith, *New Leaf* (1989). Textile pigment sprayed on cotton silk fabric; cotton, rayon, and metallic threads, 5′5″ × 2′½″. Collection of Mr. and Mrs. Donley Klein, Marietta, Ga. Photograph by Steinkamp/Ballogg, Chicago, courtesy Barbara Lee Smith. Inset: © Spencer Grant/Stock, Boston.

p. 69: See credit for page 1. Inset: © Kim Newton/Woodfin Camp & Associates, Inc.

p. 93: Alphabet quilt, pieced and appliquéd, North Carolina, c. 1900. Cotton, 5′10″ × 7′2″. Private collection. Photograph courtesy Shelly Zegart, Louisville, Ky. Inset: © Goldberg/Monkmeyer Press.

p. 121 Furisode kimono, Japan, late Edo period (1615–1868). Satin and gold leaf, length 5′3″. Given by Mrs. Hamilton Bruce. Photograph by Julia Hedgecoe. Inset: © E. Williamson/The Picture Cube.

p. 147: Jean Draper, panel from *The Four Elements* (1982). Hand-felted fabrics, surface stitchery, string, and en-

twined knotted shreds, 2′5″ × 1′4¼″. Purchased. Photograph by Dudley Moss. Inset: © Peter L. Chapman.

p. 177: Friendship sampler quilt, pieced and appliquéd, Wisconsin, c. 1840. Cotton, 6′4″ × 7′1″. Private collection. Photograph courtesy Shelly Zegart, Louisville, Ky.

p. 179: Eleri Mills, *Jess*, two wall-hangings (1984). Mixed media. 3′10½″ × 1′8″ each panel. Purchased. Photograph by Julia Hedgecoe. Inset: © Gary A. Conner/PhotoEdit.

p. 207: Anna Lou Holland and Christine Holland Ross, pieced and embroidered crazy quilt (1878). Silk and velvet, 7′2″ × 6′2″. Photograph courtesy The Kentucky Historical Society, Frankfort, Ky. Inset: © David Bitters/The Picture Cube.

p. 237: See credit for page 177. Inset: © Bob Daemmrich/Tony Stone Images.

p. 263: Sari end, Bengal (now Bangladesh), late nineteenth century. Cotton and wild silk, 3′3¾″ × 5′2″. Given by Mrs. K. Harris. Photography by Dudley Moss. Inset: © Michael Kevin Daly/The Stock Market.

D

Defensive/supportive climates, 193–198
  certainty/provisionalism, 194–195
  control/problem orientation, 196–197
  evaluation/description, 193–194
  neutrality/empathy, 197
  strategy/spontaneity, 195–196
  superiority/equality, 197–198
Defensive listening, **163**
Defensiveness, 196–197
Deference, 201
Direct definition, **44**–45, 68. *See also* Identify scripts; Self
Diverse listening styles, 159–160
Diversity
  and communication, 7–8, 22, 159, 253
  and culture, 6, 8, 22, 29, 30, 32, 50, 59–60, 81, 99, 120, 123, 127–128, 132, 136, 138, 141, 144–145, 159, 181, 201, 204, 216, 221, 253, 265, 274–275, 282, 288–289, 296
  in relationships, 203–204, 270
  and society, 6–8, 17–18, 31, 32, 48, 76, 80–83, 96, 99, 109–112, 116, 123, 127–128, 134, 140, 141, 159, 253, 276, 296
Divorce, 265, 266, 281
Downers, **66**–68.
Dual perspective, **35**–36, 86, 113–114, 116, 145, 149, 153, 160, 183, 200, 225, 227, 252, 259–260, 277, 292. *See also* Interpersonal communication competence
Dyadic breakdown. *See* Relational decline
Dyadic negotiation. *See* Relational decline

E

Eating disorders, 58, 132
Ego boundaries, **51**
Emotional abuse, 44, 287

F

Empathy, **86**, 197. *See also* Person-perception
Environmental factors, 135
Environmental racism, 137
Environmental spoiling, **276**
Equality, 182, 197
Equity, **283**–285
Ethnocentrism, **194**
Exit response, **219**
Explorational communication. *See* Relational escalation

F

Facts, 89–90, 92, 253. *See also* Inferences
Feminine communication rules, 110, 240–241, 253
Femininity, 50, 59, 140
Friendship, 238–262
  acceptance, 243–244
  closeness through dialogue, 240–241
  closeness through doing, 241–242
  development of, 247–251
  external tensions on, 254–258
  honesty, 260–261
  internal tensions on, **251**–254
  intimacy, 240–242
  investment, 239, 250
  rules of, 250–251
  support, 245–247, 261
  trust, 244–245, 249

G

Games, **212**–213
Gays, 6, 56, 57, 60, 95, 103, 104, 105, 109, 222–223, 243–244, 266, 276, 284–285
Gender, 8, 44, 52, 55–56, 57, 59, 82, 122, 133–135, 140, 209, 254, 256, 257–258, 283–285
  and conflict styles, 221–222, 281
Gender communication cultures, 8, 55, 110–111, 113, 125, 126, 131, 136, 140, 145, 148, 150–151, 152, 159, 161, 173–174, 184, 240–242, 246, 253, 258, 280–281, 287

H

Gendered standpoints, 82–83
Generalized other, 42, 49, **54**–59, 60, 62, 68, 76, 99
Grace, **233**–234, 246
Grave dressing. *See* Relational decline

H

Hearing, **149**, 150–151, 174. *See also* Listening
Heterosexuality, 6–7, 56, 59, 60, 243–244
Homophobia, 57
Homosexuality, 6–7, 59, 60, 266

I

Identity scripts, **45**–46. *See also* Direct definition; Self
I–language, 115, 143–145, 193, 254, 286. *See also* You-language
I–ME dialogues, 107–108
Impersonal communication:
  I–It communication, **19**–20, 23, 100
  I–You communication, **20**, 23, 33, 100
Improving verbal communication, 113–120
  accuracy and clarity, 117–120
  owning feelings and thoughts, 114–115
Indexing, **119**
Ineffective listening, 156–165
Inferences, 89–90, 92, 253, 259. *See also* Facts
Intensifying communication. *See* Relational escalation
Interpersonal climate, **180**–205, 214, 227, 230, 231, 259, 280
  confirming/disconfirming climates, 189–193, 199, 200, 203, 230
  continuum of, 189
  defensive/supportive climates, 193–198

N

Native Americans, 75, 109, 141
Navigating, **279**
Needs, 13–18, 23, 38, 180
   belonging/social, 15, 181, 243
   in a diverse society, 17–18
   Maslow's hierarchy of, 13, 57, 243
   physical, 13
   safety, 14
   self-actualization, 16–17, 57
   self-esteem, 15–16
Neglect response, **219**
Noise, 22, 23, 157, 166
Nonverbal communication, 29,
     122–145, **123**, 154, 189, 195
   artifacts, 133–135, 140
   chronemics, **137**–138, 231–232
   environmental factors, 135–136
   improvement of, 141–145
   kinesics, **129**–130
   paralanguage, **138**–140
   physical appearance, 132
   principles of, 123–128
   proxemics and personal space,
     136–137
   silence, 141
   touch, 131
   types of, 128–141

O

Organization, 73–76, 79, 87, 92,
     105–106, 151–152, 167. *See also*
     Perception

P

Paralanguage, **138**–140
Paraphrasing, **169**–170, 173, 190
Particular others, 42, **52**–53, 76, 85,
     99. *See* Self
Perception, 70–92, **71**, 94, 103,
     105–106, 166, 218, 231, 274
   checking, 88–89, 92
   improvement of, 86–92

influences on, 79–86
   cognitive abilities, 84–86, 92
   culture, **80**–83, 86, 92, 99
   physiology, 79–80, 86, 92
   social roles, 83–84, 86, 92
ladder of abstraction, 91
processes of, 71–79, 92
   interpretation, **77**–79, 87, 92,
     98, 153
   organization, 73–76, 79, 87,
     92, 105–106, 151, 167
   selection, 71–73, 79, 87, 92,
     151
Personal constructs, **74**, 84, 151,
     152. *See also* Constructivism
Personal qualifications, 143
Personal relationships, elements of,
     180–189
   comfort, 185–189
   commitment, **183**–184
   investment, **182**–183
   trust, **184**–185
Personal space, 136–137, 191
Person-centered communication, **35**.
     See also Interpersonal commu-
     nication competence
Person-perception, **85**–86. *See also*
     Empathy
Persons with disabilities, 61, 109,
     191
Perspective of the generalized other,
     49, 54, 58, 68, 75, 99
Physical appearance, 132
Placemaking, **280**
Prejudgment, 158
Preoccupation, 157
Process, **24**
   of communication, 24–26, 30, 37
   of listening, 149–155
   of self, 42, 51–52, 62, 65, 68, 107
   of perception, 71–79, 92
   of relationships, 292
Prototypes, **73**–74, 105, 151. *See also*
     Constructivism
Proxemics, **136**–137. *See also* Non-
     verbal communication
Pseudolistening, **160**
Psychological responsibility, **286**

Punctuation, **101**–102, 120, 252
   demand–withdraw pattern,
     101–102
   punctuating interaction, 102

Q

Qualifying language, 118–120

R

Race, 8, 54–55, 57, 60, 82, 112, 159
Reappropriation, 105
Recall, 167
Reflected appraisal, **48**, 53–54, 65,
     68. *See also* Self
Regulative rules. *See* Communication
     rules
Relational culture, 24, 26, 30, 31,
     100, 278, **279**
Relational decline, 280–282, 293
   dyadic breakdown, **280**–281
   dyadic negotiation, **281**
   grave dressing, **282**
   intrapsychic phase, **281**
   social phase, **281**–282
   social support, **282**
Relational dialectics, **185**–189, 199,
     204, 251–252, 279
   autonomy/connection, 185–186
   couples' response to, 187–189
   openness/closedness, 186–187
   novelty/predictability, 186
Relational escalation, 275–278, 293
   explorational communication, **277**
   intensifying communication,
     277–278
   invitational communication, **275**
Relational level of meaning, 27–28,
     124–127, 133, 149, 154, 157,
     164, 197, 275, 276. *See also*
     meanings
   liking/affective, **28**, 125–126, 130,
     131
   in nonverbal communication,
     124–127
   power/control, **28**, 126–127, 131,
     136
   responsiveness, **27**, 125, 130,
     154–155

Please give us your feedback

Thank you for using *Everyday Encounters*. I hope you have enjoyed reading it and have found it valuable in your interpersonal communication. In order to make the next edition even better, I'd like to know what you think about the book. Please give me your opinions on this edition by filling out the questionnaire below. When you're done, just fold and seal the questionnaire and drop it into the mail (postage is already paid). Thanks for your help!

    Julia T. Wood

1. In comparison to other textbooks you have read,
   is *Everyday Encounters* better, about the same, or less effective?

2. What are the three topics or parts of the book that you found most useful?

3. Which parts did you find least useful?

4. Did you try the skills in the "Put It in Practice" boxes?
   Did you find this feature useful?

5. Are there any other criticisms you have of this edition?

6. How can we improve the next edition?

7. Did you use a computer in conjunction with this class?
   If yes, what kind and for what purpose?

May we quote your answers to all of the above questions? ◯ yes ◯ no

Do you have a student commentary (like those included in this book) that you would like to have me consider using in the next edition? If yes, please type it up and send it to the address on the other side of this page. If your commentary is published, your privacy will be protected.

Name (optional) _____

School _____

Address _____

City/State/Zip _____

Internet address _____

Year in school and field of study _____

FOLD HERE

NO POSTAGE
NECESSARY
IF MAILED
IN THE
UNITED STATES

BUSINESS REPLY MAIL
First Class Mail   Permit No. 34   Belmont, CA

POSTAGE WILL BE PAID BY ADDRESSEE

Julia T. Wood
Wadsworth Publishing Company
An International Thomson Publishing Company
10 Davis Drive
Belmont, California 94002-9801

FOLD HERE